SENTIMENT

A MEMOIR

Cheryl Krkoč

SENTIMENT

A MEMOIR

SENTIMENT; *A Memoir*
Copyright © 2021 by Cheryl Krkoč. All rights reserved.

No part of this publication may be reproduced, stored in a retrieval system or transmitted in any way by any means, electronic, mechanical, photocopy, recording or otherwise without the prior permission of the author except as provided by USA copyright law.

To order additional copies of this book:
www.amazon.com
www.barnesandnoble.com

Published in the United States of America

ISBN *hardcover: 9781956895063*
ISBN *softcover: 9781956895070*

For Francesca

And thanks to family and friends who shared their stories, reminisced, helped me remember.

Again Again

The strings tug at my heart and choke back all its efforts. Again Again

That hollow feeling grips me

As we sit apart.

I feel your presence then, would be

Like-

Raindrops in the desert –

A commet in the sky-

No- more like

God, to one about to die.

This vanishes- then a

Voice whispers –

Can this be – one

With flesh of dust

Touched-

With things that live eternally.

Poem from Dad to Mom.

CHAPTER 1

I was born on January 22, 1951, after what my mother has described as a long difficult labor for both of us. In those days, fathers were normally not allowed in the delivery room, but because my dad was a medical student, he was able to witness my birth. After I was born, Mom was placed back in her room to recuperate. She stood up, and gobs of blood gushed out of her womb and landed on the floor. The anxious young nurse in attendance took the pad from the bed, mopped up the floor with it, put it back on the bed, and instructed Mom to sit back down on it. But Mom knew better than to do that, so she just propped herself up against the edge of the bed to avoid the soiled pad. She waited patiently until another nurse arrived and asked if she could have a new bed pad. She was always unassuming that way. As for me, I was about to begin my journey to try to make sense of where I had landed, to take it all in as best I could, but not yet able to define my experiences with words. It was only after I had gained some proficiency with language that I was able to glean information and make more sense of my surroundings. This is when I began to pick up on family stories, which I would categorize in my brain and store them safely there. Even before I was born, I had a lot of baggage. I just didn't know it yet. My senses helped me put things together. I made sure to pay attention. As far as Mom was concerned, I saw her only on the surface—just glimpses of what she hid. It was only after my brain was able to function on a more sophisticated level did I see more of what lay beneath.

My first home was built by my paternal grandfather in Elmhurst, Illinois, where a number of Slovenians had settled at the end of the nineteenth and early twentieth-century—Slovenians who came from villages near Trieste, Italy. My grandmother had been dissatisfied with the first home my grandfather built for them, so he built another that was more to her liking right next door to the first. This second home of theirs was my first—a beautiful home that bore witness to my grandfather's skill as an artisan, as did many of the homes and other structures he built in the area over the years. One of my first memories was sitting under the kitchen table and listening to family banter, which was unintelligible to me because my grandparents, father, aunt, and other relatives on my father's side spoke Slovene. My mother and uncle, who was married to Dad's sister, were left out of these conversations unless bits of English were thrown in for their benefit. Sometimes the adults spoke Slovene to prevent the children from knowing what was being said. I did pick up a few words during the time we lived at my grandparents'. I don't know the proper spelling but will spell them here as they sounded to me. Mow-chee, mow-chee meant, in loose translation, "shut up, shut up." I guess it had to be said twice to drive in the message. Then there was gee-vee-oh, meaning "a toast to a good life," which was always shouted out in unison with a glass of wine in one's hand. And last but not least was peesh-marete. The children weren't allowed to know what this meant until we reached the age of twelve. It was a sort of coming-of-age to learn this secret, and the elder children tormented the younger ones who had to wait until that special birthday. Loosely translated it meant "blow it out your ass." Or was it "blow it up your ass"? I'm not sure. To me, there was something romantic about listening to the beautiful and expressive Slovenian language. This early childhood experience and others went on to create emotional responses later on in my life when I would find myself in situations similar to those in my early years. In fact, the first decade of my life seems to have built a framework for how I managed things later on. However, for years, I didn't recognize the connection.

The first nine months of my existence in utero and the first nine years after birth were spent in the 1950s. This may be why I identify more than any other decade with this period. My earliest years seemed to have made a lasting impression. I am filled with so much nostalgia whenever I see movies, fashions, television clips, or hear songs—anything, in fact, pertaining to the fifties. It was a magical time for me.

I don't remember exactly when my sister Sandra entered the scene. She was born on April 18, 1953. As an infant, she was hospitalized for some reason. I've been told that after she arrived, I would steal her baby bottle for my own use and resorted to wetting myself again. I must have gotten over it at some point because we became the best of friends. Sandy was born with coal-black hair, which changed to white blonde over the course of her first few months. At first, Mom thought she was going bald because the blonde hair that replaced the black seemed invisible. As her hair grew in, it was naturally curly and silky. It seemed to complement her rather impish face.

My first ten years involved several moves. The first five years were spent in the second story of my paternal grandparents' home at 245 Maple Avenue in Elmhurst. Then we moved across the country to Spokane, Washington, where Dad did his medical internship. We returned to Illinois after a year in Spokane and moved in with Dad's sister, Jean, and her family. Jean and her husband, Jack, had three kids the same age as those in our family. Cindy was my age, Greg was my sister Sandy's age, and Jeff was just a little older than our new baby brother, Doug, who was born a while after our move to 140 North Myrtle in Elmhurst. This was several blocks from each of our grandparents' homes. During the time we lived there, Dad, my grandfather, and Dad's friend Joe built a new house in Villa Park on weekends. Before moving to Oregon, we spent two and a half years in the new house while Dad finished his schooling.

The town of Elmhurst was beautiful. It was named for the many mature Elm trees that grew in the area. These trees formed tunnels over the many boulevards that ran through it. There were four distinct seasons. In the fall, the trees would change color, their leaves dropping to the ground, creating piles of brightly colored leaves, and then the weather would cool down. Winter would follow with snow, sometimes five feet high, that would last for the entire season with below zero-degree temperatures. Spring would bring showers, flowers, and rainbows. Summer—hot humid days—would bring lush vegetation that grew abundantly, fireflies that lit up the night sky and crickets, grasshoppers, and frogs that created a great din. Sometimes I'd sit on the curb at either of my grandparents' houses and watch what went by on the street. One of the most interesting things was the cutlery cart—a fixture in the Chicago area in those days. The cart was horse-drawn and operated by the cutler, who put it in motion with pedals that also rang a bell. It alerted potential customers to its presence. Sometimes my maternal grandmother (Nora) would accompany us to his wagon and hand him knives to sharpen. It was all very exciting. There was a kid named Billy who lived right around the corner from us. He looked all-American with his freckles, blond hair, and broad grin. All this probably improved his sales. He had a red Radio Flyer wagon he pulled behind him through the neighborhood. It was heaped with freshly picked corn from his family's garden. He'd ring the doorbell at the side of our house. Francesca would give me change to purchase enough for all of us to have an ear for dinner, and it was sweet and delicious. The other thing I loved were the glass milk bottles delivered every few days to our doorstep. The milk was always very cold because of its glass containers. I wish they were still around.

My paternal grandmother, Francesca Brecelj, was born on September 27, 1900, on the border of Italy and Slovenija, in the province of Gorizia (also known as Gorica). My grandfather, Francesco Krkoc, was from the same region and was born on July 23, 1898. Their passports indicate that Francesca departed from Trieste, Italy, on May 6, 1921, and came to Boston Harbor, where she and her traveling companion, Victoria Cermelj, traveled by train to Chicago. The first Slovenian family to arrive in Elmhurst, the Milosts, picked them up at the train station. The women stayed at their rooming house until they found work. The Milost family also helped with that. Francesco departed from Genova, Italy, on July 22, 1922. Francesco's oldest brother, Tony, came over in 1910 at the age of nineteen and acted as a sponsor for my grandfather.

Tony married a Slovenian woman by the name of Frances-a jolly lady. They fought a lot and married, divorced and remarried three different times. Mom thought Uncle Tony seemed like a Mobster. I don't know if there was any truth to all this though. Anyway, she was fascinated with his demeanor, but also a little intimidated by him. There is also a record of a twenty-six-year-old Slovenian named Franziska Breceli leaving Le Havre, France, for America on March 29, 1910. She was a first cousin of my grandmother's and Franziska sponsored Francesca when she came to America. It was common for young unmarried Slovenian women who immigrated to the area to work for wealthy families as domestics after they arrived in Elmhurst, and that is what Francesca did. And so did Victoria Cermelj. Victoria worked for the family that created Alka-Seltzer. They were kind and helped her learn English. My cousin Cindy told me that our grandmother was sought after as a domestic because of her skills as a cook of delicious Northern Italian cuisine. A story my father told me about his mother was that she complained to the lady of the house about bedbugs in the mattress of her small attic apartment and asked to have it replaced. When she realized this request was being ignored, she put on her coat and walked out the door without an explanation. She barely spoke English and had no other prospects as far as other employment. As far as I know, she was never ever intimidated by anyone, and I never saw anyone ever get the best of her. My aunt Jean (my father's only sibling and four years younger than him) sent my father an article from the Slovenija Quarterly Magazine Volume XIII No. 1 (1999) several years ago. It tells another story about my grandmother and this first employment experience in America. I found the article with other documents—passports, birth certificates, naturalization papers, marriage licenses, etc.—that my father had given me. In the Slovenija article, there is an account of the history of Slovenes who settled in the Chicago area, written by Pauline Remec Moltzen, and includes the following story: "Wine was an important part of living to our people. In the early years, grapes were shipped from California in freight cars to the Proviso yards. Here is where our people came to get wooden boxes brimming over with luscious red and white grapes. In the 1920's, Prohibition was the law of the land, so there was an element of risk in the winemaking, especially for those more venturesome individuals who distilled a much more potent liquid. This brings to mind the story of Francesca, one of our young women whose first employment was that of maid in the home of a wealthy family. There was a bottle of wine in the icebox—no refrigerators then— and Francesca said to herself, 'I wonder what kind of wine these American's drink? ' and poured herself a small glass. When the woman of the house, who was a shrew, noticed that the wine was missing from the bottle, she heatedly berated her maid for what was hardly a major transgression. In telling us the story later, she said that if she had known her employer's reaction, she would have replaced the shortage with water! She soon found other employment with appreciative employers." Pauline goes on to say, "Today, this wine taster's son is a retired well known doctor in Oregon whose wine-tastings can be of the best vintages."[1] She is talking about my father.

My grandmother told me that she knew of my grandfather while they were still in Slovenija, but that he was popular with the women, had a motorbike, and was a good dancer, so he was not interested in her at all. "He was too good for me," she explained. She added that after they were in America, there was a limited availability of Slovenian women, so he took notice of her and they got married. Frances Vertovec, a teenager related to Dad, was maid of honor at the wedding, and at the last minute, Dad's cousins Pauline and Ade were added to the ceremony. The bridesmaid went down the aisle first, followed by Francesca—the bride to be—and then Pauline and Ade. (Pauline's mother lost her first child Rudolf, in his infancy. Then came Pauline, who was nine years old when my grandparents married. Her brother, Ade, was born two years after her, in 1918—the same day their father died of the flu during the epidemic).

---

[1] Pauline Remec Moltzen, "The Slovenians of Elmhurst, Illinois," *Slovenija Quarterly* Magazine XIII, no. 1 (1999): 50.

Francesca told me how angry she was after finding herself pregnant (with my father) shortly after their wedding night (October 10, 1925), and he was born nine months to the day after that night. Karolina (Podgornik) Milost acted as midwife to Francesca. The story goes that Dad was born in Pauline Remec's home on Addison Avenue. Pauline Remec and her brother, Ade, were not allowed to come in the house that day. The excuse given was that a friend from South America was coming to visit. Why they couldn't come in when the friend had not yet arrived was something they did not question. Anyway, the friend from South America was Dad, and his young cousins first met him wrapped in a blanket and held by the midwife. Years later, Francesca let me know that after the birth of her second child, a daughter, four years later, she took to using a diaphragm. I was surprised to hear this from her, given how devout a Catholic she was. Another story that she and other family members told was of her going to confession and the priest questioning her about having only two children and suggesting that she add to her family. She told the priest to mind his own business and left the confessional. She explained that this was during the Great Depression, and times were hard enough as it was. Adding to her family would only make matters worse. She also told me a little bit about her early life in the old country. She and the other women there could balance big baskets on top of their heads without needing their hands to hold the basket in place. She explained that this was done to get things from one place to another while still having their hands free for work. I tried it without much luck, and she told me that this skill took a lot of practice.

Francesca's passport gives her height as five foot three but I'm not sure she was as tall as that, at least not in her older years when I knew her. She seemed more Italian than Slovenian in appearance and temperament, other than her almond-shaped green Slavic eyes that she passed on to my father and all four of his children. In the summer months, she would have sweat running down her face while she worked, moving quickly about, easy to yell or curse in her native tongue, and her hands always gesturing to accentuate her broken English. She had strong arms that were often busy kneading dough for habunsa, sweet bread, and strauba. She also prepared some of my favorite meals—pasta e fagioli and polenta con salsa di salmone e pomodoro. She was usually in a housedress, with no makeup other than a bit of rouge on Sundays for mass. I was fascinated with her rouge, which was kept in a little tin in her bedroom dresser, and she would often find me exploring the contents of her top dresser drawer with the rouge container and apply some to my cheeks. She also had a carnival glass candy dish in the living room and kept it full of Hershey's Kisses. My mother would usually find a stash of the candy hidden under my pillow, and Francesca would make sure to refill the dish so that I always had a steady supply. Because of my preoccupation with the candy dish and in an attempt to curb my candy theft, my mother suggested that it would be better for me to eat apples. She said I had replied that apples were good but that candy was "good-good," and so I continued on.

All of Francesca's meals were delicious, especially during holidays. She cooked a combination of Italian and Slovenian cuisine. There was a large garden behind the screened-in summer house where we ate our meals when the weather was hot. If a bee found its way into the summer house, Francesca would smash it by clapping her two hands together. She was always quick with this execution. She grew many fresh vegetables here. My favorite is a type of lettuce called regrad (pronounced ree-ute) that grows in Slovenija. She brought seeds over with her when she immigrated and had a healthy patch for all the years that my grandparents lived in their home. I have never seen this type of lettuce here, and it has a flavor all its own. As adults, my sister and I brought regrad seeds back from Slovenija when we visited, but neither of us was able to successfully grow a good patch the way she had. Gram-ma regularly prepared special items for her grandchildren. She made what she called black-and-white cows—the black was root beer or Coke with ice cream added to the glass, and the white was 7Up with ice cream. The ice cream would create a bubbling up of the pop that would rise up over the glass and run down over the sides. This made it taste all the better. She would also announce that she was going to prepare "whippin' Jell-O," and so we'd wait and watch as she prepared the Jell-O mixture, adding cream as she worked her egg beater around the bowl to form the airy pastel treat. Sometimes she simply whipped the Jell-O without the cream before she let it set up. We would wait impatiently until the dessert had been refrigerated long enough to eat.

While she was putting the finishing touches to the holiday meals, the grandchildren would visit her in the kitchen, while the other adults were in the living room. She would pour a jigger of wine for whichever of us requested it. She would also pour me jiggers of vinegar at my request because I liked its sour taste. On one of these occasions, my youngest male cousin made the trip into the kitchen for a jigger of wine one too many times. She seemed to have lost count about how often he had returned. He began running very fast around the living room, red-faced, bouncing on the chairs and laughing hysterically. The other adults found this quite amusing but didn't know why he was behaving this way until my grandmother confessed what she had done.

My grandfather had a more Slavic appearance and a strong, handsome face with high cheekbones, a broad forehead, and deep set eyes. He had thick sandy-brown hair and a medium muscular build. There was a gap between his two front teeth, a trait that his daughter inherited. A quiet, somber man who had learned his craft as a mason in the old country, he was able to find work in his American community to help support his family. Francesco was a protégé of Frank Vertovec, another Slovenian immigrant who started a construction business in the area. Francesco improved his skills under Frank's watchful eye. Francesco would labor in a slow, methodical, and precise fashion as he worked with his mortar, bricks, and stone. He always drank warm beer as he worked, explaining that water would bring on nausea in the hot, humid summer months. After a long day of work, he would love to watch the Chicago baseball teams play on the television and read his newspaper. His favorite team was the Chicago White Sox, in spite of the fact that he lived in a region where he was supposed to favor the Cubs. He would also listen to his native music on the radio. My grandmother was initially very angry when a television was purchased and would turn her chair around so that she wouldn't have to look at it. She would occupy herself with crocheting and such, but after a while, began turning her head to sneak a glance at the television. Before long, she became an avid fan. Her two favorite shows were The Beverly Hillbillies, which she called the hilly billies, and Charlie's Angels. When she saw the moon landing on the television nothing could convince her that it was for real. "It's all fake" is all she had to say about it.

The kitchen was always warm and inviting. Cooking and baking aromas would waft through the air. Gram-ma took great care in preparing my grandfather's favorite foods. She would explain that he needed a hearty meal due to the long hours that he had put in that day. Meals were usually eaten in the kitchen. In fact, this room was really the heart and soul of the home where relatives and Slovenian friends would congregate. Gram-pa always sat in the same place. There was a toothpick holder on the table, and after a meal, he would work his toothpick around in his mouth. We all ate with great gusto around the kitchen table. It was always a boisterous and lively scene. This carried on to future mealtimes after our move to Oregon where there were no pinkie fingers in the air at our family table—unless it was Dad, who sometimes feigned fussiness and pretentiousness in jest.

Most of my grandparents' siblings immigrated to Argentina after American immigration standards became more restrictive. Neither of my grandparents ever returned to their native land nor did they ever travel to Argentina. The only sibling of my grandmother who remained in Slovenija was Maks, her youngest brother. Her sister, Marija, and brothers, Josef, Francesco, and Albin, all immigrated to Argentina. My grandfather's oldest brother, Anthony, came to America in 1910. Other of his siblings, Joshko, Olga, and Cirila, all immigrated to Argentina. The only of my grandfather's siblings who remained in Slovenija was his older brother, Rafael and Cirila's twin brother, Mrtod, who died of a congenital malady at the age of twenty-five. A sister, born in Slovenija in 1896, was the first girl born in their lineage in over one hundred years, but she died in infancy.

A few relatives found their way to America over the years. One visitor was Yanko Krkoc, Rafael's son; thus, a nephew to my grandfather. Yanko was a Catholic priest in Slovenija who looked after a small parish. He had a gregarious lighthearted disposition and was well loved in his country by his family and parishioners. Much of his work there occurred during Tito's Communist rule. Religion was tolerated by this dictator but not encouraged. Yanko sometimes commented on the difficulty of his job in this unsupportive environment. Another visitor was Irma, a niece who traveled from Argentina. When she traveled to the States, Irma was a young natural beauty whose mother (Olga) was my grandfather's sister and whose father (Josef) was my grandmother's brother. I met her when I was about nine years old when she visited my grandparents, before Dad moved us to Oregon. Years later, my grandmother's youngest brother, Maks, visited from Slovenija. He was a baker by profession, a Communist who had given up his land to fellow Communists, which resulted in criticism from other relatives who didn't approve of his political bent. In spite of this, he was well received during his visit to America. A few years after his visit, he was hit by a car while walking on the side of a road in Slovenija and was killed—not an uncommon occurrence there, where driving is done with high velocity and risk-taking behavior.

SENTIMENT; A MEMOIR

My grandparents wrote letters and often sent care packages, which my grandmother would carefully prepare for their journey, to the old country. She would describe the poverty they had left behind and that she felt that they had found the land of opportunity in America. She explained that she felt obliged to assist her family that remained in Slovenija. She often described this world to me as a "vale of tears," referring to the trials and tribulations of life from the Catholic hymn Salve Regina's line "gementes et flentes in hac lacrimarum valle", translated "mourning and weeping in the valley of tears."[2] At first, I thought to myself that she was probably exaggerating about conditions there but later discovered more about my grandparents and other Slovenians before they came to America. The First World War occurred during the time before they left the place that was then called Austria-Hungary. Slovenija was only a small province in this country. After this war, Yugoslavia emerged from the downfall of the Habsburg Empire as a union of Slavic provinces. My aunt Jean and my father told me of the hardships that family in the old country had endured during this time.

There was a Slovenian community in Chicago proper, around St. Stephen's Church on Twenty-Second Street and the religious retreat Lemont run by Franciscan priests who spoke Slovene. The

---

[2] "Vale of Tears," *Wikipedia, The Free Encyclopedia*, http://en.wikipedia.org/wiki/Vale_of_tears.

Elmhurst Slovenes often rented a room over a pharmacy in town where they gathered and partied. There was dancing and frivolity during these events. Elmhurst had forty-five Slovenian families who stuck together and looked out for one another.

My aunt, her husband, Dad, and I traveled together to Yugoslavia and Italy in 1989, just before the civil war broke out there. Jean told me family stories while we traveled through Italy. One story was about my grandmother fleeing from the Italian soldiers in the fields where she worked as a young girl and that many of the females had been raped by the soldiers. Francesca had denied to her daughter that she had been raped, explaining that the soldiers overlooked her because she was so young. My aunt wasn't convinced that her mother's denial was truthful, though. Jean also told me that there were gypsies on her father's side of the family, but that her father would never admit to it. My father told of my grandmother's mother taking in men and sewing to provide for her family during hard times, while her husband was away as a soldier. He also told of his father going into the army at the age of fifteen. My grandfather eventually found himself in an Italian prison camp. He told my father that the soldiers would piss on the bread and throw it into the makeshift cells for the prisoners to eat. Dad said that, for the most part, his father didn't talk much about the war. My brother, Doug, told me later on that when he was seventeen and our grandparents were visiting in Oregon, Francesco told him a little more about his experience as a prisoner of war. He said that other food thrown in the cell barracks went into the latrines where they had to salvage it and that they also had to resort to eating rats to keep from starving the death. Gram-pa had tried to run away to escape but was caught and returned to the cell barracks. He told Doug that although he had tried to escape, the guards didn't shoot him as he expected they might. He also told Dad that when the war was over, he and the other prisoners simply walked back home to their villages. All this gave me the impression that many families left there in droves because of hardship, but Pauline Remec Moltzen had a different impression, which she shared in her article in the Slovenija Quarterly. It reads as follows: "The Statue of Liberty inscription welcoming the tired poor and wretched refuse hardly fits our people. [They were] poor in worldly goods, yes, but young, enthusiastic, and venturesome. I am reminded of young Anna Besednjak Rebek who was a delightful woman, much loved, with great generosity of spirit. She came to this country when about eighteen. She said that a group of young people in her village were wondering what to do for amusement one day. Probably in jest someone said let's go to America."[3] And they did.

---

[3] Pauline Remec Moltzen, "The Elmhurst Illinois Slovenians," Elmhurst Historical Museum Archives, 1999, 3.

Dad had the most expressive face of anyone I ever knew. It conveyed his feelings more than any words could ever have. He almost always had a smile on his face and seemed to be on top of the world during his youth. He carried himself with a measure of easy confidence. He took after his mother's family in appearance and disposition and had an uncanny resemblance to his paternal uncle, Josef, Francesca's oldest brother. Dad didn't know this uncle because Josef immigrated to South America from Slovenija, but my grandmother had photographs of Josef to compare Dad with. He had the dark complexion and the intense almond-shaped green eyes and black hair, which Dad combed straight back, of my grandmother and Josef, but his high cheekbones and physique were inherited more from his father. Dad filled a room with the energy and charisma that emanated from him. He had a fiery and temperamental nature. He felt things deeply. Being around him was like a drug. Since my earliest awareness, I had been drawn to him like a moth to a flame. There was his emotional intensity and exuberance—his joy with life. Even as a little girl, I knew we understood one another. I would come to recognize his traits in others as I got older, and they would have a similar effect on me as Dad had. This is when I could get myself into trouble.

Dad didn't speak English when he started the first grade at a Catholic school where nuns were his teachers. This led to his having a rough start in school because his teachers were neither kind nor helpful. In fact, they were unkind to him because of his different appearance and language. And they were too humorless for his taste. He recalled one of the nuns at school telling him that when someone smells a rose and enjoys the scent, it's sinful because of the pleasure it evokes. His response to her opinion in telling this story was that she was an asshole. His best friend, Joe Remec, lived a few doors down while he was growing up. Joe's mother, Victoria Cermelj Remec, was the one who traveled with my grandmother on the ship that brought both of them to America. Dad would tell of his youth when Gram-ma was continually yelling for him to come home, which prompted him to run further away. He described his mother as a "bulldog," referring to her headstrong and fiery disposition. Dad and Joe got into trouble regularly. For instance, they slid under the fence of the Elmhurst rock quarry to explore it and discovered that there were explosives there that they accidentally set off. Dad returned home full of shrapnel in his legs. Dad would reminisce about other activities that he, Joe, and other neighborhood kids would participate in. They became proficient at the games of jacks and marbles. Dad described himself as having been a hoodlum during his youth and later on seemed to have developed some regrets about his past transgressions. In spite of his regrets, he remained cagey up until the very end of his life. He was a whiz kid too. He developed an interest in the stock market at the age of twelve and got his dad to purchase stocks on his behalf.

For the rest of his life, this remained a hobby, which became quite lucrative for him.

When Joe and Dad were twelve, they found work at a local golf course that catered to the mafia. Dad said that he got good tips but he forever developed an aversion to the game. The mafia men had prostitutes to accompany them around the golf course. Dad would witness them dragging the prostitutes into the woods and then return to the game. I guess Dad didn't think this was cool, and thereafter, he had a poor opinion of the game of golf. Later on, he and Joe liked to go the racetrack to bet on the horses. Both of them knew what they were doing.

Joe (later on known as "Big Joe") had a stocky build compared to my father's slighter physique, which led to Dad's dependence on Joe to protect him if he got into too much trouble smarting off. Joe gained even greater strength after he started his career in construction. Joe never married. According to Dad, Joe's older brother had a reputation with the ladies from the early age of thirteen, when he began seeing women in their twenties and thirties. Joe, on the other hand, didn't have much to do with women. He told Dad he would never bring anyone else into this crummy world and hence would never marry. Joe did have a romance with a woman while he was in the service in the tropics but returned home without her and lived with his mother and later took care of her in her old age.

His father died during his childhood, which made circumstances for his family even more difficult than other Slovenian families that had an able-bodied male breadwinner.

Dad took Sandy and me to the Walgreens soda fountain in Elmhurst every weekend. We would meet up with Joe and the other Slovenian men there. I loved being a part of this gathering. Dad sat us up on the fountain stools, and we would order our lime rickey and listen in on the men's conversations. Big Joe, in particular, spoiled us. He had a loud booming voice, a rough edge, and a sarcastic and cynical sense of humor, but all the kids in our family loved him. He gave us Christmas and birthday gifts into our adulthood, sending them to Oregon from Chicago. Joe had a dog named Dumb Nuts, but when kids were around, he called him Stinky. The dog went everywhere with Joe. As Stinky got older, he became decrepit and incontinent, so Joe would have to carry him everywhere and clean up after his messes. Joe finally had to put diapers on Stinky. Dad was never much for animals, especially dogs. One time, while he was visiting in Chicago, he asked Joe why he put up with Stinky. Joe told Dad that Stinky was his friend, and that's why.

When I conferred with Sandy about Joe, she asked how I would be able to get the gist of Joe on paper, and I admitted that I didn't know. She seemed disappointed with what I had written so far, so I asked her to write something for me. She questioned her ability to get anything worthwhile down herself, so I told her "Oh, just write something. It doesn't have to be perfect." It took her a while, but this is what she sent me: "Joe Remec was a loyal and true friend. He had an invincible and incorruptible moral sense, a vulnerability to human fragility but a general distrust and often even disgust of human nature . . . He was a mountain of a man—a jolly Clemenza who children were naturally drawn to. He'd bob around in the lake like a huge cork laughing while kids tried futilely to dunk him. He used his sharp and acid wit to skewer those bits of bad behavior he'd see inherent in human nature. This it seemed was maybe in hopes of improving mankind's lot if only just a little."

My mother was beautiful—a delicate, ethereal woman who had a face and figure similar to Marilyn Monroe's (especially before Marilyn became famous) but also had a quality and appearance that reminded me somewhat of Ingrid Bergman. She had a broad forehead, porcelain skin with a sprinkle of freckles, auburn hair, full lips, and what Dad called a movie star's nose that was natural. She loved to go to the movies, and this may have inspired her to dress in her stylish manner of the 1940s and 1950s. There was a shyness to her that set her apart from my father who was anything but. She tells of spotting him in the halls of their high school when she was fourteen years of age. He was sixteen then, and he remembered teasing her by asking her to show him her report card, which he discovered had straight As. Nothing came of this interaction for some time because Dad enlisted in the navy during his first year at Elmhurst College and spent the next few years overseas during the end of World War II. While he was overseas, Mom finished high school and also did factory work to help make ends meet at home and complained about the perfume factory assembly line work. The factory was not air conditioned and the temperature and humidity would rise to the nineties in the summer months. She was responsible for putting the labels on the bottles. Tabu was one of the perfumes that she could never tolerate smelling after having worked there. Mom used to reminisce about going to Downtown Chicago on the El after the end of the war was declared and told of the celebration in the streets that occurred there. I have wondered if she hoped she might spot my father returning home, as she reported seeing many exuberant sailors celebrating in the streets. By the time my father returned to the United States, she had graduated from high school and was working at a soda fountain shop on the Elmhurst College campus. He resumed college there on the GI Bill, and they picked up where they left off.

They married on September 3, 1949. Mom was working for the Public Service Company as an executive secretary to a man named Ray Nelson whom she remembered fondly over the years. Dad was still attending Elmhurst College after his return from his stint in the navy. Dad bought a leather-bound photo album (purchased during their honeymoon) with a painting of a Native American on the cover and the word "photographs" above the Native American's head. To the right of the Native American were the words "Waupaca, Wis." The pages were made of thick black paper, and Dad printed and drew pictures in white ink. In the book, he mapped out the course of their honeymoon and added sentimental and playful comments. The album also included photos and comments about their return home, their new apartment above his folks, the construction of the house in Villa Park, various family events, and the funeral of their friend Dick Wolf who was murdered in Chicago on New Year's Eve of 1950. Mom had dated Dick briefly, and Dick and Dad had been friends in high school. Mom and Dad partied on New Year's Eve with Dick and their other friends, and Dick had suggested they head down to Chicago to continue the celebration, but everyone declined for one reason or another, so Dick headed out on his own. Mom was pregnant with me. The next morning, they got word that Dick was found dead in a Chicago alley. Dad saved a slip of paper Dick gave him that night with the date, December 31, 1950, his new address, phone number, and where he was to attend college. Dad added the date of his death the next day (January 1, 1951) to the slip of paper and added it in the photo album.

After Mom found out that she was pregnant with me, she wasn't allowed to work at the Public Service Company any longer, which she said was common practice in those days. She busied herself in preparation for her new career as a housewife and mother. When Mom was about six months pregnant, she and Dad attended a costume party. She went as a clown to take advantage of her big belly, and Dad dressed as a woman with high heels, a formal dress, wig, purse, and makeup—the whole works. They were driving to the Halloween party when a cop pulled them over on the highway. He had them get out of the car. Dad was walking around with his getup as motorists whizzed by. I'm not sure he thought it was funny at the time, but he laughed about his embarrassment when he told the story after the fact. After graduating college, Dad started working for (I think) International Harvester Company but didn't like it much. His math professor, John B., from college encouraged him to apply to medical school, and so he did. He was accepted at the University of Illinois. I had colic, so I wasn't a very cooperative infant and cried all night long. We were living above my grandparents and my grandmother would come upstairs at night and complain to my parents about my crying, so my mother walked with me for hours to keep me quiet. Dad complained that he would never finish medical school. He bought a car for twenty-five dollars to get back and forth from school. It was a piece of crap. He said he could see the road through the holes in the floorboard of the car. One day it just conked out on the highway. He left it there on the side of the road and hitched a ride home.

I remember Dad always spending time with us in spite of his schooling and his work as a milkman down in Chicago. His route included all the inner city neighborhoods, and he would tell of the ones that were the most fun. He built snow slides with snow steps in our backyard and poured water on the slide, which would freeze and make the slide even faster. He also fashioned a go-cart with a lawn mower motor that my sister and I would ride around the driveway and sidewalks in our neighborhood. It went so fast that I can't believe we never had any mishaps with it. I remember him playing plane with us by holding our arms and swirling us around and showing us how to make snow angels in the snow in the winter. Sometimes we would have our pajamas on and be ready for bed, and he would pack us into the car and we would all ride with the radio on, playing fifties tunes or black jazz stations. Our destination was a small popcorn shop in Wheaton about a thirty-minute drive from home. The shop was so long and narrow that one could barely fit into it. We would each get a bag of popcorn from the clerk and drive home, eating away. Dad would say "This is the best popcorn in the world!" and we thought so too. He would also take Sandy and me out to Lake Michigan on his days off. Mom used to laugh about his telling of one of these excursions where I had to pee. He said that the water was choppy that day, and he had no other choice than to offer his felt fedora for me to use. Then he threw it into the waters of Lake Michigan and returned home hatless. When Mom wasn't around for whatever reason, he'd make meals for us and would announce that he was going to get out the "Daddy plates." Then he'd take out a box of waxed paper, tear a sheet off for each of us, and that was our Daddy plate. Cleanup was easy. He just grabbed each used waxed paper, crumpled it into a ball, and disposed each of them in the garbage. Well, you know, Dad just taught us how to have fun.

Sandy and I kept our paper dolls and their clothes in a shoe box. The dolls and their clothing, hats, shoes, etc. came inside a book. We had to cut the dolls and their clothes out before we could place them inside the shoe box. Then we would dress our dolls up, using the little tabs on the clothes, shoes, etc. to hold them in place. One time Dad brought us paper nurse outfits—a nurse's uniform and hat—from the hospital. We were like paper dolls, only for real. He also brought home Japanese candy called Tomoe Ame as a treat for us. It came in a brightly colored box with a special compartment on the bottom that had a little toy inside. The candy was an orange-flavored soft little square gelatin, but the best thing about it was that the candies were wrapped in clear rice paper. Dad would say "You girls don't have to unwrap the candy, just put it in your mouths." When we did, the rice paper would dissolve with a pleasant sensation for us, and the orange gel filled our mouths with flavor. He explained about the candy wrapper every time he brought them home for us. Looking back, I just think he liked the telling of it. Dad had a special place set up for his studying in their bedroom. I would creep in at times to say hello and visit. He always had a shiny dark brown porcelain Japanese teapot sitting on his desk. It had a delicate gold leaf and brightly colored raised dots of paint for decoration. Teabag strings hung out the top. He always told me that he needed his tea when studying in order to help keep him awake. He'd pour me a little cup so that I could join him, and we would visit one another. I still have the teapot.

Mom would put a blow-up swimming pool in the backyard for my sister and me to splash around in. There was also a deck off the living room in our upstairs apartment where we would play. It had a sandbox next to the wall with rakes, pails, and shovels. Mom also read to us. Her mother hadn't allowed her to read during her adolescence. Maybe this had something to do with Mom spending time with us in this way, to instill the love of reading that she had. Later on, she would take us to the library or a bookstore, and we would pick out books of our own. Some of my favorites were Mary Poppins (much better than the movie), the Winnie-the-Pooh series, (also better than the animated versions), and all the Dr. Seuss books (ditto). Once, while on the deck, my mother witnessed my grandfather backing out of the garage and hitting my tricycle, which I left out in the driveway. She said that he sat frozen in his car, fearing what he might discover. Mom had to run down to tell him that I hadn't been on the trike before he was able to get out of his car to inspect the crumpled wreckage.

There were two other mishaps during this very early period of my life. Dad often lamented about an incident while he was taking me for a stroller ride in our neighborhood when I fell out of it and landed on my head. The other was while I ran up and down the brick walls of the steps that led off the front porch, and I fell off. I do remember this event and the egg-shaped lump that formed on my forehead after the fact. Mom also told of mischief that I would get into in our upstairs apartment—piling the kitchen chairs one on top of the other where she would find me sitting on the top chair near the ceiling, poking holes in cakes she had prepared for one of our birthdays, and flushing utensils down the toilet, which caused considerable difficulty with the plumbing. No one in the household was aware of the cause of these problems until she finally witnessed a spoon disappearing in the bowl. Mom often described me as having always been headstrong. "You always had to get your way," she would explain, not really in a critical tone—it was just a matter of fact.

I contracted hard measles from a friend of mine from the neighborhood named Janey. She had been to my birthday party a few weeks earlier and had come back to visit me. Mom asked why we hadn't seen her in a while, and she said that she had had the measles. When Dad found out about this, he was angry that her parents hadn't warned us because there was some kind of shot to be given that might help ward off the disease or at least make it less severe. But it was too late for this to be successful as I came down with it that very day. I was very ill, and my parents feared for my life. My mother said that I didn't gain a pound for a few years after this illness. I was also plagued with frequent ear infections. The only remedies in those days were mineral oil applied with an eye dropper, a cotton ball to hold it in place, and a hot-water bottle. I still remember the long nights I lay awake with my painful ears. Eventually, the symptoms would subside, but the ear infections led to my having my tonsils removed. I was admitted to the hospital and promised ice cream after the operation was over. Unfortunately, the anesthesia made me feel nauseated, and so I passed on the offer of ice cream. Instead, my parents told me that I could have anything I wanted when I got home, and I decided that I wanted a bottle of wine. They bought it for me and would dole it out in a shot glass like Francesca did in her kitchen for her grandchildren. Wine tasted good to me.

My first home had a walkway that led to four brick steps with borders and then two more cement steps that led to the front door, which was arched at the top. There were white scalloped squares and white oblong bricks that formed an arch around the door. This led to the hallway with a set of stairs and banister that led to our apartment on the second floor. Sandy and I loved to slide down the banister. On the right side of the hallway were glass French doors with sheer curtains covering the glass that led to the living room. Upon entering the living room from the French doors, there was a stone fireplace and mantle directly across. To the right was a set of bay windows that faced the front of the house. This is where the living room sofa was stationed. There was a console radio next to the sofa. Other chairs were situated around the room, two on either side of the fireplace and the French doors with side tables accompanying them. All the furniture was covered with plastic covers to protect them from wear. There was an entryway from the living room into the dining room, which had a large mahogany dining table, chairs, china cabinet, and buffet. There were a row of windows with sheers covering the windows and curtains that were left open to let in the light. A combination bathroom and bedroom were behind the dining room and had been added on to the house to accommodate Jean and Jack after they were married. For a while, my parents were upstairs during the same time Jean and Jack occupied the bedroom suite—until a house was built for them several blocks away. The walls of the bedroom were decorated with pictures of Madonna and Child, crucifixes, and other religious paraphernalia. The adjoining bathroom is where my cousins Cindy and Greg, my sister, and I would lock the door during holidays and hang out. (This is also the room my grandmother dropped dead in years later while preparing herself for a trip to Oregon to visit our family. We were on our way out the door to drive from Bend to Portland to pick up my grandparents from the airport when we got the call that they would not be coming after all).

A swinging door connected the dining room and the kitchen, which, as I have mentioned, was the heart and soul of the house. Here, there was a turquoise table set with chrome legs and vinyl fabric on the chair seats. A window at the sink looked out on the backyard where the screened summer house and garage were located. There was a laundry chute and a built-in ironing board behind a latched door in the wall, next to the swinging doors in the kitchen, and also one in our upstairs apartment's hallway. These were used for more than dirty clothes. All manner of objects were deposited in the chute by the children that occupied the home and later retrieved in the basement where they landed next to the washing machine, which had a hand-operated wringer. Clotheslines decorated the basement to accommodate drying clothes in the winter. The washing machine had hoses hooked up to it from a deep sink for filling and emptying the machine. There were steps that left the kitchen and went to an exterior door on the side of the house, but there was also a sharp turn one could make to the right before going outside, where there were additional stairs that led to the basement.

In the basement, in addition to the washing machine that held much interest for me as a child, there were numerous interesting rooms. One was a water closet with a toilet, a sink, and a pull string for a bare bulb to light the room. This is where my grandfather would get away from the crowd and was often found shaving. Around the corner from the bathroom was a large room with shelves where my grandmother kept stuff that she didn't have room for in the upstairs part of the house. She would show me all sorts of things that she had in there. She also told me that she had stored photographs from the old country in this room that had been destroyed when the basement flooded, which happened fairly often in spite of a drain in the cement floor. (She did have some photos she had kept in the dining room china cabinet upstairs that remained safe, however, but did not include any of her parents). Another room was for wine making. The basement was large enough to play in when the weather wasn't good outside.

Next to the door in the kitchen that led outside and to the basement was another door that led to my grandparents' bedroom. This room was small and faced the front of the house. There was a small water closet off the bedroom that faced the entrance hallway. I suspect my grandfather had intended for all the bedrooms to be on the second floor but the Great Depression led to his remodeling the home and their renting out the upstairs to tenants. He may have converted an original den into their bedroom and water closet, closing off this room to the entrance hallway. It is likely that there was an entrance from the hallway to the den early on, before it became their bedroom.

When my parents married, the upstairs apartment became theirs. Because of the way the house was designed, they made use of the front door that took them to the stairway leading to the second floor. My grandparents normally used the side door that led to the kitchen, and this was also the way that friends and relatives entered. There was a doorbell at the side door so that they would know when someone was there. The upstairs isn't as clear to me in memory as the ground floor. I do remember that it was small, and so after my parents had me and Sandy, they made a bedroom for us out of the kitchen nook that had been used for a kitchen table. They attached a curtain to separate it from the rest of the kitchen. Mom decorated the nook with circus wallpaper—horses, clowns, giraffes, circus tents—and the space held a console radio, Sandy's crib, and my little mattress. The apartment was heated with radiators. It felt good to stand in front of them to get warm after having been outside during the winter months.

Because Mom had been working before she married, she was able to save up to furnish the apartment. She bought a blonde bedroom set for their bedroom that was very modern at the time. The bureau, highboy, and side tables had big brass handles. Mom also purchased a very interesting chair for the living room. It was shaped somewhat like a snail, was light gray with a flower-patterned cushion, and you could swirl around on it or slide down the sloped edge. It was accompanied by matching flowered draperies on the windows and an imitation rock ottoman with a fabric top. There was also a fifties-style end table with a glass top and an open storage shelf under the glass. It was set next to a charcoal-gray couch that had only one arm opposite the end table. Dad fashioned bookshelves with loose bricks and Formica placed against the wall by the couch. The rug was a light sea green with a swirled pattern that sat on the hardwood floors. The woodwork had been dark, but Mom wanted her new home to be "modern," so she stripped the woodwork and made it look light. She would have birthday parties for us in our apartment, with hats, blowers, balloons, cake, ice cream, games—pin the tail on the donkey, London bridge, ring around the rosie—cousins, grandmothers, aunts, and a few friends thrown in.

The deck off our living room had a wood plank floor and balusters with railing and a trellis under the railing. There were four stakes that left the brick wall with a baluster that followed. The trellis was airy, with a crisscross design and intersecting and parallel bars. Later on, it was covered with canvas to prevent grandchildren from falling over the edge. The deck looked out over the backyard, where one could see the screened summer house, the garden, garage, and the wishing well that my grandfather had built next to the summer house. There was a bucket with a pulley that we could put stuff in and lower or raise to retrieve our treasures. Behind the garage, there were pens where the chickens were kept. They served to provide eggs and Sunday meals that included a chicken dish. I have very vivid memories of my grandmother grabbing a chicken and chopping off its head on a block of wood using a hatchet, and there were times when the chicken would continue to run around the backyard without its head, blood spurting from its neck. She was very matter-of-fact about this process, but for me, it was horrifying.

Certain television shows had stuck in my mind from these early years. Mister Peepers, starring Wally Cox as a junior high science teacher, is one of my first television memories. He was comical looking, timid, and had a high squeaky voice. Mrs. Gurney (Marion Lorne) was an older, often confused English teacher and cohort of his and Tony Randall played Harvey Weskit, a history teacher at the school.[4] Then there was the show Our Miss Brooks- about a sardonic English high school teacher with her teaching cohorts and students.[5] The Life of Riley with William Bendix was another

[4] "Mister Peepers," *Wikipedia, The Free Encyclopedia,* http://en.wikipedia.org/wiki/Mister_Peepers.

[5] "Our Miss Brooks," *Wikipedia, The Free Encyclopedia,* http://en.wikipedia. org/wiki/Our_Miss_Brooks.

favorite. He was a gullible lug who got himself into trouble, often with the help of his neighbor and best friend, Gillis. His wife was Peg and his children were Babs and Junior.[6] I Love Lucy, last but not least, was probably the show that I watched the most. It provided me with the lasting impression that a married woman has to be sneaky to do what she wants in life.

At Christmastime, Mom and Dad would take Sandy and me on the El into Chicago. We got to see the displays in the department store windows and make a visit to Santa Claus at Marshall Field's. On one of these trips, I saw a different bell-ringing Santa on the street who was drunk, which confused me at first, as I had just seen the "real" Santa, so I decided that the drunk Santa was a fake.

Francesca took me to Chicago with her too when I was about the same age, three or four. I spotted a black man in the store we were in. This was the first time I had ever seen a black person. I pointed at him and said, "Look Gram-ma, that man is chocolate" in a loud voice. She tried to shush me, but I remained undeterred. It wasn't long after this event that I decided I wanted a black baby doll. I pestered my parents until they took me to a department store where I got to pick out the doll of my choice. I named her Fire. I

---

[6] "The Life of Riley," *Wikipedia, The Free Encyclopedia,* http://en.wikipedia.org/wiki/The_Life_of_Riley.

don't know how I came up with that name, but of course, one definition of the word is "fervor, spirit, ardor."[7] Anyway, I loved Fire.

Mom's family immigrated to America between the early and middle 1800s. Settlers had come because their homeland was overworked and overcrowded. Mom said that her grandmother remembered her family living peacefully with the Potawatomi Native Americans and that these people had been friendly to the German immigrants and helped them survive the hard winters. Although a treaty agreement in 1937 led to the relocation of many of these indigenous people, some remained in the area.[8] My maternal grandmother Nora's family's early settlers were farmers and later merchants. Nora's uncle (Edward) became a doctor. Her family had become affluent until the Great Depression changed their social status. Nora's father (August) ran a grocery and general store and was the mayor of Addison, Illinois.

My grandfather was born an Asche. His mother, Luisa Graue, died on April 18, 1889, shortly after the birth of her eighth child. My grandfather was not quite three years of age. His father died of a heart attack on July 9 the following year, a little over a year after

---

[7]   The American Century Dictionary, Warner Book Edition, 1995. Oxford University Press, Inc.

[8]   "Mastadons and Indians," http://w w w.dupageheritage.org. yps /chapter 1.html, under "Chapter 1," 1 and 4.

his wife's demise. Their eight children were divided up among relatives to be raised. Franz became a "poor relation" and was adopted by the Rathje family, Louis and Caroline (maiden name Fischer). Franz had Fischers in his family tree, which may account for his going to them after his parents' deaths.

Luisa's grandfather, Johann Conrad, and father, Frederick Graue were millers by occupation. They ran the Graue Mill in Oak Brook, Illinois along with the Asche family. This is where they provided food and shelter in the basement of their gristmill in order to assist slaves in escaping slavery. The Underground Railroad provided transportation to such stations which led to the eradication of slavery in the 1800's. The Underground Railroad remained active until the end of the civil War.[9]

After living with the Rathje family for about ten years, Franz moved in with his adoptive sister, Martha, and her new husband, Edward Marquardt, my grandmother Nora's uncle. I suspect that this arrangement led at least in part to my grandparents having been acquainted during their adolescence. He remained with the Marquardts until he married Nora at the age of twenty-eight.

---

[9]   Graue Mill visitors travel to Underground Railroad in Oak Brook, by Pioneer Press Staff, Chicago Tribune, August 2, 2015, http://www.chicagotribune.com/suburbs/oak-brook/news/ct-dob-underground-railroad-tl-0806-2015082-story.html

She was twenty-five. The Marquardts were well- to-do, but Franz didn't benefit financially from his association with them or his adoptive parents, the Rathjes. He did, however, get some money from the Asche family estate which he used to build a home for his new bride. Franz was sort of a jack-of-all-trades. He worked at E. C. Simmons Keen Kutter Cutlery and Hardware store and for Suburban Auto Insurance Company as an underwriter, then as a postman (one of the first two in Elmhurst), a builder, and a firefighter. His first job was in management at the York Theatre in downtown Elmhurst, and also his last during his old age when he returned as an usher. Mom and Dad would walk down to the York while living with my other grandparents when Sandy and I were little. They would get us into bed, and our grandparents kept an eye on us while they were gone. They got to go the movies for free. I also remember going there while my grandfather worked at the York. He would take our tickets and show us to our seats with his flashlight.

Mom used to tell us about her early years growing up. It sounded much different than how things are now. She described having a large console radio in the living room. In the evenings, the family would gather around the radio and listen to the presentations—often dramas, comedy shows, and even thrillers—much like television but without the visual. She also described the big tub in the kitchen for bathing. Her mother would heat water on the stove for the bath. Bath night was always on Sunday. Mom would also describe all the canning her mother did in the fall for the winter months, when the garden would be covered in snow. The canned goods had to last through the winter months until spring, when the garden would start to produce again. Her father (and later also her brother) brought home game to provide food for the family too. Mom grew tired of venison and such and during her adult life avoided such things.

My maternal grandparents lived several blocks away from us at 136 Elmhurst Avenue—an easy walk from 245 Maple Avenue. This was a much different environment than that of my Dad's parents. This was the home built by Franz shortly after he and my grandmother married. The outside had stucco walls covered with vines. There was a large screened in porch in the front of the house where a swing hung from two chains at the far end of the porch entrance on the right. Chairs and end tables were scattered across the porch, which really made it a type of living room outdoors. This is where family congregated during the warm-weather months. A table fan sat next to the front door to move the air. My grandmother would occupy the swing, but when she wasn't in it, her grandchildren would take over.

From the front porch, there was a door that led to a long hallway with a small lavatory at the end. Next to the lavatory door was an entry into the kitchen on the left. Above the small sink in the lavatory, there was a small medicine cabinet where a small brown bottle of Mercurochrome was stored. It had a rubber stopper with a glass applicator and a glass bulb on the end. When one of us would get a scrape or a cut, Gram-ma would paint some of the orange-red tincture on our "owie" to doctor us. It would sting at first but made us feel better anyway. The Mercurochrome had a distinctive and pleasant scent (at least to me), and the orange stain on our skin would hold some fascination and seemed to distract us from any discomfort we might be feeling.

On the way to the lavatory, there was a cuckoo clock on the right wall of the hallway. It had two little doors, and at each quarter hour, a little bird would pop out of one door and cheep once, twice, thrice, or four times as it reached the hour. At the hour, the other door would also pop open with another bird that would follow with a low-toned cuckoo as many times as the hour. My grandmother would pick us up and let us move the hands around so that we wouldn't have to wait for the birds to sound off on their own. This didn't agree with my grandfather, who was a meticulous and finical man. (Mom used to complain about his precision in trimming a tree—placing the tinsel one at a time, and it had to be evenly distributed. This, she had explained, took the fun out of it). Franz expected that tampering with the clock as such would impair its functioning. He didn't get very far in deterring

Nora from entertaining us thus, however. She merely ignored his protestations. My grandmother was actually somewhat slovenly. Mom would describe growing up with sticky cupboard handles and floors. Gram-ma would do her baking without cleaning up her hands after mixing sticky dough and carelessly drop things on the floor. She was remiss in cleaning up after herself in general. She often had a disheveled appearance. Oddly enough, this seemed to contribute to a kind of sensuality about her. Mom didn't seem to appreciate these opposing traits of her parents.

The living room was on the right of the hallway and the den was on the left. The rooms were decorated in the turn-of-the-century-Victorian- style heavy fabrics, dark wood, wallpaper, ornate objects, ornamentation, and oriental rugs. My grandfather had built in stained glass windows that decorated the living and dining room areas. There were built-in bookcases with glass doors and shelves partially separating the living room and dining room behind it. The den held particular interest for me because there was a large deer head with antlers hanging on the wall across from the front window and a Tiffany lamp on a desk in front of the window. There was a set of three or four steps at the back of the room that led to the kitchen. The kitchen had an identical set of steps that connected it to the den, and both led to another set of stairs at a sharp turn that led to the interior second-story part of the house.

At the back exterior of the house was a set of stairs attached to the wall that led to the screened mud room where you entered into the kitchen. To the left of the kitchen, there was a narrow hall-like butler's pantry that connected the kitchen and the dining room where utensils, china, and cooking ingredients were stored. It had a counter space below the cupboards that served as a place to put the finishing touches on the dishes being prepared. Below the counter space were drawers containing the utensils. The cupboards held the china and cooking ingredients. At the back of the kitchen was a doorframe that led to the short set of steps that converged with the other set that led to the den. There was also a door at the back of the kitchen next to the doorframe that went into the basement. The pantry and stairways held interest for me as a young child, as the house was something of a maze. The pantry was busy when there was a family dinner being prepared. The work involved was out of sight of the adult guests but not from me and my sister, who ran back and forth between the kitchen and dining room to observe the activity in the pantry. The kitchen had a small two-chaired table on the side exterior wall with windows above. There was a deep sink as one entered from the hallway. The refrigerator and stove sat at the back exterior wall.

The interior stairs of the house led to the bedrooms on the second floor. There was a small landing that had entries into each of the bedrooms and a bathroom with a black-and-white tile floor, claw-foot tub, and toilet with a pull chain. My sister remembers an additional door behind the tub that led to one of the bedrooms. There was also a screened sleeping porch that looked out over the backyard. It was open aired and screened in the summer but converted to a closed porch in the winter months with storm windows that opened for fresh air. One of the bedrooms that faced the backyard had a small closet with a narrow set of windows. This is where I remember sneaking into so I could hide out and observe the activity in the backyard, unnoticed.

The property around the house was spacious and traveled all the way to the next block, which sustained a large garden area. Behind the garage, there were cages that held raccoons that my grandfather kept. My sister and I would run through and explore the rows of vegetables and stakes in the garden. There were also various fruit trees interspersed among the vegetables, and we would pick up fallen fruits to eat. We visited with the raccoons, which seemed friendly, and poked snippets of food for them between the cage wires and watched them work their food around in their delicate little hands and nibble it up. There was a metal swing in the backyard that my grandmother spent most of her days in during the warm weather. She visited with her lady friends and family. The swing had a trellis around it with grape vines and juicy big purple Concord grapes that we would pick and eat. Next to the swing was a rock garden with an old bathtub that had been built into it.

It often had water in it for us to float our rubber ducks or toy sail boats on. Behind the mud room, there was an exterior door which opened to a flight of steps that led down to the basement. It was fun to run down these steps to get to the basement and then travel up the inside steps to the ground floor and outside again.

In her older years, my grandmother was as wide as she was tall and had large bushy black eyebrows. She liked to wear flowery dresses, hosiery, and always tucked a hanky down her dress into her ample bosom. She cut a hole in one of her black leather shoes where a bunion was so that it wasn't so painful when she walked. She blinked a lot and had a rather comical but pleasant face. She loved to eat and even had a habit of swiping her finger through the butter dish as she passed by in the kitchen and sucking the butter off her finger. In her younger years, she had been quite lovely. My mother often described her mother as having been a Gibson Girl—"The American ideal who had an ample bosom, hips, and bottom, an exaggerated S-curve torso shape with the use of a swan-bill corset, and hair piled high on her head. She was dressed in the latest fashionable attire, was independent, confident and portrayed as sexually dominant. The illustrator Charles Dana Gibson personified this feminine ideal in his satirical pen-and-ink illustrations during this time period."¹⁰ My grandmother fit the bill.

Nora would be so happy to see her grandchildren arrive that she would smother us with wet kisses, but our grandfather was usually standoffish. The first memory I have of him was when I was playing in their backyard and chasing a familiar squirrel. I chased it out toward the street where it ran in front of a passing car and was run over. After witnessing its demise, I was distraught, and after telling him what had happened, he picked up the squirrel and carefully helped me give it a proper burial. He had a collection of interesting objects in his basement, where he spent a good deal of his time. In his later years, when he worked on and off at the York Theatre, he would bring billboards home and attach them to the walls of the basement. There was also a cut-out cardboard figure of Gregory Peck from the movie The Man in the Gray Flannel Suit that came from the York Theatre. He stood in the basement and was so realistic that he was rather frightening to see as we flew down the steps. Gram-pa would also pin up clippings of jokes from the newspaper alongside the billboards. He was a taxidermist too and had various stuffed birds, squirrels, and raccoons on display. There was a small cuckoo clock on the wall that held much interest for me and my sister. So did the train track set that pulled down from

¹⁰ "Gibson Girl," Wikipedia, The Free Encyclopedia, http://en.wikipediia.org/wiki/Gibson_Girl.

the wall with operating trains. There was a room for making wine with a bathtub that was used for the process, with shelves for the equipment and bottle storage. My sister remembers Al Watts, (my grandfather's cousin's husband) who lived next door, spending time with my grandfather there making and drinking wine. Gram-pa also smoked his pipe. He had his toolshed down there where he did his woodworking. This is where he fashioned a wooden cutout that was either a duck or a rabbit depending on how one looked at it. Sandy remembered the basement as having been man's world.

Mom would drop my sister and me off at her folks after she started work at Olswang's Department Store. She told us later on that my grandmother would let us do just about anything while in her care, including coloring on the walls. I remember a large tin that held an assortment of buttons that she would let us sort through too. I was also fascinated with her telephone desk with the old-fashioned dial phone where she spent a great deal of time talking to friends and family. She let us play with it and make phone calls. Gram-ma had bad eyesight, and once, my sister tripped over some furniture in the den and cut her leg badly. I could see to the bone. I ran for Gram-ma, but she evidently couldn't see well enough to recognize the extent of damage done to my sister's leg and suggested that it was not of any concern. I was worried, and so I waited until she left the room and then called my father who left work to see what was going on. He took my sister to her pediatrician who sewed her up. Sandy remembers Dad taking her to Walgreens for a lime rickey after her ordeal. I stayed at my grandmother's until Mom came to pick me up. I suspect that in addition to my grandmother's poor eyesight, she didn't want to admit that one of us had been injured while in her charge. (According to Mom, when Nora was a child, she and her friends played a game with the sun. They all tried to be able to stare at it longer than the others. Mom speculated that this is what led to her mother's near blindness). Another time, Sandy fell asleep on the couch in the living room. She didn't see Sandy on the couch, again, because of her poor eyesight. She had covered herself with a blanket. When she woke up, she observed Gram-ma running around on the side of the house with a frantic look in her eyes. Sandy figured out Gram-ma was looking for her, so she ran outside to see her.

Sometimes Sandy and I would be dropped off to spend the night at our grandparents'. I remember being afraid to stay there. The house seemed spooky at night. My grandparents always had a boarder to help make ends meet, and one was living there during the times we would visit. I don't remember him ever acknowledging my sister or me, but his presence was felt by both of us. He had one of the bedrooms upstairs, and he would wander around at night. The cuckoo clock in the hallway downstairs was loud. It seemed to act as the heartbeat of the house, which was heard throughout the day and night. If I had to get up at night, the house seemed difficult to navigate because of all its twists and turns.

Gram-ma would read to us before we went to bed. One of the storybooks she read out of was Little Red Riding Hood. She acted out the part of the wolf during her telling of the story—which neither I nor Sandy appreciated. Then she would always say the same prayer with us—"Now I lay me down to sleep, pray the lord my soul to keep. If I die before I wake, pray the lord my soul to take." Did that mean I might not make it through the night? I have another clear memory of being with my parents, grandparents, and my sister on their front porch for a visit. Nora read an article in the newspaper out loud about a local little girl who had been found in the basement of one of the homes at Elmhurst. She had been kept down there by her parents and nearly starved to death. This story led to nightmares about basements and my being kept in one, like the girl in the newspaper article. Since my grandparents had a basement that seemed scary to me anyhow, this story seemed to further fuel my fears about what might happen to me while staying there overnight.

When Mom dropped us off to go to work, Gram-ma would ask me about what I wanted to be when I grew up. Even when I was very young, I was aware that there was tension between my mother and my grandmother. I was also aware that my parents' marriage had not been approved of by my mother's family. In fact, her parents, my grandmother in particular, refused to have anything to do with it at first. This had to do with my father's immigrant parents and with his being Catholic. My mother's family came from a long line of Lutherans from Germany who married their own kind, and to my knowledge, my mother was the only family member in this country (other than her Uncle Edgar and my cousin Ken who married a Catholic who converted to Lutheranism) who had ever transgressed this tradition. Mom followed her heart in her decision to go against her family's wishes. She went ahead, arranged for, and paid for her own wedding, which her parents finally agreed to attend. It was only after I was born that they began to accept my parents' marriage. My grandmother was eager to be involved with grandchildren that were a product of my parents' union. All this history may have had to do with my response to my grandmother's question about what I wanted to be when I grew up. I always told her that I expected to be a nun. She would say "Oh no, you mustn't say that" and then suggest other options. In spite of her objection to my choice, I kept insisting that I had plans on becoming a nun. I didn't, really. I only said this to defend myself. I also remember relatives I never got to know very well who would drop by to visit my grandmother. They would make disparaging remarks about my sister and me being "little Catholics." Even then, I knew it was meant as some sort of insult. I never mentioned this to my parents, but the comments stuck with me. A few of Mom's relatives who visited my grandmother were always nice to us, though. They brought gifts for my sister and me. These were my aunt Lena, who was the more-than-half-sister of my grandmother, and also Nora's cousins Alicia and Laura.

On one of our visits to Gram-ma Nora, Mom came back to pick us up after having gone to the dentist for removal of a wisdom tooth. Her expression upon her return stays with me. She discovered years later that the dentist had broken her jaw. She suffered with pain on that side of her mouth forever.

Mom seemed closest to the men in her family—her father, her Uncle Edgar (her mother's younger brother by seventeen years), her cousin Arnie, and her brother, Norbert. She also had good relationships with her maternal cousins, Laura and Alicia, and her paternal cousins, the three Graue girls (spinsters who lived together into their old age). These girls had a sister who died in her early childhood. Mom had also been close to her maternal grandparents, August and Malinda. She was four when August died, but she remembered him. She liked him and said that he always had gifts for her and Norbert when they visited. Mom visited her widowed grandmother often as a child. She described her grandmother as having had long black hair that went to her waist and a dark complexion. Malinda liked to work in her garden. She spoke Low German to my mother, who understood the language. Malinda died on October 25, 1953, when I was about two and a half years of age.

My grandmother's more-than-half-sister (and cousin), Lena, was sixteen years her senior. After Lena's mother (Henrietta or Helena Boeske, 1861–1887) died, her father (August) married Lena's mother's niece, my great grandmother Malinda. The union between my grandmother's parents (August and Malinda) produced Nora, my grandmother; a younger brother, Arthur (three years younger than Nora); and Edgar, a brother seventeen years her junior. My mother would tell the story about Arthur, who wandered into his father's green house and was found there passed out with heatstroke. According to Mom, he was never the same after that. He remained with his parents into his adulthood and with his mother after his father's death. My Uncle Norbert remembers that Arthur had a girlfriend that his parents didn't approve of and gave him a hard time about it. Norbert didn't know the reason why. Arthur spent the last few years of his life in the Elgin State Hospital and died at the age of forty-seven. When he was an adolescent, Norbert remembers visiting Arthur there with his father and his uncle Edgar. Arthur shared a tombstone with his parents after his death.

Mom adored her Uncle Edgar whom she described as having been a dandy in his younger years. He wore spats, remained a bachelor into his thirties, and was popular with the ladies. He would often take Mom out on the town in Chicago when she was a young girl. He finally settled down and married a woman named Alice. Edgar was a Salerno cookie salesman for many years and traveled all over the Midwest. Later on, he and Alice traveled all over the world. They never had children of their own, which left my mother for Edgar to spoil.

Nora and Franz had not been able to have children for the first ten years of their marriage. (When they did finally have their two children, they named their son Norbert after Nora and their daughter Frances Jean after Franz). Mom's cousin Arnie Asche, who lost his mother at the age of four to the flu epidemic, was my grandfather's nephew. Arnie's mom left behind not only Arnie, but also three older daughters and twin baby girls. After his mother's death, Arnold's father moved his aunt (Mary Graue Poetker) and her daughter (Laura) into his home to have them help with the older children. The twin baby girls were sent to other relatives. After a few years, the women left, and at some point, Arnold was sent to live elsewhere. My grandparents, being childless, had considered adopting Arnie. He spent a lot of time with them while growing up, but for some reason, the adoption never went through. Arnie's siblings lost track of him for some time, not knowing where he was, but census records indicated that he was with a relative of his mother's, Herman Kuhlman, during his high school years. Herman was his maternal uncle. Arnie served in the army during W WII. Letters he sent to family told of his being in England, France, Belgium, and Germany between July and October 1944. My mother told of his being a POW and being forced into a death march while there. "These were the forcible movements of hundreds of thousands of prisoners from concentration camps and POW camps near the Eastern front to camps inside Germany, away from front lines and allied forces, between autumn 1944 and late April 1945 by Nazi Germans. This was both to remove evidence from concentration camps and to prevent repatriation of POWs."[11] During this time, Arnie was shot and wounded. His family believes that this occurred in 1944, between October 30 and December 5, likely in November. Arnie was recuperating in a hospital in England when it was blown up. He sustained additional injuries and returned to the United States where he spent many months in veteran's hospitals in Iowa and Colorado. In August 1945, he was transferred to yet another hospital in Madison, Wisconsin. He lived with his wife, Ruth, on a small farm in Wisconsin, and the couple eventu-

---

[11] "Death Marches," *Wikipedia, The Free Encyclopedia*, http://en.wikipedia.org/wiki/ Death_Marches_(Holocaust).

ally adopted a son.¹² I remember Arnie visiting my grandparents, mother, and uncle when I was very young. Mom said that he was never the same after returning from the war. She grieved the loss of her cousin, who took his life in 1967.

Mom's brother, Norbert, served in India during the war too, and she felt his absence during the four years that he was abroad. This left her to contend with her mother without the support of her brother during much of her adolescent years when things between them were the worst. He was inducted into the army in March 1943. He wrote home that "[India] is like Maxwell Street, except that it is magnified a thousand times!"

"Maxwell Street is one of the Chicago's residential districts where the "celebrated Maxwell Street Market and birthplace of the Chicago Blues" and the Maxwell Street Polish (sandwich) originated. The street goes back to 1847 and "was originally a wooden plank road." Housing at this time was built for Irish immigrants who worked constructing the railroads. Other immigrant populations followed-Greeks, Bohemians, Russians, Germans, Italians, African Americans and Mexicans. The Maxwell Street Market was an open-air market where one could buy almost anything there, legal or illegal. Origin of the vendor's items was rarely questioned,

---

[12]   Pamela A. H. Kotsch, *Early Settlers of DuPage County Illinois and European Citizens: A Family Tree*, 51–57.

as they often "originated from hijacked or pirated railcars" and yards. The market thrived as a multicultural phenomenon during a time of civil unrest. Each cultural group respected and honored the other. People of different ethnicities got along there. It has been known as the "Ellis Island of the Midwest."[13]

Norbert's letter was dated September 30, 1943. He wrote that "many strange sights meet our eyes here. In fact, I could tell you many things you wouldn't believe unless you actually saw them yourself." He went on to describe his experiences there. "The natives dress in what we would call bed sheets, tucked in, to cover their bodies. None other than the very wealthy wear shoes. The natives look upon us as a very wealthy people— Sahib Rajah are the words they use . . . I remained in camp the first few days, but finally ventured forth into the native quarters to see some of the local color. It is a strange feeling to discover some of the odd things to be bought . . . for practically nothing, providing you know how to bargain . . . Laundry service in camp is very reasonable. Several days ago I sent two pairs of coveralls, a suntan uniform, suntan cap and several pairs of shorts and my total bill was 28 cents! Taxi service is very primitive; in fact, it reminds one of the stories of medieval days. One travels from camp to town in a tonga (horse-drawn cart)." While serving there, Norbert's rank was sergeant. He

[13]   "Maxwell Street," *Wikipedia, The Free Encyclopedia*, http://en.wikipedia.org/wiki/Maxwell_Street.

won the Bronze Star, a combat star, the Good Conduct Medal, and sharpshooter's and driver's badge. He discovered that his lifelong friend Richard Meissler (later to become his brother-in-law) had recently arrived in Burma, so Norbert arranged a plane trip from Assam to Burma for a reunion, many miles from their homeland.

Mom continued to fret over Norbert while he was overseas and was lonely for him during his long absence. She often spoke of the emptiness she felt during those four years. The letters I found that Norbert had written during his stay in India provided me with a different perspective about his experience during the war. I know he had difficult times there. Mom used to say how thin and brown he was after returning home. But his letters also suggested that his experience in India opened up a whole new world for him. Both Norbert and my mother were brought up in a strict and conservative Lutheran environment. Mom frequently brought up suffering abuse from her mother during her adolescence, which she often attributed to having been born to a menopausal mother, although I'm not convinced that was the only reason. She would also hint at her own suspicion about her mother having suffered sexual abuse as a child. She talked only to Sandy about this, and Mom would never elaborate. She told me once that there were periods during her own adolescence and early adulthood that she couldn't remember at all. They were blocked from her conscious memory, she explained. She added that Dad would mention some event that both of them had attended that she would have no recollection of. She told me several years ago that she had a terrible secret that she wouldn't tell until she was on her deathbed. I encouraged her to disclose this secret, but she refused. I explained that she might not be able to do so when the time came, but she still wouldn't tell me. And I was right about that. So all this remains a mystery to us, and now that she's gone, we'll never know.

My aunt Esther lived next door to my grandparents with her husband, Al, and their three children. Esther was a cousin of my grandfather's. Carol was the youngest of their children and became my mother's best friend. When Mom started into adolescence and began to have her difficulties with her mother, she took refuge at Carol's house. Mom described her mother becoming hostile toward her, often waking her in the middle of the night to scold her for some misdeed. She also described her mother as refusing to let her read, demanding that she devote her time to housework instead. Maybe some of this had to do the provincial way Nora was raised herself. And Mom always did have a quiet but fierce independent streak. During this time, Mom had hopes of going to college and applied to Elmhurst College for a scholarship. She waited to get word back, but it never happened. Years later, when my grandparents were visiting us in Oregon, my grandmother told Mom that she had opened the letter for her from the college, offering her a full ride and that she had thrown the letter away.

Mom made attempts to put all this behind her and mend her relationship with her mother. She had me and my sister spend time with her when we were small, and later on, after my grandmother had died, named our youngest sister Nora after her. In spite of her attempts and my grandmother's seeming to have grown out of her mean streak, Mom never really got over her hard feelings.

I remember going to Uncle Doc's mansion as a child. This was the home where my grandfather (Franz) had lived before he married. As mentioned, my grandfather was considered to be a poor relation and never benefitted financially from his adoptive parents, the Rathjes. Nor did he benefit from his association with the doctor and his wife Martha (Franz's adoptive sister) who were wealthy. Martha had since died and "Doc" had married a woman by the name of Dorothy. They would have extravagant Christmas parties there. Dorothy was a school principal who never had children of her own. She was from the old school and believed that "children should be seen but not heard." My sister Sandy, cousins Ken and Don, and I would be at these Christmas events. And later on, there were also my brother Doug, and Ken and Don's younger brother, John. Dorothy would make great attempts to have us all sit in chairs during the course of the evening, just like in the classroom, I guess. Sandy's and my crinoline petticoats under our party dresses made the sitting all the more unpleasant. This plan of Dorothy's didn't work out very well for her, however, because as soon as her back was turned, we were off and running. I also remember being presented with a piece of apple pie for dessert at one of her formal dinners. I didn't like apple pie then (I do now, though), and so I cried at the table but was told to eat it anyway. The highlight of the evening was to wait for Santa to arrive, alias Tom Collis, who was married to Mom's cousin (Alicia). The lights would be dimmed before his arrival to make it more dramatic and, possibly, to disguise his identity from the children. There was a beautiful tree in the alcove of the living room with windows all around. We would wait impatiently until "Santa" barreled in through the front door with a big bag of gifts, unloaded the packages under the tree, and ran back out. It was all very exciting. Dad continued on with this Santa tradition after we moved to Oregon and by then there were two additional kids in our family-Doug and Nora. Dad enlisted a friend of his to play the part of Santa, who would ring our door bell, run into our living room, drop off presents under our tree, and then run back out. Nora, the younger of the two, couldn't be convinced that Santa wasn't real for a very long time. After all, she had seem him on numerous occasions with her own eyes.

Years later, when Dorothy died, she left her money to her long-suffering maid (who came to her at the age of eighteen from an orphanage) and to various nieces and nephews, but there was nothing for Mom other than a box Dorothy gave Mom with various broken antiques. Mom kept them anyway and had them repaired.

One of the items was a lamp with a beaded fringe that had gone bad. Mom paid Sandy and me to re-bead the strands and attach them to the lamp. It turned out looking pretty good, but I'm not sure it was worth all the hours we spent reviving it.

It was difficult for me to leave my grandparents when we started out to Spokane for Dad's internship. I was five years old and Sandy was three. I have a clear memory of driving away from my first home. Other relatives had gathered there for a get-together and send-off. I was crying when we got ready to pull out of the driveway. My cousin Cindy asked why. I guess that if she had to ask that question, I didn't know how to answer her. She had never been as sensitive or sentimental as I, so it had been difficult for us to relate to each other on some levels. I guess I would have to describe her as pragmatic. Perhaps she inherited her pragmatism from Francesca.

On our trip across country, we visited Mom's cousin Irma, her husband, Robert, and their five children (two boys and three girls) in Stevens Point, Wisconsin. Irma is my great-aunt Lena's adopted and only daughter. Two of her girls were about the same age as me and Sandy. Kathy had dark hair like me, and Susie, the younger, had light hair like Sandy. They had a playhouse in their backyard like a real house that we got to explore. We left there and camped along the way. One stop was at Glacier National Park in Montana.

I remember driving into Spokane late in the day, and we had to try to find a place to rent. We drove around for hours looking at apartments and finally found a place that the landlord would rent to us. It was a very small apartment on the second floor of the owner's home. There was only one bedroom, so Dad put their bed and our bunk beds up in it. I remember waking up in the middle of the night and wondering what was going on in their bed. This may have led to my drawing a picture of Mom in her wedding dress, me and my sister side by side looking ahead, and Dad with his pants down and looking in Mom's direction. I showed my drawing to Mom who tore it up and threw it in the garbage. I was angry that she ruined it and told her that I wanted to repair it so that I could show it to Dad when he got home, but she wouldn't let me. I have always wondered if Dad ever heard about the picture.

Dad was gone a lot because of his work at Sacred Heart Hospital, but he'd often take me and Sandy to the hospital while he did his rounds and leave us with Mrs. Casey, who ran the cafeteria there, and she'd make us a nice lunch. She liked our dad and knew that he was struggling to support his family, so she would put sticks of butter in between two slices of bread and send them home with us. She also gave him leftovers from the cafeteria to take home. On his mornings off, Sandy and I would still be in our pajamas and he would load us in the car and take us to the bakery. The clerk was familiar with us and would let each of us pick out a cookie for free.

Dad was also a milkman in Spokane as he had been in Chicago. He would drive by on his way back from his route and honk the horn in front of our house to let us know that he had chocolate milk cartons for us, so we would run downstairs and get our treat.

Dad fashioned parachutes for me and Sandy while we were in Spokane. He used cloth handkerchiefs for the parachutes, wooden clothespins for the parachutists, and thread to hold them together. He drew a face to the clothespin parachutist with his black fountain pen. Then he devised a pulley system that went out our window on the second floor to the ground outside. One of us would drop the parachute out the window, and it would float to the ground below. The other would put the parachutist back in the basket of the pulley and send him back up again. We took turns being the one who would throw the parachutist out the window and the one who would retrieve him below and spent hours with this entertainment.

Dad also devised a homemade telephone with a wire connecting two tin cans. One of us would get inside a closet in one room and the other in a different closet in our apartment and talk to each other with our "phones." Another fun invention that Dad made was a periscope, using mirrors and a cardboard cylinder. He explained that this device could be used to spy on people without their knowing it. We would duck in our automobile while on rides and see what was happening inside the cars that went by.

Sometimes we tried hiding behind our couch to observe what visitors were doing without their knowledge, or so we thought. One day he dragged a truck tire home. I don't know where he got it, but he quickly transformed it into a stupendous sandbox. It sat out under a big tree in our landlord's backyard. We'd haul beach sand from the lake we'd visit on weekends, and before long, the sandbox was functional. The hot sun beating down on the rubber tire created a pleasant scent that both Sandy and I still connect to the hours we spent with our rakes, sieves, pails, and shovels in our sandbox. Dad sometimes played tricks on us too. One thing he did that Sandy and I didn't think was very funny was when he would take us on an outing and disappear when we weren't paying attention. We would eventually become aware that we were on our own and begin to panic. Then Dad would pop out from behind a corner and laugh. Both my parents came up with a scheme that involved a hoax. The plan was for Dad to come home from work and show Mom his colorful new tie. She would tell him that it was god awful and insist that he remove it. He would then refuse and she would respond by taking out the scissors and cutting the tie off. When this plan was carried out, it was supposed to incite laughter, but instead, there were tears. Years later, they would bring up their surprise at our unexpected response.

There were a few unfortunate events for Sandy and me while in Spokane. One involved my baby teeth refusing to loosen as the big teeth began to emerge. My mother was afraid this would cause my teeth to become crooked, and so she talked to Dad about it. They didn't have money to take me to a dentist, so Dad, being a medical student, asked for advice about how to go about extracting the teeth. One evening he set up the kitchen as a dental office, expecting the baby teeth to have lost most of their roots. Unfortunately, this was not the case. My sister remembers witnessing the gory details with considerable distress. I have to admit that I too experienced distress of my own. Dad found himself trying to yank the teeth out with a plier-type object. Since the teeth were firmly attached, this proved to be a difficult and bloody process. When the teeth finally came out, there were long healthy roots attached. Dad was sweating, swearing and angry that my mother had suggested this in the first place.

Another event pertained to our Ginny dolls that were an Easter gift from our grandparents. Next to the house was an empty lot where we played for hours. We took our dolls out one day for an adventure. Somehow we forgot them when we heard our mother calling for us and didn't realize until the next day that they were missing. We went hand in hand, as usual, to search for our dolls and found them covered in mud. It had rained that night. I suppose we were concerned that we would be in trouble if we brought them home that way, so we buried them. I don't remember anyone ever saying anything about the missing dolls, but they were sorely missed by us.

In those days, children spent a lot of time outdoors. At least we did. In the winter that we were in Spokane, Mom would get our skis out for us. There was a steep hill in front of the house that we could ski down, then take our skis off and climb the hill, put the skis back on and go down again. It seems that we spent hours doing this. Because I was five and Sandy was three, I was supposed to keep track of her. When the weather got warmer, we would explore the neighborhood. At the bottom of the hill where we skied, there was a grade school. We would play on the playground on the weekends and after school let out. One day some bigger boys on bikes started throwing rocks at us. I knew that I needed to protect my sister (and myself), and as they started back around the school, we ran and hid in one of the window wells of the school. The boys came back around and started throwing rocks again. The window well did offer some protection but also kept us hostage because we couldn't escape without fear of being hit. It seemed that we were there for a long time before the culprits left, and we were able to return home.

Sandy remembers our making mud pies next to the house. She wanted Mom to see them and had me run upstairs to tell her about our project so that she would come down to see the pies. She was disappointed when Mom looked casually out the window and said that she could see them from where she was. She remembers thinking that Mom wasn't too interested. I think Mom was sometimes bored and lonely while Dad was at the hospital and on his milk route. I think that this was when she started smoking. Sometimes Dad had twenty-four-hour rounds at the hospital on weekends. Once, I remember the three of us waiting on the steps to our apartment for him to return home. She was angry because we had run out of food over the weekend, and as soon as he arrived, she asked him for money so we could go to the store to shop.

There were other interns that would stop by to visit on their own or with their families. I remember John Lorang, Dick Morton, Frank Morton, Roy Moss, and another intern who was Filipino (Constancio Cleto). There were sixteen interns in all. Roy and his wife, Georgie, had five children, all about a year apart. Georgie sometimes brought them over for Mom to watch over so that Georgie could have a break. I think she paid Mom for watching her kids. I liked Georgie. She was nice.

On Dad's day off, we would all go to a nearby lake as the weather got better. There are pictures of Mom in a swimsuit, appearing even more buxom than usual. This was because she was pregnant with our brother. Sandy and I played with our turtle floats out on the lake. Dad took Sandy and me to mass on Sundays. Mom didn't go with us because she was Lutheran then. The priest at the Spokane Church would be in his pulpit, preaching fire and damnation in a loud thunderous voice. I was afraid of him. I would tell Dad after mass about my opinion of the priest, and Dad would just laugh and seem not to take the priest's ranting too seriously.

Mom took us to the set of our favorite cartoon show in Spokane. Sandy and I had watched the show on the television at home. The emcee had a routine where he would tell one of the girls in the audience that he wanted to do a magic trick where he would pour black ink on her dress and then make it disappear. Then he would take a large handkerchief and wave it over the dress, and this was supposed to remove the ink. Sandy and I had seen this trick fail on numerous occasions while watching the show at home. While we were there at the show, we were the ones chosen to demonstrate this trick. He explained the trick and pulled out his ink bottle. I grabbed on to Sandy's hand and ran for Mom, who was waiting in the wings on some bleachers with the other moms. He ran over to try to persuade us to come back on the set but we couldn't be talked into it. I certainly didn't want my pretty dress from my grandmother Francesca to be ruined.

There was another outing Dad liked to take us on while we were living in Spokane (and other places too). He'd show up with a brand new kite kit and boundless enthusiasm. Then he worked on assembling the new kite for its near future in the sky. Sometimes this endeavor was accompanied by cursing and frustration, but he inevitably got the kite flight-ready. Then we'd all head out to some wide open spaces. Dad would show us how to launch the kite by running with it to get it airborne. It didn't matter what the weather was, if there was a good wind up that day, or what particular kind of kite it was—it never seemed to get off the ground, but would rather skitter along on the ground. Sometimes it did start up toward the clouds but then, with a sudden reversal of motion, would torpedo back to earth and be destroyed. No matter what, none of us ever had any luck, but Dad never lost his delight during these kite-flying events.

We made our return trip back to Illinois in July 1957 with a stop to visit Dad's friend and fellow intern Dick Morton and his family in Nevada and then onto Illinois, camping all the way. We moved in with Aunt Jean, Uncle Jack, and their three kids. The house was two stories but not very big. My parents got the den for a bedroom. My aunt and uncle's bedroom was on the first floor, down the hall from the den. After Mom had Doug on November 26, there would be two babies in the household. (All I remember about Doug's arrival is that Dad and my grandmother Nora came to pick up Mom and the baby at the hospital. Grandma loved babies and wanted to hold her new grandson in the back seat while we all drove back home. Mom put Doug in his bassinet, and Sandy and I inspected the new addition to our family. The first thing we noticed was his dried-up umbilicus that dropped off over the course of the next few days). Now Doug would be in the den with our parents and Jeff in his parent's room. My cousin Cindy, Sandy, and I shared Cindy's bedroom upstairs, and Greg had his bedroom to himself, which was adjacent to ours. Upstairs, there was also an open sewing closet to the right of the staircase for my aunt and a small landing at the top of the stairs that led to the bedrooms and a water closet. Cindy liked to stay up late and sleep in in the mornings. She would keep me awake at night, but I would always wake up early in the mornings anyway, so I would attempt to wake her up. This didn't work because she would get angry at being wakened and then fall back asleep again. There were also huge thunderstorms in the middle of the night that would wake us girls. I don't think Greg ever noticed them. We would look out the window in awe of the backyard lighting up with a fluorescent glow and listen to the loud thunderclaps.

We also listened to the radio. (Even after we moved to Oregon, we would visit and stay at Aunt Jean's and sleep in the same bedroom with Cindy. On one such visit, "Palisades Park " by Freddy Cannon was a big hit then, and so was "Runaway" by Del Shannon. Hearing these songs still brings me right back to Cindy's bedroom and the thunderstorms we watched from her bedroom window in the middle of the night). There was a side door at the left side of the house that led to a full basement and to the left, the kitchen. The front door of the house led to the living room, which no one ever spent any time in, other than the babies who napped together there. Mostly, people congregated in the kitchen or the small den that had the television and a fold-out couch, which my parents used as a bed. The basement was lots of fun in the winter months. We would roller skate, jump rope, and just, in general, play down there. While living at my aunt and uncle's house, Dad was busy with his residency. He, my grandfather, and Joe Remec worked on building us a new house on the weekends. Sometimes Dad would take me and Sandy to the site while they worked, so we got to see our house built from the ground up.

At Aunt Jean's, I would get up at night, go downstairs to the kitchen, and get up on the counter so that I could reach the baby aspirin bottle. I loved the taste of it. I'd sit on the kitchen counter in solitude and relative darkness, eating away at one little orange pill after the other. Then go back to my bed without anyone knowing.

Money was scarce, and Dad was offered the "opportunity" to be part of an experiment with LSD at the medical school. He got paid twenty- five dollars to take a tab, which was intended to provide information about how the students would react to the drug. Dad didn't sleep for three days and nights and described a hellish experience. He said he was grossly underpaid. I often wonder if this event contributed to his emotional disturbances later on in his life. Mom didn't have a car of her own, so she was stuck in the house a lot. My aunt would go out, and Mom would be home with all the kids. I don't think Mom was very happy while living there. There wasn't any privacy for Mom, and Dad wasn't around much. I remember a big fight my parents had in the den and Dad leaving in a huff.

The kitchen was small and seemed smaller still when a card table was brought in to sit next to the chrome kitchen table to accommodate four adults, four kids, and two babies at mealtime. We all ate our dinner together when Dad was able to get away from work soon enough to join us. Oftentimes, he was absent, though. These meals were boisterous and fun for the most part. The most memorable meal for me was when Cindy, who I was sitting next to, whispered into her younger brother's ear and suggested that he pour his glass of milk over his head. I heard this and was surprised when he did it. Everyone at the table roared with laughter except for Greg, who didn't seem to like having milk all over him. Everyone except for Cindy and me seemed to think that he had done this spontaneously. The kitchen at Aunt Jean's was also a gathering place where we would get new boxes of cereal that had a prize at the bottom, in a sealed little white envelope. One of us kids would get ahold of the box and tear it open and we would fight over who would get the prize. The best of them was the plastic submarine or frogman that you added baking soda to so that it (or he) surfaced and submerged on its (or his) own in the bathtub or kitchen sink.

We did other fun things while living with my cousins. My aunt got us all tickets to the Howdy Doody show. Mom and Aunt Jean took us. We had front row seats in the peanut gallery, where we sang the theme song. Buffalo Bob would ask the peanut gallery what time it was, and we would answer "It's Howdy Doody time." The four of us got to dance with Buffalo Bob, Clarabell the Clown, and Howdy Doody himself, who was a puppet that Buffalo Bob brought to life.[14] Dad also got free tickets to the circus when it came to town, and all of us would get to go there too. The Brookfield Zoo was another frequent destination. The zoo had big orange kid carts that would hold a couple of kids at a time. We would take turns riding in it.

Other outings were to the museums in the Chicago area. My favorite was the Museum of Science and Industry. One of the best things there was Main Street, which looked just like a turn-of-the-century city with gas streetlights, cobblestone streets, an old-fashioned barbershop, etc. You had to go on an elevator that took you down to the basement to get to Main Street. On the main floor,

[14] "Howdy Doody," *Wikipedia, The Free Encyclopedia*, http://en.wikipedia.org/wiki/Howdy_Doody.

there were bottles with fetuses in them that showed the development of human beings in stages. In the first bottles, you could barely see what was in them but as one progressed, the fetuses got bigger and bigger until the last bottle, which had a term-sized baby in it. I remember feeling sorry for the fetuses that never had a chance to be born and live. One time, Dad took Sandy and me to the museum and we made a recording. There was a booth you went in to that had a microphone. You could speak into the microphone and, at the same time, watch the little yellow record being created with your own voice on it. Then it would come out of a chute when the record was complete. Dad started out by attempting to have a conversation with us that was to be recorded. This didn't work very well, as we just stared back at him, presumably shy about having our voices recorded. Dad coaxed us to talk into the microphone. "Come on girls, say something," he said, but we still didn't cooperate very much. He finally got us to sing the song he used to sing to us at bedtime with him—"Pals and buddies, you and I. Pals and buddies 'til we die." Mom and Dad got me a record player when I was about three years old. I also got a record carrying case, where I stored my yellow-colored 45 rpm's. They said that I played with my record player for hours and took good care of it and the records. I listened to the one from the museum over and over. It survived for several years before it disappeared—this happened sometimes because Mom and Francesca didn't like clutter.

With piles of mud, Sandy and Greg built a home for worms they collected in the backyard. When they showed the worm house to their mothers, the house was deconstructed. This led to their planning to run away from home while their mothers listened in. As they sat on the steps to the kitchen pondering how to carry out their plan of escape, they talked themselves out of it. Both of them loved to eat even more than the rest of us, and they began to have concerns about missing their evening meal. They also wondered what would happen when it got dark and it was time for bed, so they changed their minds. Another time, the two of them were horsing around in the living room where the babies were sleeping in the crib together. They knocked the crib over and the babies both tumbled out onto the floor. Sandy and Greg ran for cover, suspecting that they were in big trouble, which they were. Luckily, the babies seemed to be unharmed. Their mothers questioned whether this had been intentional or accidental. Sandy swears it was an accident.

My cousin Cindy attended a Catholic parochial school while we were living with them, but we couldn't afford the tuition, so I started school at Roosevelt Public School. In the mornings, Cindy would head off in one direction and I in the other. Mom took me to school the first few days, but I didn't like it much. I was afraid of the bigger kids, especially some of the boys out on the playground who would roughhouse and tease littler kids like me. I also refused to sit at my desk but instead would stand next to it. My first-grade teacher tolerated this behavior, but then I started running home during recess. Mom had to take me back to school. This went on for a few weeks until I got more used to the routine. I began walking to and from school on my own. There was one busy cross street on the way that had an underpass. It traveled under the street, and there were handlebars on the walls to help one get down the steps, through the tunnel, and then back up to the other side. Life at home remained rather hectic with everyone crammed into the house. I think that I had some awareness of my mother's discontent too. I suspect that there was some disconnect between her and us kids when we were young because I remember other family members more clearly during my early childhood than I do my mom, and now she was getting ready to have her next baby. And as I've said, Dad wasn't around much then. One day, on my way home from school, a car pulled up next to me. I couldn't see inside the car very well. A man inside the car rolled down the window and said that my parents asked him to give me a lift home. I started toward the car but became uncomfortable and frightened. I turned around and began running as fast as I could to get home. I didn't say anything about this event to anyone. I wonder now if this was because of my father's absence, my mother's preoccupation, and the general commotion in our household. Shortly after this event, the car pulled up next to me again. This time, the man said that he had some candy for me. I started running home again and didn't mention what happened.

I don't know how long it was after these two events before I was heading back from school and heading down into the underpass when a man stopped me in my path. He was wearing a black leather jacket with a lot of zippers all over it. I remember him having a smirk on his face as he stared down at me—something I'll never forget. It was a look that made me think he thought we were in this together, but I didn't think so. He asked me if I wanted to see something. I suspected that this wasn't good but nodded my head in agreement because I was afraid of what he might do to me if I didn't agree. He took his dick out of his pants, and I started to turn to run back out of the underpass, but he grabbed my arm and pushed me up against the wall. When he was done with me, he must have fled the scene, but I don't remember him leaving. It seemed as though I lost some time before I noticed myself standing in the underpass alone, leaving the impression that the man disappeared as suddenly as he appeared. I felt as though my feet were cemented to the ground. I don't know how long it was before I was able to move, but when I did, it was at a run. I got to the front door of my aunt's house and rang the doorbell. Usually, I entered the house at the side door. Mom came to the door. I must have been hysterical. I told her that a man had pulled down his pants in the underpass. She called the police. When they arrived, they looked big and scary to me too. I became aware that my sister and cousins were hiding behind the couch and listening to everything that was being said. When the policeman questioned me, I was able to tell him that a man had stopped me in the underpass and pulled his pants down but that was all I could get out. I could see Cindy, Greg, and Sandy hiding behind the couch, taking in every bit of it, and didn't want them to hear about anything else. Nor am I sure I would have had the nerve to tell the policeman any more even if no one else had been listening. I tried to give the policemen a description of the man, and I mentioned the black leather jacket with all the zippers on it and that I thought he was an adult but young. One of them told me and my mother that if I saw him again, I should go to the nearest house, knock on the door, and ask someone to call the police for me. Well, I did see him again on numerous occasions going back and forth to school but only at a distance. He still wore the black leather jacket. I never went to a house as the policeman had suggested because I was afraid that some bad guy might be there as well. Instead, I would hide behind a bush in hopes that the leather-clad man wouldn't notice me again. My mother told me years later that I started having nightmares and would wake up the whole household, yelling. I don't remember that. I never told anyone about all that happened. It wasn't just the embarrassment and humiliation. I thought if my parents knew all of what had happened to me, it would hurt them.

During this time, I would be dropped off at Sunday school by Dad. A nun was the teacher. She was mean. One day she asked the class if there was anyone who didn't say their prayers before a meal or attend mass on Sundays. I raised my hand, and she told me and the class that I better get myself to mass as soon as my Sunday school class was over. She also frequently cautioned us about the dangers of "impure thoughts and deeds, hell, and damnation." When Dad arrived to pick me up, I insisted that I had to go to mass. There was a Sunday picnic planned at my grandparents' that I didn't want to miss, but I was afraid not to go to mass. Dad had been to an earlier service while I was at Sunday school, but he agreed to drop me off. He said he would pick me up afterward. I sat in the pew crying the entire time because I was missing the party. A lady next to me noticed my distress, and she gave me a little rosary to calm me down. I attempted to return it to her after mass, but she said she wanted me to keep it. Dad came back, and I got to join the party.

On the days Dad was late picking me up from Sunday school, I would panic. I waited out in the hall after the schoolroom had been locked and all the other children had left. I think that I was afraid that some guy like the one in the underpass might show up. I wasn't quite clear on the concept of "impure thoughts and deeds" but suspected that it might have to do with my fantasies about men doing disturbing sexual things to me. I also suspect I may have been unhappy about anticipating an afterlife in hell.

I developed a crush on a boy while in first grade. I became jealous when a girl who sat behind me would flirt with him, so I decided to teach her a lesson. We had to change our regular shoes to tennis shoes for recess and leave our regular shoes under our desks. I waited until the teacher and all the kids were out of the room and put her shoes inside her desk so she wouldn't find them right away after she got back from recess. Then I joined the others on the playground. When we came back to the classroom, she started making a big stink because she couldn't find her shoes. I got scared, so I suggested that she look in her desk. Unfortunately, she didn't find them there because in my hurry I had accidentally put them in the wrong desk. Finally, the child whose desk they were in announced that he had found them and the girl calmed down. Our teacher announced that she was going to go from row to row and ask every kid in the class if they had hidden the girl's shoes. The closer she got to me, the more afraid I was. All the kids before me had denied having hidden the shoes, and when she got to me, I couldn't answer at all but could feel my face flush. The teacher gave up on this interrogation, but after class, several of the kids came up to me and asked if I was the one who had hidden the shoes. I didn't respond and decided to let them decide for themselves. Afterward, I wondered if the teacher had seen what I had done all along. A few months earlier, I had received my first communion at Immaculate Conception Catholic Church (also known as St. Mary's because it was easier to say), and I had also done my first confession. I decided that I had better go to confession again to report my impure thoughts and deeds and my hiding the shoes in the desk. I got into the confessional and heard the priest's voice behind the curtain. I couldn't bring myself to confess what I had intended to, so instead, I told him that I had fought with my sister and disobeyed my parents. He absolved me, but I knew that I hadn't been forgiven for what I had intended to be forgiven for.

Dad liked to make Halloween costumes for us. Roosevelt School had a Halloween Carnival in 1957 while I was still in first grade there, and he made me and Sandy cat costumes. The house that Dad, Joe Remec, and Gram-pa built in Villa Park was ready to move in to in the spring of 1958, and we moved out of Aunt Jean's house to our new home, the first one of our own. The year I was in second grade at the new school, Dad decided to make a jester costume for me. I didn't know what a jester was, so I asked him about it. He said it was a sort of clown that would entertain kings and his court. I wasn't sure that I wanted to be a jester, and when I arrived at school, the kids kept asking me what I was supposed to be and I said "A jester," and they said "What's a jester? " I had a difficult time trying to explain it to them. The next year (when I was in the third grade and Sandy was in the first grade) Dad made pumpkin ghost costumes for each of us. He used two sheets and attached them to chicken wire that was formed into a cylinder. Real carved pumpkins were then attached to the cylinders, and off we went. It was hard to keep the pumpkin head from falling over, so we walked to school very carefully. When I got to my classroom, the teacher asked us to guess who was who, but no one could guess who I was because I appeared to be so tall. They thought that I was one of the taller boys in the class. It was a relief to take this costume off after school because it was so hard to move around in. It was fun to wear for the interest that it evoked in others, though.

In the winter months, we would go tobogganing. We'd bundle up and put on our galoshes after dark and trek out to the big tobogganing hill. Sometimes there was a bonfire and flasks of hot chocolate to warm oneself after an exciting cruise down the hill. Then we'd climb back up the hill to start all over again. Kiddieland was another popular destination in the warmer months. It was a small scale amusement park not too far from home. There were mechanical rides as well as rides on real horses attached to a big wheel with spokes. Harnesses would attach the horse to the spokes so that they would follow one another around in a circle.

My grandmother Francesca would take my cousin Cindy, Sandy, and me to Oak Park to shop while we were living with Aunt Jean and Uncle Jack and while we lived in Villa Park. We would walk several blocks from her house to downtown Elmhurst, where we would take the bus to Oak Park. Grandma had her purse dangling from her arm and wore a housedress and black pumps. As usual, she would speak in her loud broken English. It was an adventure to go on these excursions with her. She liked to buy us fancy dresses. We would go for lunch and then return home with our shopping bags. After our family had moved to Oregon, we returned to Illinois to visit. I was just out of parochial school in Bend and to start junior high in the ninth grade. During this visit, Gram-ma gave my aunt Jean some money to take Sandy, Cindy, and me to Chicago to shop. Aunt Jean was always adventurous like my dad but more easygoing than he was. I picked out a psychedelic outfit, and my sister followed suit. Mine had a fluorescent yellow skirt with matching fluorescent tights and a long-sleeved blouse that had multicolored ovals. Sandy picked out a similar outfit with a maroon skirt, paisley tights and matching blouse. Jean and Cindy laughed at our choices. When we returned to Gram-ma's at the end of the day, she hollered at Jean after Sandy and I modeled our outfits for her. She scolded Jean for letting us buy such gauche apparel. Jean just laughed at her mother. When we started school in the fall, Sandy and I attended junior high. She was entering the seventh grade and I the ninth grade. I talked her into wearing our new outfits on the first day of school. We liked to walk rather than take the bus. The reactions were amazing. People rolled down their windows and made comments. No one at our new school had ever seen anything like these outfits. I guess this was because they were available in a big city like Chicago but not in a Podunk town like Bend. Another sidebar—Gram-ma went shopping in Chicago on her own one day. She headed into a bathroom stall in one of the large department stores there, and while she was sitting on the commode, someone reached over the stall door and grabbed her purse. She saw what was happening and made an attempt to go after the thief, but her hose were around her ankles and impeded her pursuit. She returned home smoking mad.

Gram-ma and Gram-pa also took us to Lemont (the Catholic Franciscan-run Slovenian retreat), about a forty-minute drive from Elmhurst. We would walk along a path where there were statues of the Blessed Virgin Mary, Jesus, and the saints. We would stop and do our novenas at the statues. The grottos that held the statues were constructed with split agate thunder eggs and plaster. The thunder eggs had beautiful brilliant colors and crystal formations inside. Sometimes there were loose agates that we could take home. There was also a large outdoor grotto with an altar where masses were said during warm weather. Francesca would kneel at the altar even when masses weren't being said. I remember one trip back from Lemont very well. Gram-pa was driving on the freeway, and Gram-ma was next to him in the front seat. We kids were in the back. I really had to pee and told them that, but there seemed to be nowhere to stop on the freeway. They kept telling me to try to hold it until we got home. This was very difficult, and when we pulled up in the driveway at their home, I made a beeline into the house. What a relief!

Gram-ma took us to mass in Elmhurst too. She would kneel and say her rosary while she worked her beads. She bought us each a rosary of our own. The beads were made of clear-cut glass, and she taught us how to say our rosary. Francesca had pierced ears, which she had had since she was a small child in Slovenija. This was before pierced ears were popular with Americans. She insisted that her granddaughters get their ears pierced too and said when we did, she would buy us expensive gold loops. She was true to her word, but many of these earrings were lost by my sister and me. They seemed to have a habit of falling off our ears, unbeknownst to us. We also went to the A&P market with her. This was five or six blocks from her home. She had a cart that she would load with groceries to get them back home. Her excursions to the A&P were daily because she insisted on the freshest food at the store if it wasn't coming from her garden. Sometimes we would go to the butcher and if he held up an unsatisfactory sample Gram-ma would yell "that's dog food" along with a dismissive hand gesture. This would go on until she was presented with something more to her liking. She never did learn to drive, but when she was working for the W WII home front activities in a tent factory during the forties, she signed up for a chance to win a car and won. In the newspaper, there was a picture of her being presented with her new car. When she got older, she would ask family to take her to the grocery store. This was quite an experience. Jean took her shopping one time, and Francesca got angry with her for some reason. She began throwing loaves of bread down the aisle at Jean, who was mortified. As time passed, Jean was able to see the humor in what had happened. She had a wonderful sense of humor and laugh, and it was fun to hear her tell this story.

After our house was finished, we moved into a rough neighborhood in Villa Park on Bierman Avenue. There was a field next to our neighborhood, and at the far end of the field was a train track that had frequent trains going along on it. My brother, Doug, was getting around pretty well by then, and so Mom had to tie him with a harness and rope to the clothesline in the backyard to keep him from running over to where the trains were. The land in this subdivision had been farmland, and there were still remnants of farm life around. For instance, we had a patch of asparagus along the edge of our front yard. We would pick batches to give Mom for dinner. Dad still wasn't around much because he was doing his residency and still working on the side. Mom still didn't have a car.

The Stefanskis and the Sparagnas were the families that we spent the most time with in Villa Park. Sandy was the eldest of the

Stefanski children, and she had four younger brothers. They lived beyond a blackberry block behind our house and on the way to our school. Their parents were nice, and they would take us places with their children. My favorite was the drive-in movies. Mom and Dad took us to the drive-in too. One time, the movie was about a guy who escaped from prison by looking at a knife, I think. The knife had some sort of magical power, so he could bend the jail bars to escape. It turned out that he was really a dead guy who had been buried alive and had gotten out of his grave. Then he terrorized the community. Both my sister Sandy and I had nightmares after we saw this movie. Dad thought we would think the movie was funny. The Sparagnas lived down the street from us on Bierman. They had a boy my age named Joe. I had a crush on him. We used to hold hands while we sat on the curb in front of his house. Our family used to go over to their house to visit and have a meal.

There was a huge apple tree in Sandy Stefanski's backyard. Sandy S., Sandy, and I would climb to the top of the tree and eat the green apples up there. I loved the tart taste. One time, I went too far and kept eating the little apples. My gut ached, and by the time I got home, my belly swelled until it looked like a barrel. Then the foamy green diarrhea started and never stopped. That was the last time I ate so many apples. In Villa Park we ran wild, always barefoot in the summertime. This led to frequent painful bee stings and an occasional foot cut with glass. Dad would repeatedly yell at us to wear our shoes, but we liked the feel of the dirt, grass, and even the hot pavement beneath our feet even if this often left us with the bee stings and cuts on our feet. We girls went topless too, and this was acceptable until pubescent changes occurred. Right next to our house was a large field that ran all the way to the train tracks. One summer, a brush fire got started and burned the field to the ground. It was no time, though, before new green sprouts of grass appeared—new life. We ran through the new grass, which felt soft on our feet, but unfortunately, the garter snakes liked the new grass too and would slither over our bare feet and startle us.

Hula-Hoops were all the rage while we lived in Villa Park. Sandy and I asked Dad about getting one, but he said he didn't have the money. For a while, we borrowed them from our friends. Then one day Dad came home with a Hula-Hoop for Sandy and me. We had to share it, but that was OK. I got really good at it. In fact, years later, while I was attending my twenty-year high school reunion, there was a Hula-Hoop contest. It got to be that there were only two of us left on the dance floor working our Hula-Hoops. The other girl's name was Maureen. We went at it for so long that the judge declared a tie. Everyone seemed to have gotten tired of waiting to see who would win.

One day we all went for a ride, and Dad stopped at a store that had novelties. We were looking around the place, and Dad discovered some tins of fried grasshoppers and boxes of chocolate-covered ants. He bought some for us, and we all got back in the car. He told us how good they would be, and they were. The grasshoppers were crunchy and salty, and the ants were sweet and chocolaty with a hint of bitterness to them. When we got back home, we attempted to share with the kids in our neighborhood that we were friends with, but no one else wanted to try them, so we got to have them all to ourselves.

Dad got some hand-me-down bikes for me and Sandy right before we moved to Villa Park. Sandy's was the right size, but mine was too big. I had to stand up to work the pedals. The bike made a clunking noise while I rode it, but it got me around. In the winter months, our next-door neighbors made a real igloo that they let us play in. They had a teenage boy who was mowing the lawn one day and put his eye out when a rock flew up and hit him. This made me fearful of lawn mowers.

There were other kids in the neighborhood who were mean. One lived about a block away, and he had a cast on his arm. Whenever Sandy and I went around the block to play, he would chase us with the cast and try to hit us with it. Another kid came by one time when Dad and I were out on the back porch in the summer. I knew the kid from school. He tried to pull my dress up right in front of my dad. Dad told him to get lost. The worst thing, though, was when I was returning from my Blue Birds meeting after school and got into a skirmish with a bunch of bigger boys who started heckling me and then began to chase me. They pushed me to the ground, piled up on top of me, and started punching me. I felt one of the kids' fingers near my mouth, and I bit it as hard as I could. He yelled like a banshee, and all the other boys jumped off me. When they figured out he was yelling because I bit him, they started running after me, but I was a fast runner and got to my house and down the exterior basement stairs. They followed me into the basement, and my mother heard the ruckus from upstairs. She got a broom and waved it around at them until they left. I never had any trouble with them again but worried that they might try to retaliate.

Mom bought us clothes that were embarrassing to wear while we were in Villa Park. She bought Sandy and me gray baggy pants with flies, like boys' pants have, and also black boys' galoshes with big buckles on them. We got teased unmercifully because we had to wear this stuff.

I felt guilty about an incident that had to do with one of the boys in our neighborhood. A bunch of us were ripping around, and someone came up with the idea to tie a kid to a tree. He had to be talked into it, but he finally agreed. So we found some rope and tied him up good. This was OK at first, just for fun, you know.

He then decided he wanted to be untied, but we all decided with group-think to leave him there for a while anyway. He yelled and hollered, and we ran off. A few of us finally came back and untied him, but he was still mad at us. I don't blame him.

One time, at school, I got very panicky when I thought that my teacher was keeping us late and worried that I would be late getting home. I kept looking at the wall clock and wondering why she wasn't telling us it was time to go home. I finally realized that I was reading the wall clock wrong.

In the summer we loved to work our way through the square block of wild blackberries behind our house. The bushes had sharp thorns, but we would go inside and pick the berries anyway. We got cut up, but it was worth it. There were tons of fireflies that lit up the night sky. My cousin Ken collected them in a glass jar and said he was going to send them in somewhere and get paid for his trouble. I just liked to watch them. In the fall, there were piles of colored leaves to play in and bonfires to get rid of them. In the winter, the snow would pile up higher than our heads. We had galoshes and snowsuits, so we could barely move on our way to school. In the spring, when it rained, we walked to school with our umbrellas, and if there was a good wind up, we'd run, and the umbrellas would get us a bit airborne.

Mom and Dad wanted to get away by themselves, so Francesca came to watch us. Doug was a toddler and very active. The day Francesca got to our house, I didn't feel well. She prepared soup and salad for us, and I told her that I didn't feel well enough to eat it. She insisted that I try some of the dinner she had prepared. I vomited all over the table. This was the beginning of a very long weekend for us all. When my parents returned, she was waiting at the door with her bags packed and didn't even say goodbye. She just went out to the car and asked Dad to drive her home.

Mom had the mumps while we were in Villa Park. I remember her lying on the couch in the living room for days. She never got up, that I remember. Dad would come home at his lunch break to check in on her and us. For the most part, we ran around and did what we wanted. Since I was the eldest, I tried to manage my brother as best I could. If it got too bad, I just put him in his playpen or I'd try to entertain him. We had a cardboard puppet theater and puppets, and we would regularly have our puppets perform. We wrote out dialogues and story lines beforehand. We also had a cat named Blackie. Blackie was a smart cat who would go to the refrigerator and tap on the door when she was hungry. She had a litter of kittens, and when we went camping, we left her and her litter in the basement with food and water, but it must not have been sufficient because when we got home, Blackie was hysterical and the kittens had open sores all around their necks. Dad was very upset about this situation and felt responsible for their fate. He decided that he had not prepared them for our absence properly. He had to get rid of the kittens. We also had a rabbit that once had a litter of fourteen bunnies. We would open the lid of the hutch outside and peer in to observe the bunnies. She divided them into three groups—the two smallest in one group, eight in the middle group, and the four largest in the last group. She would nurse the biggest first, and if anything was left, she would nurse the middle group, and then finally the last. The smallest two died first, then the middle group and finally the last four. She seemed to have been trying her hardest to save the strongest four that had the best chance, and then the other eight. I guess it was just too much for her to try to feed all those bunnies. My sister and I didn't know what to do with the bunny corpses as they dropped off one by one. There was an incinerator that was used to burn leaves, paper, and other stuff next to the hutch. We decided to cremate the dead bunnies by putting them in the barrel. A few months later, we noticed that the hole in the bottom of the barrel held the remains of the bunnies. Sandy and I decided to find a little box that we lined with soft cotton, like a little coffin to save the remains. However, after handling the bones and fur, it became apparent that the odor was gag worthy, and it transferred to our hands. We attempted to wash our hands to get rid of the smell, but it lingered. We decided to bury the remains instead of keeping them.

Right before Dad was done with his residency, he began to lose feeling in his legs and then was unable to walk at all. He was admitted to the hospital for tests. Later, he told me that he suspected he might have multiple sclerosis and thought to himself, "Here I am in debt, ready to start my practice, and what will become of my family if I'm unable to work?" It turned out that he had some other form of neurologic disorder, which could go in different directions. One was that he would continue to deteriorate and become non-functional, and another was that he would recover. Dad did slowly improve and regained his feeling and ability to walk, but I became aware of residual effects of his episode. He thereafter walked with a drop foot. Dad had also suspected he had an undiagnosed case of polio as a child. He had a deformed toe from early childhood that he later attributed to the disease. I have also wondered about the potential effects of radiation, which he worked with a lot at his job. While he was a radiologist, the guidelines to protect practitioners were not what they are now. Dad would show me how his fingers were deformed and lacking prints because of the radium treatments he did. He would develop difficulties later on, and I wondered if some of the afflictions he had suffered were caused by all these things.

We left Villa Park after Dad finished his residency. We started out across the country in our black Volkswagen bug. It had a small luggage compartment behind the backseat where Doug sat during our trip. Sandy and I were in the backseat, and Mom and Dad were up front. Our tent, sleeping bags, blow-up mattresses, pots, pans, and camp stove were all on the luggage rack on top of the car. Our other belongings were placed all about inside the car, including our potty-chair. Dad was in a hurry to get across the country because he had interviews set up along the way about potential jobs as a radiologist. We sang songs while we traveled, and Sandy and Doug would fight in the backseat. If one of us kids had to pee, we often used the potty-chair in the car. Then Mom would throw the contents out the window, which built up after a while on the outside of the car. If someone had to crap, and there was nowhere to stop, we would go in the potty and wait until we could find a place to dump it. One time, Dad asked me to dump the contents of the potty in the outhouse at a campsite we drove into. I went in and accidentally dropped the potty in the hole. I returned to the car and told him that I had been spooked by a snake in the outhouse, but he didn't believe me. He thought I made up the story to keep myself out of trouble. I don't remember whether there really was a snake or not, but at the time, I think I thought there was. We had to go to a nearby town and go through a bunch of stores to find another potty. Another time, Dad got stopped by a cop for going too fast while there was a full potty in the car. He must have taken pity on Dad after smelling the inside of our car and seeing us kids in the backseat. He didn't give him a ticket. On the same trip, Dad went the wrong way on an exit. He knew it wasn't the right exit, but he had missed the right one and was trying to get back on track. A cop put on his siren and lights and pulled us over. Dad did get a ticket that time.

We would find a campsite and set up camp at the end of the day's drive. Dad would go to his interview. Mom cooked us a meal on the camp stove. We'd try to get a good night's sleep and then deconstruct camp, pack up the car in the morning, and head out again. Our last destination was Bend, Oregon. We stayed for a week at Todd Lake and camped up in the mountains. It was sort of like our first home in Oregon. Todd Lake was very cold, but we swam in it anyway. There was also a path around the lake that we hiked on. There were tons of pollywogs and baby frogs all around the periphery. Valerie Ellis and her family were staying there too, and we made friends with her. Sandy lost a gold ring from our grandmother Nora while swimming in the lake. It was a child's ring and an antique. We dove into the icy water, searching at the bottom of the lake, but we were never able to retrieve it. Maybe it's still down there somewhere. Dad would go down into town for his interviews with the radiologist who was looking for a partner. He met with him several times throughout the week. Sometimes we traveled down from Todd Lake with him, about a half-hour drive into Bend, and hung out in town parks while he was busy. One day a local dentist struck up a conversation with Dad in Drake Park, across the street from where the dentist lived with his family. He invited us to dinner, and we accepted. These were the first people we were acquainted with in Bend.

Dad accepted the job, and so we headed back to Illinois to sell the house, pack up our belongings, say goodbye again to our relatives, and head back to Oregon. There was a big going-away picnic/party at Francesca and Francesco's home. My maternal grandparents were also invited. Gram-ma Nora looked sad and cried the whole day, anticipating our leaving. I wasn't too happy about leaving either. On our three drives across the country that summer, Dad decided to take a few detours so that we could have a little vacation as we drove. We camped at Yellowstone National Park, saw Old Faithful blow, and toured the geysers and hot springs that smelled of rotten eggs. We found a swim hole to cool down, and several bears joined us. Then we traveled to Mount Rushmore in South Dakota to see the four presidents' faces carved into the rock—Thomas Jefferson, George Washington, Theodore Roosevelt, and Abraham Lincoln. On our southern sojourn, we saw the Grand Canyon in Arizona. These memories are still clear in my head.

The terrain, as we entered Central Oregon this time, struck me as desolate, stark, forbidding, and void of color. This impression was going through my head while Dad was exclaiming how wondrous the mountains and landscape were. I think Mom had more my impression. She had a complicated family that she was leaving behind but also, in some respects, a support system. I think Dad was escaping from his past. In Oregon, he could leave his immigrant background behind. My parents were also leaving behind some of the family conflict with Mom's relatives related to their marriage and religious and ethnic differences. I was leaving my family and first home, so why was he moving us to this godforsaken place anyway? But Dad was off and running—nothing could stop him now!

So far, I had learned that life could be exciting and fun, or dangerous and that, in nature, living creatures don't make it out alive.

Josefa Brecelj

Ernesto and Josefa Brecelj with
Joseph/Francesca/Francesco

Francesca with Siblings

Francesca with friend in Slovenija

Alojsija Krkoc

Francesca

Joseph and Alojsija Krkoc

Francesco in Army   Francesco 8 days in the Army

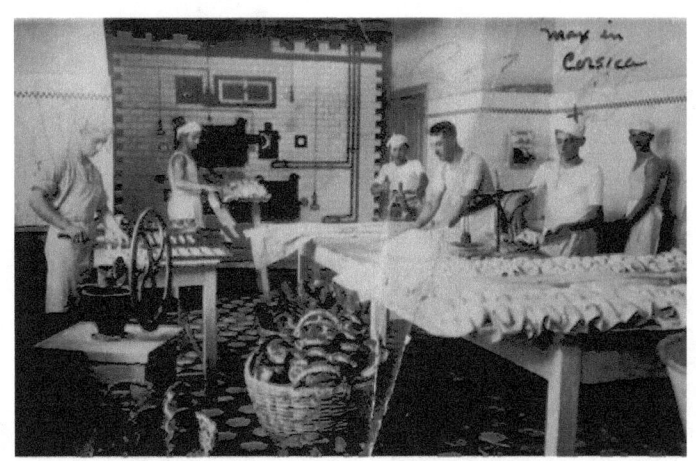

Francesca's Brother Max in Corsica

Francesco (top left) with
family two days before Immigrating

Victoria Cermelj and Francesca

Francesca and Francesco's Wedding (Left: Ade Remec, John Areo/ Mr. Vertovec, Frances Vertovec/Pauline Remec)

Francesca and Francesco

Uncle Tony and Francesco

Francesco with Dad

Dad in Backyard

Francesco with Dad and Jean

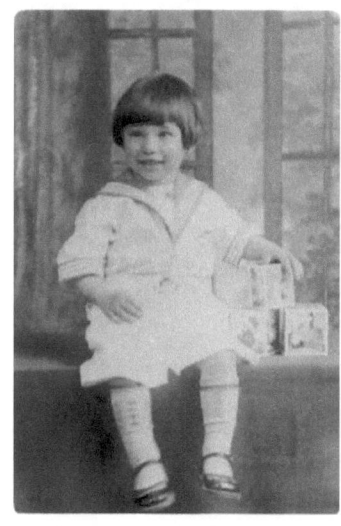
Dad with Blocks

Francesca with Dad and Jean

Francesco with Jean (top)

Joe and Bill Remec and Dad

Joe and Dad on Rock Wall with Girls (bottom)

Joe and Dad on bikes

Dad and Jean

Our House

Our House

Family Photo

Grandma Home from Work

Summer House

Nora's Mother - Malinda
(Marquardt) Weber

Nora's Father -
August Weber

Nora's Childhood Home

Franz's Biological Mother - Louisa (Graue) Asche

Franz's Biological Father - Wilhelm Asche

Nora

Franz

Franz (in back) with Nora (on right) and cousins

Nora and Franz Wedding

Nora

Nora with Friend   Nora's Brother Arthur

Nora's Family at swing

Weber Family Portrait

Nora, Esther and Kids

Franz with Mail

Franz with Coat and Hat

Nora with Norbert

Franz, Nora, Norbert

Franz and Nora on Lake

Franz and Nora on Porch Swing

Family and Friends in Back Yard

Nora, Norb and Franz

Norbert on Trike

Mom's House

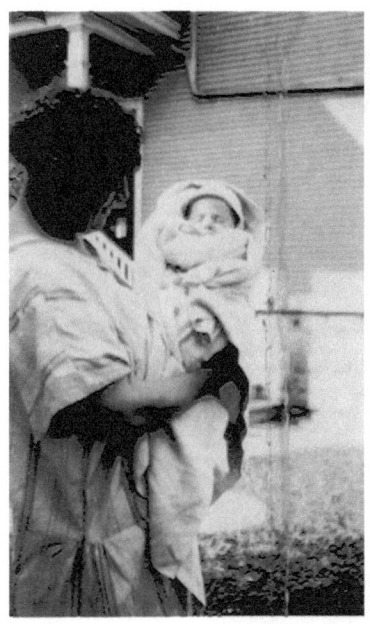 

Nora with Mom   Mom with Bouquet (1931)

Mom Worried

Mom with Sun Suit

Mom and Edgar (on left)

Norb and Mom at Christmas

Mom at Christmas

Mom with Flowers

Family Photo

August Weber with his Dog

Granny in her Garden

Nora's Brother Edgar

Mom and Norbert

Family Photo (1937)- Nora, niece Irma (right)-
(left) Malinda, Lena, Norb, Franz-
Mom in middle Front

Rathje Family

Norb with his Dog

Mom with her Buggy

Mom with her Dog Sandy

Mom with Friend in Chicago

Norb in Army

Mom looking Haughty

Uncle Tony

Gramma wins a car

Gramma (on right) with Angelina Brecelj and Mary Podgornik

Dad next to Car

Dad with
(Joe on Right) Buddies

Joe Remec

Dad laughing

Dad and Aunt Jean

Mom at Brooke Field Zoo

John B.

Mom and Dad

Mom and Dad

Mom at rectory

Dad and Mom at their Wedding Reception

Wedding Cake

Joe and Jack at Wedding

Joan and Victoria Remec, Dick Wolf

Wedding Helpers in Dining Room at Mom's House

Helpers in Pantry

Mom and Dad on Honeymoon

Aunt Jean in tree   Aunt Jean looking Sultry

Jean with a Beau

Dad and Me

Mom and Me

Mom and Me

Mom on our Deck

Dad on our Deck

Just like Mom

Me on Ottoman

Ken and Me

Ken with His Parents

Our Car

Mom, Sandy, Me

Dad, Sandy, Me

Me with Sandy's Bottle   Me with Broom in Front of Summer House

Our Car (with me in Foreground)

In our Pool

Dad snaps a photo of Sandy and me through our bay window on his way to work

Sandy in Her Crib

Sandy and Me on Rock Tub

Sandy at our Sandbox

My Fifth Birthday

Cindy, Me, Sandy　　　　Cindy, Greg, Jeff

Move to Spokane

Camping at Glacier Park

Dad, Sandy and Me

Me and Sandy

Intern's Wives

Dad at Ski slope

Dick Morton

Swimming in Spokane

Kitties at Roosevelt School

Trip to Brooke Field Zoo

Cindy, Jean, Greg

Jeff, Cindy, Greg

Mom with Pin Curls

Doug on Picnic Bench

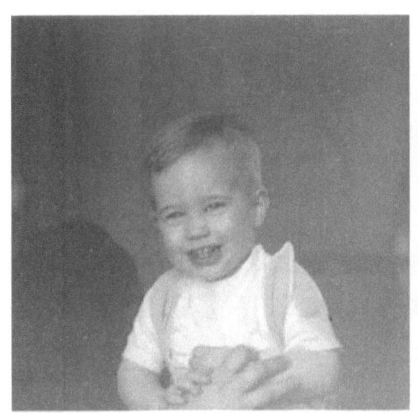 

Doug   Doug in Villa Park

Doug, Me, Sandy

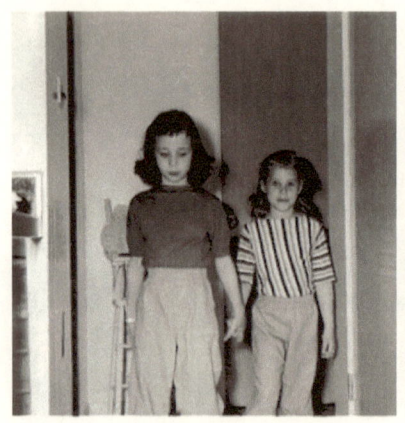
Sandy and Me in Villa Park

Sandy and Me at Window

Sandy and Me at Floor

Sandy with Blackie the Bunny

House in Villa Park

Gramma, Me, Doug at Christmas

Cindy and Me on Bike

Grampa reading paper

Grampa on Sofa

Leo on Trike

Leo and Darren

Top Row
Uncle Tony/Aunt Frances/Grandpa/Grandma/Dad

Middle Row
Jeff/Jack/Jean/Irma/Doug/Mom

Seated
Greg/Cindy/Me/Sandy

Leo's Parents

CHAPTER 2

In Bend, we found a house to rent on the corner of NE Tenth Street and Norton. It was green stucco and had an irrigation ditch running through the backyard. In the summer, we caught pollywogs that eventually turned into frogs. There was a large backyard with numerous pine trees. A large picture window in the living room looked out over the backyard. Norton Street, which ran along the north side of the house, was really only a dirt road then. That summer, Sandy and I spent much of our time at the public pool, where Mom would drop us off. Doug was still too young to go along. Sometimes we would ride our new bikes around the neighborhood and to the pool. Mom bought us two-piece swimsuits before we left Illinois. They were the new thing in the Chicago area, but unfortunately, they weren't anything in Bend. Both Sandy and I were shy about wearing them but set out on our first trip to the pool with the new suits in hand. The kids at the pool made fun of us, but we didn't have any other suits to wear during that first summer, so I guess the other kids had to get used to them. There was a boy about my age who would hold my head underwater and splash me. I found out later on that he was in my fourth grade class at school.

After we moved into the house on Tenth Street, Dad came home one day with a plastic pet turtle bowl lagoon aquarium and a few little red- eared slider turtles. We filled the turtle bowl with water and were delighted with our new pets. The bowl had plastic steps that the turtles could use to climb to the little island on top. We added colorful rocks to the bottom of the lagoon's water. A plastic palm tree stood on the island to keep our little friends company. They really were fun little pets. One could purchase them at a five-and-dime or through mail order. I'm not sure how Dad came about acquiring them. Sandy, Doug, and I would let them out on the grass in our front yard to play and get their needed sunshine. One fall day, one of the turtles got away from us. We looked far and wide but could never find the little guy. We were all sad about his disappearance and had finally, over the winter months, almost forgotten about his suspected demise. Mom went out to garden at the first signs of spring and started digging in the mud. She turned over a rock, and there was our little friend. Mom brought him inside to show us. He appeared to be frozen but we ran some warm water in our bathroom sink and made a little lake for him. At first, nothing happened, but we continued to add extra warm water to the sink, and finally, his hands and feet started to emerge from his shell. Then his head poked out, and finally, he began to swim around in the sink. When we were sure he was fully recovered, we reunited him with his long lost companion in their turtle bowl home. When we flew out to Chicago for a visit that summer, Doug insisted on taking our turtles along. He couldn't be deterred from his insistence on taking them, so Mom got a Chinese container for them to travel in. Doug got on board with the container, and no one seemed to care or notice until he took one of the turtles out of the container and lost him. Then Doug had a big stink on the plane about his lost turtle. The stewardesses made announcements about the lost pet and everyone on the plane looked around for the turtle. The little guy made it all the way to the back of the plane, and one of the passengers yelled out "I found the turtle." Doug was so happy to have him back, and he made sure to keep track of him during the rest of the flight.

Dad had enough money for us to attend St. Francis School, which we thought was great because our cousins had been able to go to Catholic school while we were in Illinois. I started out fourth grade at St. Francis School with Sister Josephine Mary. This was already my third school, and I didn't know anyone except for the boy, Mike M., who held my head underwater and splashed me at the pool during the summer. I was shy, so it took me a while to find friends I liked. There was a group of girls that I finally made friends with, though. It was sort of a clique, but there really wasn't any snobbery in the school during the fourth grade, and I got to know everyone in my class. We played square ball or jump rope on the playground at recess. The nuns continually cautioned us about avoiding impure thoughts, which left me feeling uncomfortable and guilty, but I was a conscientious student and had fun at school too. Our class went to the church to practice songs that we would be singing during masses. We sang in the choir loft that looked out over the congregation. If you didn't have a hat on upon entering the church, the nuns pinned a paper towel or Kleenex on top of your head with a bobby pin. Not having a hat in church was a serious offense if you were a girl. There was a narrow winding staircase in the vestibule that led to the choir loft. It had an organ that was played to accompany our songs. The choir teacher was a nun who told me not to sing. She suggested I pretend to sing but not make any noise. So that's what I did, and I didn't sing out loud after that for a very long time. Before that, I thought I had a pretty good voice. I certainly was exuberant when I sang songs, and Dad praised me, my sister, and my friend T. when we sang as a trio and played the piano to accompany ourselves in our living room. In fact, Dad even went so far as to say that we sounded professional, so I never did get why I was told I had to be quiet in the choir loft. Maybe he was unrealistic about our potential.

At St. Francis, Sandy and I had to go around the Bend neighborhoods, knock on doors, and try to sell chances to whoever was interested, and that was usually nobody. The chance could lead to winning something big, like a car, but no one seemed to think they would be a winner. Usually, they just said no and closed the door. We also had bingo games at the parish hall. They were fun, but neither Sandy nor I ever won anything. Dad showed up for the bingo every now and again and always won. He'd buy three or four cards at a time and work them all at the same time. He'd get prizes for us, usually big stuffed toys that we loved. One time he got each of us a gray stuffed pony. He had the luck of the Irish, and he wasn't even Irish.

Father Steven was the parish priest. He liked me and would call me up to the front of the class when he dropped in and press a five dollar bill into the palm of my hand without the other kids noticing. He would tell me he thought I seemed sad and serious, which may have prompted him to be especially kind to me. He even went so far as to ask my parents about his concern for me, but Dad reassured him that nothing could be further from the truth. I suspect Father Steven saw me more clearly than even my family did. One time, he called in the afternoon when I was home alone. I asked who it was, and he suggested I guess who it was. I hung up the phone, thinking it was some sort of obscene phone caller. I felt panicky. He called right back, and I was reluctant to answer, but I did because I thought it might be a family member. He quickly explained that he was the caller and apologized for having unintentionally frightened me. Father Steven kept in touch with me even when I entered college. Sandy went to confession once at St. Francis Church while she was in second or third grade. She ran through her litany with the priest, left the confessional, and ran into Father Steven on the way out. He asked where she was going, and she replied that she had just done her confession. He let her know that there was no one in the priest's booth while she was in hers because he was just returning to his post. But she heard the priest conversing with her while in the confessional, and so she told him that she didn't need to go back in to say her confession to him.

St. Francis School was a couple miles from our home, but I preferred walking there rather than going to the bus stop a few blocks from home. There was a boy who would harass me while I waited there for the bus. I finally had enough and punched him in the stomach real hard one day. He ran away crying and never bothered me again. Around the corner from St. Francis, there was Shaffer's Ice Cream Parlor. We stopped in there on the way home to grab an ice cream cone. The best was their licorice ice cream. Dad also worked near downtown, where school was. We took piano lessons from the nuns down in the basement of St. Francis School. There was a choir section in the middle of the basement and about six individual piano rooms with closing doors around the periphery. This is where the lessons were held. Piano lessons were torture. After the lessons at the end of the school day, Sandy and I would go to Dad's office downtown. He would give us some money to go across the street to the Trail Ways Bus Depot Restaurant to have a Coke and fries before he was done with work. Then he would drive us home. But some days, Sandy and I would take leftovers (which were in brown paper lunch bags that Mom prepared for us every school day) with us into the restaurant and then slide into a booth. It was a more comfortable place to eat than at Dad's office. Then the owner, who was a friend of Mom and Dad's, would come over and tell us to leave if we weren't going to order anything. Another time, we started pushing the buttons on the jukebox all at the same time. Each booth had its own jukebox. Well, it started smoking and making weird sounds, so we left as fast as we could.

When Doug got a little older, he had to take piano lessons too, but instead of learning to read the musical score he just had Sandy or me play the piece for him when Mom and Dad weren't around. He had an ear for music that we didn't. So while we trudged along with our dreadful practice, all Doug had to do was listen to our rendition once, and then he could play it. Mom finally figured out that he couldn't read a note of the score, and she also figured out how he was able to play the piano—much better than us girls.

After the first year in Bend, we left the rental on Tenth Street and moved around the corner to 1314 NE Ninth Street. The selling point for Dad in the purchase of the house was that there was a view of the mountains. He loved the mountains. Our cat was pregnant and traveled back around the corner to have her kittens in her old home. She found her way into the master bedroom of our old house on Tenth Street and had them on the master bed's pillow. The new renters brought the cat, kittens, and pillow over in a box. This cat had kittens again later on at our new house, and this time, she had them in our kitchen. We got to watch her give birth. The kittens came out of her inside little clear sacks with water in them, and she licked the sacs off her kittens, which remained wet and slippery. The new house had a family room with a niche that had a garage- type door to hold a saddle. The previous owners had kept their horse's saddle in the niche and their horse in the backyard, in a makeshift stable. Dad converted the saddle niche into an elaborate bar, where he stored liquor bottles, glasses, and related paraphernalia. He also decorated the walls with jokes cut out of the newspaper, napkins from various restaurants and bars they had frequented, and other mementos.

At Easter that year, when we ran around the house hunting for eggs, we came upon a big box with baby chicks. Dad built a chicken coup in the backyard for when the chicks got bigger. However, the chicken coup was bigger than it needed to be, so we talked him into converting the coup into a playhouse. The chickens still had some space to lay their eggs and nest. The new playhouse had a second floor that one could get to by way of a ladder inside. The ground floor had enough room for three sleeping bags. I would ask one or two friends over, and we would stay overnight inside the converted chicken coup. It was easy to sneak out in the middle of the night. We would walk all over the neighborhood and spy on the houses of our friends. Dad also found a really long extension cord for our only wall phone in the house. This was to allow family members to walk to various rooms while we used the phone. There was no such thing as cordless phones in those days. I, in particular, loved to talk on the phone. Sometimes I'd just sit up against the wall in the hallway and talk away, but if I wanted more privacy, I could pull the cord into my bedroom and close the door. We could even take the phone into the bathroom that was right next to our long extension-corded hall phone.

At Halloween, we'd get together with our friends at someone's house and head out with a pillowcase. Bend was pretty small in those days, so we could get around to most of the neighborhoods and had a full pillowcase of candy by the end of the evening. We would usually be out until about eleven o'clock. When we got a little older, my friend Mary R. got her driver's license, and so she drove us around in her car with some other friends too. We might park and go to a few homes for candy. Even though we were a little old for trick or treating, people usually gave us candy anyway. One year, a group of boys drove by and pummeled us with eggs.

One year, for Christmas, I got a microscope from my parents. It had slides that you could put just about anything that would fit on it. There were tools to make thin slices because the specimen had to be thin enough to see through in order to examine it under the microscope. Then a smaller thin piece of glass was added to the slide to hold the specimen in place. Dad showed me how to prepare the slides, which opened up a whole new world to me that had previously been unseen with my naked eye—a drop of water, for instance, with all the living creatures that inhabited it. Dad's enthusiasm was contagious, and so I explored all sorts of items—cloth, salt crystals, hair, dust, etc.

In the winter we all went skiing at Mount Bachelor. In those days, there was hardly anyone up there. We still didn't have too much money, so Dad's partner's wife would give us her kid's hand-me-downs, which included ski wear. There was a T-bar in the old days that you would catch with your butt on its way by, and it would carry you up the hill. There was also a rope tow that you had to grab on to, which pulled you up the hill. The guy who ran the T-bar was a cute college student who rented the guest house behind our big house. Since he knew us because he lived behind us, he was fun and playful with us when we got on the T-bar. Later on, he went to Vietnam, and when he returned, he wasn't as happy as he had been before he went over there. Mom and Dad went up on a weekday one time while we were in school. The snow was heavy, and she stopped by the lodge to check her bindings and put the proper wax on her skies, but something wasn't right because her skis were sticking as she started down the mountain. She was near the top when Dad noticed that she was not behind him. He saw her up above and climbed back up to her to see what was wrong. She had a compound spiral fracture in five places. The ski patrol brought her down and took her back to Bend and to the hospital. Sandy and I were at our ballet class when Dad picked us up. On the way home, he told us what happened. When we got home, I cried because Mom was gone, and Dad gave us Chinese TV dinners that tasted bad. The next day, though, he started preparing turkey soup with a frozen carcass from Thanksgiving. He let the pot with the bones simmer on the stove for four days and nights. Then he added rice and vegetables and served the soup for our dinner. It was the best broth that I've ever had then or since. For the days Mom was in the hospital, Dad resorted to "Daddy plates" again. Mom came home, and she was confined to a chair in the family room because of her cast. Doug was about four years old then, and he seemed to know that she couldn't get up from her chair very easily, so he pretty much did whatever he liked. When Mom finally got the cast off, there was old skin and long hair all over her leg. For a while, the leg was smaller than the other. It did improve after some time but was always shorter than the other one after that. She had to have all her slacks altered so that she didn't look lopsided.

Gram-ma and Gram-pa took the train out from Chicago and brought Cindy and Greg along. We met them up in Portland, visited the Rose Garden, the Zoo and OMSI (Oregon Museum of Science and Industry) and then drove back to Bend. This started a tradition of my grandparents visiting us every other year, but after a while, they started flying out. Initially, Gram-pa was fearful of flying because of the planes he saw go down during the war, but he got over his fear. After their first visit to see us, they came by themselves.

Our first big family vacation was at the Seattle World's Fair in September 1962. We stayed in a cheap hotel because the nicer hotels' costs were inflated because of the fair. There were many sights to see. We rode up the Space Needle, wandered through the cultural center where I purchased souvenirs that I still have—a Chinese doll with a cloth face on a stand (the porcelain dolls were too expensive), and a shellacked black jewelry box. Dad told us that he heard that both Elvis Presley and Ricky Nelson were filming or performing at the fair. From that point on, I was preoccupied with spotting them. Dad was amused by my fervor. I was on the lookout constantly, but we came across Elvis only by happenstance. He was shooting a movie scene, which involved going down a set of stairs with his costar. There really weren't a lot of people watching them, so I was able to squeeze through so that I stood right next to the steps. The two had numerous takes, so they would descend and climb the stairs again and again. Each time, Elvis would stroll right by me. I was in seventh heaven. During the filming, Dad bought Doug a helium balloon that he had been pestering him for. The balloons were being used in the shoot but were also for sale. He tied the balloon around Doug's wrist so he wouldn't lose it, but Doug wanted to hold the balloon on his own and said he wouldn't let go. He made a big stink about it. As soon as he had his way, he let go of the balloon and we all watched it fly into the sky and finally disappear. He was tearful about his lost balloon, and I was sad about Elvis's disappearance after his shoot was over. In spite of my efforts, I never was able to spot Ricky Nelson.

In the summer we always went to the Deschutes County Fair and Rodeo in Redmond, Oregon. One time, Dad asked Sandy and me to go down to Erickson's Grocery on Greenwood (a few blocks from our house) to pick up some snacks for our ride over. We were both wearing our rubber flip-flops, and on our way back, we ran across Greenwood, which was in the process of being re-tarred. Our flip-flops got stuck in the tar. We tried to pull them out, but the tar was too hot for our bare feet, and so we ran home without them. Dad asked what happened to our flip-flops, and we told him. He went on and on about how we could have neglected to notice that the street had wet tar on it. Then we all proceeded to the fairgrounds, where Dad just so happened to step right into a juicy wet cow pie that covered his shoes. So we got to ask him the same question he had so recently asked us, and he took it with a sheepish grin.

Two other frequent destinations during the sixties were Lincoln City at the Oregon coast and Portland, Oregon. The Oregon coast still holds a special place in my heart, not only because of its beauty and serenity but also because of fond memories from my childhood and early adulthood there. Initially, we stayed at the Ester Lee, but one time, while we were there, Dad went on one of his morning runs along the beach and spotted a new place hanging over a cliff. He jogged up and spoke to the manager, who provided him with a brochure and a tour. The new place had been fashioned by connecting two old homes overlooking the ocean. The original owners had decorated the apartments with Scandinavian tole painting. He returned from his outing with the brochure in hand and proclaimed that the next time we traveled to the coast, we would be staying there, and we did ever after.

When we first started going up to Portland, we stayed at a Travelodge outside the city proper. That's what we could afford. The motel had a big sleepy bear on the sign. There were two stories and an elevator that took you to the second story if that's where you wanted to go. One time, Sandy and I were just having fun in the elevator, going up and down. We started pushing all the buttons at once, and then the elevator made a loud crashing noise and started jerking around with us still inside it. At first, the elevator door wouldn't open. I remember being afraid we wouldn't be able to get out, but the door finally started working again. After a while, we stayed right downtown. The theaters in Downtown Portland were ornate, with velvet curtains that opened to reveal the movie screen and often had additional sheers underneath that would also open. Broadway held the most theaters—the Broadway, the Orpheum, the Music Box, the Rialto, and the Paramount. The Oriental, one of the most ornate theaters ever built, was at Grand and Morrison. There was also the Aladdin on SE Milwaukie. Ushers with flashlights would show you to your seats. Some of my favorite films that I saw in Portland were My Fair Lady and Doctor Zhivago, but there were many others.

We had fine meals. Ryan's was a restaurant in Morgan's Alley that we would frequent often. Mom and Dad knew the bartender there who would make them killer martinis. When Mom took Sandy and me to Portland to shop for school clothes, this is where we would stop for lunch. Family trips would include dinners at the London Grill or Trader Vic's in the Benson Hotel. Trader Vic's was cave-like, with torches lighting the restaurant. The décor was fashioned after the fifties and sixties tiki culture, with its rattan furniture and brightly colored fabrics.[15] There were unique cock-

---

[15] Tiki Culture", *Wikipedia, The Free Encyclopedia*, http://en.wikipedia.org/wiki/tiki_Culture

tails (their mai tai being the most popular) and exotic cuisine.[16] I thought it felt like being in the tropics. At that point, I had never been to the tropics, but I got some idea what it might be like. Dad would say that we must try the special beef that was prepared in an ancient type of Polynesian oven. He wasn't kidding when he said it was out of this world. He was so impressed with the oven that he fashioned one in our backyard. He built it with bricks as he had learned some masonry from his father during his growing-up years. He told of his father's general dissatisfaction with his masonry, however, because Francesco was a perfectionist about his work and never thought Dad's measured up. The brick oven Dad built didn't really work very well- but he had given it a try.

The London Grill offered English and French cuisine—numerous game dishes and flaming desserts which were all delicious. At first, there were only male African American waiters and then only male Middle Eastern waiters, but there were objections by others because these jobs were sought after, so after a while, men and women of different ethnicities were hired, although female staff remained scarce. There was also a restaurant, café bar, and toy store on the top floor of Meier & Frank department store. We ate at the café bar for casual meals and at the restaurant for a more formal lunchtime meal. There was a great view of the city in the restau-

[16] "Trader Vic's," Wikipedia, The Free Encyclopedia, http://en.wikipedia.org/wiki/Trader_Vic%27s.

rant. Here, there were all-female older English waitresses that all looked alike— matronly and frumpy. Crumpets and tea were available. During Christmas, Santa hung around outside the toy store, and inside, there was a train that ran around the periphery of the ceiling. One of the first places we stayed at in Downtown Portland was an old hotel, the Park Haviland, which eventually ran hookers through it, but it was fun before that happened. We found out about it when Mom and Aunt Lois (Ken's mom) stayed there one night. They had men carousing in the hallway and knocking on their door all night long, asking to come in. It was torn down several years later. After the hookers arrived at the Park Haviland, we started staying at the Mallory Hotel, which had a simple charm, or the Benson, which had a lavish lobby, a piano bar, and the two restaurants.

We also frequented the Lloyd Center in Portland. We had moved to Oregon in the summer of 1960, and the monstrous mall, touted to be one of the largest worldwide, opened on August 1 of the same year. Of course, Dad had to take us up to see it as soon as he heard about the opening. What I remember most about our many visits to the mall over the years were the ice skating rink that we always got to skate on and the Jewish delicatessen. Spectators, including Mom and Dad, lined up above to look down at the skaters below. We always got big Reuben sandwiches when we ate at the deli. I can't remember the name for sure, but I think the deli was called something like The Pink Elephant or The Pink Hippo—I'm not sure. It seemed there was an emblem at the entrance that pictured the dancing elephant or hippo in a tutu.

Sometimes Dad worked in Madras, about an hour's drive from Bend. At the end of his day, Mom would drive up with us kids, and we would meet him at his workplace. We'd leave the extra car there and head up to Portland where we would go to Celebrity Attractions at the Civic Auditorium on SW Clay Street. Sometimes it was a ballet, concert, or a play. Musical groups from around the world also came to perform. The shows ended at about ten or eleven, and then we would drive back to Bend in the middle of the night.

We went up to Cultus Lake with Dad's partner and his family one summer. Governor Mark Hatfield was in the next cabin and heard a funny sound coming from our adjoining cabin. Later, he and Dad talked, and Dad explained that they had been using the ice pick to chip ice for their drinks. Dad said he found Governor Hatfield affable. During this trip, Ron Howard from The Andy Griffith Show was staying at the lake too. He was about twelve years old. Somehow, we kids wound up getting in a fight with him, and we started throwing rocks back and forth. Later in the day, we decided to take the row boat out. Mike (Dad's partner's son) didn't want to go, so Sandy, Peggy (Dad's partner's daughter), and I went.

A storm blew in, and we dropped one of our paddles and drifted out to the middle of the lake. We got to a shallow area of the lake and got out to try to push the boat to shore, but the wind was too strong. Mike came to check up on us and pulled us ashore. He gave us a hard time about how ditzy we were.

Dad traveled far and wide for his work in those days. Radiologists were hard to come by, so he and his partner covered a good portion of Oregon, east of the Cascade mountain range. The area east of Bend was mostly rural, but Dad, being the city slicker he was, still never found it difficult to relate to those he ran across in this stretch of the state. Maybe it was the rural setting his parents left behind when they left Slovenija, or the blue-collar upbringing he had in this country. Dad often offered free care or reduced rates to those patients who had difficulty paying. For all these reasons, he was popular with his patients, and they repaid his kindness with favors.

Every fall, we drove over to Eastern Oregon for potatoes after the harvest with commercial machines. Whatever was left behind was for us to gather and dig up—some misshapen but good to eat anyway. Orchards were offered for our picking too. And later in the season, one of the farmers offered his pond to us for ice skating. It was always calm and quiet on those nights as we sped around the natural rink. Dad could never pass up any tree in our own neighborhood that bore fruit, some of which were rotting on the ground from neglect. He'd take us for a walk to the tree, and we filled paper bags to the brim. He never asked permission, but no one ever seemed to object to our scavenging. These outings continued on into my adulthood when his grandchildren were often included in these expeditions.

Dad was always a crazy driver. He spent hours on the road with his work, and one night, on the way back home, he rolled our black Volkswagen. He found himself upside down in a ditch on the side of the road and crawled out through a broken window. Other than a few nicks and scratches, he was unscathed. Another mishap involved a mushroom- hunting expedition where he went on his own to a secluded forest area. He unintentionally disturbed a hornet's nest, and they went after him in hot pursuit. Hundreds chased him through the woods, swarming around his head. As he ran, he tripped over a fallen log, injured his leg but kept on running 'til he found a river and dove in. He remained underwater 'til his adversaries gave up the hunt. I still remember clearly how he appeared when he walked in the kitchen—his swollen face that looked like a balloon, his slit-like eyes, and his dizzy affect. He took to his bed. His leg was never quite the same.

Mom and Dad went out of town frequently for Dad to attend medical meetings or just to get away and have some time alone.

Being the city guy that he was, Dad knew how to explore just about any city they visited. Mom was always a good sport, for Dad would challenge her conservative upbringing. For instance, he often dragged her to jazz clubs in the cities they frequented, where they would be the only white folks in the place. One time, they had a particularly good meal somewhere in Portland, and they jaywalked across some street. I suspect that they were somewhat inebriated, so when a cop drove up, he attempted to give Dad a ticket. Dad must have failed the attitude test because the next thing they knew, they had been thrown in jail. Mom was in her own cell, separated from Dad, and remained so for the next few hours. Dad wasn't afraid like Mom had been, only furious. They were finally let out after Dad paid a stiff fine. He thought about making a formal complaint during the weeks after the fact but thought better of it.

We had an assortment of sitters. Mrs. Henches was the first. She was a nice old lady who lived nearby in a shack with her husband. He was nice too. He had a shop in their backyard, and he would take us out there and show us his train set that ran along the ceiling. He also carved our first names and our last name initial out of wood. He varnished the carvings, and we kept them in our bedrooms. Mrs. Burmbach (boom-boom) made us homemade Barbie doll clothes. Mrs. Hamby was a good sitter too. She lived out in the country on Hamby Road, named after her relatives. She would bring over a marble board game, Aggravation, and set it up on the dining table where we would play for hours. Sometimes she took us out to her farmhouse so we could see the farm animals she had there. Other sitters were Mrs. McClartey and Mr. and Mrs. K.—Doug's friends Stewart and Scot's grandparents.

We also had younger sitters who were fun. One was Kathy, the daughter of the pediatrician in town. One day Kathy made popcorn for us in a pan on the stove. She added a bunch of oil and it caught on fire. She had to pick up the pan with a pot holder and take it outside. She dropped it on the cement steps to our back door and the grease left a big spot, so when Mom came home, she wasn't very happy and knew we had been up to something. It seemed that every time Kathy came over, we got into mischief. So after a while, Mom avoided having her come over to sit. A college-aged woman also sat sometimes too. She was one of Dad's technicians. She was a beauty—tall with a dark complexion, black hair, and big brown eyes. I was thirteen, but she treated me like an adult and would confide in me about some personal feelings she had. For instance, she was in college but said that she thought guys her own age were immature. She added that she preferred older men. I always remembered her saying that to me.

One time, Sandy and I wanted to make homemade puppets, but we couldn't find any material to make them. We both searched the house far and wide until Sandy discovered a pair of Dad's pajamas that he only wore when he was really ill. She took a pair of pinking shears out of Mom's sewing box and cut one of the sleeves off and then folded the pajama top back in the drawer. Dad didn't discover the missing sleeve until years later when he turned up sick. This time, he laughed at the strangeness of the shorn sleeve and puzzled over its corruption. He suspected Sandy was the culprit, but she didn't confess until a lot later. There were other things Doug did, though, that he didn't take as well. For instance, there was an antique lamp with tassels as pulls in our living room. Doug sat on the lounge chair next to the lamp one evening and decided to wrap the tassels around the bulbs. When the lamp was turned on later by some unsuspecting family member the tassels started to smoke, burn and scorch. Dad wasn't too happy about all this. Neither was he at another time when Doug and Sandy were throwing pillows around in the living room and one of Doug's landed on the crystal brandy decanter and the matching long-stemmed etched glasses. The set was demolished, and Doug didn't hear the end of that for a long time.

John B. was the professor who encouraged Dad to go to medical school. He was Dad's math professor in undergraduate school. The two remained friends for life. John was a "confirmed bachelor." He planned a trip out to Oregon every two years like clockwork. Mom dreaded it. She liked John OK, but he and Dad would drone on at the dinner table about theories, mathematics, physics, chemistry, and the universe in general. I guess John B. was some sort of intellectual. He had that look in his eyes—sort of dreamy and far out in space. If someone had a conversation with him or asked him a question, he'd tilt his head up slightly, gaze up at the ceiling or the sky, and remain silent for an extended period until he formulated the proper response. As kids, we just thought he was kind of weird. When Dad went to work during his visits, he was left with Mom. They really had nothing to say to each other because their brains didn't work the same. Sometimes we would find John B. out in the middle of our backyard where he'd pull a lawn chair and remain for most of the day, just staring at the sky without uttering a word. He just liked to think. Then on the weekends, when Dad was home, we'd all drive around and see the local sights. When John was in the army, he was assigned to the intelligence unit. This was because of his sharp mind and fluent German. One of his jobs was to interview German prisoners of war. Later on, John was asked to be a part of a research team in Washington, DC, and participated in the work to advance computer technology in 1950. He was that smart. When John B. got older, his old Chicago neighborhood had an influx of African Americans. Some of the white folks from the old neighborhood left, but John remained. He said he had no trouble with his new neighbors and, in fact, got along with them fine. When he was a young professor, he devised a grading system that is still in use today by some educators. That is, he would have papers come in with numbers only so that he didn't know whose it was. This, he said, made grading less likely to be guided by personal biases. I know Dad always felt a debt of gratitude for John having had faith in him and encouraging him in his pursuit of higher education. Dad always tried to pay this debt back with kindness toward John and his own encouragement of others he thought could benefit from the kind of encouragement John had provided him.

The Pilot Butte Inn was a landmark in Downtown Bend. It took up an entire city block. My friends and I would stroll by it frequently and admire the lodge, with its river rock and board-and-batten siding. Windows had awnings on the south side of the lodge. The gabled roofs and window surrounds lent the inn character. The entrance had a trellis with vines covering it. There was an old-fashioned barbershop on the Wall Street side. The back of the building looked out over the Deschutes River. The inn dated back to 1917 when it was built in what was then the small developing lumber town of Farewell Bend.[17] It was a regular location for holiday parties and dances and even had famous guests who stayed over. The actor who played Paladin in the Have Gun—Will Travel television series stayed there while filming episodes in the area.

---

[17] "Pilot Butte Inn, Bend," *The Oregon History Project*, http://ohs.org/education/ oregonhistory/historical_records/dspDocument.cfm?doc_ID =A899DBFF- B7F9-D3E1-52F6536DDF2123D8.

This was a show about a bounty hunter who traveled wherever he was needed. Doug, in particular, was eager to meet the actor (Richard Boone) because he was such a fan of the show. Mom and Dad took all of us down to the inn so that we could meet him. He was in the large lobby wearing his character's attire when we arrived. My brother got up the nerve to go and ask him for one of his cards that read "Have gun, will travel." Doug kept the card for years, and as far as I know, he still has it. To me, the inn always seemed to be the highlight of our small town. So it was sad when it fell into unscrupulous hands and disrepair. There were attempts to revive it in the late sixties and early seventies, but there was a recession going on, so nothing came of these plans. I was home from college when the demolition of the building took place. A ball and chain crashed into the building over and over. My witnessing its destruction felt like witnessing an execution. Anything built in its spot since the inn's demise looked atrocious. Maybe the inn's spirit is in play here.

My best friend was one of eight children in a big Catholic family. Initially, she lived near the Catholic Church but later moved out a ways, several blocks from my home and also near the KGRL radio station. I would spend almost every weekend at her home, or we would stop by at mine on our way home from school. Sometimes she stayed for dinner at our house. She liked to call my dad Frankie. She was born with a hole in her heart and was known as a blue baby. She was very ill as a small child, but when she was six, she had open heart surgery to fix the hole. She was one of the firsts to have such a surgery. This improved her status, but her first six years without enough oxygen taxed her lungs, causing them to become enlarged and damaged. She continued to have bluish skin and lips. She tired easily. Her home seemed more relaxed than mine. Dad could be intense and demanding at times. So I spent a lot of time over at her house.

They had a basement family room that Mary R. and I took over on Friday nights when I stayed over. We watched The Tonight Show Starring Johnny Carson with popcorn and soda. Mary R. was the sixth of eight children in the family. They were a funny lot. Because there were so many kids, they all talked loud and over one another. Mary R. had a quirky sense of humor. When we were in high school, she was in the band. In fact, all eight of the kids in her family had been in the band during their high school days. Her oldest sister H. played the French horn. She even played it at one of her brothers' wedding. Mary R. played the clarinet. When we were in high school, there was a band concert one evening so I went to show my support. There were bleachers set up for the band members in the auditorium. There was one band member (a large nerdy girl) who Mary R. didn't like. I think she didn't like her because the girl was first chair and Mary R. was second chair. But there they were seated right next to each other on the top row. During the first number, the girl fell backward off the bleachers and landed behind them with a tremendous crash. This created quite a commotion. Everyone in the band ceased playing, and Mary R. couldn't contain her laughter as she glanced down behind the bleachers at the girl. The girl wasn't hurt, so she dusted herself off and returned to her seat. The music resumed, but Mary R. was never able to regain her composure after that.

The house was split level, and Mary R.'s bedroom was upstairs in a long line of bedrooms. There were twin beds in her room, and she slept in one with her dog, and I slept in the other. Her brother Tim would come in and bug us. One time, he came in and dared us to drink a shot of some liquor. I never had a problem with hard liquor, so I drank it right down. Then Mary R. tried but didn't fare as well. In fact, Tim and I thought the shot might kill her because of her bad heart and the way she was coughing, sputtering, and carrying on. Another time, their mom talked Tim and his friend into taking us to the drive-in. We thought this was exciting at first, but during the movie, they made us sit in the backseat and told us not to bother them.

Mary R.'s neighbor had a horse named Ginger that was a plug. He let us ride Ginger. We would get up on her back together and ride around the neighborhood. Sandy also had friends who had horses, and so we started asking Mom and Dad if we could have one of our own. They took us out to see a horse—one that one of Dad's technicians (who was also our neighbor) recommended. I took a trial run with the horse, and it took off running. I knew it was too much for me but was afraid to say so, thinking this might be our only chance to have a horse. Dad was a city slicker, so what did he know about horses anyway? Sandy took a ride too, and it was decided that we would purchase the horse. The horse's name was Lady. Lady was getting older but was a thoroughbred. This may have accounted for her spunkiness. Lady was boarded at Dad's partner's acreage about a half mile from our home. When I rode Lady in their pasture, she would take off with me and run right up against the fence and pull her head down to the ground in an effort to slide me off her back. She was usually successful. Another time, she bucked me off while I was riding her in the field. I fell right on my head and was knocked out. When I would take her out for a ride out on Eighth Street, she would decide that she wanted to go home, and there seemed to be nothing I could do to change her mind. In those days, Eighth Street was a common thoroughfare where many equestrians traveled. The last time I took her out on Eighth Street, I had gone down a dirt side road and started back home when she took off and ran right in front of a truck traveling down Eighth that almost ran into both of us. I got off her, walked her home, and never rode her again. Sandy, however, figured out how to manage Lady and won some ribbons at the county fair.

Mary R.'s parents let her live as if she was a healthy child. She wasn't coddled because of her condition. However, as her friend, I was aware of her restrictions. If we walked home from school, she was winded easily, and we would have to stop for rests frequently. We got into only two disagreements during the time I spent with her. One was related to a bike ride we were on, and I got impatient and took off without her. She struggled to keep up and taxed herself. When I got to our destination and she caught up with me, she was angry that I left her behind. The other time was when we were working on our homework together at my house. I had a habit of convincing her (and myself) that a math problem was so- and-so when it wasn't. Somehow this wound up resulting in our scribbling on each other's papers and then tearing them up. It took a few days to get over this incident. Dad warned me early on that she wouldn't live through high school, but I didn't believe him.

At St. Francis School, Mary R. and I had boyfriends in the sixth grade. .We didn't actually talk to our boyfriends though we developed crushes on two of our classmates, and word got around. These two best friends, Arlie and Andy, sent word back in agreement with the matches. One day out on the playground, Arlie started horsing around with me. He would jump in front of me, poke at me, etc. I started jumping around playfully too and inadvertently grabbed on to his dick beneath his salt and pepper cords. We stood there for what seemed like an eternity—my face bright red with embarrassment and his with a sly smile. Later on in my life, I would recollect this event and learn that our life's paths had developed similar courses.

Mary R. and I went to Girl Scout day camp one summer with a bunch of other kids from school. One of the girls in our group was from a school in La Pine, and she was more "mature" than the rest of us. In fact, she told of her sexual escapades with her older boyfriend. The rest of the girls were put off by the girl's tales, but I was fascinated and hung out with her to hear more about it. We all spent the last night in a tent. We started sneaking around the other campsites, but something spooked us, so we sped back to our tent and stayed put. We were convinced that a criminal or a ghost was stalking us.

The next year, we were older, so we got to stay at camp for a whole week. Our scout leader had us all shop for our own food, and we all had to stock a large ice chest with our purchases. Unfortunately, our ground beef got maggots in it, and the rest of the food spoiled. Our leader was kind but not very organized. Nor was she much in the way of supervision. I remained hungry for most of the week. On the final two days of camp week, we were to hike from the base camp up to Green Lakes and spend two nights up there. Mary R. and I started out with the rest, but she was unable to keep up. We decided to go back down to the base camp at her speed, spend the night, and then go back up at her pace the next day. This would allow us to have one night at Green Lakes with the others. We made it to the top at about sunset the next day. It was cold that night because of the elevation. There seemed to be a shortage of sleeping bags, so the other Mary suggested that we zip two bags together so the three of us could share the bigger bag to keep warm. The bags didn't zip together very well, and it was so cramped in the bag that before long, I crept out of the bag and attempted to sleep on the ground with just my clothes on. It was not a very restful night, but the night sky was spectacular up there, and we saw numerous shooting stars. The next morning, we hiked back to the base camp, and I returned home where I had a shower and some good food. Dad may have been influenced by my tale of near starvation during my week at camp because, later on, he created a stash of freeze-dried food for Doug after he was invited by a friend of Dad's to accompany him and his son on a mountain climbing expedition. Dad knew the guy was a cheapskate and wouldn't bring enough food. He advised Doug to hide his stash-not share it-and Doug heeded his advice and was grateful as the other two remained hungry during their adventure.

Doug went to kindergarten in Mrs. Bowlus's class. She had a school across Greenwood Avenue that was about six blocks from our house. There wasn't much traffic in those days, so he walked there and back on his own. Mrs. Bowlus also taught tumbling, gymnastics, and piano lessons for older kids, so Sandy and I got signed up for these things too. This was after the piano lessons with the nuns. I didn't really like tumbling. There was a trampoline that I was supposed to do stunts on, and I used such things as the vaulting horse and the balance beam. I didn't like to practice piano either and especially didn't like the recitals when parents would come to see the students. Sandy and I would get cold feet and flub the numbers. We would rather play outside with each other or our friends, ride bikes, and explore the outdoors.

In those days, there were plenty of wide open spaces. We rode our bikes to the swimming hole at Tumalo State Park in the summer. We built forts in the woods. We walked over to the KGRL radio station and hung out with the deejays there, and they played our requests. Andy was our favorite deejay because he was so cute and nice. I have always loved music, so one day while I was at Erickson's Grocery down the block, I spotted a form you could fill out to get "The Twist" record in the mail if you just sent in a few dollars, and sure enough, the record came in the mail about a week later. Chubby Checker was featured. I liked to do the Twist, and after a while, I could get all the way to the ground and up. Later on, I danced the Twist with a partner.

In the meantime, Doug was becoming quite the bicyclist. He got a unicycle for Christmas, and in no time, he was riding all over the neighborhood. He would even ride up Pilot Butte with his unicycle. He also got a BB gun, but when he pumped a couple of shots into Sandy's butt with it, that was the end of his gun. He got a carbide cannon from Joe Remec too. He would load it with carbide and then add water, and it made a loud canon sound. He added too much carbide one time, and it exploded in his face and singed his eyebrows off. He and his best friends Scot and Stewart (brothers), who lived across the street, got into the house that was being built next door to ours and turned on all the faucets. The house was flooded, and Mom and Dad got a call from the builders. In spite of this, they went to the same house a few weeks later and put their hand- and footprints in the newly poured driveway. Our parents got a call about this too.

Dad would get frustrated with Doug at the dinner table because he couldn't sit through a meal. He was only about five, and our dinners were lengthy every evening—usually two or more hours long—and Doug was a hyper kid in the first place. Doug would fidget at mealtime and ask to be excused from the dinner table to go play. On one occasion, Dad told Doug that he could leave but that he was banned from the dinner table, so in the future, he could just go down for his meals at a nearby burger stand. He wouldn't have to sit at the dinner table anymore, he explained. Dad gave him money every evening, and Doug would head out to the burger stand where he would order his meal and have his burger and fries.

It took about a week before Doug got tired of the same thing every night and promised to try to sit still during meals, but that still didn't always happen.

Mom prepared gourmet meals every night that would take her half the day to make. Dad was the one who encouraged her to develop her culinary skills. He noticed, when they started going to San Francisco for his medical trainings, Mom was able to detect every ingredient in each dish they ordered. She had a good nose. So she would be able to return home and make these dishes without a recipe, but Dad bought her gourmet cookbooks too for her to experiment with. Mom's sweet breads with garlic tomato sauce and her orange duck were some the best food I've ever tasted. She would prepare the orange duck for Dad's birthday because it was his favorite. She would spend two days preparing this meal. Another thing that Dad became aware of on their trips to the city was that some of his mother's dishes, such as polenta that he had grown up on, were going for exorbitant prices in the restaurants and that they were Italian dishes for the most part. He was unaware that his mother cooked Northern Italian cuisine. One time, while they were in San Francisco in a high rise hotel, Mom and Dad sat in front of the window enjoying the view. Mom just had her brassiere and underpants on. Dad noticed a guy in another high rise with a pair of binoculars pointing in the direction of their window. Dad told Mom that the guy across the way was checking her out but she didn't believe him so he waved at the guy and the guy waved back. Then Mom knew Dad was right and so she retreated from the window.

During our evening meals, Dad would ask us about our day, compliment the chef, rave about our meal, and expound on his life theories. One piece of advice that stuck in my mind was his conviction that family business stays in the family—with business meaning anything that pertained to our family and its members. So if we went on vacation, we didn't' tell anyone about it. We didn't discuss difficulties, arguments, or past history with outsiders. I wasn't sure at the time why Dad was telling us all this, but upon reflection, it seems that he didn't trust the establishment, and for good reason. He was considered an outsider in his youth, and so our secrecy was our protection. Family was the only place where one could really feel safe, or so he thought. Another meal discussion that sticks out in my mind is Dad's description of the beauty of a pregnant woman—in particular, my mother. Being the doctor that he was, he had little reservation about describing in detail the changes in a woman's body during her pregnancy— in particular, her vulva and vagina, which were so enticing to him. Mom never objected to his discussion of this topic. What it left me with was a positive opinion about pregnancy that later served me well. I was lucky enough to have married a man who had the same opinion as my father.

St. Francis was OK until I got in the seventh grade and had Sister B for a teacher. She divided the class in half. One side was for the girls, and the other was for the boys, and we weren't allowed to interact with the other side. She liked to play sports with the boys on the playground, and it seemed to me that she would flirt with them. Teachers usually liked me but not Sister B. I would put teen magazines in my desk at school, and she would look in our desks to make sure we didn't have anything prohibited in there. Prohibited was anything that she didn't like. She found my magazines and threw them away. Another time, she accused me of cheating on a math test, tore my paper up, and threw it in the garbage. I cried at my desk, and Mark W., a fellow classmate, sneaked up to the garbage pail while Sister B was writing on the blackboard, got my scraps of paper, and sneaked them back to me. I was able to put the pieces together and then copy the answers on a new sheet and hand it in. I hadn't ever cheated before, but after this incident, I decided that I would try it. Mary R. agreed to conspire with me. We would hollow out pens so that we could put notes in them and pass answers back and forth. It looked as though we were borrowing a needed pen. We successfully cheated this way and never get caught.

Things got progressively worse as the year wore on. I started ratting my hair, as it was the popular style at the time. Sister B didn't like it and hauled me out of the classroom and into the girl's bathroom where she took a brush and tore out the rats. (This is currently the bathroom at McMenamins Old St. Francis School Pub). My friends and I would submit requests to KBND radio station for songs that we would dedicate to friends or crushes. Sister B listened in to the same radio program at night and would call those of us who had submitted requests out in the hall the next day and scold us for having done so. We were told that we were not to do this anymore. So we started using code names, which I guess really defeated the purpose. Patty H.'s mom agreed to let Patty have an afternoon boy-girl birthday party, so she invited her friends from school. I was so excited that I would be able to go to this party because boys would be there, but Sister B found out about the party somehow and called all our parents to call the party off. I was really angry with my mother who didn't stand up to Sister B. I started having stomachaches at school and complaining that I didn't want to go to school in the mornings. I really did have stomachaches and often felt nauseous before I had to go to school. Mom sent me to the doctor who couldn't find anything wrong with me. I think that she finally figured out what was wrong—Sister B. I still had to finish seventh grade at St. Francis though.

I developed mixed feelings about Catholicism. On the one hand, the sexual mores and prudish attitudes of the church's clergy were off-putting. My experience with Sister B didn't help either. On the other hand, I was drawn to the spirituality that was represented by the efforts put forth historically by parishioners in their artistic expressions of their faith, the magnificence of the cathedrals that suggested the fervor of their belief, and maybe also to bring others into the church. I also liked hearing the mass in Latin and the ceremony which lent a feeling of mystery. My grandmother's religious fervor also likely influenced me. It seemed to me that the ideas of peace and love were good ones, but that it was people who often used religion to their own advantage that always led to corruption. Dad didn't seem to take his religion too seriously. He would frequently fall asleep in church with his head bobbing up and down during mass. Or he would make faces at kids who looked back at him to entertain them. One boy was hit up alongside his head by his mother for laughing at Dad's faces during mass, and then Dad felt bad. However, he always said that his Catholicism was one thing he would never give up, that he recognized all that his family had lost in leaving their homeland, and that his religion was one thing he was determined to hang on to. He seemed to maintain his struggle between fitting in here and clinging to his roots.

Mom started attending mass with Dad early on in their courtship. She marveled at the similarity between the Catholic and Lutheran services and questioned the lines drawn between these and other denominations. This may have led to her consideration and eventual entry into the Catholic faith. I remember her taking instruction during evenings at the rectory and her baptism after we moved to Bend. Mom and Dad explained to us the importance of being united in one faith within our family. I'm not sure how much my father's influence had to do with her decision. Once she was Catholic, she became almost fanatical. I wondered if she had guilt about giving up her Lutheranism. When her parents came to visit, she cautioned us not to say a word about her conversion. When they were visiting, she attended Lutheran services with them. Later on, she seemed disappointed that her sacrifice wasn't always appreciated by some of her offspring, namely Sandy and me, who drifted away from the Catholic Church.

I decided to try out Mom's cold cream that she kept in her bathroom. I guess I felt like I was a grown-up, being in seventh grade and all. After a few days of using her cream, I developed a bad case of acne. I don't know if it was the cold cream altogether or if my age had something to do with it too, but it lasted for years. Mom would tell me that by the time I was sixteen, it would all be cleared up, but that didn't happen. She had a bad experience of her own with acne as an adolescent. She said that a doctor did X-ray treatments on her face, which resulted in her skin turning black after a few days and then falling off. In spite of this response, the doctor continued with these X-ray treatments, which didn't do anything as far as clearing up her skin. Mom suggested all sorts of remedies for me. She got me a sunlamp that I later ended up taking along with me to college. My colleagues would tease me about my sunlamp. It didn't help. It just gave me a sunburn. I tried all sorts of acne scrubs and soaps to no avail. Once, the guy from Troy Laundry who delivered Dad's dress shirts asked me if I had the measles. It was humiliating. When I started dating, I'd try to make sure to present myself in dark places so no one would notice. Parking at night was a good choice. If I was inside, I'd try to dim the lights or simply turn them off. All this didn't help my self-esteem. I still remember Mom telling me that my experience had a positive aspect to it. She explained that being self-conscious about one's appearance builds character. It helps instill empathy for others who suffer imperfection, and I think she was right. I also got very sick about the same time and had to go to my dad's office to have tests done. I had to drink a barium drink so that they could see my insides, and it was decided I had a kidney infection.

I began to notice a general feeling of apprehension that seemed to hang around for lengthy periods of time. I couldn't identify any real cause. It may have been around earlier on but I didn't have a conscious awareness of it. This feeling was also accompanied by a tendency to feel hyper-aroused by sensual experiences—colors, music, tastes, smells, or doing something risky with my friends. Was it pubescence or something else? I also became aware of "going away." It seemed to be like some sort of trance. I'd lose track of time and then come to again. Others have pointed this out to me over the years. I'm not always aware of it myself.

This is also about the time Mom had her talk with me about sex. According to her, I have always asked curious questions, which she generally ignored, from an early age. But this time, she brought up the topic. I still remember we were in the kitchen alone, and she was ironing. She announced that it was time for us to have a discussion about the birds and the bees. I noticed that she seemed a little uncomfortable about having this discussion at all. Our talk consisted of her telling me that when you marry, it's the wife's duty to make sure her husband remains sexually satisfied. That was it. That's all she had to say about the topic. It was OK, though. I already knew a lot more than she would have expected, for whenever I found myself alone in our house, I'd pore over Dad's pertinent medical books, especially one called Ideal Marriage: Its Physiology and Technique by Th. H. Van De Velde, MD, which included just about anything and everything you'd ever need to know about the subject.

There was an entry in my junior high yearbook from a classmate who lived a block away on Eighth Street. His name was David K. He was goofy and a cutup in class. Sandy and I had received a gift of real walkie-talkies for Christmas, as opposed to the tin can and string sort of our Spokane days. At school, I discovered that Dave had a walkie-talkie too so we would chat on them during the evenings and weekends. He wrote the following in my yearbook: "Cheryl, It's really been great knowing you this year. I think you're the cutest girl I've ever seen (except for Janet). It's really been the best year ever and you helped make it that way. May God bless you. Love forever, Davie. P.S. get on your walkie talkie tonight at 9:00 P.M. O.K.? P.S.S. You've got a nice house-auf wiedersehen."

My friend Janet wrote the following retort on the opposite page: "(Reserved for Putt). Cheryl- David's second best girlfriend- for a little bit of conceit maybe the best girl won! Ha-Ha. My goal this year has been to keep you honest. Have I succeeded?-no! I'll always remember the hay ride. We had such a neat talk. And everyone we talked about-Wow! It would sure fill a gossip column! We've given each other so much advice it has just been great . . . For Hick Day we'll really have to get a wild outfit. Maybe we could be Siamese twins or something! This summer we can have a blast-summer geology and afterwards. Boy if we go to the beach and spend the night who knows what might happen. Maybe we will have a bunch of classes together next year and torment the teachers as we have Mr. Wilson." (I don't remember ever doing that). "The poor man-never to forget the duo that marred him. I'm terribly anxious to hear of your plans for snagging boys.-Bet they are exciting-suppose they'll work? We should steal a car and practice driving this summer if we run out of things to do. Don't forget the milkshake—30 cents at that. Love always, Janet. Just an added note—I'll have to come to your church again. Maybe I won't be so scared the next time. Let's never end this great friendship—I really got to know the cool Cheryl this year and can't wait 'til next year. Janet."

Dad hired a college guy to do some tree trimming, lawn work, painting, etc. at our house in the summers. I was thirteen, and the guy was seventeen and already attending college. He was from the East Coast and drove out with a buddy to do some rock climbing at the famous Smith Rock right outside of Redmond, Oregon. He had a minor mishap there and wound up at Dad's office for an X-ray. They got to talking, and Dad agreed to provide him with summer employment. He was around most of that summer and was the first guy that I knew was attracted to me. He would flirt and show off. I was likewise attracted to him but also somewhat intimidated by him. He was older and seemed dangerous in some way. He would leave for college after the summer was over and then return again the next summer.

I remember wanting my period to start. After all, my friends were talking about it out on the playground. Some of them didn't like it, but I thought I would. It finally did start when I was fourteen, and I was very excited about it. On the first day, Mom had given me a few pads, and I went into the bathroom to change. I was still nervous about the whole operation and left the used pad on the back of the toilet. As I left the bathroom, Dad was heading in there. I remembered the pad, but it was too late because he had already closed the door. When he came out, he smiled and said "I guess you're all grown up now," and I was mortified. Mom also took me to The Smart Shop in Downtown Bend and bought me some training bras, but my girlfriends had bras with real cups that seemed better to me. I went downtown one day and called Mom on a pay phone in front of The Smart Shop. I told her that I was planning to stop by and grab a few new bras for myself. She said that I already had some, but I told her that I needed a different kind. I saved up some money of my own doing chores, so I was able to go in and buy them. I guess I couldn't tell her all this face-to-face. Mary R. and I also thought we were too thin, so we went down and bought some Weight On. Our plan was for her to come over to my house in the mornings before school, so we could both take a pill without our parents knowing about it. On the first day she came over for her pill, I left the box out on my dresser, and Mom found it while I was at school. When I got home, she had thrown it all away. She told me that it wasn't safe to use pills like this. She said something about the pills having tapeworms in them, but that didn't make any sense to me. Maybe she was thinking of pills that were meant to have people lose weight. I wasn't happy about paying for the pills and having them thrown away. Mary R. and I decided we'd just start drinking lots of milk shakes to put on some weight, but that didn't do any good either. They did taste good, though.

I figured out early on that males have dominion over and are considered more important than females. This made me wish I was a boy for a while, for all the privilege and freedom it would entail. But all this didn't stop me from developing an appreciation for being female and a fascination for all that femaleness had to offer, much in the form of sensual experience. My musings accelerated and exhilarated after my menarche. I liked the little period cramps that felt a lot like the pain you feel when you push a loose baby tooth up against your gums with your tongue when you're a little kid. Then there was the warm feel of blood gliding through the vagina, then leaving it in a gushing flow or a quick spurt. Later on, I would marvel at the complexity of the female body—the womb, like a spaceship providing all the nutrients and oxygen to sustain life and provide a safe place for the growing alien inside, then the body opening like a flower's bloom to expel its seed, and the breasts that take over in a carefully orchestrated chain of events after launching. Oh, how giving birth is like a gigantic orgasm and then some. The monthly cycle, so akin to all of nature and creation, felt as though I belonged to the moon. The female cannot escape her oneness with Mother Nature. Ovulation mimics the state before orgasm, creating the same sort of tension right beforehand—an agitation for gratification that can lead to desperation or even violence. I believe women are more sexual than men. Their bodies are designed to propagate the human race. The female sex drive is more complicated because of the more all-encompassing nature of her sexual being. This goes largely unrecognized because males are often more demonstrative about their own sexual experience and often unconcerned about the female counterpart. But I expect some men do know something of the female psyche and often either ignore it or try to suppress it, for it has a truly powerful and dangerous potential.

I would come to discover the orchestration of the womb, the vagina, and the vulva in the sexual union—the womb's spasms of pleasure deep inside me in unison with those of the velvety vagina grasping the male member, drawing it closer to the female center of conception; and the moist, swollen, and seductive vulva, with its sweet and earthy scent. How all these parts transform over the course of a lunar month—the menstruation offering another form of pleasure—a sharper, stronger scent, an even more velvet- like wall of warm comforting blood for the intruder—a bloody, sensual, and raucous mess. And during the fecund state, the female organs take on the most sensual state of all—ripe, luscious, full vulvar lips, and caressing, serene, viscous, and generous walls that grasp and hold dear. Then comes the fecund womb, already in its desired state but still eager to respond with violent spasms that disrupt the inhabitant's peace but enhances the lover's pleasure.

My friend T had a younger brother who was my sister's age. Both of them were kind of wild. T's mom would take us to Cascade Bowl next to St. Francis School downtown on Friday nights. She played in her league, and we hung out in the locker room. There were benches to sit on. We gossiped, looked through magazines, and got food at the concession stand. While we were friends, for some reason, some of our mutual friends decided that we should ignore T. I thought this was stupid, so I began hanging out exclusively with T until the ban on her was dropped. I remember a trip to Portland that her mom let me go on with T to visit her aunt and cousin. They had a basement where T's cousin hung out with her friends. She was about fifteen and looked flashy. She was flirtatious and brazen with her male chums down there in the basement. I thought I could never be like that, but I wished I could. It took quite a while, but I would.

My friend Paula was more advanced in the area of sexual development than me. She was preoccupied with boys and had their attention. I would walk home with her after school. She was openly flirtatious with an older guy who lived next door to her, and he reciprocated the attention. She was "making time" with him. I think that she must have felt sorry for me because I was not only very shy about boys but also didn't really attract much attention from them. I was also told by others that I had an air of aloofness that put guys off, but this was really only my shyness. At any rate,

Paula told me that a boy named Johnny was interested in me, and that he wanted to meet me at the Tower Theatre where Paula was to meet up with her older boyfriend. Well, I got as put together as possible for my first "date." We waited in the lobby at the Tower, but Johnny never showed up. I was disappointed but also a little relieved because the thought of meeting him made me nervous. I began getting romantic letters from Johnny, and I wrote back to him. At this point, I began to look forward to meeting him and asked my go-between, Paula, to intervene. This is when she told me that Johnny was made up, not a real person at all, and that she had manufactured him and written the letters herself in order to make me feel better. I didn't feel better when I found out he wasn't real, but I did appreciate her gesture.

Sandy and I took ballet lessons at the Mary Cowden School of Dance Arts after school for three or four years. It was only a few blocks from St. Francis, so we could walk over after school. Mary Cowden had been a ballet dancer in San Francisco or somewhere like that and, in her later years, had dedicated herself to teaching ballet and other dance. She was very theatrical, and her toes always pointed outward because she had worn ballet shoes and danced for so long. She always wore scarves around her neck and waved her arms about to accentuate her speech. One year, I was in The Nutcracker that required a ballerina outfit—a tutu. Another year, I wore a Chinese outfit. The year I was in the Chinese outfit, I was getting ready for my number backstage when I noticed itchy blisters on my back. At first, I thought the blisters were poison oak, which I had had before. But this time, it turned out to be chicken pox, so I had to go home without performing. The recital was right before school was out for the summer. We drove back to Illinois for my grandparents' golden wedding anniversary. Sandy came down with the chicken pox on the way out to Illinois, and the hot weather made the pox spread over every inch of her body. My condition got better. The party was at my cousin Ken's house. At the anniversary party, I wasn't that interested in the reason for the party. I was more interested in hanging out with my cousins—in particular, one of Irma's sons, Jimmy, who was a second cousin, so it seemed he wasn't off-limits because of the second cousin thing. He was a few years older, and he flirted with me down in Ken's basement, but it really didn't amount to much. The next day, though, I fantasized about how I might get in touch with him and get some kind of romance started. This was one of the first of many incidents where I would get carried away about an infatuation.

Eighth grade was better than seventh. My teacher was Sister Mildred Marie. She wasn't great but was better than Sister B. Mary A. got to have parties in her basement. Sometimes they were slumber parties. We would stay up all night, and I would go back home the next day, tired and crabby. After a while, Mom wouldn't let me go to overnighters any longer because of this. Sometimes, boys were invited to the parties. One time, there was a Halloween party there. My friend Paula came over to my house beforehand to create a costume for me. She used hair spray and ratted my hair so that it stuck up like a beehive on top of my head. She put big freckles on my face with an eyebrow pencil. I wore a short blue jumper and held a big lollipop. I'm not sure what I was supposed to be. Someone brought chew to the party and dared me to put some inside my lip. It gave me the whirlies, and I felt like vomiting. It was the first and last time I tried chew. Mary A. and I would go to her house sometimes when her parents weren't home. Her dad was scary and her mom seemed downtrodden. One time, when we were there at her house, her dad drove up, and she freaked out and told me I had to hide in her closet or she would get in big trouble for having me there. So I did. It seemed like I was in there forever. He was standing right in front of the closet door where I was hiding and giving Mary A. a hard time—probably not as hard a time if he had found out about me hiding in the closet.

Before eighth grade was over, my maternal grandmother died in Illinois. We left for Illinois before school was out. Nora was in bed and seemed to have tried to use the phone. The receiver was off the hook when she was found dead the next morning, hanging over the side of her bed. This was on May 17, 1965. We flew out for the funeral. I remember Sandy and me being left alone with my grandfather in the kitchen. Mom must have gone to make arrangements for the next day. There was a tornado outside that blew at the front door. The wind caused banging and whistling sounds. Gram-pa kept talking as though Gram-ma was still around. In Illinois, the funerals are formal, with a few days of the wake when there is the viewing of the body and people coming to pay their respects. I went to Gram-ma's wake and knelt in front of the casket. I had never seen a dead body in a casket before. I cried and cried, but I think it was less from my own grief over the loss of my grandmother than from the awareness of the complicated grief and suffering of my mother. I may also have felt sad that Nora had been so fond of me, and I seemed to have had an inability to return her affection as much as I might have and that she had remained a mystery to me. She seemed to have dark secrets that I never got ahold of. I sensed some sadness about her. She seemed a complex and troubled lady that maybe no one ever understood. When I studied old photographs of her, I noticed that she clings to her husband. She looks at him with adoring eyes. She shows affection to her niece, her more-than-half-sister Lena's daughter, which I didn't see in her manner toward my mother until she and Mom were both older. Francesca was an open book. Nora was a closed book. I began to understand during the funeral that difficult emotional experiences were deepening the degree of my emotional intensity. I became drawn to those I recognized on some level as sharing a similar disposition to my own. Mom remained in Illinois after the funeral to take care of family business. The following week, we drove back up to Portland to greet her at the airport. We met her at the terminal, and she was covered with hives. She seemed distraught and looked troubled.

I started school at Cascade Junior High in the ninth grade. Along with me, Mom transferred Sandy into the seventh grade from St. Francis, and she took Doug out of the third grade there because he was having difficulty with the nun who was his teacher. He was enrolled in public school too. Cascade was about a block from St. Francis School, so the change didn't take much getting used to as far as location was concerned. We were able to leave our dreaded parochial school garb behind and wear regular clothes. As a fashion aficionado, this was a big deal for me. I kept some of my friends from St. Francis and also made some new ones. Some of the St. Francis kids going into the public school system (Cascade Junior High) wanted to get into the popular group there. I wasn't too interested in that, and in fact, I resented that some of my St. Francis chums were so desperate to get acquainted with the popular kids. This all led to a reorganization of cliques during the ninth grade. I was and still am on the introverted side, and as far as friendships went, I was prone to develop more emotionally intimate friendships rather than become involved in a desperate attempt to be in the right group. The kids I gravitated toward tended to be somewhat quirky and "intellectual," if there is such a thing in junior high. Occasionally, though, the cliques would mingle, so I did get to know most of my classmates.

There were fun things at junior high. For one thing, comingling between boys and girls was not prohibited as it had been at St. Francis with Sister B. There were noon dances. I would attend these events and enjoyed the music but was never asked to dance. There were also armory dances downtown on the weekends (where the library is now). Paul Revere and the Raiders was a group that frequently played at the armory. They would come into town in a black limousine that would slide through Downtown Bend. I didn't get asked to dance at these events either, but it was exciting to hang out there with my friends and listen to the music. To me, it was a sexually charged environment that I enjoyed. During weekends and after school, we would gather at someone's house and then walk to Downtown Bend, where we would stop at the Skyline Steakhouse for fries and a Coke. On Friday nights, we'd all meet at the Tower Theatre for a movie with hopes of meeting up with some boy there. A frequent party spot was Maxine's house. Her parents were easygoing. My friends and I would mingle and hang out there with other junior high kids.

Cascade started a contest that involved a seesaw. It was erected near the junior high on the corner of Franklin and Bond where there used to be a service station. There was a parking lot next to the station, and this was where the seesaw was. The goal was to break the Guinness Book of World Records for continuous seesawing. This involved students signing up to take turns for two-hour intervals. The transfer from one person to the next involved having one person slide off as the other got on. This sounded fun, so I'd sign up with a friend and we'd head out to take our turns. I preferred the middle-of-the-night shifts because there weren't as many other kids milling around, and it was fun to walk downtown at two or three in the morning to get on the seesaw. Sometimes the next kids wouldn't show up, so we would have to ride up and down until someone came to replace us. I heard that we broke the world record, but I don't know whether this is true or not.

Things didn't go well in Illinois with my grandfather after Nora had passed away. My uncle called Mom, and it was decided that my grandfather would come to live with us and see how that would work out. Maybe this was because Mom was home during the days and could keep track of him. Well, things didn't work out with us either. Franz became even more confused in his new surroundings and would take off for walks and get lost. Mom really didn't seem to have much propensity for geriatric caregiving and, for that matter, not much for caregiving in general. She kept the house clean, ironed, cooked, and was pleasant to us all, but when anyone was ill, we were on our own. Anyway, it didn't take long before Gram-pa was in a nursing home. My sister remembers visits when he was tied in a chair and that Mom was unnerved by his predicament but with no real remedy to change matters. I must have been preoccupied with adolescent adventures because I don't remember much about his being with us or seeing him in the nursing home. He didn't last long there. He died of kidney failure. This was on January 21, 1966, one day before my birthday. Mom flew back to Illinois with his body. It was so frigid there it was impossible to dig the hole in the ground for his burial. Dad stayed in Bend with us while she was gone.

In the summers, my friends and I would take to the water. Tumalo State Park was one frequented spot. We rode our bikes all the way there and back. It was quite a climb on the way back, so I would have to get off my bike and walk it up the steep grade. When we got there, we'd spread out our towels and swim, play cribbage and sunbathe. We usually had a transistor radio to listen to music. There were also lava tubes that traveled underwater in a section of the river. Some of my friends would shoot through the tunnels and come up the other side, but I never got the nerve to do this. I may be fortunate because some guy who was too big tried to get all the way through and got stuck in the tube. Paramedics had a heck of a time getting his body out of the tube. Needless to say, he didn't survive. We also did inner tubing on the canals that ran outside of town. There were waterfalls that we'd go over too, and sometimes the inner tubes would topple over, and we'd wind up underwater. Then we'd drag the tubes back and start all over again. No one wore life preservers in those days—at least we didn't.

Sandy and I shared a room with twin beds at the front of the house, and we would horse around at night. One thing we did was get in bed with each other and pull the covers over our heads. We hid a flashlight and my red-and-white transistor radio with its earphones and listened to the radio when we were supposed to be sleeping. We would take turns with the earphones and change channels with the use of the flashlight. Mom and Dad would check in on us, and they either ignored our shenanigans or were clueless about what we were up to. I don't know. Cocktail parties were in vogue in the sixties, and if Mom and Dad weren't entertaining at home on weekends, they were going to their friends' homes for parties. Mom and Dad's parties were the wildest, and Sandy and I would be kept up by loud music and carryings-on by the adults. As the night wore on, Dad would get his African music going before the guests called it quits. On one of these nights, to amuse ourselves, Sandy and I ran back and forth from one bed to the next. After the move to my own bedroom, all this fun stopped. I suspect that my complaints about Sandy showing her friends my underwear drawer with my training bras in it may have had something to do with my parents' idea for me to have my own bedroom. I was moved into Mom and Dad's old bedroom after they had an additional room built on back of the house—a master bedroom and bath. I missed sharing a room with my sister, though.

Mom and Dad were enjoying their new bedroom suite. They had a bay window that looked out onto the backyard, which had lots of trees and flowers. Sometimes they liked to stay in bed late on weekends. If the door was closed, that was a sign for us kids to stay out. We usually occupied ourselves with television, reading, or just horsing around. Mom and Dad got amorous one morning and the shades were open on the bay window. There was a hot air balloon show, which occurred regularly in the area, that weekend, and they didn't notice right away that one of the balloons had landed right in front of their bay window. The group peered in through the window at them. Just about the time Mom and Dad noticed the group looking in astonished, the operator set the balloon and its occupants back up.

It was about this time that something went wrong at work with one of Dad's patients. Another doctor who had done a preliminary evaluation gave Dad some wrong information that led Dad to proceed with his diagnostic test. His patient had complications. The other doctor told him about his mistake about five years after the fact, but in the meantime, Dad became despondent. Our house had a long hallway that led from the front door all the way to the back of the house. This hallway led to the four bedrooms, and after my move, I was right next to my parents' new master suite. This made it impossible for me not to hear Dad crying night after night. My heart broke for him. I didn't know what was wrong. He became irritable and demanding. I remember, after he got word that I had not done as well as expected on my achievement tests at school, he brought home college calculus and trigonometry books to tutor me in the evenings. He would get angry if I didn't understand what he was talking about. I was expected to go to my room after dinner and study until bedtime every weeknight. Mom told me as an adult that while Dad was having his emotional breakdown, he would be so irritable she would sometimes take us back to the guest house for our meals and the rest of the evening in order to spare us his wrath and provide him with some time to himself. I don't remember this but don't doubt that this may have happened. I remember one summer day when we were out on the back patio, Dad was saying things, but none of it made any sense. It worried me at the time, but I didn't know what to think of it. Looking back, I think he was having a psychotic episode, but luckily, this was the only one I was ever aware of. Mom confided later on that she fell out of love with him during this time and had to pray to get her love for him back. I also came across a bill from a sanitarium in the valley with Mom's name on it. This was when I had arrived home from school, and no one was in the kitchen. The bill was folded on the counter when I took a look at it. This perplexed me too because

I hadn't been aware of her having been gone, unless a hospitalization was hidden under the guise of one of their vacations.

Mom and Dad had picnics in our backyard on Sunday afternoons when the weather got better. They sat on a blanket on the lawn and would have a bottle of wine between them and then put some steaks on the grill for dinner. We had a television out on the deck and also a fire pit, so when it got cooler in the evening, we could remain out doors and watch television in front of the fire. We had the summer house in our backyard that had been used as mother-in-law quarters by the previous owners of our home. It was a place where I would entertain friends, and it also acted as a guest house for visitors. My grandparents would inhabit the summer house when they visited in the summers. We sometimes rented the place out too and one of my junior high teachers, Kathy, rented it during the time that Mom and Dad were having their picnics. On one particular evening, two of Kathy's friends came by-my German teacher (Herr M.) and my physical ed teacher (Miss M.). Dad invited the teachers to join them, and he brought out extra bottles of wine and divided the steaks into smaller pieces to accommodate his guests. The party started getting raucous about the time that Mary A., her twin brother, and a few of my other friends showed up to visit. They were all amused by our teachers partying at my house. Well, after a while, my friends left, but the party carried on, and the adults moved into the house after it got cooler outside. Sandy and I peeked around the corner in the hallway into the kitchen where everyone had gathered. Herr M. had a glass of wine in his hand and was weaving around-backwards, forwards, side-to-side, in a wide circle-with his feet planted firmly on the ground, until he took a sudden face plant on the ceramic kitchen floor. It was a sight to see. He was out cold. He had arrived on his moped, which remained parked in front of our house for three days with his sandals draped over the handlebars. Kathy, Dad and Miss M. loaded him in Kathy's Volkswagen and took him home. The next day at school, all three of the teachers were absent, and Herr M. was out for three days altogether. I wasn't about to provide any explanation for this, but Mary A. did, so everyone at school knew what had happened at my house the night before.

A month or so later, Dad's parents came from Illinois to visit. They usually visited every other summer and stayed in our guest house. The Wednesday picnic group had started up again and, on the particular Wednesday that my grandparents went along, the picnic was to be held on a dinner train that ran from Bend to Prineville. Fortunately for me, I was busy that night, but Sandy and Doug attended with Mom, Dad, and our grandparents. It turned out to be a train ride from hell. I heard back that Dad tied one on and was so intoxicated that he got into a big argument with his father on the train ride and in the car on the way home. Sandy remembered that the two of them argued in Slovene, so no one other than Dad and our grandparents could understand what was being said, but she figured it wasn't good. Sandy remembers that after the shouting was over, Gram-ma sat in the backseat of the car—silent and wiping her eyes with a Kleenex and then nervously tearing it up into little pieces. Doug said he was mortified. My grandparents wouldn't talk to Dad for a few days afterward. We still don't know what the argument was all about.

During their visits, Gram-pa would walk down to the M & J Tavern on Greenwood, read his newspaper, have a few beers, and then walk back home again. It was during a summer visit about six years after the dinner train fiasco that Gram-pa decided that the patio Dad and family had built from shale rock (gathered and transferred to our home from the mountainous area near Todd Lake) needed to be covered. Creation of the original patio happened shortly after our move to the Ninth Street house. Mom complained to Dad about the red cinders—the only semblance of a patio—outside our back door. The cinders were tracked into the house by everyone and anyone who entered at the back of the house. So Dad decided to try to please his bride and, at the same time, create a new patio that was to be from the indigenous building blocks of Central Oregon. Creation of the original patio had required weeks of drives to and from the quarry-like area, loading the rock into our station wagon and then unloading it in our backyard. Then there were months of fitting the irregular rocks in cement for the end-product. Sandy had a red rock that she was particularly taken with and helped Dad find a prominent spot to venerate it. They chose the juncture between the walkway around the side of the house and the patio behind it. Dad was proud of the patio, which he (and we) had created with his (and our) own hard work and effort. But his father had criticized it from the get-go, and the patio had become a bone of contention between the two of them over the years. Gram-pa did have a point though. This home improvement project was like all the rest of Dad's. The finished product was uneven and difficult to navigate across. So Gram-pa started his project in spite of the fact that he was dealing with a cancer that eventually killed him and that Dad wasn't too enthused. He worked long hours with Doug (or even Leo) helping. This type of work was not meant for girls or women—lucky for us! The patio had the same precision that all his brickwork had, and it was easier to walk on than the old patio that remained underneath, but there was something sad about covering up the old one, and I think Mom thought so too. I have often wondered what people who might discover the rock beneath the brick in the future might think of it, but I'll have to say it's a hell of a foundation. I have also wondered if the fight in the dinner train earlier on had anything to do with the patio—a symbol of Dad's father's disapproval of him.

Gram-ma worked in our yard, cooked big meals for Gram-pa, and went shopping at the grocery store. She never saved leftovers.

Mom and Dad couldn't figure out at first why our garbage cans were bursting at the seams by the time they needed to be taken to the curb—until they looked inside. I guess the years of not having enough to eat led my grandmother to squander food, so she threw a lot of it in the garbage. Someone would have to take her to the store to buy more food. One day, Leo agreed to accompany her. He later described her storming around the unfamiliar store, frustrated that she couldn't find the things she needed. One item she was after was a canister of bouillon cubes that she called "Cubans." She tried to convey this to the store clerk in her broken English, but he had no idea what she was talking about. She became even more frustrated when she asked him where the "hrapes" were. She sounded as though she was being attacked as she shouted "hrapes" over and over again. Leo finally explained to the clerk that she was looking for grapes. In the same vein, she called her grandson Greg "Hreg," herself "Hrem-ma," and the government, was the "hoverment," and so on. I figured out later on that Slovenian G's sound like H's, so when she read a word starting with a G she pronounced it as an H.

Our guest house was also used as a hangout for me and my friends when it wasn't being rented out. It was a house set up like a studio apartment with a combination living room/bedroom, a small kitchen, and a bathroom with a large closet at the back of the house. We had sleepovers back there. One time, Mary A. and

I had the idea to tape a break-in. We used my tape recorder that my friends and I often used to create scripts, one of which was played on the local radio station after we submitted it for airtime. Originally, Dad had purchased the recorder so that we could send tapes back and forth to our relatives in Illinois. He also sent the same recorder to my grandparents. They would tape holiday gatherings and send them back to us, and vice versa. I still have some of them and treasure being able to hear the voices of my family members who are no longer with us. The tapes would include commentary by my father about the advantages of living on the West Coast and frightful piano performances by me and Sandy. Dad would prompt us kids to tell about our adventures, but Doug was the only real cooperative participant. In fact, Dad would yell at him on tape about how he was talking too much and interrupting others. He would say "Give the girls a turn" even though we weren't all that keen on having one. Mom's voice was never heard on any of the tapes. I'm not sure if she had refused to talk or if Dad intentionally or unintentionally didn't include her. Anyway, back to the break-in. Mary A. and I were setting up for the slumber party. We taped loud break-in kinds of sounds and hid the recorder in the bathroom where there was an outside window next to the toilet where someone could potentially climb through. The plan was for one of us to excuse herself to use the bathroom and then turn on the tape, which had a few minutes of time gap before the sounds would start, with the intention of scaring everyone else. We finally decided, after much deliberation, to include Mary R. in on the hoax because we were afraid that she might get so scared she would have a heart attack. So we told her. It went off without a hitch. The rest of the girls ran around screaming, and so did we so that we looked like we were scared too. Mary R. got so caught up in the scam that she started hyperventilating, so we told everyone what we had done, and everyone laughed and calmed down.

A friend of Dad's also worked at the hospital. We started going to Montana on vacations with him and his family. His wife was a petite and pretty black-haired woman with full lips and big blue eyes. One of their daughters was the same age as Sandy. A son was about Doug's age, and they had two other kids. Dad's friend's father had been friends with an old hermit who lived in the mountains of Montana—a gold miner who built several log cabins by hand on his property. He was a friendly old guy. He spent months on end alone in his cabin in the mountains and traveled to town occasionally for food and supplies. He liked liquor, so Dad and his friend would bring him a few fifths of something or other, and he would drink it in one sitting. This led them to dole it out in smaller portions, lest he drink himself to death. He had a spittoon next to his easy chair and would spit his chew in it. All his cabins had woodstoves, and there was no indoor plumbing. There were a few outhouses scattered about his property. He would show us kids how to pan for gold and would even accompany us on excursions into the mountain areas with streams. We had some success in our efforts, and Dad eventually had gold pins made for friends and family from the gold we had panned. (I wore one of them to Dad's funeral). We would also go hunting for huckleberries, and Mom and Dad's friend's wife would make huckleberry pies on the woodstove in our cabin. There were ladders that the hermit built of wood that went up the sides of some of the trees. I'm not sure what the purpose of these was. I decided to climb up one, and a spoke broke and a nail left a gash in my arm on the way down. A scar still marks the spot. Another time, there was a violent thunderstorm, and we took cover in one of the outhouses. The lightning struck so close to the outhouse that the ground shook, and it felt as though there was electricity all around us. The sound was deafening.

We also spent time with the wife's parents at Flathead Lake and went water skiing there. I had a crush on the eldest boy of the couple, but as usual, he didn't seem too interested in me. I think he thought I was a twerp. I was a string bean, and before the vacation that year, I bought a two-piece bathing suit that I thought was pretty snazzy. The top was white with little black stripes, and the bottoms were black with little white stripes and a black belt with a buckle on top. But the best part of the suit was that the top had hard cups inside that made me look as though I had a bosom when I really didn't. I thought this might attract my crush, but when it didn't, I still liked the suit anyway. After we got home, Mom put the suit in the dryer and shrunk the cups, which, in my opinion, ruined the suit. I was really mad at her. I don't think she got why. She probably couldn't relate.

It's not long after this trip that I noticed that Dad's friend would come by to visit when Dad wasn't around. Even when Dad was around, Mom would drape one arm around the back of her dining room chair so that her breasts (which were ample) would stick out in Dad's friend's direction. Maybe Dad wasn't' aware of this, but I was. I was also aware that there was friction between Dad and Mom since he had become moody and irritable after his medical mishap. Things got worse after one of Dad's friends made a comment to Mom about Dad's involvement with some woman. Mom confronted Dad at the dinner table one night about what she had heard, but he vehemently denied any wrongdoing. I'm not sure she was convinced of his innocence, but I know I wasn't. All this may have had to do with Dad becoming more distant toward his friend, and eventually, the friendship seemed to dissolve. With Dad, there was definitely a double standard. I suspect that with Dad, being in love would have been a necessary component of any romantic relationship he got into—be it Mom and/or anyone else.

Mom had a thing about her hair. I remember her wearing curlers or bobby pins around all day long during the time we lived in

Illinois. She would tie a scarf around them so that they were less noticeable, but that didn't work very well. When it would be time for Dad to come home, she'd take the curlers or bobby pins out and comb out her hair so that she looked nice for him. A while after we moved to Oregon, she started going to the beauty shop once a week to have her hair done. Mrs. B was her beautician and she coifed Mom's hair in a beehive, which was popular at the time. I had preferred her 1950s style. With the beehive, she had to wear a hair net while she slept in order to keep it in place. She also had a chopstick-like instrument that she used to prop up her hair in the mornings. This was maintenance until her next appointment, and she couldn't wash it in the meantime. I had developed super oily hair—inherited from my dad—and always washed it at least twice a day, so the thought of Mom waiting a week before a wash seemed weird to me. When I was in sixth grade, Mom got me and Sandy curlers. Some were pink plastic with a plastic bar to hold them in place. Others were wire with bristles that stuck out from inside the wires. Then you would have to put pink plastic sticks through the curlers to hold them in place. I would put the curlers in with wet hair before bedtime. They were so uncomfortable that I often woke up in the middle of the night and threw them all over the bedroom. The next day, my hair would be sticking up all over the place. On the nights that I left them in, there would be a line where the plastic bar held the curler in or where the wire curlers missed the hair by the scalp. Then my hair would look like I still had curlers in. Later on, Mom bought me a wiglet to enhance my hair for dances and other special events. I wore one to my junior homecoming dance, and I felt like a fool.

When Dad and Mom took me to San Francisco, Mom took me to a beauty shop to have our wiglets integrated into our real hair. Dad picked us up after the beauty shop outing to head for dinner. It was windy that day and Mom's wiglet blew right off her head and ran down the sidewalk. Dad sped up and left us behind because he didn't want to be seen with someone whose wiglet had blown off and was running down the sidewalk. Mom also had me and Sandy go to Mrs. B for special occasions such as school formal dances. I clearly remember going in for my senior prom. I showed her a picture of how I wanted my hair to look. She said she was busy and there were people in front of me. By the time she got to me, she just took a curling iron to my dry hair and created tight Shirley Temple curls and called it a day. When I got home, I tried to make my hair look as best I could, but it still looked dumb. Sandy had similar experiences with Mrs. B and has commented to me that when she did her own daughter's hair, it always looked a lot better than when she did ours. As time went on, I made a decision that when I went away to college, I would never be caught dead with any sort of curlers in my hair. I didn't want any guy to catch me wearing those things, and I didn't want the discomfort and trouble either. Nor would I mess around with any sprays, styles, wiglets, perms, etc. I would just wash and cut my hair when needed and give it an occasional brushing to keep it in place, and for the most part, I kept this promise to myself.

When Mom got older and only my sister Nora was left at home, she got a pixie cut, or so I heard. Sandy had come home to visit right after Mom's cut and commented to Mom how much she liked her new hairdo. Sandy called me after her return home and asked if I had seen Mom's new hair yet. I said no. Sandy told me it looked very cute on Mom and to check it out. So I went over the next day or so, but I didn't see any pixie cut. In fact, Mom's hair seemed to look worse than usual. I even brought up the topic to Mom about Sandy's description of a new hairdo, but Mom acted as though she didn't know what I was talking about. I called Sandy back and let her know how my visit had gone. Sandy started questioning her own sanity. It seems that Nora had also seen the new haircut and witnessed Dad's disapproving comments, after which Mom donned a wig and never went back to her real hair.

In spite of Dad's emotional difficulties, he still took us and our friends skiing. Sometimes we would also get to take friends to the coast for the weekend. One time, I got to take my friends, Mary R. and Mary A. Sandy took her friends, who were sisters, Kathy and Vickie, and Doug got to take a friend too. Mom cooked all the meals for everyone. Still, Mom was reserved and quiet. Photos of her taken on this vacation suggested that she was preoccupied. In the summer, my parents were part of the Wednesday Picnic Group, which was started in the late fifties by George R., who had been stricken with polio in his twenties. He invited his friends to Wednesday evening summer picnics that took place in various parks in the area. He hoped to keep his social life active in spite of his disability. This group is in operation to this day, although the crowd has slimmed down considerably due to member mortality. Children of couples in the group were welcome. I sometimes asked Mary R. to come along with me to these events. Dad drove our Volkswagen at the time, and he stored his red X-ray goggles in the backseat, along with the X-ray films that came in yellow and black cardboard boxes. Mary R. and I would sit in the backseat to and from the picnics. These events always involved a lot of alcohol, so the rides home were wild. The two of us would put on the goggles—there were always at least two available—and they created a red aura around everything in sight. This made the trip home seem fantastical and less frightening. I have to admit that we both laughed about the predicament we would find ourselves in on these trips home.

High school was next—Bend Senior High. Fortunately for our class, they started what was called the module system that year. This involved reorganizing classes the same as in college to allow for time to study and socialize at school. This system allowed for much more free time than the conventional format, which required students to go directly from one class to the next. It also made it easier to get into trouble—probably the reason that the school went back to the conventional schedule the year after I graduated.

My clique in high school consisted of friends from my St. Francis days and also new friends picked up from junior high—Janet, Susie, Annette, and Christi. These were the kids I spent time with in and out of school. Annette and I were the two in the group who were the most interested in boys. For this reason, we decided to branch out a bit. We weren't sure how to go about this, but we decided to start by attending Friday night dances at school. I didn't get asked to dance but enjoyed the music, the disk jockey, and the excitement. There was a Sadie Hawkins dance (named after a comic strip character in the L'il Abner series) coming up in which the girls were supposed to ask someone and participants were supposed to dress up as hillbillies. About the same time, our school broke up into groups and worked on homecoming floats for the downtown parade. I decided to ask a guy who lived around the corner from my house and got up the nerve to call him. I had been on a school field trip the summer before to Crater Lake and sat next to him in the boat on the lake, so his name was the first thing that popped into my head when deciding who to ask. He told me that he was going to be out of town that weekend, but I saw him working on one of the floats the day before the dance and spotted him trying to hide from me when he saw me and my friend Annette walk by his house on our way to her house, also close by. I decided not to bother trying to go to the dance, but a girl in my class named Vickie suggested that I call a guy named Leo, so I did. He told Vickie previously that he liked me. His mother told me that he had gone out of town for the weekend. When he found out that someone had called after his return home (he really was out of town), he didn't know who had called. I hadn't provided his mother with my name.

At Christmastime, Leo and his friend Doug Herland were in a letterman's booth selling See's Candies for their basketball team. I (and a few friends) went over to talk to them. Leo leaned back in his folding chair, and it toppled over with him in it. I knew he was embarrassed but couldn't help laughing anyway. He admitted to me later on that he had developed a crush on me. He also admitted much later that while my friends and I were working on our float a few months earlier, he had pelted me with an egg that hit my mustard-colored parka. He didn't know whom he hit until he saw me at school with the parka on. Leo finally got around to telling Vickie that someone had called him to ask him to Sadie Hawkins but that he had been out of town. She told him it was me, so he decided to ask me to the basketball homecoming dance called Cupid's Carousel. But before that, he decided to see if he could meet up with me at one of the Friday dances. Vickie suggested that I attend a particular Friday night dance. She said that someone wanted to ask me to dance, so Annette and I went. Vickie didn't say who it was. We hung around for a while and another guy asked me to dance. Leo arrived late and when he showed up, I was already on the dance floor. Leo asked Vickie what was up, and she told him that the other guy had asked me to dance, so Leo cut in. We had a few dances, and later on that night, I ran into him out at Shakey's Pizza Parlor. At school, Vickie let me know that someone was planning to ask me to the homecoming dance but, again, didn't say who. I went to Portland with Mom and Sandy on one of our shopping trips a few weeks before the dance and bought a dress for the occasion in spite of the fact that I hadn't been asked yet and didn't even know for sure who was going to ask me. A few days before the dance, I was at my locker with a few of my friends when Leo walked up with his posse of friends surrounding him, broke away, and asked me out. I said yes, and that was that. So I was about to have my first date.

I got all dressed up for the dance, and my brother put on his military gas mask (he was into G.I. Joe stuff) and said that he was going to tell my date that he had to wear it because I had bad gas. I complained to Mom and Dad about what he was threatening, and they kept him in the back bedroom until we could get out the door. We had to double date because Leo was only fifteen and didn't have a driver's license yet. It was fun at the dance. We had some slow dances where he held me tight. I could feel his hard-on pressed against me. Our song became "I Had Too Much to Dream (Last Night)" by The Electric Prunes. "She's Not There" by The Zombies was another favorite. After the dance, the four of us headed to Shakey's Pizza Parlor. We sat by the window and watched the people heading toward the restaurant from the parking lot and tripping over the parking blocks that were hidden between the cars. It seemed like every other patron tripped on their way in.

My brother finally got to meet Leo one day when he came by to see me. Doug was about nine or ten and was with his friends Scot and Stewart, riding around the neighborhood with their Sting-Ray bikes. On this particular day, they saw Leo get out of his car and head toward our front door, and they surrounded him. Doug demanded to know what he was doing there, and Leo said he was there to see his sister (me). Doug explained that he and his friends were the Ninth Street Gang, and he guessed it was OK if Leo saw his sister, and then they rode off down the street.

This is about the time that Dad and Doug built a soap box car for the local Soap Box Derby. They worked out in the garage to come up with the perfect design with the intention of placing well or even winning the race. Dad, as usual, wasn't very patient with the project or with Doug, but they persevered. The result was the

"G. B." (printed on the side of the green soap box car) —translated as the "Green Booger" because that is what it looked like. The race was always held on Revere Street, just a few blocks from our house. There was a fairly steep grade that ran down to Highway 97 (also known as Third Street). Hay bales were positioned in front of the finish line near the highway to prevent the soap box cars from running into the busy street. Sandy, Mom, Dad, and I stood on the sidelines as the cars flew by. It was truly exciting, especially when Doug took first place, which allowed him to qualify for the race in Salem, Oregon. Dad and Doug worked hard to refine the car for the next bigger race. We all traveled over to Salem, but Doug didn't win this time. There was just too much stiff competition.

When I was still attending St. Francis School, we were made to participate in some team sports—nothing I was ever interested in. Field hockey was one of them. I always had my stick in hand and jumped around on the sidelines in order to avoid any contact with other players on the field. In spite of the gym teacher's efforts for me to participate more fully in the endeavor, I continued on with my avoidance behavior. I always had As and Bs in my academic classes, but the exception on my report card was always my C in gym class. Things didn't improve after I started high school. It was early on in my relationship with Leo that he and his buddies hid in the balcony overlooking the basketball court to spy on me during my feeble attempts to participate in the game. I clearly remember dribbling the ball around the periphery of the court in a similar manner that I had developed on the hockey field earlier on. Leo later expressed his amusement at my arm and hand movements to block my opponent's advances. He would describe my stiff arms flailing about—one high above my head and the other at my side—and directed toward the floor and then changing to the other direction. I didn't mind him making fun of me because I didn't care if I was any good at these sorts of sports anyway.

I was a Catholic girl who still believed I would go to Purgatory if I French kissed. After six months, Leo finally got up the nerve to kiss me, but when things progressed to French kissing, I objected and explained that French kissing was at least a venial sin. He thought I said menial and commented that if it was menial, it must not be that important. When I explained it was venial and not menial, he wanted to know what a venial sin was, so I tried to explain it all to him—that venial isn't hell-worthy but mortal is, and a venial sin can wind you up in Purgatory. He thought that my explanation was funny and convinced me to ignore my conviction about Purgatory, venial sins, and such. It didn't take me long to let go of my worry about French kissing, but after the first time I was felt up, I was embarrassed and avoided him at school all day. When I finally did run into him, he didn't say anything about the night before and acted like nothing had happened, so I eventually got over my embarrassment.

There were study rooms with doors at school, off the library, and we would go into any one of them that was empty and make out in there. We also did the same on the oval in front of the school. Sometimes Mom made me a sack lunch for school. Leo and I would head out with our lunches to the oval in front of our high school during the warm weather. Whenever I had an orange in the sack, I'd peel it, section it, and put a section in my mouth, halfway in and halfway out, and then offer Leo the half on the outside. He gladly accepted with a kiss that resulted in his having his half for himself. But one time, I accidentally bit his lip and drew blood. After that, he was a little leery of my offers, so he resorted to a more genteel approach. I got called in to Ms. McDougal's office and was told I had better not be seen out on the oval making out anymore. Leo got called in by a male administrator and given the same instructions. Well, since there was an open campus, it wasn't very hard to figure out that all we had to do was leave. We would go to the nearby Juniper Park and make out there. Better yet was Leo's home in the afternoons when his parents were at work. We'd also drive out in the sticks and make out in his parents' car at night. If I had to pee on these dates, I was too embarrassed to say so. I would hold it as long as I could, and if things got too bad, I would say that I had to run in for something at one of the convenience stores. He would drive me to one and wait in the car for me. Then

I would sneak into the toilet and go. While I was in the store, I'd buy something to make it look good.

But Leo wasn't without his own religious hang-ups. He was raised Southern Baptist due to the influence of his mother. As a child, he used to hide all his underwear to avoid going to church, but she simply had him go in his pajamas to solve the problem. Later on, while in junior high, their Baptist minister, who routinely drove around town to check things out, spotted Leo in line at the Tower Theatre for a movie. This was prohibited, and so was dancing, drinking, or any other sort of tomfoolery. When he next attended Sunday school, the minister brought him up in front of the class and chastised him for being at the movies. When Leo said it was none of his business, the minister grabbed him by his shirt, and then Leo socked him in the jaw. His mother got a call saying her son was no longer welcome at the Baptist Church, but she did make him find another that would take him. As soon as he went away to college, that was the end of his churchgoing but not the end of his tomfoolery.

Mom had to teach me how to drive because Dad yelled too much. She and I had some rocky rides—literally. We went off on some dirt roads a little out of town for me to practice, and I accidentally stepped on the gas instead of the brakes. We went skittering along over the rocky road at high speed. Another time, she was showing me how to back out of our driveway. I would always turn the steering wheel the wrong way. When I got onto our street, instead of going forward, I accidentally put the Volkswagen in reverse, and we started backing down the street. There was a car coming up the street, and when the driver saw what was happening, she put her car in reverse so that both of us drove down the street in unison until I figured out what I was doing wrong. We had to go out to the DMV seven times in all before I finally got my license. I usually had a tall somber tester who wore cowboy boots and hat. He made me nervous when he sat next to me in the car and took notes while I drove. Parallel parking was particularly taxing. On one of our trips out to the DMV, it started snowing on the way, and by the time we got there, it was like a blizzard, so we were told to come back another day. There were a few instances where it was lunchtime by the time we got to the front of the line, and we had to leave. I finally passed after Mom gave me a tranquilizer before my test.

Since Mom had such a great time teaching me how to drive, she decided that I ought to have the same privilege. So I got to teach my sister. We went out one evening at dusk to a track out south of Bend to practice. She got behind the wheel and drove around the track several times. She wanted to drive back home because she was feeling pretty confident, so I let her. She pulled out onto Highway 97 and started back home. Something didn't seem right, but I didn't know what until I noticed cars coming in our direction at high speed. She had pulled out into the wrong lane. I said, "You're in the wrong lane," and she swerved to miss an oncoming car just in time. Another time, she drove into the A&W Root Beer stand in front of Pilot Butte. There were posts with radios where you were supposed to make an order, and then the waitress would bring the food and/or drink out on a tray that attached to your partially rolled down window. But Sandy ran over the post, so things didn't work out so well for us that day.

Sometimes Leo and I would drive up Pilot Butte, which was a lover's lane of sorts. However, this spot had problems because his friends had a habit of going up there and harassing couples in their cars. Our dates would include bowling, dances, and movies. One of Leo's best friends was M. We would double date with him and girls he went out with. One time, we went over to Leo's house, and his parents had gone to bed. M. and his date proceeded into the kitchen, and after I followed them in there, I was surprised by what was going on. We also double dated with Leo's friend C. and his girlfriend. Once, he got mad about his record player because it was skipping, and so he threw a bottle at it and broke everything—the player, the bottle, and the record. C. had a little sports car. One day he took Leo and me for a ride. We were all cramped in the front of the car. I was sitting on Leo's lap. We turned off Greenwood and headed down Wall Street when the car filled with smoke. C. swung the car to the curb, and we all barreled out. I had hit the wires with my knee and they crossed and caught on fire. Both doors were open and the smoke continued to pour out of the car. C., being the excitable person he was, laughed, jumped up and down, and shouted next to his smoking car.

C.'s folks would let us take their camper out on weekends, and we took it up to fishing holes. He wasn't much of a fisherman, so Leo would have to set his hook for him. We all caught catfish. There were a couple of beds in the camper, so each couple would grab one. We also got together with him later on in the summers when we were home from college.

During high school, instead of having sitters stay with us when Mom and Dad were away, I was put in charge of the household. Mom would stock the kitchen cupboards and refrigerator with lots of good food for my stint as head of the household. This unpaid job wasn't always easy. Doug and Sandy got into it on a regular basis, and my job was to keep the peace. Doug got so angry at her one time that he took his baseball bat and chased after her, and when I started to intercede, he also brandished his weapon at me. I was finally able to talk him into giving up his bat. Another time, Sandy and I decided to bake a homecoming cake for Mom and Dad's return. I wanted to remove the cake pans in the oven for fear she would have difficulty with the pot holders, but she insisted on being the one to remove the pans. As I feared, she dropped the second one on its way out, and it tipped over on the floor and broke into pieces and crumbs—maybe it was the power of suggestion. We attempted to put it back together and frost the cake, but it didn't look very good. Another frequent incident while they were gone was our getting locked out of the house. Sandy and Doug would chase each other around, inside, and outside the house and would eventually try to lock the other out. This led to everyone being locked out, including me. Of course, we never seemed to have a key outside in order to get back in, so we would have to go over to our neighbors, the Riches. Cliff and Laurie were both high school teachers. Cliff would come over and take our back door off the hinges so we could get back in. After this happened three or four times, Cliff asked our parents for a key that he would keep with him, and so it became easier to get in after that. All he had to do now was unlock the door.

After my sister Nora was born, there were other complications when Mom and Dad left. Invariably, she would become sick about a minute after our folks' departure. It would usually be an ear infection or the flu. I would call Nora's pediatrician who would either have us take her to the Bend Memorial Clinic at 419 Greenwood where he would meet me after hours or he would come to our house. Once, she had such terrible diarrhea that I panicked. I had been unable to get ahold of the doctor right away. The fluid stool would run down her legs and right through her diapers. Every time I changed her diaper, the same thing would happen. As I traveled around the house with her, the fluid stool got everywhere—on the floor, the bathroom counter, all over her, and all over me. I finally called Leo, who took pity on me and came over to help out. He didn't really know what to do either. Finally, the doctor arrived.

Doug and Nora were both the family pranksters—Doug was usually the instigator, and Nora was more often the one deciding to get even. Nora was only about three years old when he wanted to get into the bathroom one day and decided to bug her. He pounded on the locked door and asked her if she was taking a Nora. Her high little voice could be heard from the other side of the bathroom door, yelling "No, I'm wiping my Doug." One time, we were all coming back from a Mexican restaurant and he farted on her in the car. She decided to get even. After we got home, he hunkered down in his favorite lounge chair in the living room and ate some ice cream bars from the freezer. Leo was hanging out with him and noticed Nora creeping along the floor and behind furniture in a stealthy manner. Leo remained silent so as to see what she was up to. Suddenly, she jumped in front of Doug, let one out, ran for cover in her bedroom, and locked the door behind her—lucky because Doug was in swift pursuit. He retreated to the living room, as he knew he'd been had.

Numerous pranks persisted and became more and more elaborate. Nora had been bothered by a Peeping Tom looking through her bedroom window and complained to Mom and Dad about it. This gave Doug an idea. He got his friends Scot and Stuart to help him with a photograph of himself. He stood outside Nora's bedroom window, pressed his face against it, and had them take a photo of his face from inside her room. Then Doug got it printed and blown up, taped it to her window, and drew her shades. When she got around to opening them his monstrous face was staring in at her, and she ran out of her room screaming but figured out pretty soon what Doug had done. She still has the photo. The head of one of Dad's spit roasted pigs also found its way onto one of the posters on Nora's bed, and she was greeted by it on her way into her room one day. Then there was the time he took a duck's foot from one of Dad's hunting expedition bounties and taped it inside one of Nora's schoolbooks. It wasn't until she opened up her book in the classroom that she saw it and shrieked out loud. But she didn't want to tell anyone what led to her outburst. She was just too embarrassed. When we went on one of our beach trips, he'd sneak down in the mornings before anyone else was awake and wrote a huge "Nora is a bo-bo" in the sand. When the curtains were drawn in the morning, there it would be, and we would all laugh. She would rush down, erase her name with her little feet, replace it with his, and return with a big smile on her face. I think Nora enjoyed their jousting just as much as Doug did.

After Nora started middle school, she attended an evening dance chaperoned by some of the teachers there. Sandy and Doug decided to sneak over to the school and spy on her. They found a low window without blinds that looked into the gym. Nora was out on the dance floor when she spotted their faces peering in at her. She made nasty faces at them, so they ran back home, laughing all the way. Nora was mortified. When Nora was a freshman in high school, she dressed up as a boy for Halloween. Dad's famous mustache was part of the costume, which Mom carefully attached with spirit gum, and off Nora went. After a while, the mustache started to itch and the other kids at school didn't even recognize her and thought she really was a guy, so she called Mom to come get her. But Mom didn't seem interested, so Nora had to stay all day at school with the mustache. She still complains about Mom's refusal to save her from her discomfort and humiliation.

A trick Doug played on every female in the house involved a contraption that he found in the trick store he and Dad frequented in Portland—a little plastic bulb with a spigot on it that he placed under the rim of the toilet seat. I went into my parents' bathroom to pee more than once and was surprised when the water in the bulb went the opposite direction to what I expected. It felt like I was wetting myself but I couldn't figure out why until I discovered the gadget. I didn't have to guess how it got there, though. At times, the rest of the family got into the game too. Mom served up rubber chocolate to us one time. She arranged them on a doily in a pretty candy dish and suggested that we all try one. When we stuck them in our mouths, they were chewable but not edible, and it took us a while before we figured out we'd all been had. Sandy visited Nora once, and Nora put a sign on Sandy's back that she unknowingly wore around all day long. It read "I'm a butt eye." When Sandy went shopping that day, a woman shopper in the store tapped her on the shoulder and let her know that she had a sign on her back and handed it to Sandy, who was embarrassed after becoming aware that any number of people may have read it during that day. Sandy also tried to retaliate against Doug for his getting into her room all the time by rigging a pail of water above her bedroom door for him. But the prank backfired on her because she forgot something in her room before school, forgot about the bucket, and the water soaked her instead.

During the summers, college guy would return to our house for summer work. I was getting older now, and he started to see me as dating material. I was still dating Leo but didn't consider the relationship to be exclusive, so I agreed to go out with college guy after he got up the nerve to ask me. One day, he came by our house to visit. We were in the living room, with the door to the kitchen closed, and snuggling up together in the lounge chair when Leo came to the back door to see me. Doug saw what was going on and ran around to the other entrance to the living room at the front of the house. He told college guy that he had better leave because Leo was in the kitchen, and so he had to skidoo. I guess Doug was protecting Leo's turf, or maybe he was just trying to avoid a showdown.

College guy liked to take me to the drive-in for obvious reasons but was really quite shy in spite of his intentions. He would put his arm around me and eventually kiss me. One night, we drove up Pilot Butte. We were making out, but he stopped himself from going further, got out of the car, and walked around on top of the Butte for a while. I couldn't figure out what he was doing. Then he got back in the car. Neither of us said anything.

We explored Central Oregon. He had a dream of building a house that blended into its environment, and the materials around its location would be the stuff of its creation. I have to say that he would get so carried away about this dream house idea that I got bored with the subject.

My relationship changed with Mary R. after I started dating. I just didn't have as much time for her. I took a typing class one summer at the senior high per Dad's encouragement. He said that his lack of typing skills when he started college made this academic transition difficult. The teacher's comment on my report card read "She developed excellent skill and had a very fine test at the end. Well done!" Mary R wrote this comment underneath: "But she spends too much time talking to the boys. Please watch her." This comment was indicative of her sense of humor, but I also suspected that she felt neglected by me. One night, she stayed over. We were in my double bed, and I was awakened when she pretended to be Leo and get cozy with me. I didn't know what to do, so I asked her what she was doing. She acted as though she didn't know what I was talking about. No more was said about this event, but I thought about how I should handle it. I decided that our sleepovers in my bed needed to end, but I would stay at her house because I had my own bed there in her room. I never said anything to her about not having her stay overnight at my house any longer. It just didn't happen. In fact, nothing was ever said, period. We remained friends, but I have to admit that I continued to feel a little careful because I wondered if she was in love with me.

Leo's family had come from the South to homestead in Oregon. His dad, Welborn, lost both his parents by the time he was sixteen. His brother was twelve. Welborn went looking for a wife as soon as possible. Leo's mother, Frances, had lost her father when she was a child, and her mother struggled to support their five children after her husband's death. When they married, Welborn's brother lived with them until he went into the service. Welborn ran a ranch outside La Pine, Oregon. The owners of the ranch were wealthy Californians who came up to visit and be waited on. Welborn was a real cowboy, and Frances kept the house, fed the ranch hands, and worked out in the fields. The couple had seven children, and Leo was the youngest. While they were still on the ranch, Leo just about shot his older brother, Daren, with a bow and arrow. Daren had taken Leo's bow for their cousin to use and wouldn't let him go on their excursion. So when they got back, he grabbed his bow and arrow and was about to shoot Daren when their sister Gwen stepped in between them. Another time, Leo got some chicken shit on his Hula-Hoop. He showed it to Daren, who suggested he just wipe it on the handmade sweater that Gwen was wearing and was supposed to be in the state fair the next day. Leo asked, "Are you sure she won't care? " Daren said, "No, go ahead. She won't care." So he did, and Gwen started yelling and carrying-on, and then their dad came out to ask what was going on. Gwen showed him, and then Leo got a swat and a lecture.

When Leo was ten, his parents moved into town, and Welborn got a job at the county road department. His mother went to school, got her LPN degree, and started working at the hospital. Only his youngest sister was still at home with Leo. By the time we started dating, all his siblings were out of the house and married. His youngest sister was overseas with her husband who was in the service. When she became pregnant, she came home to have her baby. His parents were conservative, and so Leo had an early curfew. They sent his pregnant sister with us to the drive-in one time. She was mortified, but if she had refused to go, then we wouldn't have been able to go either. So she sat in the backseat. The good thing about her was that she suggested we drop her off at home after the drive-in and then take off on our own. So that's what we did. We went out in the sticks to make out. When their parents heard her come home, they assumed that Leo was with her.

Leo began talking marriage while we were still in high school. In fact, he told our classmate who had arranged our first date that he intended to marry me before we even met. I guess he was infatuated with me, but I also think marriage would be his attempt to catch up with all his older siblings, but of course, he never would—catch up or fit in. My dad, on the other hand, encouraged a college education and discouraged any serious romances. I was the eldest, and he had big plans for me. He was so enthralled with his career as a radiologist that he thought it would be in my best interest to follow in his footsteps. Science, math, and physics were, in his mind, the way to go. I lumbered along in these classes and did all right with the help of my math teacher, Mr. Hegg, whose door was always open in the math lab for tutoring. However, I enjoyed the courses in the humanities a lot more.

Leo's family didn't really encourage higher education. I think he was influenced by my dad about college. In spite of Dad promoting college and career, he also expounded on the benefits of Mom being a homemaker, and he expected her to be home when he wanted her there. She decided to take up golf and had me go to our first golf lesson at the Bend Golf and Country Club. I knew right off that it wasn't for me. She persisted with her lessons, though, but when she started actually playing and wasn't home to prepare Dad's lunch and whatnot, her story was that he made life miserable for her so she quit. And then there was Dad's low opinion of golf because of his twelve-year-old experience as a caddy. What would be going on out at that golf course anyway? This all remained a bone of contention between them. Mom was known to hold a grudge, and did, about her feeling bullied by Dad. At any rate, the mixed messages I got about career versus mother/ homemaker created a quandary for me as time went on. Whose steps was I supposed to follow after anyway?

Leo came over for dinner one evening, and Dad was surprised when Leo told him about an accident with his bike when he was twelve. He was on his way to his baseball game, got hit by a car just as he approached the baseball field, and had gone over his handlebars, his head smashing into the curb and fracturing his skull. He remembered his coach tending to him while he sat on the ground, trying to pick gravel out of his elbow. He vaguely remembers a ride in the ambulance to the hospital but seeing only the outside of the ambulance that he was in. He was in a coma, and Dad was the radiologist in the hospital who did his X-rays. Neither of us knew Leo then, but Dad remembered him when he told the story. Dad told him that the doctors, including himself, didn't know if he would survive, and if he did, what would be left of him brain-wise. But he did survive and didn't seem to have any obvious repercussions. There were other mishaps in his history. For instance, he chopped his nose nearly off with a hatchet in the barn when he was three while trying to pull it off its nail on the wall. His mother was alone with no car and so she taped it back in place. When Welborn returned with their pickup truck a few days later, she took Leo to see a doctor, and he said that if he had stitched it up as he would have done, the results would not have been as good as the results of her "doctoring." There is only a very thin line, barely noticeable, on the side of his nose. He also tried to see what was inside a golf ball, and when he punctured the outer shell, the acid in the middle of the ball flew in his eyes. He had to wear patches over them, and no one knew whether he would see again. His oldest sister (Pat) was nearby and knew how to handle the situation. Her quick thinking may have saved his eyesight. He was lucky again.

Dad had a cousin, Emil Brecelj, who was quite the rounder. Mom and Dad took each of us on our trip to San Francisco when we were sixteen. Dad would get ahold of Emil, and we would have a day with him. Sometimes Emil would bring a mistress and sometimes his ex-wife. When I was there, he brought Marilyn, a mistress who was dark haired, voluptuous, and pleasant. We took in the sights and ate at a seaside restaurant at midday. When Sandy went, Emil brought his ex-wife, a stunning redhead even in her middle age. With Doug, they went out for dinner, and this time he had his ex-wife with him again. Emil may have been less inhibited than when my sister and I were there because we were young girls. But with Doug, Dad and Emil got loud and obnoxious in the restaurant, and Doug was disgusted with it all. Years later, Emil drowned while out on a boat with his son. There was suspicion that there had been foul play. While I was in San Francisco with my parents, Dad took me down to North Beach. In the mid-sixties, this area was full of zoned-out drug addicts with vacant eyes. The place scared the crap out of me, which, I guess, was Dad's intention. I'm not sure I would have had an inclination to use drugs without this experience, but it made a lasting impression. I also remember walking down by the waterfront with my parents and seeing the actor Robert Vaughn (from the television series The Man from U.N.C.L.E) walking right by us. I made eye contact with him. Dad recognized him too and encouraged me to ask for his autograph, but I was too shy. I did turn around, though, and followed him to get a closer look before he dropped out of sight.

Mom told me once that established people in Elmhurst considered Dad's family to be low class. In fact, as I got older, he would tell me the same thing. Dad's ambition to rise in his social standing was reflected in his ambition for his children—me, in particular, being the eldest. There were the piano lessons, ski lessons, ballet lessons, concerts, fine dining, and also his high expectations for our personal achievement. He had limited success in his endeavors regarding his children, though. We were not always cooperative. Not to say we were openly contrary, but none of us seemed to have inherited his level of ambition, but then none of us had his childhood experience as the son of immigrants either. He was sometimes so impressed with his accomplishments that he would tell us that none of us would ever be as successful as he was in any area of our lives. His hubris could be downright irritating, but at the same time may have led to our general feeling of never measuring up to his expectations and, at the same time, not wanting to disappoint him by surpassing him in his achievements either. At first, I think he overestimated my potential, but after a while, he seemed to have developed a resignation about my shortcomings. But deep inside, I felt I had disappointed him. On the other hand, I knew nothing could damage his love and loyalty for me, and I just loved my dad's side of the family the way they were. They seemed earthy, sensual, fun loving, and exotic.

As Dad got more affluent as a doctor, he redefined himself. This played out in his newfound interest in such things as fine food, wines, and culture. Being exposed to such things had their advantages, but something was also lost. His embarrassment about his background and ethnicity removed him somewhat from the positive aspects of his origins that I felt I had to hang on to. In spite of himself, his true nature would erupt, and these were the times that I loved him the most. It seemed that he always struggled with this. Sometimes the two forces merged.

He would become enamored with all sorts of interests. Mushrooms— he bought books about mushrooms. We went hunting in the woods for them before mushrooms were in fashion, he cooked with them, and he became an expert about them. Wine— he had a wine merchant in Portland (Ray Selich) that he would visit every time he was there. He went to wine tastings, savored different wines in restaurants, and became an expert on wine. The Joys of Yiddish by Leo Rosten—he read this book from cover to cover. He began sneaking Yiddish words into his vocabulary and sneaked into Jewish weddings and bar and bat mitzvahs if he came across one in whatever city he and Mom were visiting. He would say that no one seemed to notice that he hadn't been invited, and he would have a great time. Games People Play—this book was popular in the sixties. Dad would expound on the topic presented in this book—that is, how people interact in unhealthy ways and how true he felt the book's theories were. He loved to write poetry and dabbled in artistic pursuits on an amateur level. His creations were scattered around the house—wood carvings from drift wood he collected at the coast, paintings of San Francisco, and framed pictures made of buttons and velvet for Christmas. He and his friend from the hospital came across a huge tree trunk and had it delivered to our house. It was placed in cement on our patio and was supposed to act as a table. They counted the rings to determine how old it was. Dad had an inexhaustible amount of energy.

Some of dad's enthusiasm involved projects with us kids. One day he brought some plaster of paris, gauze, and straws home from the hospital. Then he instructed us to take turns lying down on the kitchen floor. He then soaked the gauze strips in the plaster, inserted a straw into each nostril of whichever of us was there, applied Vaseline Petroleum Jelly to our faces, and then proceeded to place the gauze strips strategically across our faces until a mask was created. Then he instructed whichever of us was on the floor to remain very still until the plaster dried. In the meantime, he said we could breathe through the two straws. Mom called his creations death masks, and she thought they were creepy. He couldn't convince her to have one done, and they all seemed to end up in his "study" where all his weird stuff had their final resting place. Two places he liked to take us were Darrell's House of Music in Downtown Bend and the record department at Meier & Frank in

Portland. That's where they used to have record booths. You could ask the clerk to play whatever was of interest, and sure enough, the music was piped right into the booth. This helped us decide if the album was worth a purchase or not. Dad loved Thelonious Monk, Miles Davis, and Louie Armstrong, among others. He seemed to lose interest in buying albums after the record booths went out of fashion. He would complain that there was no way of knowing if the album was any good or not-so why should he buy any-and I could see his point.

Another place we frequented was Skjersaa's ski house. It was only about six blocks from our house on Ninth Street, so we would walk down after dinner in the winter when it was dark and check out the merchandise. Sometimes we'd buy some ski gear or clothing and then hike back up to the house and call it a day. Along with the ski gear he might purchase for himself, he also came up with some outlandish getups for the ski slopes. He got into Western motifs—belt buckles, string ties, cowboy boots, and such. He decided he wanted to wear his cowboy hat while he skied down the Mount Bachelor slopes, but the drawback was the cold weather, so he went down to Betty Sans Alterations and had her sew a wool scarf onto the cowboy hat. He tied the scarf under his chin to hold the hat in place, and he was set for the slopes. This is also about the same time he started applying appliques to his casual clothing. He thought that some of the doctors' designer shirts with their signature emblems were corny, so he made his point by cutting out big flowered Ks and stitched them on his sweatshirts, sweat pants, etc.

Dad would scout out all sorts of places to purchase different food and drink. When he and Mom went to New Orleans, he visited Angelo Gendusa Bakery on Rampart Street. He made big orders and then had them shipped home or would freeze them and then drive back with all sorts of breads and rolls in ice chests. It was the best bread I ever ate. Dad had explained that the climate in New Orleans and the expertise of the bakers there were responsible for the bread's excellent quality. Every time we went to Portland, we visited the farmer's market. His favorite spot there was Policar's Fish Stand, run by Ralph and, later, his son. Again, he would drive over the mountain with his ice chests and then make large orders of fresh fish and seafood for our return trip. He got to be good friends with Mr. Policar and his family. He had a source for lamb in Tony Euriser in Burns, Oregon. In his suit and leather overcoat, Dad would drive over after work in Burns and help Tony load five or six whole lambs into the back of his Jaguar. He also purchased a set of fourteen framed arrowhead collections from the Pine Room Tavern there, run by an elderly couple. He had tried to purchase the set for years, but the couple remained steadfast about keeping it. They had collected the arrowheads during their youth and displayed them in their tavern for many years. After the husband died, Dad approached the wife again about purchasing them, and she finally agreed to sell them. She asked for $3,500 but Dad said he wouldn't accept the offer but would accept an offer of $5,000, which the widow gladly agreed to. The woman's only stipulation was that the arrowheads remain in the original frames, and Dad gave his word that he would keep this promise. He first decided, as he got older, to donate them all to the High Desert Museum but was told that they intended to remove the arrowheads from their frames, so he reneged. Instead, he gave them to us kids. Sausage making became another preoccupation of his. He got a recipe from a doctor friend, bought pig intestine and a machine to stuff the ground meat into the intestines. They tasted god awful, but he kept pumping them out anyway. When Sandy was in her late twenties, she drove up from Eugene (where she was working) to Portland and visited Mr. Policar. She asked him to wrap up some fish for her and paid him for it. When she brought up Dad's name, he asked her for the wrapped fish back, wrapped some fresher fish and gave it to her without a word of explanation.

Wherever Dad went, he formed connections. "If you head down to Ryan's in Morgan's Alley (in Portland), tell Pedro I sent you and that you're my daughter," he'd say to me. So I did, and Pedro would make me a killer martini. This wasn't until I was of age, but Dad had known Pedro since the early sixties. Mom and Dad would also frequent The Clothes Horse in Portland. They met Bill Berry there (a clerk in this high-end store) and made friends with him. Bill would meet my parents at The RingSide Steakhouse out on Burnside. Sometimes Sandy and I would be invited to these gatherings, and Bill would choose a drink that he thought fit our personalities. He was quite flamboyant. I remember him strolling in once with a full-length fur coat. Harry's Bar at Century City in LA was another of their frequented spots. Dad had a favorite waiter there, a Slovenian named Bruno who would show them a good time and bring plate after plate of specialties of the house for them to try out. The two would exchange stories in their native tongue. Mom and Dad took me there once so that I could have the experience too.

Dad took heed of the publicity about nuclear threats that circulated in the sixties. I'm not sure how seriously he took the news stories about all this, but this gave him an excuse to do one of his favorite things—shop. He started stocking the larger of my two closets (which he wired with 12- volt lighting) in my new bedroom. I had one for my clothes and shoes, but the bigger walk-in closet was taken over by Dad, who filled it with large quantities of dried fruit, canned goods, dried beans of all sorts, etc. He also liked to get a bargain and would buy dozens of rolls of toilet paper, paper towels, or any other household item that was on sale. It drove Mom nuts. Sandy had a particular affinity for the apricots. She would sneak into the big closet in the middle of the night and eat a bunch of them. This created some gastric problems for her but also cleared up her acne. She didn't know why this occurred but later on discovered that apricots have a large amount of vitamin A.

Dad developed other varied interests. One was mountain climbing. He decided to be trained by Lou Whittaker who had climbed Mount Everest and taught mountain climbing skills on Mount Rainier. His twin brother had been the first American ever to summit Mount Everest. When I was in high school, Dad would suggest that we pack a lunch and hike up Mount Bachelor during the summer months. He loved this excursion and marveled at the sight as we reached the summit. We would eat our lunch, drink a little wine out of his flask, and then head back down the mountain. We rarely saw another soul up there. I wasn't as enthralled with these outings as he was, but I enjoyed his enthusiasm and company. These excursions may have sparked his interest in mountaineering. He took Sandy and Doug with him for lessons on Mount Rainier. I never did this because I wasn't well during the time he and my siblings had this adventure. He didn't think I had the strength to manage this feat, and he was right. After the instruction, the three headed up the mountain with their guide and other pupils and successfully made it to the top with numerous of their group dropping out before reaching the summit. Doug thought it was a great adventure, but Sandy was miserable the entire climb in spite of the fact that she did make it up and back.

The Thomas Crown Affair, starring Steve McQueen and Faye Dunaway, came out in 1968. We all went to see the movie while in Portland. The movie was about a cat-and-mouse romantic relationship between Thomas (Steve McQueen) and Vicki (Faye Dunaway). Thomas plans a bank heist just for the fun of it. It involved an assortment of persons he hires to carry out the robbery without any of them ever knowing who he is. Vicki is the investigator for the bank's insurer who investigates the case and suspects Thomas right away. Dad was intrigued with the character Tommy Crown, and for good reason. He was just like Dad. Dad laughed throughout the film, and the resemblance between Tommy and our dad didn't go unnoticed by the rest of us either. After he saw the film, Dad decided to try some of the things that Tommy had done. Luckily, robbing a bank wasn't one of them. But he booked dune buggy rides for all of us when Mom's brother and his wife visited that summer. This was at the coast, and the rides were truly thrilling. I was surprised when my very conservative Aunt Lois was exuberant during the ride. Dad always did say she was a good sport. The next thing he did was take glider lessons. After he got the lessons under his belt, he took us out for glider rides out at Sunriver. I couldn't believe it when the plane let go of us and how loud it was during our ride. I had expected it to be quiet, but the wind blowing by the glider made so much noise that you could barely hear what the person next to you had to say. Mary R.'s oldest sister, H, got wind of Dad's glider interest and decided to sign up for a ride herself. Mary R. went out with her sister to see how it went. H got in the glider with the pilot and up they went, pulled by the plane. She wasn't up there very long when she got motion sickness and barfed all over the inside of the glider. The irritated pilot descended as soon as possible. H brushed off the incident, and the pilot had to hurry to get the glider cleaned up for the next guest. Leo and I went to see Thomas Crown in Bend after I'd seen it in Portland. We were amazed by the kissing scene between Tommy and Vicki in the middle of their chess game. We made efforts to imitate them when we went parking after that.

Later on, Dad got on a kick about gold jewelry. He'd find stores that were going out of business and buy them out. Then he'd wear several gold chains at a time around his neck and give them away to family and friends. I remember when I was in Italy, where the men tend to wear gold chains (often with a crucifix or an Italian horn), I thought that he would fit right in. His father had a ring that Slovenian men who have an affiliation with some sort of secret society wear. Francesco passed the ring on to Dad, and later on, Dad passed it on to Doug. I wish I knew more about its significance, but this is imparted only to the one who wears the ring.

All about Mom: Dad was full of it. Mom was just the opposite. I will have to describe her as humble, lady-like, shy, and soft-spoken. She was never snobbish. When Dad had plans to buy a Rolls-Royce, she told him to forget it. When he bought her an expensive and flashy fur coat, she neglected to wear it and finally had it altered so that it appeared less pretentious and more sporty, but even then, she rarely took it out of the closet. This said, she also wasn't a pushover as time went by and had a stubborn streak a mile long. In her own quiet way, no one ever really got the best of her unless it was either her mother or her own self.

Some instances come to mind to demonstrate these qualities, and some had to do with other doctors' wives in our community. Mom had a peach ultra-suede suit that she liked. She bought it at Nordstrom in Portland. She always went to Chris Gibson, who knew Mom's taste in clothing. Mom never really liked to shop for herself, and going to Chris made the task easier. Chris would bring in an assortment of clothing for Mom to try out, and she would choose from Chris's selections. But Mom did enjoy taking Sandy and me to Portland for shopping trips. These were the times that Mom seemed happiest with us. Her focus was to hang around with us while the two of us perused the store's merchandise and tried stuff on. If we couldn't decide between one item and another, she would say "Why don't you just take both of them," so we would. But let's get back to the peach ultra-suede suit. Mom frequently wore the suit on Sundays for mass. On one occasion and while wearing the suit, another doctor's wife slid into the pew next to her with the same suit and told Mom in a loud voice that she had just purchased her suit on sale and at a fraction of the cost Mom must have paid for hers. Mom just looked at her for a minute and whispered, "Well, you'll never be seeing me wear mine again." And she didn't. She gave it to me, but I didn't wear it either. It was sort of too bad Mom never wore it again because she looked a lot better in it than the other doctor's wife did.

A second doctor's wife story involved Nora and Sandy. This doctor's wife told Mom she wanted Nora to be a flower girl for her daughter's wedding. Later on, she called again to let Mom know she could send over Sandy to clean the toilets at her home in preparation for the wedding reception that would be held there. Mom let her know that not only would Sandy not be coming over to clean any toilets but also that Nora wouldn't be a flower girl in the wedding either.

After Sandy and I left home and Nora and Doug were still living at home, Mom developed even more nerve. There was a situation with one of Nora's "friends" who was a doctor's daughter. One day Nora's friend came to visit. She gave Nora an egg and explained that if she kept the egg in a box under a heat lamp, the egg would hatch a chick. Nora was diligent in her care for the egg, expecting the desired result in so many days. But Mom grew suspicious of the girl's claim and inspected the egg (while Nora was at school) by cracking it open and found it was hard-boiled. She went down to Eastern Oregon Mills, where she purchased a poult (baby turkey), and placed it in the box. Nora was thrilled when she got home and called her "friend," who soon came over to visit. This "friend" insisted that the bird was hers because she had brought the egg over in the first place. Mom told Nora to give the girl the box with the bird in it. When the poult grew big enough for her friend's mother to figure out what had happened, she called Mom and insisted that Mom come and get the bird. Mom said she didn't plan to do that, so she told Mom she intended to come over and return the bird, but Mom said, "No, you're not." And that was the end of it.

Mom and Sandy started meeting in Portland while Sandy was attending the University of Portland (UP). They would shop together and always went to Nordstrom, where Mom purchased her skin cream, 2nd Debut. Mom always had delicate porcelain skin and had finally found a lotion that agreed with her. The lotion came in a beautiful cut glass bottle that she always displayed on her bathroom counter. Sandy accompanied Mom to the cosmetics counter where she made her usual purchases of 2nd Debut. But this time, the cosmetics assistant told her that they didn't carry such an inferior product any longer and that she would have to go to somewhere like Payless if she wanted to find it. Mom replied,

"Well, good. It'll be cheaper there than it was here," and that was the last time she visited the cosmetics counter there.

Sandy came home for summer break and got a job at a local grocery store. She turned out to be one of the slowest checkers on the face of the earth. Her manager would prod her along, but nothing could really speed her up. All this was nothing new because she always was and remains slow-moving. Mom often likened Sandy to her father, Franz. Sandy also has a deadpan affect (also like Franz), which may have also further irritated her boss. A while after her stint as a checker, she and a friend visited the store when Sandy's ex-manager was acting as a checker, and they went through his line. Her friend commented about Sandy having worked there before, and he replied that she was mistaken, that he would never have hired someone as ugly as Sandy. She went home and told Mom what the manager said. Mom didn't say a word, got in her car, and drove down to the store. She found the manager there, and I won't repeat what she said to him, but it wasn't good. She told Sandy what she said to him. Sandy told me later that she felt sorry for the guy after Mom got through with him.

Mom and Dad had a chalk drawing done of Nora by a local artist friend of theirs. Both of them liked it. But Dad, being like he was, thought it would be a good idea to spray lacquer on it so that it wouldn't get smeared. Mom told him to just leave it alone, but he persisted and just had to take the framed chalk drawing out in the backyard, along with his spray can. When he returned with the still-wet drawing Mom said, "Well, now it looks like she has a beard." Dad protested, telling her that after the lacquer had a chance to dry, it would be fine. But it wasn't. The drawing, which had been showcased in the family room, was moved to Dad's study. He had claimed my old bedroom for himself after I moved away to college. He kept all sorts of stuff in there, especially things Mom didn't particularly like looking at. One of his doctor friends had given him a gag gift that he mounted on the wall—a rotten apple-looking face whose eyes moved back and forth and whose mouth spit water while cackling when his tie was pulled. It too had initially been hung above the fireplace in the family room. Now the chalk drawing would take its place next to the rotten apple man, never to leave this room again.

After I got married, Mom loved the fact that Leo had become a lawyer. The two of them always had a special relationship with each other. They would kid around and say they had to stick together in order to have some leverage when faced with the Krkoc bunch. Mom would call Leo with various requests for legal advice and a strong arm if necessary. One of Nora's friends was planning to marry, and Mom called Meier & Frank in Portland to order a place setting of silverware from the bride's registry. The bride's gift arrived, and she called Nora, amazed and pleased that the gift from Mom and Dad was the entire twelve place setting. Nora was amazed too and told Mom, who said that she had only ordered one. Mom called Meier & Frank about the mistake and was told there was nothing they could do about it. The store employee suggested that Mom call the bride and ask her to return the merchandise to the store for a refund. Mom said the store should be doing just that, but they still refused. Mom called Leo who presented himself as her lawyer. He too suggested that the store contact the bride to explain their mistake. The bride never knew about any of it and kept everything, and Mom got her money back minus the cost of the one set she ordered. The store must have decided they didn't want to call the bride either. She depended on Sandy's husband too. She didn't know much about auto repair and knew that mechanics are famous for fleecing women who they perceive as knowing nothing about the topic. In Mom's case, they were right. So Mom would ask him to write down terminology and questions to be asked so that when she took her car in, she appeared knowledgeable. This worked well for her because then the mechanics didn't think they could get anything over on her.

Mom could give the impression that she was vain. Dad even said so when they were older. But I don't think so. I know she was aware of the power she had over some men, including Dad. Her natural beauty offered her benefits when it came to the opposite sex, and this is what I think motivated her to try to maintain herself. She was also very aware of Dad's popularity with the women, and she had always had her suspicions about his dalliances, which were well founded. And Dad sometimes made uncomplimentary comments to Mom about her aging. So I think her vanity was really only her insecurity.

Mom and Dad decided to have me go on American Heritage during the summer between my sophomore and junior years. Mom took me up to Portland for an orientation a few months before I was scheduled to go. She was pregnant with my sister Nora then. A lot of people just thought that Mom was gaining weight because in those days, women approaching forty didn't usually get pregnant, but my parents had planned the pregnancy. In fact, Mom had a miscarriage before becoming pregnant with Nora. They even talked about having another after Nora but decided against it. Leo would come over to pick me up for a date and Mom would usually be in her full-length dark blue velvet bathrobe. He didn't even notice that she was pregnant! Right before my American Heritage trip, I expressed my concern to him about the possibility that I wouldn't have a chance to see my new brother or sister before I left, and he didn't know what I was talking about. I had to explain about Mom's pregnancy. I don't think he believed me at first. I commented that I found it peculiar that he hadn't noticed. Doug, on the other hand, did notice. He was ten at the time, and once, when we all went to mass on a Sunday, he asked Mom if she wasn't a little bit embarrassed to be seen "like that." She told him no. Well, Nora was born on June 5, 1967, and so I got to see Mom and my new sister in the hospital before I left. Dad drove me up to Portland on June 8, and I got on the train on June 9. My Aunt Jean got pregnant about the same time that Mom had a miscarriage before Nora was conceived. They always seemed to have had babies around the same time. Jean's pregnancy was difficult this time, and there were serious complications after the baby girl was born. Surgeries were required. The infant died in hospital. When Mom found out she was pregnant again, both she and Dad worried about the outcome because of Mom's age and Jean's fate. But Nora turned out to be fine. Years later, I spoke with Jean over the phone after she was diagnosed with a cancer that eventually killed her. She cried about her baby girl all those years later. Dad said she never really got over it.

I was the only person slated to go on the American Heritage trip who wasn't from Portland, Eugene, or Washington State, so when I was dropped off to get on the train, I didn't know anyone. Most of the kids were older than I was and seemed more sophisticated. I eventually made the acquaintance of a Jewish girl (Janis K) and two un-identical twins (Randi and Sarah J) that I liked, and the four of us stuck together throughout the trip. Most of the other kids intimidated me. (I would spot Janis years later-after we were both married with children-in the General Store at Sun

River Resort. I approached her and asked if she had gone on the American Heritage trip in 1967 and she replied that she had. She remembered me too and we discussed briefly what had transpired in our lives in the interim. I always remember a face). I wrote the following in my itinerary booklet: "Today I got on the train alone and sat alone the first half hour of the trip until I got the nerve to ask J---- if I could share her seat. Then I met the two boys who came from her school and soon it was time to get ready for bed. We all struggled down the hallway to a lav(atory) that I expected to be much smaller. It was fun getting ready for bed with ten other girls plus two advisors in the small room. Well finally we were ready for bed, but no one seemed to want to sleep so the trip was becoming . . ." (That's as far as I got). There were a few rules to be followed, such as no drinking in our rooms, and I was amazed that these kids made a habit of breaking all the rules they could. After we got to Chicago, we spent the rest of the trip on buses. There were many historical stops—DC was the first. I remember the White House and Mount Vernon the best, other than the visit to the U.S. Capitol Building where I met Edward Kennedy. He signed a photograph of himself for me. Then we headed to Charlottesville, Virginia, where we saw Monticello. I fell in love with the place and fantasized about living there. We also went to the University of Virginia, which so impressed me that later on, when considering colleges, I thought about this university but was too timid to consider going all the way across the country to attend there. We also visited Jamestown in Williamsburg, Virginia, and headed to New York City.

I was reluctant to visit New York because I feared I wouldn't return home alive, but this was the place that I really fell in love with. It was so exciting, and I found the people there interesting and friendly. I think I felt more at home because of the ethnic diversity—something that was lacking in Bend. New York felt more like Chicago to me, only even better. We got to explore Manhattan on our own in the evenings. The eighteen- year-olds on the trip loved this because they were legal in New York, so they were able to get into the bars and clubs. The stock exchange sticks in my mind too. We stood above the arena and watched the excitement on the floor below—all the men in their suits, exuberant and wild with good news from the lighted board on the wall, with ticker tape flying around the room. The New York experience opened up my world. I didn't realize it yet entirely, but the city's vibrancy reflected my own heritage and ethnicity—a city that has such diversity and history that no other place else on earth may compare.

Boston was our next stop. What I remember most about Boston was Durgin-Park—an old restaurant that was known for grumpy waitresses, peanut shells one could drop on the wooden floorboards, and good seafood, the lobster in particular—and the

Boston Pops, where I heard a woman with the most beautiful voice—the only voice that ever gave me goose bumps. Then we went to Harvard, Sturbridge, and Philadelphia. At Sturbridge, my period started without my knowing it. I was with my three buddies—Janis, Randi, and Sarah. They suggested a stop at the bathrooms, and when I got in the stall, I noticed that blood had soaked through to my skirt. They were aware but didn't want to come right out and tell me. I yelled out from the stall and told of what I had discovered. One of them gave me a sweater to tie around my lower half so that I could get back to the bus for a change of clothing. The other memorable part of Sturbridge was the stockades that each of us tried on for size. We took pictures of each other in them. In Philadelphia, I remember walking to the Liberty Bell. While I was gone, I got the following letters from home:

From Dad (June 17, 1967): "Well Cheryl it's like the good guys and the bad guys on T.V.—Just remember if you do what is right in your own mind that is what matters. It is what is right for you that counts—'per drinking parties.' We all miss you around here and refer to you frequently with pride as the adventuresome one. Mom always sets your place at dinner absentmindedly. Miss C. was here Thursday night-kept us up till 2 A.M. per her usual conversation. Weather here has been on the warm side so the weeds you can harvest when you get home are doing well—looking forward to your return with fatherly love, Dad. P.S. Got your card—thanks. P.P.S. Some report card, pal."

From Mom (Tuesday, June 20): "One more week and you'll be in Chicago and practically home. We called Grandpa last night and he knows when, where and how and almost to the second of your arrival. We were unable to call him on Father's Day so we got the call through last night. We were so sorry to miss your call—just went to the D . . .'s for a few minutes to see their new dog. Everyone had just left and it was close to 9 o'clock. Sunday was a very hot day and most of our Baptism party was in the backyard—baby joined us too. Dad and I have been wondering if you will be able to see Kosygin today. We're enjoying your trip right here in Bend as much as we hope you're are doing. Kathy moved out Saturday and I had her for dinner on Thursday. She stayed her usual lengthy time and left about 3 in the morning which gave me enough time to feed the baby and almost be ready for the next day. Ho! Ho!— as Oscar would say. We did enjoy the evening and she brought me some large flowers she had made. Time for the mailman, xx, Mom."

From Doug (postmarked June 22, 1967): "Dear Cheryl, I hope you are having a good time. I'm on little leagle (league). I am not old enough to be on it but Mr. Dexter took me thar (there). Love, Doug."

I took the train back from Chicago on my own after I stayed on in Elmhurst a few extra days to visit my relatives. Mom and Dad greeted me at the train station in Portland. My luggage was missing, so we had to drive up a week later to pick it up. After I got back to Bend, Yanko and Aunt Jean (cousins) came to visit. Leo had just gotten back from a vacation of his own. We took them to a carnival that was going on in the Safeway parking lot on NE Third Street (Highway 97). This was my first meeting with Yanko. Jean and Yanko had a special chemistry. They both had the same sense of humor and adventure and laughed and teased each other continually. Yanko talked me into a ride on the Rock-O-Plane. This ride was like a Ferris wheel, but instead of the traditional seat, there were cages that one could twirl with the use of a steering wheel inside the cage. That is, twirl all the way around on its axis while the Ferris wheel also moved. The cage could go forward, backward and upside-down. This combined movement lent itself to extreme fright, at least for me. Yanko took charge of the steering wheel and made the cage go all the way around. I protested with "Stop," and in his broken English, he would smile and say "More?" I would say "No, stop," and he would say "More?" and on it went. The more I protested, the faster the cage went. Finally, the ride was over, and Yanko laughed at my distress, and I had to laugh too after I was able to get off the ride. While I was up there with him, I could see Leo and Jean laughing and pointing down below me. When I got off the ride, Yanko tried to talk Jean into taking a ride with him too, but she laughed and said "No way." Dad was still really not himself during Yanko and Jean's visit. I felt that Jean especially was aware of Dad's irritability. Yanko had never met Dad before, so maybe he thought Dad was just that way. I think that even Dad had some awareness near the end of their visit and was remorseful about not having been a better host.

The summer between my junior and senior years, college guy was back in town. I started seeing him again, but I was still dating Leo too. One afternoon, Leo stopped by to visit me, Mom, and Dad on the back deck. It was a hot sunny day. He came around the side of the house, saw college guy, and left. This made me nervous. He went down to the Snack Shack, a burger stand on Eighth Street a few blocks away, and called me. He gave me an ultimatum—he would drive by and pick me up, and we would have a discussion about college guy. I told college guy that I had to go, and he left. Leo asked me to choose and said, "It's either him or me." A few days later, college guy and I went up Pilot Butte, and I told him I couldn't see him anymore and why. He said that he wanted to marry me when I was a little older and cried about our breakup. I'm still not sure why I did what I did. Maybe I was a little afraid of college guy, and Leo seemed more stable and dependable. Leo and I did have fun together. But nevertheless, I didn't like cutting things off with college guy nor did I like having been given an ultimatum by Leo.

All my friends were getting summer jobs, so I decided to do so as well. Previous to this, Mom and Dad had been satisfied with and encouraged our working at home. We spent hours weeding flower beds, painting, doing housework, etc. and were paid well for our efforts. My first real job was as a waitress. The manager there was a tall mustachioed cowboy who was mellow and cordial. His son worked there too. We waitresses wore long flowery dresses and frilly white blouses. Money started disappearing from the till, so the manager called all of us in one at a time to confront us about the theft. I actually suspected another waitress. When I got in his office, he was behind his desk and asked if I was the one who took the money. I was innocent, but as usual, when accused of a misdeed, I always felt and acted guilty. I could feel my face flush as I denied everything, so I was concerned he wouldn't believe me. It turned out that his son was the thief, and the manager apologized to all of us after he discovered the truth.

I also worked the following summer at the Skyline Steakhouse in Downtown Bend on Wall Street. I walked in looking for summer work, and the manager told me that he had just fired someone the day before, so he gave me the job. I was to start the next morning. Well, the fired waitress was a friend of the owner and got her job right back in spite of the manager firing her. The rumor was that she'd been drinking on the job. She showed up the next day too and didn't like the fact that I was there. We were supposed to store our receipts in a slot at the back of the restaurant and retrieve them at the end of the day. It was busy that day, so I had lots of receipts, but when I went to get them at the end of my shift to turn them in, there were only four or five. The manager asked me what was up. I told him that I had placed a lot more in the slot throughout the day and that I couldn't account for the missing receipts, but I knew that I had put them all there. I didn't want to come right out and accuse anyone, but I had a pretty good idea how they went missing. Another of the waitresses, a young girl there, wasn't very friendly either. It was a good lesson for me about the general pettiness and competitiveness that people get involved in. It made me promise myself to try not to get involved in such things if I could help it. Then there were the patrons. Most were nice and friendly, and some were regulars you got to know. There were also the pompous obnoxious types, usually male. One of them came in one evening and started giving me a hard time. I didn't know how to handle him. I went over by the kitchen to calm down. The kitchen staff were my favorites. They liked to laugh and joke and didn't take things much too seriously. One of the older waitresses offered to take my table for me after the manager started yelling at me about my customer, so I let her and was able to avoid him after that. I was able to stick it out through the summer, and the old waitress who'd been fired finally accepted my being there.

I started having bouts of nausea, diarrhea, abdominal cramping, and high fever. At first, I thought that I had a flu bug, but then I started to notice a pattern of returning symptoms. Usually, symptoms would subside, but I would continue to feel tired in between bouts. Symptoms would return at four- to six-week intervals and became more severe. I couldn't get out of bed because of severe malaise. Dad wasn't one to pay much attention to his kids' health issues. I think he never wanted to accept the fact that anything was really wrong with us, so he generally ignored it. However, after three or four episodes of this illness, he took notice and sent me to a friend of his, Dr. Woods, who was considered to be the best around. My white blood count was sky-high and other labs were off. The doctor suspected pancreatitis but wasn't sure. He was also unable to get accurate labs when I wasn't acutely ill. So he told me to come back when I had another attack.

I was in AP biology and English classes. Mr. E was my biology teacher, and he took his class to the Oregon State University Marine Science Center (a research and teaching facility near Newport, Oregon) for five days every spring. We studied sea life over there and stayed in the OSU (Oregon State University) barracks, which included rustic shelters with wooden bed frames to throw one's sleeping bag on. A few parents went along as chaperones. Mr. E was great. He was a romantic too. For instance, he picked field flowers next to the highway on the way home to give his wife upon his return. While we were there, I developed a crush on one of the guys from my biology class who was on our trip. When we got back to Bend, he told some of his friends that he liked me. Leo found out, and his friends backed the guy off. I didn't know this had happened until a few years later. When I did hear about it, I was irritated. But getting back to our biology trip—we all wore waders when we went out to collect sea anemones in the channels near the shore of the ocean. The water would rush in around us and had a powerful current to it. One wave went high enough to allow water to rush into my waders, and I was underwater in no time and felt cemented to the floor of the ocean. The water continued to rush over my head. If two of the guys next to me hadn't turned me upside down so that the water drained out of the waders, I'm convinced I would have drowned. The following year, Mr. E took the next class over. A sneaker wave caught them unawares in the same spot we had been the year before. Three boys perished. He never took another group over after that.

Mary R. had never had a date, and so when Leo and I planned to attend the senior prom, I asked if he might find a date for her. He asked a nice guy who really hadn't dated either. He was a cowboy type that classmates called Sod Buster to differentiate him from another guy in our class who had the same real name. They called the other guy Cougar. Mary R. was excited about her date. On the day of the prom, she asked me if I'd like to head downtown to help her pick out some ribbons for her hair to match her dress. We decided to eat lunch at the Skyline Steakhouse first. She told me that she didn't think she would get to college as she had hoped— something about not having enough money to go. This didn't make sense to me because all her older siblings had attended OSU, so why wouldn't she. I told her that I thought she would go, but she remained skeptical. The prom was held at the Sunriver Resort Great Hall—a beautiful setting. The hall had high ceilings with exposed beams, a large stone fireplace at the far end of the room, and a balcony overlooking the main floor. Tables were decorated with springtime ornamentation. The Great Hall was built in 1944 by the Army Corps of Engineers and had been a part of Camp Abbot Army Base. It was originally the officers' mess hall.[18] When Leo and I arrived, I saw Mary R. and Sod Buster, and I told her how lovely she looked. She was beaming. Later on, Leo and I were in front of the fireplace and noticed a hubbub on the far side of the room. I ran over and Mary R. was on the floor. She and her date had just had a photo taken by the photographer there. The thought ran through my head about what Dad had said about her

---

[18] "Camp Abbot," *Wikipedia, The Free Encyclopedia*, http://en.wikipedia.org/wiki/Camp_ Abbot.

not getting through high school alive. They hauled her off into the bathroom, and my English teacher wouldn't let me in to see her. After a while, an ambulance came and took her to the hospital in Bend. I told Leo that I wanted to follow the ambulance into town, and so we did. We ran into the lobby of St. Charles, which used to be on Hospital Hill right downtown. A classmate was on duty that night and told me that Mary R. was dead. Leo had booked a room for us for after the prom. He had champagne glasses and flowers decorating the room. Unfortunately, the evening was not what he expected, but we stayed there until about three in the morning, and then I went home and woke my parents to let them know what happened. They had been very fond of Mary R. and were shocked by the news in spite of the fact that Dad had predicted her premature death years earlier. But I don't think he expected that it would be on prom night. As time went by in my life, I came to respect Dad's ability to predict a person's death. He was never wrong.

I was still struggling with my mystery disease. The doctor had not been able to determine what it was or how to treat it due to its unpredictable course. After Mary R.'s death, I found myself in bed again, so I was unable to attend her wake. I managed to get to the funeral, but I didn't go up to the casket to see her. There was a gathering at her family home afterward, and all her friends attended. Right after the funeral, my family had planned a trip to Disneyland. I had never been there before and don't remember much about this vacation other than the fact that my biology teacher, Mr. E wanted me to take the AP test so that I could get college credit, and it was being offered in Bend when I would be in California. So he arranged for me to take the test at a high school in Anaheim. Dad had to drive me there in the morning, and I spent the whole day with the test in front of me, but I didn't really have the energy to try. I pretty much checked boxes just to get through it. When I returned to Bend, I think Mr. E was disappointed in my test results. I felt bad about this because I really liked him and knew how devoted a teacher he was. But it was just too bad a time for me to care about such things.

During high school, some of the guys in our class of 1969 formed a club called Drinko '69 for obvious reasons. Members had cards made up that said Drinko '69 on them. I still remember sitting in the Bend High Library with Ms. M, the librarian in charge. Mary R. and I were sitting at our usual table at the back of the library next to the study lab with some other friends. Mary R. continually reorganized the bulletin board behind our table to annoy Ms. M. The magnetic letters would be rearranged to say something other than what was originally there—usually something comical. Sometimes Ms. M would catch her in the act and start toward the back of the library. Everyone could hear Ms. M's heels clicking along as she headed down the library toward our table, but Mary R. would dodge out the study room door, head back around to the front door of the library, lock the door, and then lock the study room door. Then Ms. M would be locked out of the library. This happened on a regular basis. The library is also where Mary R., a few other friends, and I decided that we should have a club too. We took out a sheet of paper and experimented. We came up with the 54 Club-upside down. This was supposed to look like someone's butt on a toilet—this concept being similar to the significance of the 69's sexual connotation. We invited our friends to join and everyone did. Now our class of '69 (or '54) was ready to graduate, but Mary R. was not to be among the graduates of our class.

On graduation night, after the commencement ceremonies, Leo and I went to a party. We hadn't really done this before, spending most of our time together or with our own friends who were from separate cliques. Neither of us had been drinkers or used drugs in high school. Some kids did, but it wasn't as prevalent as it became a few years later during the seventies. But at the graduation party, there was liquor, and Leo drank quite a bit. After the party, we parked, and he tried to force my head into his lap for oral sex. This really pissed me off, and I told him to take me home. It seemed that the liquor brought out the aggression in him, and I was surprised by it. He had always been a little cocky but never aggressive. (This also brings to mind our handball matches while we were in undergraduate school at Willamette. He would hit the ball as hard as he could so it went right past me. I complained that his serves were too much for me, but he continued to lob them past me. After a few matches like this, I let him know that this would be the last time I'd be playing handball with him).

Dad encouraged me to go to college out of state and not where Leo was going. I agreed with this because I wanted a chance to be on my own. I thought about the University of Virginia, but that seemed too far away. I liked Seattle ever since I saw Elvis there, and we had also been back a few times after that for vacation. So I applied to Seattle University, a private Catholic school in Downtown Seattle. In the meantime, Leo was heading to Willamette University (WU) in Salem with a full ride football scholarship. He got hurt the first week of practice but got to keep the scholarship anyway. He also lived and worked at the blind school near campus to pay for room and board. I headed to Seattle with my parents a few weeks later. There was a dinner for parents and students when we got there. We sat with my new roommate-to-be and her parents, and a male student and his parents. I disliked this girl from the start and the guy went on and on about how cool my dad was. I asked the girl about the fact that she smoked as I had filled out a questionnaire about my living preferences from the school during the summer. She explained that she had filled it out the opposite of how she was—that she was a nonsmoker, nondrinker, etc. During the first week at SU, she invited me to come along to a party she was attending, so I went. There was a separate darkened room at the party where a female stripper was featured. She dragged me in with her and sat us down in the front row to cheer the stripper on. We were the only femmes in the room other than the stripper. I decided to leave and return to Bellarmine Hall—my dorm.

The guy I met at the dinner asked me out the first week on a first date. All he talked about again was how cool my dad was. On our second date, he drove me out in the middle of nowhere and attempted to have sex with me. I wasn't cooperative, but he continued his advances. I got out of the car and started walking. He told me to get back in the car, but I continued to walk. I don't know what I would have done had he driven away—it was so desolate out there. He kept driving along beside me, and I finally agreed to get in the backseat of his car. He drove back to campus, but I could tell he was angry. I didn't agree to go out with him again, which must have made him mad because he would get drunk and call me at night and then call me names. Another guy asked me to go to an overnighter. I thought this was a party where everyone danced all night long—sort of like my old slumber party days in junior high—so I agreed to go. The party was on an island with a lodge on it. We took a ferry there. There was dancing and a slight French guy asked me to dance and then go for a walk in the woods with him. I thought he was sexy and started imagining what we might do in the woods together, but all of a sudden, he just took off. Maybe I was too eager, and it showed. I found out that the party included bedding down, and my date expected me to bed down with him. We did make out, but I told him he had to sleep outside my sleeping bag. The next day, I had a big hickey on my neck, and not long after that, I developed an infection there. I went to the infirmary and they gave me some topical ointment and said to wear a Kotex to cover the sore, so I had to wear a scarf or turtleneck to cover the Kotex, but there was still a bulge that was noticeable.

It didn't take too long before I met some people I liked and decided to ditch my roommate. I was convinced of this after she poured baby powder all over me when I was ready to leave for a date. She would also get back in after a night of partying, wake me up, and jabber for hours even when I told her I wanted to sleep. My future roommate (Patty) had a roommate who was a friend of my roommate. Patty didn't like her roommate either, so we decided to trade. We also decided that we wouldn't take no for an answer, and after the first term, we switched. Patty had a loud voice and was funny. She was a nursing student. She bought blue fuzzy feet-shaped rugs for our dorm room. There were some other girls we were friends with too—Lynn, Jan, Marcia, and Kathy. Lynn was from San Francisco and had a Volkswagen. We'd pile in on the weekends and head to Vancouver, British Columbia, where there were tea and coffee houses with good jazz and blues musicians in addition to some strange street people.

Practical jokes were a frequent pastime in Bellarmine Hall. My favorite was one played on me. Our phone rang, and so I scurried across our dorm room to get it. When I picked it up, to my surprise, the phone kept ringing. It seemed really weird and caught me off guard. The pranksters had taped the receiver buttons down. Another one involved having smoke blown under the door of our rooms from the hallway. The room would fill up with smoke until we opened the door and extinguished the source. There was also a panty raid. The guys involved sneaked up the fire escape and pounded on the door. I was the one to run over to see what was up. One of the guys pleaded with me to let him in, so I did. They ran through the rooms of the girls on our floor and grabbed whatever underwear they could find. Someone said they had seen what I had done, so I hid in my closet until all the commotion was over. Unfortunately, someone ratted on me, and I was called in by the dean of women, who suspended me for three days. I used the time to catch up on my homework.

It was 1969, so there were war demonstrations—sometimes mobs of people took over Downtown Seattle or our campus. There was also a bomb threat once, and our dorm had to be evacuated in the middle of the night. We all stood outside Bellarmine Hall with our pajamas and bathrobes until we were told it was safe to go back to our rooms. Since we were right downtown, there were frequent scuffles right outside our dorm, often resulting in someone being taken by ambulance to the nearby hospital on the hill. My folks would visit occasionally and take me to a French restaurant, The Brasserie on Pike Street. You had to enter by going down a broad set of stairs to a room with white pillars and black-and-white checkered marble floors. One time, as we were leaving the restaurant, a black man fell down the stairs and landed right in front of our feet. He had a stab wound. Since Dad was a doctor, he checked him out while restaurant staff called an ambulance. We waited until he was taken to the hospital. My folks took me shopping in Downtown Seattle too, but the clothes were so bad (it was the late '60's after all)I didn't find anything to buy, so I stuck with my cords and T-shirts. Sandy visited too. We put bobby pins in her blonde wet hair one night in the dorm, for fun and to see what would happen, and the next morning it turned out to be a blonde Afro. She and I explored Seattle with her hair like that.

I studied hard all week long. Since I was a bio major, I had calculus and chemistry that I struggled with and didn't like. On the weekends, we'd go to the Tabard Inn—a campus nightclub—or to an upperclassman's apartment to party. There would be liquor and marijuana. Sometimes the marijuana made me paranoid. I remember being at Tabard Inn once and thinking the police were coming for me. I also had a few bad times after drinking too much, which all led to the conclusion that I needed to slow down. This is when Jan set me up with her brother who was attending the University of Washington (UW), and we dropped by his dorm where there were scary things going on—hard-core drug users in small dark rooms with black lights and psychedelic music. It wasn't my scene. On another night, Lynn, Patty, and I accepted a ride from some UW guys while we were in Downtown Seattle, and they took us to a fraternity party. One of the guys led me to a vacant bedroom, and when I said I didn't want to be there, he got mad. We girls said we wanted a ride back to our dorm, and they took us back, but they weren't too nice about it. After a few months, I knew I liked my liberal arts classes a lot better than my science classes. I was flunking chemistry and couldn't get myself to want to try any longer, so I decided to do what I did in junior high when I wanted to buy my own bras. I used the pay phone in front of Bellarmine Hall to call home and tell Dad I was changing my major. I hung up before he could argue with me about it.

A Chinese guy asked me out, and he took me to a movie called Myra Breckinridge with Raquel Welch—not a good first-date movie to see. The movie was based on a novel by Gore Vidal with the same title. It had a reputation for being one of the worst movies ever made, and it lived up to its reputation. Time magazine was quoted as saying the film was "about as funny as a child molester" and that "it is an insult to intelligence, an affront to sensibility and an abomination to the eye." Even Gore Vidal commented that the movie was "an awful joke", and the film historian Leonard Maltin commented that it was "as bad as any movie ever made"[19]—all true. My date asked me out for the next weekend. In the meantime, Leo called to let me know he was coming up for the weekend. I told him that I had a date, and he suggested I cancel it, so I did. I called the Chinese guy and asked him for a rain check, but he seemed insulted and hung up on me. I didn't know this for some time, but Leo was dating coeds from the very start but still got annoyed if I dated anyone. In fact, he dated a coed named Karen who was considered his girlfriend at WU. When I came to town, he'd ditch her for the weekend. I found out about her after a while but was OK about his dating her. After all, that's what I wanted to do at SU, but it never amounted to much. Jan had set me up with her brother for the one date. Jan and Eric arranged for us to double date, and my date was Jerry (a friend of Eric's) who had a girlfriend out of state. They had an understanding that they could date other people. I also went out a few times with another friend of Eric's—Dave Bender. He was an artist type, and I liked him. I'm not sure there was much chemistry, but we enjoyed each other's company. Dave took me to see Ray Charles. I had seen him with my parents in Portland a few years earlier, and his performance had been electrifying. This time, he stumbled onto the stage and had to be escorted off. We made the best of the rest of the evening.

---

[19] "Myra Breckinridge (film)," *Wikipedia, The Free Encyclopedia*, http://en.wikipedia.org/wiki/Myra_Breckinridge_%28film%29.

After Leo started his second year at Willamette, I told my parents I wanted to visit before I headed up to Seattle. I told them Leo was arranging for me to stay in one of the girls' dorms, but this wasn't true. Our plan was to head to the coast for the weekend. A week before, he had tried to have sex with me in his parents' living room. I protested, saying that I didn't think it seemed very romantic and suggested a weekend coast trip for that purpose before I would head up to school. After Mary R. died, I had concerns about dying a virgin, which I didn't want to happen. I was ready to lose my virginity. I drove over to Salem, and before we left for the beach, we went to Meier & Frank department store, which had a pharmacy. We casually perused the aisles in the store for contraception and tentatively handed the package to the cashier. When we got to Lincoln City, we checked into a motel. I was sore for a few days after, but the first time was pleasant. After the weekend, I headed up to Seattle U.

When Leo came up to visit me in Seattle, we would go to the farmer's market and eat at Ivar's on the Pier for fish and chips. For special occasions, we'd go to the Mirabeau at the top of the Seattle-First National Bank Building. The restaurant was located on the fiftieth floor and had a spectacular panoramic view of the whole city. The waiters were very attentive and came to the table to light Leo's cigarette every time they saw him pull one out of his pocket. We had our first Baked Alaska there, which made us so full that when we got back to the room, all we could do was lie on the bed for the rest of the evening. Sometimes we'd book a room at the Sorrento near SU. On one occasion there, I was making a lot of lovemaking noise, and our windows were open over the courtyard. Some guy in the next room yelled out "Are you all right over there?" I answered, "Yes, just fine." Bellarmine had rules about curfew, so if you were late getting in, there was trouble. But if you signed out for the weekend, there was no problem. You just had to make up a place where you were going.

I took trips down to Willamette some weekends too. I rode the bus back and forth. Leo's friends were mostly guys that also worked at the blind school. Willamette was conservative with frats and sororities, but the blind school atmosphere was different. The employees' student rooms were in the basement. I stayed in Leo's room for the weekends I visited. We'd go to the Pancake House nearby for breakfast. Sometimes we'd head over to the coast and eat at the Pixie Kitchen which was an all-you-can-eat seafood joint. It had a carnival atmosphere with mirrors in the entryway that deformed one's appearance when you stood in front of them. There were also photo booths that produced a row of photos from behind a curtain. Behind the restaurant was a fenced fantasyland where pixies rode around on a train. Sometimes I'd stick extra scallops in my purse for later on, but by the time we got back to Willamette, the food was soggy and cold.

I didn't really trust contraception, so I became anxious about my periods starting. This probably led to their not showing up on time. I went to see my doctor with concerns, and he gave me a pill to take that got it started. After that, it was fifty-some days late, and so I called Leo about my fears. I headed back to Bend for Thanksgiving with my friend Lynn from college, and the first thing I did upon my arrival home was to greet Leo at our front door and whisper to him that my period had just started. The news made the weekend much more relaxing.

Two of my favorite courses at SU were music history and contemporary art history. In my music course, we had study lab. We went to the lab and used headphones to study a musical arrangement while listening to a piece and also following it with the score. It brought the music on the page to life. The notes of the score and the sound became one. Art class was exciting too. It opened up a whole new way of looking at the world and complemented all the other courses I was taking at school.

My biology teacher, George Davis, was a mentor to me. I continued with my biology classes in spite of my change of major because I enjoyed them. When I told him I was planning to leave SU to move closer to my boyfriend and there were plans for marriage, he said I was making a mistake. His feeling was that I ought to finish up at SU and continue with my schooling beyond undergraduate school. During my two years at SU, Leo kept insisting I transfer to WU. He gave me an engagement ring during my time at SU, and I returned it saying I wasn't ready to be engaged, but he persisted, and I finally agreed a second time. When I think back, I suspect that my mother's role as a homemaker led me, at least in part, to my decision. So I was off to WU for my junior and senior years. I would start my senior year married.

Fun with Joe – July 1961

Joe and the Guys – July 1961

Jeff

Greg

Mom and Doug at Mt. Bachelor (1960)

Rathje Family Photo (1960

Portland with Cousins

Leo (age 9)

Sandy and Me

Mom and Sandy Cooking

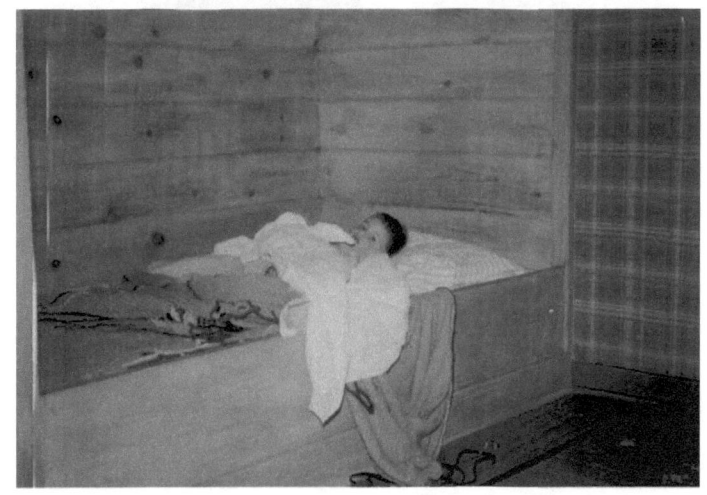

Doug in Bed

Easter Chicks

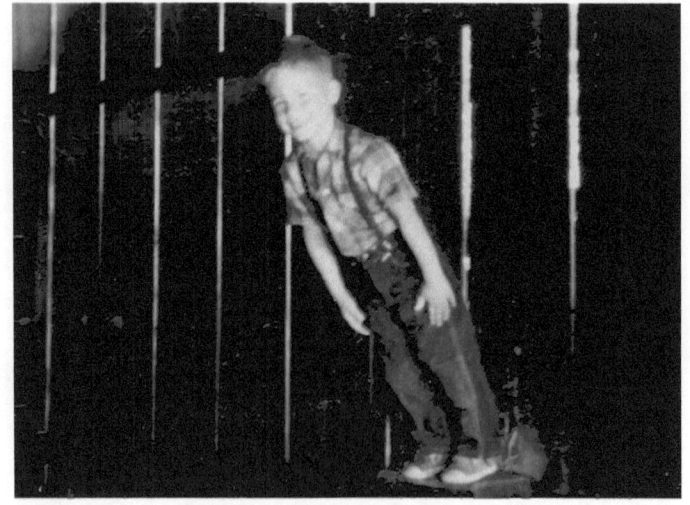

Doug at Uncanny Canyon

Crater Lake

Crater Lake with Mom

Doug and Me with Curlers

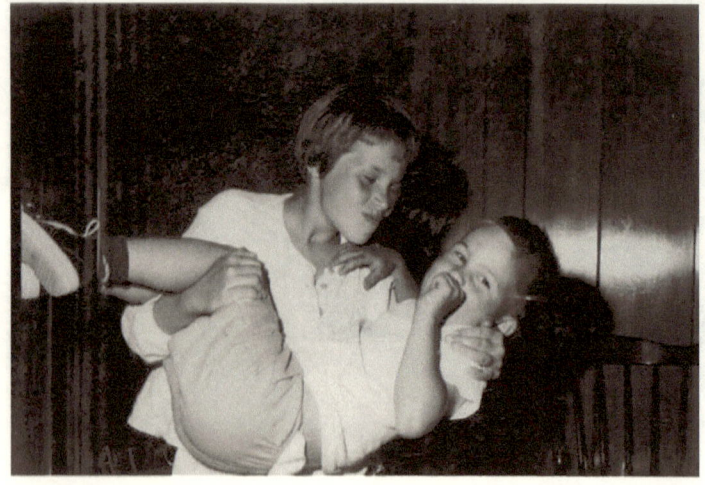

Sandy and Doug

St. Francis in Seventh Grade

Doug and Mom

Doug and Mom ('64)

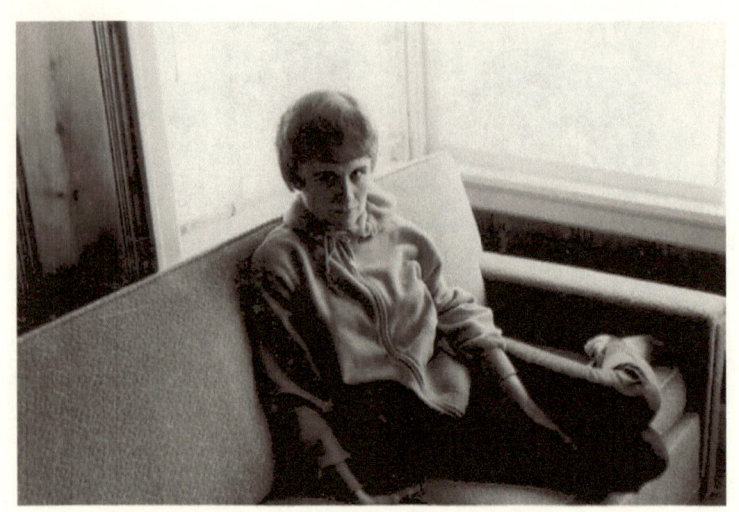

Mom ('65)

Me ('65)

Sandy ('65)

Doug Fishing

Nora and Mom (1967)

Me on the phone in Hallway

Doug and Nora

Nora and Doug

Nora and Dad (69)

Family Photo

Me- High School Graduation 1969

Sandy-College Girl

CHAPTER 3

Leo enlisted his WU girlfriend, Karen, to find a place for me to live at WU, so I wound up in Lee House with mostly freshman girls who had been unable or unwilling to pledge a sorority. The frat/sorority thing was new to me because Catholic universities don't have them. There was a wide variety of goof balls and misfits at Lee House, the goofiest being my roommate. Her dad had wanted a boy when she was born, and when she turned out to be a girl, he named her after himself anyway. She was as wide as she was tall, with small delicate hands and feet. Her mom would send care packages, which included an assortment of goodies—candy bars, chips, cookies, etc.—that she stored in our room. Our room was for studying and socializing, not sleeping. The dorm had a sleeping porch, and I was assigned a lower bunk. It was weird sleeping in a cold room (because windows were kept open) with a bunch of girls who moved in and out all night long. My roommate had a large assortment of suitors that came and went. They were mostly small skinny guys. While she was entertaining them in our room, she'd lock me out. I'd pound on the door and call for her to let me in, but she would just say "Come back later" and, in general, ignore me. I could hear her carrying-on in there. So I really didn't have a place of my own. In the dining room, no one really talked to one another, so I'd eat by myself and then try to figure out what to do next if I couldn't get back in my room. But there was one coed who lived at Lee House that I saw coming and going but never got to know very well. She was on the second floor, and I was on the first. Her name was Susie. I didn't know it yet, but our paths would cross again a few years later.

My sister Sandy started college at the University of Portland, a private Catholic school, when I was a junior at Willamette. Leo had a weekend job driving the Willamette bus for field trips, so I decided to go see Sandy. I didn't really have much, if any, experience with freeway driving, so the trip to Portland was frightening, especially when it came to getting off on the U of P exit. I did make it to campus, though, and we decided to head down to the city center for the day. We started talking while I was working my way to our destination, and I got onto the wrong exit. We drove around and around until we finally got where we wanted to go, with a few close calls in the meantime. Sandy had a roommate who was short and buxom. She was gregarious and funny too. Sandy said some of the guys at school would grab at her friend's boobs and call her a cow, which she laughed off in public but cried about when she would get back to her dorm room. She fell in love with a guy who didn't return her feelings, which also made her cry. Sandy would get frustrated with her because she borrowed Sandy's shoes and stretched them all out. She also squeezed herself into Sandy's clothes and did the same with them. I also met another of Sandy's friends at college who was a true nymphomaniac. Sandy informed me when we were alone that her friend couldn't resist anything that wore pants (unless it was a girl). I'm not sure she was a good influence on my sister. Sandy brought her home for Christmas break, and she and Mark, her temporary boyfriend from high school, found a date (Mike M.) for Sandy's friend so that they could double date. They went up on Pilot Butte, and she went after Mike M. He didn't protest. Sandy and Mark could see what was going on in the backseat, and pretty soon her friend's cowboy boots started kicking the back of Mark and Sandy's heads.

While Sandy and I were still attending college in the Willamette Valley, Dad and Mom invited us up to Portland for a weekend. I took the bus up from Salem, and we all met in Downtown Portland. Dad had his favorite restaurant there, L'Auberge. The food there was great. The four of us wandered around downtown for a while, and then Dad suggested we have lunch at the restaurant. I questioned whether we would be able to get in without a reservation, but he didn't seem too concerned. We headed on in after a brief walk. The host asked for the name and Dad pointed to a name on the guest register and mumbled something unintelligible, so we were surprised when we were led to a table. We all ordered our favorite on the menu and had a bottle of wine to share. About fifteen minutes later, a couple came in, but there were no empty tables. The staff seemed confused and told the couple they couldn't account for there being no room for them. They offered to pull out a table for them from a back room and fit it in somewhere, but the couple left in a huff. I know we should have felt guilty, but the meal and the time spent that afternoon was so much fun that I couldn't help but feel glad that Dad had secured our table with deception.

Leo was renting an old house with a college friend. I'd go over there on weekends where I could cook meals and stay over with Leo in his bedroom. The guy's girlfriend would come by too. She was best friends with Karen, so she didn't like me much. She was also a feminist, so she'd get irritated if I cooked meals, did dishes, and cleaned the house up. She thought the guys should do all that because it was their house after all. I felt fortunate to have a place to escape from Lee House on the weekends, so I was glad to pitch in. It sort of made me feel like it was my house too, which may have been part of the problem. His friend's girlfriend decided to move in with her boyfriend, which meant that Leo (and I) would have to move out. He didn't argue much because he didn't want to live with her (and nor did I). So Leo moved in with his blind school friend Rob and a few other guys out on Mission Street. I decided I didn't want to stay at Lee House any longer, so I went and talked to the dean of women and told her that I would be getting married during my second semester and needed to get settled in a place, so she agreed to let me leave Lee House. I found a little second-story apartment in an old reconstructed house a few blocks from Leo's. My housemate across the hall was a classmate, Nathan R. At first, I thought the place was haunted or something because, at night, the bed shook. It wasn't until I talked to Nathan, who was experiencing the same thing, that I decided I wasn't going crazy after all. We found out from the landlord that the creek that ran by the old house was compromising the foundation, causing the house to settle.

Leo and his roommates' house was not very clean. I guess it was a typical college guy's place. I didn't like spending much time there because of too much guy energy, but I'd walk over at night to sleep there sometimes. I invited Leo to stay at my place, but he didn't want to, so I didn't see much of him. And I didn't know many people, so I was lonely. I met a coed from back east named Sue. She was from a wealthy family back there, and her father was some sort of famous surgeon. She didn't like her dorm living either, so she agreed to move in with me. It still felt like I was living alone most of the time, though, because she was gone a lot—I'm not sure where. I liked to cook in my apartment because I could make whatever I liked and didn't have to please anyone else. Sue made her own meals, which were granola kinds of meals. Sometimes

I would find her in the closet meditating, which seemed a little odd to me because, at that time, it was a new concept—at least in Oregon. All in all, though, she was an easy person to live with.

One weekend, Leo and I were invited to a party in Portland by some people we had known in high school. When we got there, I didn't like the vibes. There seemed to be a lot of drinking and drugs going around. I was passed a joint and took a hit so as not to look like a square, but this turned out not to be a normal marijuana joint. Pretty soon, I couldn't walk or talk. Leo knew something was wrong and asked the host, who told him that horse tranquilizer had been added to the joint. Leo had to pick me up in his arms to get me out of there, but before that, he let the guy know what he thought of him. This guy ended up in the penitentiary later on. It took hours before I felt normal again, but this experience taught me a lesson to be more careful about what was passed on to me at parties.

I began studying a lot of Russian lit with a Professor Berczynski. I took as many of his classes as possible because he was good. He liked to party with his students too. He would flirt with me and Leo, so we suspected he was bisexual. His favorite author was Fyodor Dostoevski. Too much exposure to him and other Russian and German writers left me practically suicidal. Existential concepts intrigued me, though. They weaved in and out of many of my other liberal arts courses—philosophy, theology, art, music, and psychology. I guess Berczynski's exposure to his subject matter may have had the same effect on him as it did on me because a few years after we graduated, he ran himself over a cliff in his sports car.

Another influence was seeing Alan Watts, a visiting scholar to the university. He sat in a comfortable chair in the student union building and visited casually with students who gathered around him. I remember his wise weathered face and calm aura. He was mesmerizing. His ideas agreed with me. Alan ran a Zen monastery in California and ascribed to mysticism. He said during his talk that "sex and mysticism always have a tendency to go together, simply because the kind of people who are sufficiently sensitive to have a mystical attitude toward the universe are also sensually sensitive. A person who likes poetry, painting, and music will also be sensuously attracted to other like human beings ... (and) the emotion we call falling in love arises with terrific strength. Instead of trying to get rid of it, this emotion's energy is used to increase spiritual power.[20] Some of these ideas I had never heard in Catholic school. He was known for his dislike for religious outlooks that he decided were dour, guilt-ridden, or militantly proselytizing—no matter if they were found within Judaism, Christianity, Hinduism, or Buddhism. He was criticized by those who believed that zazen

---

[20] "Wallulah Nineteen Seventy Three," published by the associated students of Willamette University in Salem, Oregon 63: 59.

can only be achieved by a strict and specific means of sitting, as opposed to a cultivated state of mind available at any given time. He responded to his critics with the following comment: "A cat sits until it is tired of sitting, then gets up, stretches, and walks away."[21] (Maybe it was the more accepting notions about human nature that appealed to me, as opposed to the focus on guilt and sin that I had been exposed to earlier on). I didn't get entirely into the mystical scene, but it did provide me with an opposing frame of reference from what I had grown up with to this point. I was surprised when I heard that not long after I had seen him, he died in his sleep on November 16, 1973, at the age of fifty-eight.

No one I knew could shoot the shit or spin a yarn like Leo or his brother Daren. This talent may have had something to do with their family's roots in the South. Both of their parents' families left for Oregon where they homesteaded. (Come to think of it, their mother, her siblings, and all her kids had the gift of gab too). Anyway, one of my favorite stories that Leo told was about his great-uncle Jack—his dad's uncle. I still remember when Leo took me to see Jack at Bachelor Butte Nursing Home around Christmastime—the winter before we got married. Leo's dad suggested he get a bottle of bourbon at the liquor store for Jack and leave it at the nurse's station. The rules there were that Jack could

---

[21] "Alan Watts," *Wikipedia, The Free Encyclopedia,* http://en.wikipedia.org/wiki/Alan_Watts.

have two shots per day—one in the morning and the other in the evening. Instead, Leo bought two bottles—one for the front desk and one for Jack, who responded with a big smile and told Leo "You always were my favorite nephew" in his peculiar manner of speech. Jack was born with a cleft palate, so he had to hold his tongue up against the roof of his mouth in order for his speech to be understood at all. His comment really sounded more like this: "Ooh awwahys were myee vaverte nefeww." Jack took a big swig, wiped the top of the bottle off, and handed it to me. I, in turn, took a big swig and handed the bottle back to him. Then he said to Leo, "By god, boy, she's a keeper." Or more like this: "Bye go', boey, cheche a keeper." It didn't take me long to notice Jack's roommate in the next bed. He was a man that looked to be in his early to mid-forties and had what I might describe as a thousand-yard stare. Jack explained that he always looked that way because the guy had been in some sort of terrible accident. To me, it was unnerving, but old Jack just seemed to take it all in stride. The next morning, Leo's dad got a call from the nursing home to report that they had found Jack in a near comatose state as Jack had downed the whole bottle in one sitting. Leo told his dad in defense that he bet Jack slept like a baby.

Jack loved the ladies, and their age didn't seem to matter too much to him, and neither did their appearance or their integrity. He lived a life as a cowhand, logger, trapper, and mountain man—

he came to the wedding of one of his nieces in buckskins. In his later years, he lived in a small apartment in town near the river, a few blocks from Leo's home. Leo would pick him up and take him to his house so that he could watch the football game. Uncle Jack, Welborn, and Leo would settle in. Jack didn't really understand the game of football but said he loved to watch "them big ol' men just arearin' up against eaa'other." In his older years, he was all hunched over after suffering injuries in an automobile accident, but this didn't stop him from standing up as straight as he was able and putting his hand over his heart when the national anthem was played. When he was over for dinner sometimes, Leo's mother would make a meal for everyone, and when she complained that it didn't turn out just right, he would always remark with a rebuttal, such as "Rock biscuits and water gravy—just the way we like it."

While Leo was practicing law, he heard stories the lawyers and judges at the courthouse told about an old guy that was arrested for poaching deer out of season. The story went that when this gentleman was advised of his crime, he readily admitted to it, explaining that "them widows and kids need the meat." He was such an agreeable and honest fellow that the judges always found themselves dickering with Jack about how to resolve the issue. It didn't seem to matter how many times old Jack was dragged into court. He always wound up back again for the same offense. On one occasion, the judge said it would either be twenty-five dollars or four days in jail. Jack said it would have to be the four days because he didn't have twenty-five dollars. Then the judge asked how much he did have, and so Jack emptied his pockets and told him he had seven dollars and so many cents. The judge then asked for the sum in his pockets, but Jack countered with an objection—he had promised to buy a few of his cronies a beer right after court and explained that if he had to pay the seven dollars and so many cents, he wouldn't have enough to honor his promise. So the judge offered to accept five dollars as payment, which Jack gladly agreed to. After the telling of this story, Leo asked the name of the old guy, and he was told that it was Jack Parker. The folks at the courthouse were surprised to find that Leo was, in fact, his great-nephew. It wasn't too long after our holiday visit at Bachelor Butte that the old guy passed away.

I got through my junior year and spent my summer at home preparing for my wedding. Leo was having gastric problems, so maybe he was having some misgivings about our upcoming nuptials as well. Mom went all out cleaning for the big event and, in the process, fell off a ladder while washing our outdoor kitchen windows and fractured her spine. That didn't stop her from making to-do lists for everyone involved, and so the planning and preparation continued. Mom was told she was lucky she didn't end up in a wheelchair on a permanent basis. My grandparents came for the wedding. My grandmother spent weeks cooking and baking.

The wedding was at St. Francis Church on August 26, 1972, and the reception was held in our backyard. The weather was hot. Dad hired Luigi, an Italian accordionist from Portland, to play. After Leo and I had our wedding dance together, other dancing ensued. It was fun to see my grandparents dance. Francesco was such a good dancer. He swept Francesca around the dance floor—our new brick and cement patio. Then I danced with Dad, while Leo danced with Mom, and then everyone else joined in. Francesca made sure her food was featured at the buffet. She even went so far as to put some of the others' contributions back to the kitchen or refrigerator. Leo's parents and other family attended. His father beamed. Our friend Mike and Mark (Sandy's sometimes boyfriend and, later, her husband) were bartenders. The kids sneaked beer from the keg while the adults weren't looking. Friends came from Seattle U and Willamette U, along with friends from high school. It was fun, but I really didn't know what I was doing. I still didn't get that I was going to be married—whatever that meant.

Leo's friend M attended with Peggy, who had been recently widowed and with a baby daughter. M and Peggy's husband had been friends in high school, and the three had been overseas together in Germany while the guys were in the service. When they returned, Peggy's husband took a job at the quarry in Tumalo. On his first day on the job, he tipped his quarry truck over and was crushed to death. M had been supportive of his friend's widow after his death, but during our wedding, the relationship seemed to have moved beyond friendship. I wasn't too surprised a few months later when she confided to me that she was pregnant and that they had married. Mary A. was another one of the guests. Our old piano in the guest house, purchased from St. Francis School years earlier, was dragged out onto the lawn and C, one of the groomsmen, played into the night. The guy I had danced with in high school before Leo got there to claim me was at the wedding too. He stole a bottle of champagne before he left that night. It exploded in his sports car the next day, leaving a hole in his convertible top. When Mom and Dad went to bed that night, presumably after all the guests had gone, they discovered one of the guests (Leo's friend Doug Herland) sitting on the bathroom floor. He asked if the reception was over, and they told him yes. He thanked them for the evening and then ambled down the hallway to the front door. Or so I'm told. We were long gone by the time things got really raucous—off to the Metolius to start our honeymoon.

It was hot at the Metolius. George R., the picnic group creator, had offered his vacation home on the river for the first few days of our honeymoon. From there, we traveled in our yellow Karmann Ghia (a wedding gift from my parents) up into Canada. On the freeway between Portland and Seattle, a semi started changing lanes, and the driver didn't see our little car. Leo swerved to avoid being hit, and we found ourselves between a concrete barrier on one side and the truck on the other. A driver in a truck behind us honked, and the semi drew back into its lane just in time. We almost didn't get to go on our honeymoon, or anything else for that matter. We visited Vancouver, British Columbia, and then traveled up to Victoria and stayed at the Empress Hotel. It was quiet and peaceful there—crumpets and tea in the afternoons, a walk through the Butchart Gardens, the wax museum, and fish and chip dinners. One of Leo's groomsmen had given us a lid as a wedding gift, and Leo haphazardly threw it in our luggage. We didn't think about it until we were going through customs on our way back into Oregon. The inspector started going through our luggage, and he asked Leo to open up the ones he pointed to. When he got to the one with the lid in it, my trousseau was on top and Leo explained that we were on our honeymoon. Luckily, the conversation about our honeymoon that ensued ended the search.

Our honeymoon was interrupted by the start of school, so after the first week, we headed over to the coast from Salem. My idea about marriage was that I got to have sex morning, noon, and night. I think when Leo figured this out, it freaked him out, and after the weekend at the coast, our sex life faltered. Another marital problem evolved around our personality differences, which were considerable. He was extroverted, which led to his inviting every Tom, Dick, and Harry to our house all weekend long for beer and football. I couldn't get away from it all except to go for long walks. My idealistic view of my parents' marriage led me to assume that marriage meant spending lots of time together—alone with each other. I guess I didn't factor in the time Mom spent without Dad around when he was in school. After he was a practicing physician, though, Dad did come home from work for dinner and spent time with his family on weekends. In my marriage, this often didn't happen because Leo liked to party with his friends. I'm still not sure about how or why things changed from our high school years, when I had his undivided attention, and when I was at SU, when he pursued me relentlessly. Maybe the chase had been successful and was over. It seemed that a battle of wills ensued between us that lasted for years. Not to say that we didn't have good times, but friction continued to crop up. Near the end of our senior year, Leo talked about graduate school for art. He loved sculpture. Maybe this would have been a good path for him, but my view of marriage was that it was time to settle down. Again, I didn't consider my dad's years of schooling but was focused on starting a family, which my parents had done right away. However, my generation had begun to put off domestic life and marriage in favor of freedom to extend personal pursuits, travel, etc. It was all so confusing. I suspect that I didn't see domestic life fitting in with graduate school in the arts, and maybe I did have some awareness of my mother's loneliness during Dad's school years. Leo's brother offered to have Leo work for him at his stationery store in Bend, and so that's what happened. It was as if each of us was following our own family script without our even being aware of it.

After graduation, we lived with Leo's parents and had a house built in a new subdivision. We did a lot of the work on the house during the weekends, which cut costs. I became focused on getting pregnant after we moved into the new house. I had a silent fear that it might not happen because it hadn't happened so far. Before I was married, I used spermicidal foam or a diaphragm, but I never trusted those methods that much. I also had an IUD placed right after I got married. This had been recommended by Dad. I went to the public birth control clinic in Salem and spent three hours waiting. Leo dropped me off at the clinic and was supposed to pick me up after I was done. I called to let him know that I was still waiting. When I finally got into the room where the procedure was to take place, I noticed a strong unpleasant female odor. This seemed to me a bad sign. Then the doctor came in and asked if I had had children yet. When I said no, he said that he didn't recommend IUDs for nulliparous women because of the difficulty in placing it and other potential complications. I sat up on the examining table and told him that maybe I shouldn't be doing this after all. He pushed me back down on the table and said "Well, it's too late now." The pain was terrible, and the whole year it was in me, I had heavy bleeding and cramping. I finally had it removed, but before I did, there was word out that IUDs could lead to infertility. All this may have added to my trepidation about conceiving.

Our friends M and Peggy from high school invited us to a bunco party. After moving back to Bend from college, it felt like we were living in suburbia and had turned into a middle-aged couple overnight. So when our friends from high school invited us to the party, we accepted. There were a lot of high school chums there that we hadn't seen since graduation. Mike M. (who had held my head underwater at the pool when we first moved to Bend) contributed a box of hard liquor for the party. As the night wore on, it seemed the guys there were competing with one another to determine who could drink the most. This became alarming to me as I witnessed the guys guzzling bottle after bottle of hard liquor. I told Leo that I thought he had had enough, which prompted him to drink all the more. I just wanted to go home, but he was the one to decide when that would happen.

When we got out in the parking lot, I told him I thought I should drive, but he insisted that he would. A few of his friends standing by supported this plan. I should have refused to get in the car with him, but I did. We made it home safely but not because of his driving. It was only luck. I was really angry by the time we got home and let him know how I felt about the terrible evening. This prompted him to push me down the hallway that led to our bedroom. He had never been aggressive with me like this before. I decided to retreat and leave him alone. I also decided that I wouldn't be going to any more bunco parties in the future. The next morning, I filled him in on the events of the night before. He didn't remember all that much. I told him what I thought of his behavior. He continued to drink, which remained a problem, but he was never overtly aggressive like that again. It was all reminiscent of my experiences growing up with my parents and their parties that got out of hand.

I set up housekeeping and got a part-time job as a receptionist for an optometrist. My breasts got tender, and I developed this intense anxiety. Then my period started, but my breasts stayed tender. I suspect that I had an early miscarriage and got pregnant so soon that I never had another period in between, but it was still too early to think I was pregnant. It seems all this may have contributed to a hormonal imbalance. On Thanksgiving morning, we were still in bed when the phone rang. Leo answered it. He had a short conversation with the person on the other end, hung up, and told me Mary A. and a car full of other students from U of Oregon had perished in a fiery crash late the night before. The students had been heading home for break when a driver in a pickup truck with acetylene and oxygen for his welding business crossed the centerline. It was discovered later that he had been driving back from a local tavern. A burned spot on that stretch of highway remained for years. I hadn't seen her since my wedding. Friends gathered for her funeral a few days later.

I kept in touch with old chums from junior high and high school— mostly my non-Catholic friends Annette, Christi, Janet, and Susie. My St. Francis friends were either dead or had disappeared. I was matron of honor for both Annette and Christi's weddings. At Annette's wedding out at the Metolius, I was a nine-months-pregnant matron of honor. I had a dress made that could work for either of the conditions I might find myself in for the ceremony. I went up to Portland for Christi's wedding, held in her home. Janet was off to graduate school and her best friend Susie was in law school. Both of them waited until their thirties to marry and both adopted two girls.

I began to suspect I might be pregnant and went to my gynecologist on December 10, 1973, for a rabbit test. On December 14, the doctor called to confirm my pregnancy. I called Leo with the news, and he came home from work that night with flowers. I was ecstatic. I loved being pregnant—especially pregnant sex. I felt sensual, womanly, and cared for. Dr. R had been my gynecologist even before I was married. I had gone to see him for my premarital exam, and upon my exit from his office, I had been handed a card with the results. I didn't look at it until I got into my car in the parking lot and was horrified when I saw that the box marked X indicated that I had a venereal disease! How could this be? After reviewing my history to myself, I decided that there must be some mistake, so I headed back into the doctor's office and showed my card to the receptionist. She took the card with her to discuss with my doctor, and they both came out to reassure me that he had mistakenly marked the wrong box. I was relieved. During my pregnancy, I have to describe myself as having been neurotic. I was convinced that I might inadvertently ingest something that would harm my baby. I had all sorts of fears, in general, about the outcome of my pregnancy. When I made my visits to Dr. R, he was always very reassuring and took as much time as I needed to answer any questions I might have on the subject. At some point, he told me that I was narrow in the pelvic region, which could present problems with a vaginal delivery. I still remember asking him how he knew this, and he had replied that he could tell by just looking at me. He gave me about a 50 percent chance of a normal delivery after he had me X-rayed. He agreed to let me go into labor and see what would happen but cautioned me that I would likely have a long labor. In spite of his reservations, I was determined to have this baby vaginally.

The night before I went into labor, I attended a donkey baseball game (baseball players on donkeys). Leo and Sandy's boyfriend Mark were participants. After we got home, Leo and I made love and went to sleep. I woke up at exactly 4:00 a.m. with labor pains.

I called my doctor at 5:00 a.m., and he said to go to the hospital when contractions were five minutes apart. It was a quiet and crisp morning on our way. As we drove up Hospital Hill, we could hear someone screaming out of an open second story window, and I thought "That might be me pretty soon." We arrived at exactly 7:00 a.m. In the hospital, I was put in a gown, given an enema, and had my crotch shaved—the nurse cut my labia with the razor. Leo joined me after the prep. I felt euphoric and lost my sense of time throughout my labor. An hour felt like a minute. There was such a surreal and mystical quality to the process. Leo coached me with my breathing, and I dug my fingernails into his arm with each contraction. My doctor held my hand and reassured me. He had plans to leave to do rounds, but after he checked me, said "I'm not going anywhere." He seemed very surprised that his expected long labor for me was in fact progressing very rapidly. Dad was doing rounds at the hospital that morning too and came in with a single red rose for me. Dr. R smoked in the labor room. There were ashtrays all over for him to use while he checked on me. He wore his usual cowboy boots and string tie until he had to change into scrubs. In the delivery room, I could feel the baby moving down through my body and, with each contraction, feel my cervix opening for him. I went from five to ten centimeters in five minutes and was rushed to the delivery room with barely enough time to deliver my baby (at 10:01 a.m. on August 9, 1974). The doctor handed him to me—wailing, bloody but beautiful. Stitches seemed endless. I got the shakes and became impatient. I asked my doctor how long it would take to sew me up, and he said, "You want me to do a good job, don't you?" I did, so I shut up.

The rest of the day was peaceful until the other girls started to arrive in the four-bed ward. We named our baby Byron Johnathan. I didn't sleep at all for the three days and nights at the hospital. The nurses marveled at my energy after just having had a baby. Two of the girls were first-time mothers like me, and the last girl to arrive had just had her second. She had been in Washington State and had gone into premature labor, which was stopped with medication, and then moved to Oregon where she obtained my doctor for her care. I remember her telling us after her baby was born that she was one of those people who doesn't feel physical pain, so when she had her contractions, she had to hold her hand on her abdomen to tell how far apart they were and when to push. The rest of us didn't think that was fair. I saw her baby in the nursery—big, beautiful, with black hair, and perfect like my own baby. But hers had inhaled fluid into his lungs in Washington, and it had caused pneumonia. He didn't survive. Our doctor came into the ward at about three in the morning on our second night there. He pulled the curtain around her bed and told her the bad news. She sobbed and wailed, so he arranged for her to be moved to another floor where she could be alone and wouldn't have to see our babies. Things were quieter in our ward after that.

I wanted to nurse, but I didn't know much about it. The nurses discouraged it, and while baby Byron was in the nursery, they fed him with a bottle. They also didn't bring him in during the middle of the night for me to try to breastfeed him. This left me with engorged breasts and no nipple. He was used to the rubber bottle nipple and became angry when I offered mine which was, as I said, nonexistent. After three days, we returned home. As stupid as this may sound, friends started calling about the baby, and Leo invited them to visit, and I didn't know any better than to object. A friend of ours from college spent the first few days back home with us. So I was expected to entertain him as well as try to learn how to take care of an infant. Others followed. Even though I had taken care of my siblings—in particular, my little sister Nora—I was ill-prepared for motherhood. (Now that I think about it, caring for Nora wasn't all that easy either). With my new baby, I was scared to death. Even the prospect of using a diaper pin left me in a panic. I might accidentally stick him with it! I continued my attempts to nurse, but to no avail, and after three weeks, I resorted to a bottle and formula. He was colicky and cried day and night. After the three days and nights without any sleep in the hospital, I had become exhausted after returning home, and I was still getting very little sleep. I was pretty much on my own. Leo went to work.

Mom sent over Nora, age seven, to help out. Leo's mom would visit and jostle Byron around and wrap him tightly in a receiving blanket, convinced that this would calm him, but it didn't. Sometimes I would go out on the curb in front of the house to get away from the crying. I left his bedroom window open in case I heard something untoward. I became anorexic, not intentionally but because my exhaustion left me without any appetite. I also became seriously depressed and anxious—poor Byron and poor me.

Mom asked if I would tutor my brother Doug because he wasn't doing well in math. I think this was because he wasn't interested in it but rather with his friends, bike, girls, etc. So he started coming over to our house in the afternoons. He resorted to all sorts of antics to avoid our tutoring lessons. If I mention what some of them were, he'd be mad at me, so I won't. I noticed that he was also angry, not at me but at Dad. He would rant and rave about him. I felt that his distress went beyond irritation but bordered on his being troubled. I went to Mom about this and suggested that if things didn't change between Doug and Dad, that they might have a big problem on their hands. Mom must have listened because she got back to me and said that she had talked to Dad.

Dad started taking Doug to Portland on weekends so they could spend time together. Unfortunately, on one of these occasions (when Doug was sixteen), the two of them went night skiing on their way to Portland at Mt. Hood Meadows. Doug was in flight, and he and another skier collided in midair. Doug complained to Dad about facial pain and suffering, but Dad continued on to Portland, determined that they would enjoy the weekend. While in Portland, the two visited a cigar shop, and Dad bought them some cigars for the trip home. They ran into Dad's friend who vacationed in Montana with us. He told Dad he thought Doug needed medical attention. On their way home, Dad had Doug, with his broken face, drive the car over the pass while the two of them smoked their cigars. By the time the weekend was over, Doug's face looked like he was a prizefighter who had lost his match. Dad took Doug to the hospital the next day, and X-rays determined that he had serious facial fractures and was taken directly into surgery. The next day, I visited him at the hospital. His head looked like a discolored balloon, and his eyes were little slits he could barely see out of. I cried. So maybe my speaking to Mom didn't do as much to improve Doug's life as I had hoped. This brings to mind another event involving cigars that occurred years earlier. Doug asked to try one when he saw Dad smoking one. He was about four years old at the time. Dad decided to let him try, anticipating Doug getting sick and avoiding such things in the future. However, Doug smoked the whole thing down to a nub and asked for another.

When Doug was seventeen, he went out in the desert with his pal Stewart, the two of them trying out Stew's new dune buggy. It tipped over and the roll bar was missing. Doug fractured his neck but didn't know it right away. When he went home, he complained to Dad, who didn't seem that concerned, and so Doug didn't go in to have it looked at until the next day. I think Mom finally took him in. After he was X-rayed this time, he was put in a neck brace immediately and taken into surgery for his fractured neck. Go figure. Doug has speculated that Dad wanted to make him tough. If this was the case, I think Dad went too far.

While I was continuing on with domesticity and motherhood, Sandy dropped out of college temporarily to go to Germany with her friend Carol. Sandy was leaving a few romances behind that may have been, in part, her motivation to go. In her freshman year at U of Portland, she was involved with an abusive guy that she dumped and then took up with Mark, the guy she knew from high school. She was on and off again with him. In her first letter to me from Germany, she wrote, "Sorry I haven't written before this. I didn't have your address and I still don't. I called Mom on Tuesday night to tell her that I decided to stay here until April. She was in a real fine mood—after yelling at me for not writing, she told me 20 minutes of news from home (all bad). Because no one had heard from me she cried herself to sleep out of worry . . . ." (Mom had a different version than Sandy's-Mom stating that Sandy was incommunicado during her entire stay in Europe). I started getting other letters from her that concerned me. She and Carol were working on an army base as cocktail waitresses. Sandy was a slender, leggy natural blonde who attracted a lot of male attention. She wore her jeans incredibly tight, and she could pull it off. In one letter, she described a man chasing her around with a knife after hours in the basement of the tavern where she worked because he was jealous about someone else she was seeing. Then she started writing about medical concerns, and it didn't sound to me as if she was getting proper treatment there. I wrote to suggest she hightail it home, but I don't think the letter reached her in time. She later wrote that she was getting my letters late because I hadn't written "airmail" on them or provided enough postage. Her symptoms subsided, and she and Carol started traveling again. This time, they purchased Eurail passes to Holland and Denmark, and Sandy became sick again on the train and wound up in a Copenhagen hospital with meningitis.

Sandy was the first in our family to travel to Slovenija. She went by train on her own, not knowing a word of the language. She had written to our cousin Yanko about visiting, and she had arranged for him to meet her at the train station. On the train, the conductor offered her a sleeping compartment, but later on after she had fallen asleep, he sneaked in and attacked her. She had to yell, holler, and fight to get him off her. She said she had thought he was trying to be nice when he had offered her the berth. When she got to her destination, Yanko wasn't there. Without being able to communicate, it was a long arduous journey to find her way to his rectory. After she got there, the two flew around in his little car to visit all the relatives. They also traveled over the border into Italy. She wrote to me that a neighbor of Yanko who had moved to Australia was home visiting his parents and could speak both Slovenian and English, making it easier for her to communicate with Yanko and our other relatives. She described Yanko's village in a letter as follows: "It is so different there. In Yanko's village, few people have cars, bathtubs, or even toilets. Everyone owns chickens and a milk cow and they transport their farm goods with wooden carts pulled by oxen. The landscape was beautiful and there's no pollution (air, water, or noise)."

She went on to describe her homesickness after her return to Germany—"By the time you get this letter Thanksgiving will be over. How was it? Did you go to the coast again? It makes me homesick thinking about Thanksgiving. I miss everyone (Mark too). Byron will be all grown up by the time I get home. I'll miss Christmas turkey. The weather is miserable, there's no T.V. or radio-What am I doing here? I think all this foreign air has gone to my head." A few months later she wrote again—"I just got your Christmas card. It's January 6. I don't know if you mailed it late or if the mail is just really slow. I got a letter from Dad too. It took him two months to write—I was beginning to think he forgot about me or something. In both letters was mentioned that I was in Egypt . . . Anyway I never left Stuttgart. Even if I had been invited [by Carol] I couldn't have gone because I have that job and I work six days a week. I've been here alone for 2 ½ weeks and I was so lonely and homesick on Christmas you wouldn't believe it. Things are going pretty well. Work is really fun. That place is a real zoo. The people all drink so much they make Dad and Leo look like tea teetotalers. Even I'm starting to drink too much. Every night after work I have 5 or 6 drinks waiting for me . . . How is Mark doing in school? Have you talked to him or seen him at all? I wish someone would give me advice on what to do. I can't do it alone. I don't want to stay here forever but the thought of coming home and having to face the music scares me to death . . ." It seemed to me that Sandy had some ambivalence about Mark.

But then there was another member of our family that traveled to Slovenija about the same time. Our cousin Greg was also attending college, dropped out with a couple of college buddies, and off they went to Europe. Greg, like Sandy, was the middle child, which may have induced a more haphazard lifestyle. Anyway, he and his friends started out in Ireland then traveled to England with their tent and backpacks in tow. It was nighttime, and they found their way in the dark to a campsite and pitched their tent. But they were wakened in the morning by the sound of something hitting the outside of the tent. When they emerged to explore the cause, they discovered that they had settled down for the night in the middle of a golf course. Golf balls were the cause of the assault. They decided to buy a "piece of shit car" to get from England to France and for the remainder of the trip, but when it started having trouble, they stopped at a service station. The mechanic advised they refrain from driving the car because it was an accident waiting to happen. The boys didn't know how to dispose of it, so they found a junkyard, filled the gas tank with sugar, and struck the car's exterior with a hammer so as to discourage anyone else from trying to drive it. They separated when Greg decided to find his way to Slovenija but had given both of his friends Yanko's address. All three of the boys arrived about the same time. Yanko did what he always does. He was always hospitable, and so were the rest of the lot. He took them to sites of interest and to see the relatives. Greg remembers visiting our grandfather's brother, Rafael (Yanko's father), who Greg described as a very old man that looked like Gram-pa. Yanko, being the Catholic priest that he was, became the family's core—in Slovenija and even reaching across the continent to family in both North and South America. Not only was he a welcoming influence when family visited him, but he also traveled to see family abroad who had left. Later on, Greg would also travel to Argentina to meet family there. It was in Argentina that he met another of Gram-pa's brothers who Greg said greatly resembled our grandfather too.

In the meantime, Leo had been selling office equipment out of his van and got acquainted with some lawyers in town who encouraged him to go to law school. It had been something he had thought about before. Besides that, his job bored him. So he applied. I was worried about how we would manage this because Byron wasn't even a year old. He was put on the waiting list at Willamette University but accepted at the University of Puget Sound in Tacoma, Washington. We went up to look for an apartment there, and the prospects were dismal. Just in time, he got a call about being accepted at WU—a week before school started. We sold our house, and he went over and found an apartment. The next week, we moved. I cried when I saw the apartment. The carpets had just been cleaned and were still wet, and a stale cigarette smell lingered in the air. The apartment was located in what was known as felony flats because families of people in the local penitentiary waited there for their imprisoned family members to return. In spite of all this, I got to like the apartment because it was well laid out and spacious.

Previously in Bend (when Byron was only four months old), I heard a thump in his room while we were still in bed one morning. I told Leo I was going to see what was going on. I found

Byron on the carpet, on his back with the wind knocked out of him. We still have no idea how he managed to get out of his crib on his own. We turned his crib upside down so that the legs stuck up in the air, so if he fell out again, he wouldn't have as far to fall. When we moved into the new apartment, we did the same thing with his crib. However, Salem wasn't dry like Bend, and this time we placed the mattress on a not-quite-dry carpet. A few months later, I noticed something black that seemed to be growing on the wall above his crib. I decided it was mold, and so I pulled the mattress away from its resting place, and to my horror, the carpet and underside of the mattress were covered with mold. I panicked and called Leo. We had to scrub everything down and figure out how to place the crib so this wouldn't happen again but also keep it low to the ground. After all this, Byron developed an allergy to mold. His pediatrician suggested putting shallow pans of formaldehyde in each room, closing up the house and letting it stand for forty-eight hours. We had to evacuate and stay elsewhere, but it did seem to help. The formaldehyde must have killed the mold.

After my initial adjustment to our move, I loved college life in spite of the fact that I wasn't attending myself. In fact, this made it even better. Leo's exposure to law school afforded us with good friendships and a social life. I felt alive again. One of our new friends was Susie B. from Lee House. She had since married her childhood sweetheart, Tom P., who Leo met in one of his classes.

The first time they came over together, I said to Susie, "I know you!" and she said, "I know you too." Another member of the group of friends that formed was Nathan, who Susie had dated in undergraduate school and who had been my next door neighbor in the apartment that shook. Leo and I had run into Nathan while we were on our honeymoon in Victoria a few years earlier. Another friend's girlfriend was still back East, and so we had him and Nathan (the bachelors) over often for meals and company. Later, the girlfriend moved to Oregon, and they got married during law school—on Valentine's Day in Reno, in fact.

We took Byron everywhere with us during law school. His only friends there were adults until I got into a babysitting co-op. He was well received by the law school crowd. He was a somber child. He often had a deadpan expression but, to go along with it, a wry and dry sense of humor. For instance, when he was only a year and a half, friends came over to visit one evening. Our friend Tom was sitting next to Byron who looked over at him with a frown and said "Tom, you farted" in a loud voice so everyone could hear. Tom denied having done so, but everyone chided him for trying to blame it on a little kid. Byron had a hollow square plastic toy with cutout shapes on it. The object of the toy was to put corresponding shapes in the right cutout. Byron would challenge the guys to a timed contest, and he won every time. I worried that I might fall short as far as protecting him from the dangers that lurked out in the world and that I might also not have a handle on setting limits and providing the right amount of discipline. I was also an impatient person, somewhat like my dad, and resorted to yelling at times. I have questioned whether or not my shortcomings had to do with his serious nature.

His father, on the other hand, never had a problem with him. Was it because Byron recognized the gender difference and knew he wouldn't get away with anything with his dad? I used to take Byron to his favorite park in Salem with a playground. When I told him it was time for us to leave, he protested—in fact, refused. I would try to get him back in his stroller, but he'd stiffen his legs to make it impossible for me to get him into it. So I would have to resort to pushing the stroller with one hand while holding onto him with the other and dragging him back home. I decided to try time-outs, which were suggested to me. I would announce that he had to spend some time in his room. Then I could hear him tearing up the place while he was in there—literally tearing up all his books and breaking his toys. It seemed that he might have regretted this at some point, but the loss of his belongings never seemed to bother him. Matters always became worse when Leo was absent, especially for long periods during his study for finals. When this happened, all hell broke loose, and there seemed to be nothing I could do about it.

Leo adored Byron, and Byron seemed smitten with his dad. One day Leo was fixing the bathtub surround and using some chipboard, which he had purchased at the local hardware store. Byron stood patiently observing his dad. I could hear him ask "What's that, Dad?" and Leo told him he was working with chipboard. After that, Byron repeated the words over and over—"Is that chipboard, Dad?" "Chipboard, Dad?" "Chipboard . . . chipboard . . . chipboard . . . chipboard, Dad?" He must have liked the sound of the words. Leo made him a tool chest of his own, and we found a plastic drill and jigsaw that made noise when you pulled a string and other tools—plastic hammer, screw driver, etc. He spent hours "working" with his tools. From a very early age, we could take him to a restaurant, and he sat quietly for hours, listening to adult conversation. This was usually when my parents would invite us out. He seemed a little man of few words. Maybe his being the firstborn had to do with all this. When he was only a few years old, his favorite songs were "Lazy Bones" and "My Walking Stick" by Leon Redbone and "Bungle in the Jungle" by Jethro Tull. He would say "Play Wazy Bones, Daddy." It took until Byron was an adult for us to start communicating and understanding each other better. I think his experience as a married man with children contributed to this. And I began to recognize the similarities between us that may have contributed to our difficulty with each other—introversion and a quiet but headstrong personality. There seems to be a pattern on my father's side of the family developing. I don't know how far back it goes, but it is evident as far back as I have knowledge about these family members. My grandmother was the firstborn who bore my father as her firstborn. My father then had me, a girl and his firstborn. Then I had Byron, a boy and my firstborn. Then Byron had Sage, a girl and his firstborn. All of us share similar personality traits. I'll have to wait and see if the pattern continues.

After the first semester of law school, we moved to a little house with a fenced backyard near North Salem High—1155 13th NE—so that Byron would have a safe place to play. It became party central. No one had much money, but we had fun in spite of this—maybe even more than if we had. The law students formed a softball group with the Pickle Emporium Tavern for its sponsor. Byron was the team mascot, and he wore a T-shirt with a pickle man on the front like the players. He loved pickles in general, so he loved the shirt even more. There were lots of school parties, and my favorites were the fifties theme parties with poodle skirts, greased back hair, and swing dancing. We all found 1957 Chevy cars to drive to the dances. We were at a particularly raucous one of these when Leo slipped on some beer on the floor, did the splits, and then split his pants from front to back, exposing his black brief. He seemed unscathed by the event and continued dancing. We also had BYOB parties at our house with Frisbee contests in our full basement. This involved having the lights out with the goal of hitting someone on the opposing team with the glowing Frisbee to score a point. Our friend R always smoked a cigarette while playing this game and couldn't figure out why she kept getting hit.

Susie P. and I once won a bet when someone told us that if you're drinking, swallowing a spoonful of mayonnaise will result in barfing. Susie said that we could do that without barfing –"Can't we Cheryl"?, she asked. "Sure" I replied, and we proved it by downing a big spoonful each without the others' expected result. Then Susie said that, in fact, we could even down a spoonful of mustard without any problem, so we did that too. Another pastime at our parties was listening to Dr. Demento's radio program. Dr. D featured strange songs, some of which none of us had heard of then or since. One of our favorites was "I'm My Own Grandpa," and yes, this is possible, as described in the song. Another favorite was "The Freckle Song" by the Pearl Trio/ Larry Vincent. It starts out-"She has freckles on her butt, she is nice". Tom and Sue had holiday theme parties at their apartment. A pumpkin carving contest was always included for the Halloween theme parties that remained a fixture for years after school ended. There was a downside to our partying, however, especially when parties occurred at our house. They often went on until early hours of the morning. I had to get up with Byron by four or five o'clock in the morning because he was an early riser. Other partiers could sleep in. Sometimes I would get so desperate for sleep that I left our house to get away from the noise and tried to sleep in our car, but that never worked very well.

While on 13th Street, Byron liked to play out in the backyard. Someone who had lived there before us had buried garbage there, unbeknownst to us. Well, Byron discovered a bottle of insect repellent that had worked its way above ground. When he came to the back door, I noticed what smelled like perfume on his breath. I asked him if he had put anything in his mouth, and he showed me the bottle. It was empty. I called poison control, and they told me to get some ipecac. I ran down to the pharmacy and gave it to him, and we waited 'til he vomited. He liked to play in the bathtub with his toys, so I would fill a bath during the day. On one occasion, I went in to check on him, and he was in the process of swallowing shampoo. I called the ER, and they told me to bring him in. We sat in the waiting room for what seemed like forever. Then there was quite a commotion. Police and medical personnel flew in with a man on a stretcher and all manner of drama occurred. The press showed up. Holly Holcomb, the Oregon State Police Superintendent, had been shot. We finally got our turn as far as being seen. I was told that with shampoo, ipecac is not recommended. They just gave him a lot of water to flush him out and told me to expect some diarrhea. Byron liked fire engines. We got him a Tonka fire engine for his birthday, and he played with it for hours. It had an extending ladder and a hose that sprayed real water when you hooked it up to a garden hose. He also loved trains and ambulances and would imitate such noises whenever he heard them. We got him a horse on a platform with springs that he liked to ride. He named him Nugget. When he was angry at one of us or thought he was in trouble, he jumped on Nugget and rode off, yelling, "Go, Nugget, go."

Law school beach trips were a frequent occurrence. The most memorable was one in which four of us couples decided to rent an ocean home for the weekend. We looked through the paper and called to book a place that sounded perfect. When the time came, we drove over to the coast and explored the neighborhood where our vacation rental was located. We drove by almost palatial homes with beautiful exposure to the coast line until we found the right address on a minuscule little house with no view. It was so small that we didn't know how we'd all fit in. S and R took the basement because they had a small son. This didn't turn out too well for them, though, because it was dark and dank and had spiders everywhere. Leo and I had an alcove off the living room that had a curtain to separate it from the main part of the room. We got this because we had an even smaller son. The other two couples slept on the living room floor with sleeping bags. The kitchen (behind the living room) was so narrow that only two people could fit in at a time. In addition, it rained most of the weekend, so we spent a lot of time watching TV or playing board games. In spite of all this, we had fun. Another time, the guys went to the coast to do some crabbing with their crab rings. They returned to our house with a few big ice chests full of crabs and not sure what to do with them. So people started calling everyone they could think of, and pretty soon there were about thirty people stuffed into our little house. The crab water boiled over on the stove and filled the kitchen, and guests grabbed crabs, slapped them on paper plates, and ate all over the house. The next morning, our kitchen floor and living room carpet were soaked with crab juice. We worked on cleaning it as best we could, but there was always a hint of sea scent in our home after the event. I can't say that it was unpleasant, though. It simply smelled of the sea.

Sometimes when Leo and his law school chums formed study groups for finals, he would suggest that I go home with Byron to visit my parents. After all, his sisters always made frequent visits home like that. But my visit home turned out differently. On one occasion, I took the bus home to surprise Mom and Dad. Mom suggested I stay in the guest house and do my own cooking back there. I thought I would be included in evening meals, but this wasn't the case. After a day or so of sitting back there with Byron with nothing to do, I got a ticket back to Salem and called Leo from the bus depot to tell him to come pick us up. He didn't understand why the visit had been cut short. Mom had given my room to Nora as soon as I moved out. I started to get the idea that returning home, unless invited, wasn't acceptable. Mom had initially lamented my college departure, so none of this made sense to me. Maybe she got used to the idea of all her kids leaving and that she might just like it, or maybe she was just nudging me out of the nest. There was one other unannounced visit that sticks out in my mind. Dad was on one of his hunting trips when I went by in the evening, and Mom was sitting in the family room in front of the television in her bathrobe. Her speech was slurred. Then she stumbled and weaved back and forth down the hallway toward her bedroom. This was the first of numerous times I would see her so inebriated. Nora was still living at home and later confided in me that she had dealt with the same type of occurrences with Mom.

This is also about the time when Doug started college at Oregon State University. Mom drove over for "Mom's Weekend." Moms of the students were guests for the weekend and their kids were supposed to entertain them and participate in social activities and events. After Mom got there, she remained in her assigned dorm room for the extent of the weekend in spite of the fact that Doug tried to persuade her to join in on the festivities. But none of his pleas did any good. This all led to our wonder about what in the heck was going on with Mom. She had a hysterectomy a few years earlier that seemed to have thrown her into a funk, which she never really seemed to recover from. Another time, Mom unknowingly drank some punch at a party that was laced with LSD and had flashbacks after that. Of course, there may be other factors that none of us will ever know about.

All this didn't stop Doug from having fun at college. He had a propensity for losing toenails while engaged in his athletic pursuits. When this happened at college, he made a toenail necklace that he boxed up and mailed to a female friend of his. Some of the college girls had a crush on him and would bake brownies for him and leave them in his locker. But one of the guys in his frat was jealous, and so he put laxatives in some brownies he cooked up, placed them in Doug's locker, and made up a note as if the girls had made them. Doug ate some, shared some with some of the guys in his frat, and the brownies nearly killed him. After he got out of the hospital, he began to suspect what had happened after he found out the friends he had shared the brownies with had developed milder symptoms. He found out who had done him in, and so he and the few buddies sneaked into the guy's room and sewed dog shit into his mattress. It took quite a while before the cause of the odor was discovered by the culprit.

When Doug came home for a break, I was also in Bend while Leo was studying for finals at law school. I asked if he might want to head down to the Woolen Mill for a beer. He was enthused about the idea but questioned how he could get in because he wasn't twenty-one yet. We thought about it awhile, and it may have been Dad who suggested we make use of his famous mustache. So we attached it on Doug's face, and off we went. We found a table in the pub. Doug was nervous about giving the waitress our order, so I offered advice about how he might approach the topic. We practiced a little before the waitress arrived, and by the time she arrived to take our order, he acted like a pro. Our drinks were delivered and everything was going well until one of his teachers from high school, sitting at the bar, recognized Doug and came over to let him know he'd been had. The teacher didn't rat him out, though, so we spent the rest of our time at the pub with our drinks. From that point on, Doug made regular visits with the help of the famous mustache. Dad purchased the thing years earlier when he saw it at some store and decided to play a trick on his mother. He had one of us take a picture of him with it on and sent it to her in the mail. She called after receiving the photo and said "Where did you get the fake mustache?" Dad decided he wasn't as clever as he thought he was, but in spite of this setback, he kept it anyway. After he died, I discovered it in the top drawer of his bureau. He never did get rid of it.

We drove over the mountain on our way to Bend in November 1976 for Thanksgiving. It just so happened to be Doug's nineteenth birthday too, and so Dad planned a birthday party for him. Doug invited Scot and Stuart, and we were there with little Byron. I think one of the reasons Dad planned the party was so that he could try out his recently assembled pig pit—an idea he got while at a stockholder's meeting with Mom at the Coco Palms hotel in Kauai, Hawaii. Dad did the rock work for the pit, and then he and Leo built the wooden roof for cover the next summer and a machinist friend, Les Gribskov, fashioned the spit and motor. Everyone gathered at the kitchen window as he and the guys headed out to attach the pig to the spit. It was snowing that night, and the snow on the ground lit up the night sky. Two-year-old Byron peered out the window in awe at the men working. The pig was secured and began to turn on the spit. The guys returned to the kitchen, and everyone gazed out the window in anticipation of a fine birthday meal. Then the spit started to gyrate in a peculiar manner, and the pig's body twisted in two different directions at once then split in two and fell in the fire beneath with a great grease-induced explosion. The flames roared and leapt to the wooden roof. Then the backyard lit up like a torch, and the guys ran out with pans and shovels to throw snow on the flames. Byron made loud fire engine sounds as he stared in amazement, as the rest of us did. He was of the age when siren noises held much interest, and he had a repertoire at his disposal—ambulance, fire truck, police siren, and train track alert. Wee-ooh, wee-ooh, wee-ooh. When the fire was finally out, the remains of the pig were mostly charred. Dad sadly lay what was left on the kitchen counter—enough that was edible for a small taste for everyone, and that was all. Family and guests had to settle for the dishes that Mom had prepared to accompany the pork, and of course, the birthday cake. It didn't take Dad long, though, to consult with Les on how to improve on the pig pit. In no time, it was up and running with the help of a stronger spit, motor, and a tin movable lining for the wooden roof. Then there was nothing to stop Dad from trying all sorts of things on his spit.

We went home for Christmas break during that winter too and stayed at Leo's parents' home. One afternoon, I returned from an outing and overheard his father talking to his mom in the kitchen. He was telling her that he wasn't feeling well. I tucked that bit of information away and only later reflected back on what I heard that day. After our return to Salem, we started getting calls about Welborn's health problems. He had had an accident on his loader shortly before he retired from the county road department. (After his cowboy years, they had moved to Bend so that they could find jobs with benefits). The loader accident led to his developing a gangrenous gallbladder, which is likely, at least in part, the reason he had complained of feeling poorly a few weeks earlier. In addition, it was discovered that he had an aneurysm ready to burst without an intervention—namely surgery—but the infection had to be under control first. He was literally a ticking time bomb. Dad called one evening to tell me that if Leo wanted to see his father alive again, we needed to come back to Bend right away. When I got off the phone, I relayed this message to Leo in so many words. But he didn't want to go. He called his dad on the phone while he was in the hospital, but Welborn had trouble talking. I think Leo was in denial about the seriousness of the situation, and that if he didn't go home, everything would turn around. Unfortunately, that didn't happen.

I got a call on the morning of February 9. It was his mother, and she told me that Welborn had just died. Leo was in class, so I went directly over with Byron in the stroller. I opened the big double doors of the lecture hall. Everyone turned around to look at me. Leo said later that when he saw me at the door, he knew what that meant. A friend of ours, Mike L., followed him out of the hall and asked if there was anything he could do for him. We went home, and this was when he broke down and wept uncontrollably. I tried to hold him, but he seemed inconsolable. We went back to Bend for the funeral. After our return to Salem, I secretly started to think about having another baby. After all, Byron was two and a half already, but I knew Leo would want to get out of school before he'd even consider such a thing. On the other hand, a baby might bring some joy to help make up in some part for his and his family's loss. So I told him that it was too early in the month to get pregnant, so we wouldn't have to worry about birth control. It really was a little early, so I wasn't sure anything would happen, but it did. I didn't say anything about suspecting I might be pregnant until I went to the doctor and found out for sure. When I broke the news, his response was mixed, but secretly, I was thrilled, and so was Leo's mother. This baby became her lifeline and, I believe, her favorite grandchild.

Thetford was a lodge out in the woods owned by Willamette University. It could be rented out by students for weekends. Weekend parties were scheduled, and lots of law students, significant others, and kids attended. There was a large space on the main floor that included a kitchen. An open staircase led to a narrow landing with railings and with a bathroom door at the center of the landing. On the opposite ends of the landing were two large bedrooms with bunk beds. On one particular weekend, some of the guys were playing poker while the women and kids started getting ready for bed. One friend (R) was eight months pregnant, and I was just pregnant, both of us with our second child. She had gone to bed and was in one of the lower bunks in the bedroom on the right. I had just found an empty bed on the top bunk. Another couple had gone to bed together in the other bedroom, and the wife was also pregnant, about four months along. One of the guys below playing cards noticed a naked woman head into the bathroom from the bedroom on the left, and so all eyes waited until she would be coming back out. When she did, it was obvious that she wasn't a woman after all, but a guy with long hair. He was the one with the pregnant wife back in their bed. Well, he headed toward the bedroom on the right, and everyone downstairs laughed and waited to see what would happen. I spotted him on his way into our bedroom from my top bunk and as he worked his way through the lower bunks to find his wife. He snuggled up against the eight-months-pregnant friend, put his arms around her, and felt her immense belly—much larger than his wife's. She turned around and yelled, and he high-tailed it back to his room. The guys below laughed after seeing his naked body and flowing hair streak by, and so did we.

There were two other law student wives who had children, so I spent time with them during the days. One of the women (R) met her husband while he was stationed in Europe during the Vietnam War. R had a child by a first marriage when they met and had been told that she would be unlikely to conceive again in the course of her second marriage because of some sort of birth complications that had occurred. She told of her horrific birth experience on the army base there. She was in the hospital for about a week afterward, and there were some women with preemies who couldn't nurse, so she agreed to let the hospital staff pump her breasts for extra milk to feed these babies. She described how, upon returning home, the milk just kept on coming, and she became engorged and developed breast infections. She would describe to us girls what had become of her breasts after their ordeal—resembling socks with sand in the bottom. When she became pregnant again, a surprise to her and everyone else, she fretted about another birth. I suggested that I could coach her in Lamaze techniques, and she agreed. She didn't want to bother with formal training in this area. So we met at her house or mine for instruction. When the time came, we got word that she had gone to the hospital. According to her husband, things hadn't gone very well, and she had to be sedated. The baby was born by cesarean section. He weighed eleven pounds—the biggest newborn I had ever seen.

The other woman was a daughter of a career military officer, and it showed. She and her husband met while he was enlisted during the Vietnam War too. They had a son close in age to Byron. She got me involved in a babysitting co-op where a group of moms would trade child care for one another. She also advised me about nursing and hooked me up with La Leche League, which resulted in my success in nursing my second baby. We traded sitting often because our little boys enjoyed each other's company. She also started a book club, and I agreed to be a member. Members were to read the assigned book and meet bimonthly. We brought our children to her home, and they played outside while we discussed our books. One day, one of the little boys started hitting her dog out in the fenced backyard, and she witnessed this. She ran out and started yelling at the kid. When his mother saw what she was doing, she went out and pulled her son away from our host, and they started shouting at each other. The rest of us just stood in the kitchen and watched this play out in the backyard. The mother of the little boy announced that she was leaving with her child and wouldn't be returning. One after the other left until I was the only mother left other than my host. I didn't know what to say, so I said nothing. That was the end of the book club. But we still took turns watching each other's kids. I always rather admired her direct no-nonsense approach with others, and I found that, although it wasn't in my nature, I did better with her when I did the same with her. After both of us had our second child, she felt comfortable watching my infant. One time, when I went to pick the kids up, she let me know that my baby had been fussy, so she had offered her breast and this had worked like a charm. She still had breast milk for her own baby—nothing like having a wet nurse at your disposal.

Sandy returned from Germany and, surprisingly, started up with Mark again. However, her friend from Germany was still interested and began calling our folks' home. His name was Herman. Now Herman also sent tapes to Sandy proclaiming his undying love. She let me listen to some back in our folks' guest house, where she was living temporarily, and I have to admit, I was impressed with the guy's ardor. I asked if she might consider maintaining a relationship with him, but she said no because this would require her to remain in Europe. Unfortunately, Mark was waiting for her one day in the guest house where the tape recorder was, and so he listened to one of the tapes from Herman. The two decided to marry, but it seems that his hearing the tape further complicated their relationship.

Leo, Byron, and I stayed with Leo's mother for part of the summer between the second and third law school years. Sandy had worked at the Woolen Mill Tavern before going to Germany, and so when she returned, we'd go there for fun. She still knew some of the staff there from before. One night, we all headed down there. I was drinking only club soda because of my pregnancy, but everyone else was drinking beer. After a while, the club soda and my condition made me feel like I had to pee a lot. I had to keep going to the bathroom, but at some point, I got tired of getting up so often, so I guess I held it too long. I finally couldn't hold it any longer, but when I tried to go, nothing happened. I went back to our table and told Leo I needed to go home because I wasn't able to pee and thought a warm bath might help. When we got to his mom's, she was asleep. I tried running the tap in the bathroom to get things going, but that didn't work. So I drew a bath and sat in the warm water, but nothing. I was starting to panic because my discomfort was mounting. I decided to call home for Dad. He had been asleep but told me to meet him at his clinic where a catheter kit was available. So Leo and I went. Dad gave me the catheter kit and wanted to know what I wanted to do. I didn't really want him to insert the catheter, so I told him I'd take it with me, but this decision was difficult to make because I was suffering so. After we got to Leo's mom's house, I had to wake her up. She was an LPN, so she knew how to manage the situation. It was still weird to have my mother-in-law doing this. I couldn't believe the amount of urine that she collected in the pail next to the bed! It was such a relief, I can't even put it into words. The experience taught me never to hold my pee again, which led to my going in public if necessary—no different from what sensible Europeans do anyway. Later on, Dad told me that when he had worked in the ER, guys would frequently present there with over full bladders. Dad's theory was that they were too macho to be seen peeing too often while at the taverns. These guys got the same treatment in the ER that I did. Dad also said that my enlarging uterus sitting above my bladder had contributed to my predicament.

Out of the blue, Mom called me in Salem to tell me she wanted to send me to Chicago to visit Francesca and Francesco. I wondered about her motivation related to this sudden trip. Were either of my grandparents ill? Leo's mom agreed to watch over Byron while I was gone. I was five months pregnant and reluctant to leave my three-year-old, but it seemed the plans were made. So off I went. I still remember the flight very well. With takeoff, the noise or the change in elevation seemed to have disturbed my unborn baby. There was a flurry of motion inside me to let me know that something had riled him. And during our descent, the same thing occurred. It was as though he was doing somersaults in there. This was on August 16, 1977, and while in flight, there was an announcement that Elvis Presley had just died. I recalled years earlier having seen him at the Seattle World's Fair in 1962. I had also witnessed his decline on television and in magazine articles, and it all made me sad.

After I arrived in Chicago, my Uncle Jack picked me up at the airport and took me to my grandparents' home—my birthplace. Everything seemed in order. Gram-ma stormed around in the kitchen while Gram-pa read his newspaper at the kitchen table. Aunt Jean and my cousin Cindy took me to Chicago the next day. We visited the Museum of Science and Industry, and I got a computer picture of myself done there. I sat in front of a camera, and out came my face made up of computer symbols. It sort of reminded me of being there with Dad and Sandy years earlier and making the record "Pals and Buddies." Mom had encouraged me to visit some of her relatives as well. I sat in the open porch with Aunt Esther—my paternal grandfather's cousin—the one who had been a second mother to my mom (in fact, maybe more of a mother), and Mom's best friend Carol's own mother. Esther was blind by that time. This was related to her having taken Contac tablets for her allergies, or so my mother said. She talked about her friendship with my grandmother. She was as delightful as ever. I also visited Mom's spinster cousins at their home. They had been reduced from three to two with the death of one of the sisters, having lived together all their lives. The two remaining made me tea, and we chatted about family history—they were quite the gossips. My uncle Eddie picked me up one day and took me to his home for a dinner that Alice had prepared. Then I got to see about three hours' worth of slides of their vacations all over the place. I saw Uncle Norbert and Aunt Lois at their house one night too. Then there were Aunt Jean, Uncle Jack, and Joe Remec, Dad's best friend. Ken and Kathy took me to Chicago for shopping and lunch. Ken mentioned that they might visit at Christmas time, but I told them I might be awfully busy having my new baby. They were flabbergasted. They hadn't even noticed that I was pregnant! The next day—my departure day—Gram-ma made me breakfast at the kitchen table. Gram-pa was nowhere in sight, so she ran around the house looking for him so that he could say good-bye. Then I heard her yelling at him to come say good-bye to me. He was hiding in a back room, but he finally emerged, tearful, for our farewell. I understood his reticence about facing me that day. He was never good with family departures, for when he left his family many years earlier, he never saw any of them again. Then I was back on the plane and headed back to Oregon. Leo picked me up on the other end at the airport. We stayed in a hotel, before our return to Bend.

Sandy and Mark's wedding was at St. Francis, and the reception was at Aspen Hall in Shevlin Park in October 1977. Mom, Sandy, and I had gone to Portland a few months before the wedding to shop. I still remember Mom trying on a full-length lavender dress, which was low cut at the bodice and showed off her ample bosom. Sandy and I thought she looked great in it, but she was skeptical. She wanted to know if it was too flashy. We reassured her that it wasn't and that she ought to buy it. When Mom arrived at the wedding, I'll have to say that she and the dress were a big hit with the male population there. The fact that some of the men were inebriated made matters worse. Sandy and Mark had some sort of disagreement before they arrived at the reception, and they were late. In spite of this, the bride was beautiful, and the groom was handsome. I was matron of honor and about seven months pregnant by then. Byron was the ring bearer and Nora was the flower girl. The reception became raucous. Dad and his chums were betting on their arm wrestling contests. The ride home with Dad was frightening, as we weaved our way up the steep grade out of the park and through town before we got home.

Back to school for the third year, my second pregnancy left us out of some of the law school social life, but Sandy, Mark, and Doug and his new girlfriend Diane from OSU, where Doug had started college, visited often on weekends. Law student friends visited and often mingled with our family members. One thing that really bothered me during this pregnancy was that Leo had put a dead TV out on our back steps. It remained there, and I had difficulty navigating around it as my girth spread. I asked repeatedly for him to move it. After a while, it felt like I was nagging, so I decided to move it myself. This resulted in a back strain that I endured throughout the rest of my pregnancy. In retrospect, I should have kicked the damn thing off the step.

When I was about seven months pregnant, we would meet up with other law school friends at the Ram Pub. My friend Peggy had given me some of her maternity clothes for my pregnancy. One was a navy-blue short sheath that I wore to the tavern. I got up to pee, as I had learned my lesson about holding it. It was hot in there too, so I decided to get some fresh air outside before returning to our table. Some guy followed me out. He made small talk at first and then asked if I wanted to go to a party he was heading to. This seemed odd to me considering my condition. I asked myself if he had noticed my bulging abdomen and decided to point it out to him. He started apologizing profusely and then ambled down the sidewalk, presumably to his party. I have to say that I was somewhat flattered that he had found me attractive—at least from behind.

I had a good gynecologist when I first moved to Salem. In fact, I had gone to him when I had one of my major pregnancy scares, and he had helped me out with a morning-after pill. My friend Jan from Seattle U and Eric, now her husband, had moved to Salem when he started law school at Willamette. She was expecting her first baby. We palled around together, and she recommended her obstetrician whose office was closer to my home than my doctor's, so I decided to switch doctors. We only had one car at the time, and Leo usually took it to school. I got around with a stroller for Byron and the groceries I collected while on our outings. Jan introduced me to the university pool, and after that, I became an avid swimmer. My swim team experience during my pubescent years had put me off the sport. After I started going to the new doctor, I grew to dislike him. He seemed arrogant and cold. Looking back, I wish I had returned to my good Salem doc, but I didn't.

All our law school friends, other than Tom and Sue, left for Christmas break by the time I was expected to have my baby. The days got closer and closer to Christmas when we had planned to go to Bend for the holidays. But nothing happened until December 22. I felt contractions in the morning. I felt weepy, sitting at the table with Byron, knowing he would have a new brother or sister soon. I called Leo at work. We took Byron to R's and went to the hospital about 11:30 a.m., but I was sent home. This labor was different from my first, which had progressed with a regular course. This time, my labor would start and stop and did so all day long. By 5:00 p.m., we decided to pick up Byron, but when we got to R's, my contractions started up again, so we went back to the hospital. Again, I was sent home, and so we picked up Byron and some chicken pot pies on the way home. I had been working part time in the nursery at the YMCA with a young girl, Cheri Swanson, who had also agreed to stay with Byron while I had the new baby. Around 9:30 p.m., the contractions became more regular, about ten minutes apart. Leo and I started watching Johnny Carson, and around midnight, I was about to give up and go to bed when the fourth contraction at six minutes apart broke my water as I got up off the couch—it soaked me from the crotch down, leaving a puddle on the living room floor. I called Cheri. By the time she arrived, my contractions were down to three then two minutes apart. I was getting anxious because my first labor had been so fast and because now my labor had really kicked in.

After prep at the hospital, things went fast. My breathing controlled my contractions, but the shaking between, I couldn't control. The nurse checked me again at five centimeters, and then one more contraction and it was time for the delivery room. My bearing down was difficult to control. I also lost control of my breathing, but my nurse helped me to get going again. She insisted on giving me some medication to slow the process because the doctor wasn't showing up. I said I didn't want it because I wanted to remain alert, but she gave me the shot anyway. With five or six hard pushes, the baby was born. My doctor ran in just in time to catch him coming out (at 2:21 a.m.). He had been born so fast that he was distressed and had to be whisked away to have mucus removed from his airway. Then the doctor left abruptly. We inspected our new son—his wrinkled forehead, brown downy hair, and long eyelashes. He looked quite different from Byron. For some reason, I thought they would look alike. This baby looked beat-up, and I attributed it to his more traumatic delivery. I was glad it was a boy. I had always felt so close to my sister Sandy. I hoped my first two same-sex children would develop a similar bond. A few minutes after Cam's birth, the medication kicked in, and I felt drowsy, which really pissed me off. We named our baby Cameron Joseph. The only visitors in the hospital were Tom and Sue. Tom marveled at it all and asked curious questions about the birth. Sue tried to shush him, but he persisted with his questions. This wasn't unusual for him, as he is a very inquisitive person. I answered his questions as best I could. Unlike my first birth when I was at the hospital for three days, I was discharged in the morning of December 23—only hours after having given birth. Cameron went home in a big red Christmas stocking like the rest of the holiday babies in the ward. After we got home, all hell broke loose. Cameron had his days and nights mixed up, so he was up and alert all night and slept during the day. People suggested I make loud noises to wake him up or jostle him around, but nothing worked. Leo tried to help with the new baby's care, but he came down with the flu. We had missed the first Christmas ever away from home. We decided to leave for Bend on December 26 to visit and get help. We stayed at Leo's mom's house again. This time, her help was valuable because she allowed me to get some needed rest. And being the nurse she was, she also tended to her son's ailment. We got back to Bend in time to see Sandy and Mark off to DC. They came over to see the new baby. Mark was to be pursuing a political career, and DC was the place to do that. We also went over to my folks to receive presents for us waiting under the tree and to present them with gifts and a new grandson who had traveled over the mountain with us. After the few weeks in Bend, we returned to Salem for the last law school semester.

By this time, we had moved to 263 17th Street SE off State Street. Our other house had been put up for sale, but our landlord had given us some time to find a new place. With our budget the way it was, our prospects were limited. One ad in the paper looked promising, but "no children" had been included in the property description. Three local physicians' wives had renovated the house for the purposes of renting it out. We decided to call in spite of the no children clause. We brought Byron along and pleaded our case. The women fell in love with him and agreed to rent to us. They had noticed I was pregnant, so they showed me how I might use a little laundry room nook as a nursery for the new baby when the time came. The house on 17th was OK but I never warmed up to it as I had the house on 13th. We had a next-door neighbor who seemed peculiar to me. When I was out in the backyard alone, he made some strange comments that I thought I had misinterpreted at first. He couldn't possibly be commenting on Leo's crotch, could he? I tried to avoid the guy during the time we lived there. When it came time for us to move after graduation, Leo's mother came to help us. She had gone around the periphery of the house to check and make sure we hadn't left anything behind and discovered a garbage can tipped upside down, hidden by bushes, and pushed right up against our living room windows-next to the weird neighbor's house. She announced that we must have had a Peeping Tom while living there. We went out to investigate. Leo got up on top of the garbage can and said he could see the whole living room through the gaps in the curtains, including where we usually made love or walked around naked. I suggested that this probably explained the comment the neighbor had made after we first moved in. All this made me glad we were leaving. The move back to Bend was arduous, having a small child and an infant. Friends were scarce when it came to needing help moving, so it was up to Leo and his mom who insisted on packing and repacking every box. I kept Byron and the baby occupied for the most part. The moving van was finally ready to go. We didn't get back to Bend until late. Leo's brother John helped unload everything into their mom's garage. We were to remain there until other plans could be made.

Leo went to work, and I was at his mom's with Byron and the baby. She followed me around all day long, offering help and sometimes helping when I didn't want it. For instance, when I hung diapers out on the clothesline, she followed behind me and re-pinned them "the right way." Frances was a talker, to say the least. Even when I was in the bathroom, she stood outside the door and talked to me through it. She suggested I get a job across the street at the Western Union Office for the evening shift and offered to watch the kids while I was gone. I went over to apply and was hired just like that. The owner had been a neighbor of Leo's family for years, and I knew her too. Her name was Fay. She showed me the switchboard and gave me a brief description of how to work it and then left. I was there alone when all the calls started coming in. There were flashing lights and cords that I was supposed to plug in to the right outlet in order to connect the calls. I was overwhelmed and started putting the cords willy-nilly. Then I just left. I guess I was at this new job about thirty minutes in all. Besides, I didn't want anyone else taking over with my kids.

Leo got a job in the DA's office and went up to Portland for six weeks to study for the bar at his sister's and then took the test. After he returned, we waited for the results. I came back from a walk with the kids in their buggy one day, and Leo was home in the middle of the afternoon. When I saw the look on his face, I guessed what the news would be. He had flunked the bar. This didn't surprise me too much because he pretty much slid through law school, rarely going to class and cramming for tests at the end of semesters. I lost it, anticipating a more lengthy stay with his mom and an uncertain future. We found out a few days later that he lost his job with the DA because of the failed test, but he found another job with a couple of lawyers who agreed to have him clerk for them. The pay was minimal, but I let him know that I would be looking for a rental so we could move out. I told him that if he wanted to stay at his mom's, I was planning to leave anyway. I found a little place to rent on Harmon. The months there were bleak. Cameron got a bad flu. Then he developed chronic ear infections. I took him to the pediatrician who prescribed antibiotics, which never really cleared up his ears. He cried all night long and fussed all day long. Leo took another month off work to study for the bar again. He used my parents' guest house to study. In the meantime, I was falling apart. I wept and sat huddled on the kitchen floor all day long. I couldn't eat. I thought about running away. I thought about being dead. I don't know how I took care of the boys. I had noticed after Byron was born that my lack of sleep had led to either hyperactivity, such as I experienced in the hospital after he was born, or a lethargy that replaced it after I got home which turned into a full-blown postpartum depression. I began to notice that something always seemed to happen to my brain whenever I was sleep deprived—it went haywire. This time, it was even worse. Months went by with me in this state.

Mom and Dad offered to take me to Portland for the weekend, and Leo agreed to watch the kids. But I couldn't relax in Portland either. That was another manifestation of my "condition"— debilitating anxiety. Cameron's doctor finally referred us to another doctor about the ear problem, and this doctor recommended tubes. This scared me because my baby would have to be knocked out at the hospital to place them. We decided to go ahead with the operation after a few months when his condition didn't improve. After the procedure, I remember him being placed in my lap, looking soggy and limp. Then he vomited all over me. To my amazement, shortly after this, he perked up, and we were even able to take the boys out to a restaurant to celebrate.

While we were still on Harmon, life remained sketchy. Leo had developed a condition where boils developed in his groin during his college years. Dad told us that he was familiar with such conditions, and that sometimes they could become systemic and dangerous. He had seen such during his medical training. Leo finally went to a doctor who recommended surgery this time to excise the boil. Antibiotics had been tried in the past without success. The surgeon was a friend of Dad's. After Leo got back from surgery, I brought him home. He took the afternoon off from work to recover. He lay down on our couch in the living room while I prepared dinner. When he got up off the couch, it was soaked in blood, and as he walked around in the living room, blood was everywhere. I suggested he lay down on the linoleum floor in the bathroom to contain the blood and called his doctor's on-call service. The doctor told me to get a Kotex and have him hold it in place. I questioned whether this would work but told Leo, who did what I was told. Well, this only seemed to make matters worse, and I started to become alarmed, so I called his mom. She came right over, and as soon as she saw him, she said he needed to get to the hospital right away. This time, she called the doctor. She knew him because she worked at the hospital as an LPN. She told him that we would meet him at the ER. She stayed with the kids, and I drove Leo there. He put on a pair of sweat pants for the ride, and I put a thick blanket under him in the car, for the bleeding was getting worse by the minute. When we walked into the ER, the staff behind the desk came running to us. By this time, he was soaked with blood from the waist down. They asked us if he'd been in a car accident, and we told them no, he had surgery earlier in the day. The doctor arrived shortly after us, and Leo was taken in the back. I was asked to remain in the waiting room. It turned out that an artery had been nicked and needed a repair. In the surgery room, the doctor cursed when the cauterizing equipment malfunctioned. It really had been a life-threatening event, but luckily, neither of us was aware of how serious it had been until it was all over. Leo remained weak and pale for a while after all of it. For my part, it was difficult for me to eat for a few days. It all made me feel nauseous.

There is one other event during our Harmon experience that comes to mind. Byron had been jealous of his friend in Salem before we left for Bend because his friend had contracted the chicken pox. For some reason, Byron thought this was some sort of interesting condition. (He called them the chicken hawks). The boys played with a few neighborhood kids a few doors down on Harmon. They came over one day, and the little girl was getting over a bout of it herself. A few days later, Byron broke out. I got calamine lotion and took a picture of him covered with the pox and the lotion and with a frown on his face. Cam was next. He was still in diapers, and the pox seemed to thrive in the moist environment of his diaper area. He was covered from head to toe and, in particular, his groin. I took a picture of him too. Leo passed the bar the second time around, and so he got a raise and was able to practice law. I slowly started to recover from my funk.

Cameron not only looked different from his brother. Their personalities were different too. He was easygoing and kind of goofy-a cute little guy after getting over the beat-up appearance after his birth. We shortened his name to CJ. It just seemed to fit. Byron had concerns about his brother having a bald head, so we reassured him that his brother would eventually have more hair. When it did grow in, it was wavy, wispy, and light brown. Byron's hair had always been black and coarse and with his angelic appearance to go along with it-that could be deceiving. Cam was always agreeable. If we went clothes shopping and I asked him about a certain pair of pants, shirt, or shoes, he eagerly tried them on and said he liked them. With Byron, it was a different story. He wanted to pick out his own stuff. If we asked Byron to do something—pick up his toys, for example—there was usually an argument. With Cameron, he always agreed to do whatever was suggested and then just didn't bother to do it. This trait drove Leo nuts, probably because he's the same way. CJ was affectionate. He liked to cuddle. Byron was independent and didn't like to hang out in anybody's lap for very long. In spite of their differences, they usually got along. We got CJ a baseball cap that said "Why be normal?" on it. It fit him to a T.

Byron came downstairs one night and told us that his brother wouldn't let him sleep because he kept talking about seeing a green line. We went up to check things out. CJ lay on his bed and explained that he could see a green line in front of his face. He wanted to know what that meant. We asked him more about the green line, and he described it as glowing. He continued to ponder its meaning. We told him we weren't sure what it meant. We decided to tell him that an explanation for the green line might be elusive, so maybe it was best just to call it the green line and leave it at that. So that's what he did. As an adult, he explained that it was the aftereffect of the overhead light in his room having been turned off. Who knows?

While CJ was a toddler, he had a few unusual mishaps. He had to keep his tubes in his ears for over a year. The doctor had fashioned molded earplugs that were form-fitted to his ears to prevent water from entering. We were told that caution was necessary during bathing or swimming to keep any water out of the ear canal, lest he develop an infection. The plugs had to be in place every time he was exposed to water. The inside of his ear must have felt itchy to him or something because one morning, he was coming down the staircase working a knitting needle around in his ear. He was wearing his leopard print pajamas that his grandmother Frances got for him at a garage sale. I called his ear doctor who said to bring him right in, so I loaded the boys in the car, and we raced over to the doctor's office with Cameron still in his leopard attire. The assistant sat him up in the examining chair that looked enormous compared with his little body. He sat quietly and looked around the room. The doctor came in while his assistant remained. He looked inside the ear canal and announced that there appeared to be something in there-right up against the eardrum. He added that the knitting needle didn't appear to have injured anything.

His assistant handed him an instrument so that the object might be removed. The doctor slowly and carefully removed the object. He and his assistant studied it with perplexed expressions on their faces until the assistant announced that the object appeared to be a tooth. Everyone in the room except for Cameron burst out laughing. The doctor said that this was the first time he had ever practiced dentistry. I explained that I suspected that the tooth was his brother Byron's. Byron had lost a baby tooth about a month before and had put it under his pillow for the tooth fairy. I remembered having felt for the tooth while placing his money under his pillow while he slept. I couldn't locate the tooth and assumed it had fallen on the floor and been vacuumed up in the interim between the tooth's placement under the pillow and my sneaking in with the money. I added that I suspected that Cameron may have been envious about Byron's tooth or at least felt it was a valuable commodity and decided to put it in his ear for safekeeping—until he might have an opportunity to cash in on it.

Another time, Cam was upstairs and found the snorkel, mask, and fins that I used up at Elk Lake to explore the sights below the water's surface. He was playing upstairs with friends Amy and Andy, visiting from the babysitting co-op. Their mother had dropped them off that morning. Cameron donned my mask, snorkel, and fins. The mask had prescription lenses because I'm nearly legally blind without them. This seemed to have been part of the problem as he tried to navigate the stairs with all in place. I heard a loud crash coming from the stairway. He had fallen down the stairs and into our heavy beveled glass front door. He was covered in blood. I found its source—a gash on his forehead. I'm never very good in emergencies of this nature, tending to fall apart, so I ran across the street to my neighbor (Joyce) and the friend of my parents. She offered to drive us to the hospital, recognizing that I was in no condition to do so, especially since I also had to bring my babysitting charges with us. After we got to the ER, Cameron was stitched up and no worse for wear. I called Amy and Andy's mom and explained what had happened, and she came to fetch them.

Joyce and her husband were Danish. There were many Scandinavians who settled in the Pacific Northwest because of the lumber industry, and they all stuck together. Joyce was the consummate neighbor. I could knock on her door anytime, and she'd invite me in for coffee. She was always able to lend me anything I needed to borrow. I don't think I ever asked for anything she didn't have in her well-stocked kitchen. Once, I borrowed saffron for a dish I was trying out and was surprised when I went to the store to buy some to replace what she had lent me. It was about nineteen dollars for a little bottle. Another time, my stove went kaput right in the middle of preparing dinner. I walked across the street and asked if I could borrow her oven to finish baking my dish. Instead, she suggested I bring over what I had and we could all have a buffet at her house. So that's what we did. Another time, I forgot to shop for my Christmas dinner on its eve, so on Christmas day, I headed to the store and found after driving all over town that not one was open. It just so happened that friends left a few pheasants on our back porch that day. Then I ran over to Joyce, and she scrounged up all she could to complete our holiday meal—canned yams, frozen peas, etc. Not our typical meal, but it sufficed. Both Les and Joyce were chain-smokers, and they also liked to party. They had a yearly holiday party, and we always walked across the street to join in on the festivities. One of her specialties was her Danish goose, accompanied by various pickled dishes. And then there was the aquavit, which was brought out during the holiday and accompanied by a Danish toast. Everyone would raise their glass and sing in Danish whether it was understood or not. On one year, the aquavit was poured in Styrofoam cups before the toast. I guess that's all they had that year. Everyone raised their Styrofoam cups in unison, but the aquavit started to eat through the bottom so everyone drank it down real fast. Those who weren't quick enough lost their drink to the floor. Les was the one who had fashioned the pig pit workings for Dad. He always called Joyce "the old woman." He was the slowest talking, moving, and working man I have ever come across. I remember him starting a painting project across the street. His plan was to paint around all the windows in the house. It took a whole day for him to get one window done, so this project lasted a while.

Cam was a little older when he and his brother would ride bikes in front of our house. This was about the time that bike helmets began to emerge in bike shops. Leo and I purchased one for each of the boys, especially because of Leo's own pubescent bicycle mishap that had led to his coma. Cameron remembers thinking the helmet was lame but agreed to put it on anyway. The boys were accompanied by other neighborhood kids who fashioned a jump with wooden boards on the street to get air and did wheelies on the curbs. Pretty soon, Byron came running into the kitchen saying that his brother had flown over his handlebars. Cameron remembers his skull reverberating inside the still-intact helmet, and from then on, he was a believer. He escaped with cuts and bruises, but I suspect that his head wouldn't have fared so well had he gone without the helmet.

After Leo started work as a lawyer, our financial situation improved. He wanted to buy his parents' house, and his mother agreed. She decided to buy a smaller place a few blocks away with the intention of having assistance from us and being near her grandsons. I'm sure she would have preferred for all of us to live under the same roof, but my past experience with her told me that this wouldn't work out. We also continued to keep in touch with law school friends and would get together frequently at nearby resorts or travel to one another's homes. Couples were starting families, so there were new babies. Still, Leo was gone a lot, and he continued to party and socialize while I was home alone a lot with the kids.

Mark and Sandy: Sandy's marriage with Mark was short lived. She returned to Oregon from Washington, DC, in 1979. Mom found out Sandy had moved out of her and Mark's shared home and was living with a coworker from her veterinary office. Mom told her if she didn't come home, she would come and get her. So Sandy flew home and stayed in Mom and Dad's guest house until she found work in Eugene, a government position approving farm loans. She moved there the day before Mount St. Helens blew up and spewed volcanic dust all over the Pacific Northwest. She liked working with the down-to-earth farmers that she visited to do her assessments. When she left DC, she went without taking anything with her, but after her return to Oregon and after her husband had returned to Oregon too, she visited him in Portland where he was starting law school at Lewis & Clark. Dad had insisted that she get some of her wedding gifts back. When she arrived at Mark's place, their belongings were still in boxes that he had moved out with him. The box with her wedding china contained only broken pieces of what had been plates, cups, saucers, etc. He had just thrown it all in the box before his move. Her job ended because of political changes that closed down her office. She moved to Salem and found other work. She drove to Bend frequently on weekends to visit.

Sandy and Mark went out a few times in their senior year in high school. From that point on, he was obsessed with her. They both went off to different colleges—she to the University of Portland and he to Oregon State University. Sandy had been a late bloomer while in high school but blossomed about her senior year. Other than a few dates with Mark in high school, she hadn't gone out much at all. This seemed to have led to her surprise and delight at finding out that an assortment of young men were in hot pursuit of her in college, and she took advantage of her popularity with the opposite sex. Mark remained in the picture, however, and either he would come up and visit her from OSU or she would go down from UP to visit him.

During their courtship years, Mark would join our family for dinners at our house. Dad was into creating an atmosphere of opulence at mealtime, which didn't go entirely unappreciated by us kids. Dad was interested in just about anything, and one thing was food. During the sixties with Julia Child, French food came into fashion, and so Dad bought all these French cookbooks for Mom. (This didn't limit the kind of food we were served though. Mom prepared any and all kinds of ethnic meals that she would often spend hours on every day). On one particular evening when Mark was over, she had prepared artichokes that sat whole on the plates with little porcelain shell-shaped dishes with drawn butter and lemon to dip the leaves and heart in. Artichokes are fairly common nowadays, but back then, they were almost unheard of and impossible to find in Bend. Dad would purchase them at the farmer's market in Portland. Mark was from a meat- and-potatoes family. While he was having dinner at our house, everyone started eating the artichokes, which he was unfamiliar with. I was across the table from him and noticed that he popped a whole leaf in his mouth and started chewing on it. He had a funny look on his face. I'm sure he must have been wondering why anyone would want to eat something so tough. Pretty soon everyone noticed what he was doing, but no one wanted to embarrass him. Dad finally said, "Mark, you don't eat the whole thing," and demonstrated how it was done. Then everyone at the table laughed, maybe partly just to cut the tension, even Mark. Another time Mark came over, Mom had prepared oysters on the half shell. These were also accompanied by the porcelain shells with a dipping sauce. Mark popped one in his mouth and grimaced as he attempted to eat the oyster, but it was too much for him. He got up, ran to the back door, and spit the oyster out on the snow-covered lawn. Mom followed him outside, concerned, and said, "Oh, that's OK, that's OK, Mark. I'm so sorry."

In Sandy's second year at UP, when her friend Carol decided to take off for Germany, Sandy agreed to leave college behind for a while to accompany her friend on her travels—I think, in part, to get some distance from Mark, who remained in hot pursuit of her. After her return a year and a half later, everyone was surprised when she started up with him again. Now she would transfer to OSU, and they started living together. During the summers when they both moved back to Bend and when Mom and Dad were out of town on vacation, Mark moved in with Sandy until right before their return. I dropped by there one day and heard loud lovemaking sounds from Sandy's bedroom, and I'll have to say that I was impressed. I sneaked out without their knowing I had been there, and I didn't disclose my discovery to Sandy until recently.

When they got married in October 1977, there were signs of trouble ahead at the wedding. The wedding guests and family waited impatiently for the bride and groom at the reception. It became obvious after their late arrival that neither of them looked happy. The summer before they married, Sandy had been working as a barmaid at the Woolen Mill. She was popular there too with the male customers, and whenever Mark showed up, he got jealous because of her friendly manner with them. There was also the man in Germany she had the love affair with, who continued to call her from there, wanting her back. I think she still had feelings for him too, but with her impetuous and fickle nature, she had taken off from Germany without so much as a "howdy do." Mark had become aware of this other obstacle in claiming Sandy. She perceived Mark's jealousy as irritating possessiveness, but she went ahead with the wedding in spite of it. In December of the same year, they moved to Washington, DC, where he began his political career on Capitol Hill, working for his home state congressmen. I remember their departure from Bend well. I had just given birth to my second child in Salem on December 23 and arrived in Bend on the evening of December 26 for Christmas break. We stayed with Leo's mother. Sandy and Mark came over to say good-bye before their departure the next morning.

Mark had a dry wit and a dark side. Leo and I spent a lot of time with Sandy and Mark during our college years. Salem and Corvallis weren't that far from each other, so on weekends, we often visited back and forth. They would often be included in college parties, in particular, when Leo was in law school. Mark liked our boys, and they liked him. He and Sandy were Byron's godparents. He brought gifts for both boys when he visited. Sandy would confide in me that she noticed that when he was with his parents, he often showed contempt for them. This was difficult to understand, particularly in regard to Mark's father, who was a simple and kindhearted man. Mark had come from a blue-collar middle-class family. He was highly intelligent. Maybe that had something to do with it, I don't know. One thing that really bothered Sandy was how Mark was at Christmastime. She would be invited to his parents' house. Mark's gifts sat under the tree while everyone else opened theirs. His dad would ask Mark if he was going to open his gifts, but Mark would just ignore him. Sandy was amazed when weeks went by and the gifts remained unopened. After they moved to DC, he started doing the same thing with her. She finally told him that if he didn't open his goddamned gift, she would never again bother to buy him another. I'm not sure she stayed long enough to carry out her threat.

Sandy had a job interview when they first got to DC and told Mark she needed to be there at 8:00 a.m. They only had one car. Sandy waited for him to get ready to take her to the interview before he went to work, but he dawdled about, hanging out in the apartment in his socks and underwear until she knew she'd be late. She left, got in the car, and drove herself to the appointment, leaving Mark in the apartment half-dressed and without the car. Another time, while they were still in DC, Sandy got a call from our aunt Jean inviting them to Chicago for the weekend. Jean and other relatives there hadn't met Mark, and so she was planning a family dinner so that everyone could get to know Sandy's new husband. After Mark heard about the invite, he told her he had work left over but that she should fly over, and he would catch up with her a few days later for the dinner party. So she flew out, and they all awaited Mark's arrival, but he never showed up. He didn't call. He just didn't come.

Mark accumulated literally hundreds of parking tickets while in DC and never paid them. He'd just throw them in a drawer where they would accumulate. It got so bad that The Oregonian newspaper printed an article about Mark's negligence in paying his fines and that jail time was a possibility if he continued to ignore them. This was all newsworthy because of his political career and affiliation with the Oregon congressmen. The article went on to report that only two out of all the fines had ever been paid. What the news reporter didn't know was that it was Sandy who had discovered two of the tickets that hadn't made it to the drawer with the rest and paid them, not Mark. She was worried that her husband might get in trouble if he ignored them, which she expected he might do. She didn't know about the rest of them. It was only after she moved back to Oregon that the news about the tickets broke. She read about it all and had a good laugh about what had been a part of her life with Mark and that she was the only person who knew the whole truth.

Mark was the sort of drinker who drank until he passed out. He never drank during the week while he was working but saved his binging for the weekends. In spite of this, he maintained a long impressive political career. But for Sandy, it became intolerable.

She described having to load his unconscious body into the back of their car and driving him home on numerous occasions after some event. It became apparent to her that she rarely saw him. He became immersed in his political career and in his drinking and partying. I think Mom also figured things out—Sandy's loneliness—and so she would fly Nora out to stay with Sandy. The two of them spent time together exploring the city when Sandy wasn't at work. She was employed at a veterinary office and liked the job. She had thoughts of becoming a vet herself, but this never materialized. Anyway, Nora also became aware of Mark's absence from home during her visits.

Nora met Sandy's friend and neighbor on one of her visits. He was gay. He would try to talk Sandy into dressing in drag and going out with him to the bars as his date. He thought Sandy would make a handsome man that he could show off to the other men in the place. But Sandy wouldn't go for it. When he found out she had a brother, he told Sandy that if he looked anything like her, he must be gorgeous, and when she showed him a photo of Doug, he was convinced. But he only had Nora as a visitor, and he didn't seem too interested in her. In fact, Nora was a little afraid of him. She was a small-town pubescent girl who had never seen anyone quite like him. It wasn't only that he was gay, though. He also had some peculiar traits. He worked in the autopsy department of a hospital. He was responsible for replacing body parts into the cadavers and sewing them up after the autopsies. Sandy wasn't sure if the specimens in bottles in his apartment were real or not, but he said they were. Nora saw the specimens, and they looked real enough to her that it freaked her out. He offered to have Nora stay with him while Sandy was at work, but Nora would have none of it. On the day Nora was to fly home, Sandy had car trouble, and her neighbor offered to drive them to the airport. He was recovering from a hangover that morning. The three of them got into his convertible with the top down in freezing weather, and he drove eighty miles per hour on the freeway to get there in time for Nora's flight. Nora was as white as a ghost by the time they got there.

After Sandy left for Oregon, Mark went on a real bender. He spent the night out cold in the bottom of a stairwell in the city and was found by the cops the next morning covered in blood and still unconscious with a concussion. So he had his demons. Their separation and eventual divorce didn't end their relationship entirely, though. A few years later, Mark was in town and came to visit us at our house on First Street in Bend. I remember him reminiscing to us about Sandy around the kitchen table. "Being with Sandy is like always being on a first date." It happened that Sandy was in town then too and showed up at our house that evening. It was like old times. I didn't know it then but found out later that she and Mark had sex in his car right in front of our house that night. There were also other times that their paths crossed. I know she kept in touch with him by phone until someone stole her purse with her wallet that had his number (and Herman's from Germany) in it. It was only after Sandy married Dave that they lost touch with each other, but Mark still kept in touch with Leo and Doug.

In April 1980, Mom and Dad invited us to Hawaii. Dad was a shareholder in the AMFAC Corporation, and he and Mom had enjoyed wonderful experiences at the stockholders' meetings at the famous Coco Palms hotel in Kauai. Dad transferred a few stocks to me so that Leo and I could travel with them for one of the meetings there. Leo's mom often called to let us know that we ought to get out and enjoy ourselves and that she could keep the boys, so we took her up on her offer, and they stayed with her while we were gone. Leo had never flown before. Mom and Dad were coming from San Francisco, and the plan was to meet in Honolulu at the airport and then head to Kauai together. The flight over was top-notch with Hawaiian stewardesses, food, and music. When we arrived in Honolulu, we had a close connecting flight, so we had to run a long distance through the airport to catch the plane for Kauai. I had a black-and-hot pink floral dress and black high heels with netting and ankle straps. By the time we got to the terminal, the dress was drenched with my perspiration and the heavy humid air, and my feet ached. But there were Mom and Dad, anxiously awaiting our arrival. We made it just in time. We boarded the miniscule propeller plane. In those days, the landing strip in Kauai was practically nonexistent. The landing was frightening. The plane seemed to take a nosedive toward the ground and then taxied to an abrupt stop with an explosive sound accompanying it. After we got off the plane, we were met by Hawaiian men and women who put beautiful leis around our necks and played Hawaiian music for us—melodious sounds that matched the island breeze in the palms and the surf on the sand—music that would follow us throughout our visit. Then we boarded the shuttle to the hotel. The warm balmy air, lush vegetation, and beauty of the island were mesmerizing. We traveled along the oceanfront, which presented us with a beautiful sight. It also presented a view of vacationers walking along the beachfront. Leo, looking out the shuttle's window, remarked that he had just seen Robert Hays from the television show Angie. I said, "Oh, you did not," but he insisted that he had seen him.

When we got to the hotel, Grace Buscher-Guslander, the hotel's proprietress, greeted us, as was her usual custom at the hotel. She showed us around the property before showing us to our rooms. I had never seen anything quite like the Coco Palms. The lobby was primitive in some respects—in the style of the Natives' simplicity with island artifacts as decoration and a bit of kitsch thrown in. The high cathedral ceiling held palm green beams with stained glass windows on each end. The pattern of the glass was also simple—rectangles of different sizes with various shades of color that let in the sunlight. From the beams over the windows, there hung various-shaped large beads of wood strung together with wooden dowels. A set of steps underneath the window led to a landing where ancient artifacts were displayed in glass cases. The staircase and landing rails were white and decorated with wooden carved fighting shields. On the landing was a wall made of lava rock beneath the window. Our suites had giant clamshell bathroom basins. The story goes that "some of the ladies from the mainland complained to Grace over drinks that they had snagged their nylons on the sharp edges of the shell ... [and] Grace snapped back, 'No one at the Coco Palms wears nylons.'"[22] The suite's walls were painted a deep sea color, which lent the space the illusion that one was underwater. The sheers at the open-air windows blew softly in the breeze. The grounds had three pools—Palace, Queen, and King—surrounded by exotic fragrant flowers and palm trees with a coconut grove behind the lagoon that ran through the resort. It all seemed magical and mystical. There were three restaurants on the property—the Lagoon Dining Room, the Coconut Palace, and the Seashell Snack Bar. The snack bar was across the highway on the shore. My favorite was the Lagoon Dining Room, which was open- air and overlooking the lagoon. (This is the same lagoon that Elvis Presley and his costar floated down on a gon-

---

[22] David P. Penhallow, *The Story of the Coco Palms Hotel: The Grace Buscher Guslander Years* 1953–1985 (Rice Street Press, Lihue, Kauai, Hawaii. 2007), 49.

dola-type boat as he serenaded his girl in the movie Blue Hawaii). Elvis often performed on the stage in the bar of the Lagoon Room when he visited, whether for work or just play. The resort became a frequent destination for him and many other celebrities over the years, probably due to Grace's hospitality and the resort's charm. Deborah Kapule was the wife of King Kemehameha II. After he was taken prisoner to Oahu, his wife Deborah ran "a hotel on the banks of the Wailu River, near the present location of the Coco Palms ... On this sight, she built the present lagoon to keep fish caught in the ocean fattened for eating and fresh ... Deborah's hotel was known for its ... hospitality ... The old timers told Grace that Queen Deborah roamed the grounds of the Coco Palms at night and was a protector of Graces' beloved Wailua ...."[23] A later owner, Mr. Lindemann, planted the coconut grove at Wailua— "finding the Hawaiian coconut much less use" ... than (those) in the South Seas, sending all the way to Samoa for the seed nut.[24] This was the birth of the beautiful Coco Palms grove, (later) touted as the largest in the islands.[25] "Moikeha, a ruler in the thirteenth century, brought drums from Tahiti to use in religious ceremonies. It was chanted that the sound of Moikeha's drum could be heard throughout the river valley. Grace ... installed a drum in the grove

---

[23]   Ibid., preface, 2.

[24]   Ibid., 2.

[25]   Ibid., preface, 5.

to signal the beginning of her nightly ceremony. For as long as Grace lived, the sound of that drum was held sacred, primitive, and as integral to her Coco Palms as the beat of her heart."[26] Grace also noticed "local fishermen . . . walk into the ocean and out onto the reef holding torches high . . . The sight of the torches glowing out on the reef, lighting up the crashing waves, formed the germ of the idea for the torch lighting ceremony [that became famous] at the Coco Palms."[27] The nightly ceremony combined the sound of the drums with the torch lighting. A curse of the Coco Palms was the notorious flooding that occurred on a regular basis. It's location on the island seemed to attract the storms.

Dad made sure we knew about the bartender who was stationed at an outdoor bar near one of the pools and also pointed out the pig pit on the property that was used as a rotisserie for whole pigs or rows of turkey—this was his inspiration for his replica of the Coco Palms pig pit assembled in our backyard at home. The bartender made a great mai tai, and we sat ourselves down by the pool with our drinks. Dad came up behind us with a big smile. "Where do you think you are, paradise?" he asked us. We answered yes in unison. After our drink and a quick swim in the pool, we all headed to the Lagoon Dining Room. It was a perfect day. We got a table looking out over the lagoon and ordered. I

[26] Ibid., preface, 1.

[27] Ibid., preface, 11.

was thrilled with the iced tea because it was strong the way I like it and served with a pineapple stick inside the glass, which lent a sweet but not-too-sweet flavor to the tea. The waiters showed us how to take our leftover food and throw it into the water. There were tons of gigantic orange and black carp that leapt into the air to catch the food in midair or fought over it among themselves underwater, creating a great turbulence on the water's surface. (The restaurant was such a special place for me that I would sneak out first thing every morning and head down by myself to enjoy one of their special iced teas). After lunch, Dad led us to the shore across the road from the Coco Palms to show us how to body surf. He was like a little kid in the water, so excited to demonstrate his technique for us. We practiced for a few hours in the hot sun, so we all developed a good sunburn. Willie was one of the staff there who had accompanied us to the resort on the shuttle, and he told us what we needed was some Cool Aloe that could be found and purchased at the gift shop. So that is what we did. It was some sort of coincidence that Leo and Willie had both gone to Willamette University at the same time, and they remembered each other.

That evening, there was a special party for the stockholders. Dad had described how elaborate these events had been when they had attended in the past. The party was held outside, and the first thing I noticed as we arrived was that, in fact, Robert Hays was in Kauai. Not only that, but he was also at our party! Guests mingled and added buffet food to their plates. I found myself right next to the actor but never got the nerve up to say hello. I guess I didn't want to disturb his vacation. (Later on, when we were checking out, he was in the lobby doing the same. Leo encouraged me to ask for his autograph because I guess he knew I might like to meet him, but I missed my opportunity again because I felt foolish even thinking about it). At dusk, I witnessed my first experience with the torch lighting ceremony. Drumbeats beckoned us to the coconut grove. Beautiful young Hawaiian men in loincloths ran in unison among the palm trees through the coconut grove, swinging their torches in circles above their heads and lighting the torches interspersed among the palm trees until the whole grove was aflame. It was a spectacular sight that I looked forward to seeing every night for the rest of our stay, which made me feel, in some way, more connected to the magic, spirit, beauty, and history of the island.

The next day or so, we walked to the Kinipopo Shopping Village down the Kuhio Highway from Coco Palms. Dad had raved about the mahi mahi burgers he had had before at the fish stand there, so we all ordered one and sat down on one of the picnic tables to wait for our lunch. Our name was called, and Dad went over to get them. Mom, Leo, and I started eating ours with no problem, but Dad announced that his was raw, became angry, and went back to the stand and started yelling at the cook who was very apologetic and offered to fix Dad's sandwich or make another. I was mortified as Dad refused the offer and stormed back to our table. The rest of us offered some of our sandwiches, but he refused that too and just sat and sulked for a while. I have to say that Dad would get so excited to share experiences with his family and friends that he got disappointed if something didn't measure up to his previous experience(s). I wondered if this is what all his anger was about, but it still didn't excuse his behavior. I also had been unaware during our lunch that he'd been getting calls the previous night about Francesca. She wasn't doing well, and before our vacation was over, he would be leaving for Chicago from Hawaii two days early.

During our stay, we also took the famous Smith family–operated barge ride up the Wailua River to the Fern Grotto landing. From there, we hiked through the rainforest to the Fern Grotto, the wettest place on earth and also where more marriages are performed than anywhere else in the world. The falls were surrounded by a stone grotto carved out by the water's centuries of pounding motion. It was a sobering and awesome sight. On the return trip, we were treated to the boat-bound hula show where no one escaped a hula lesson on board. One night at Coco Palms, we attended the Larry Rivera show at the Lagoon Lounge Stage. He sang and played the ukulele, and his attractive daughters danced the hula. Leo was impressed. I was too but also a little jealous as he went on and on about the dancers, one in particular. Looking back on it, the trip had opened my eyes to a whole world out there that

I had been unaware of and to the fact that I was feeling my own life was in a rut. I began to feel a sense of urgency about experiencing everything that I possibly could with the time I had left. My thirtieth birthday was looming right around the corner. The young dancers brought this to light. By the end of the trip, I had decided I didn't want to return to Bend at all. I told Leo I would stay on in Hawaii, he could return home, get the kids, and we could relocate to the island. He finally talked me out of this plan. But before we left the islands, we flew from Kauai to Honolulu for a few days. The city was multicultural, bustling, but at the same time relaxed—"Hang loose, brother."

What I remember most about Honolulu were Waikiki Beach and the market place with a representation of people of every size, age, and ethnic group imaginable, and the nightclub show in the Bora Bora Room at our high-rise Amfac Hotel—the Waikiki Beachcomber Hotel—featuring island dance. The most impressive to me were the Tahitian men—barefoot, massive, and muscular with black flowing hair and fiercely painted faces— dancing with their scissor-like leg movements and chanting in unison, flinging their clubs and fiery torches and swallowing the flames. They came out onto the stage in two rows with an assortment of elaborate costumes made from indigenous plant parts and colorful textiles. Depending on the dance, the men wore a shawl (tahei) and belt (hatua), head garland (hei upo'o), neck garland (hei), dance skirt (more), or loin cloth (maro) in various assortments. The music that accompanied their dance included drumbeats, chanting, and conch shell blowing.[28] This all seemed to echo the island's natural sounds and spirit. Our last evening meal was at Rudy's Italian Restaurant. Dad announced that he would have to fly to Chicago right after dinner because of his mother's health. Our plans had been to have the Sunday brunch at the famous pink Royal Hawaiian Hotel on Waikiki Beach the next morning. By the time Mom, Leo, and I had our brunch, Dad was already in Chicago tending to Francesca.

After returning home, I knew I would return to Hawaii at some point. A restlessness emerged as I was entering my next decade of life. I was feeling caged in and cooped up. The experience in Hawaii made me want to do it all.

---

[28]   Jane Freeman Moulin. Dance Costumes in French Polynesia, 421 and 423.

Francesca in Oregon (1970)

Francesco in Oregon (1970)

In college at Blind School

Me and Leo

Ken, Me and Leo

Dad, Doug Mountaineering (1970) (Mt. Hood)

Dad, Doug, Lou Summit (Rainier) (1972)

Wedding with Leo's parents

Mom and Dad

Wedding Photo 3

Wedding Photo 5

Wedding Photo 4

Wedding Photo 6

Wedding Photo 7

Wedding Photo 8

Wedding Photo 9

Nora

Sandy

On our Honeymoon

Kathy and Ken

Me and Byron

Byron

Byron's New Brother

Leo with Cam

Boys in Chair

Boys with Frances

Boys in Bath

Mark and Sandy in Salem

Mark, Byron, Leo

Doug and Diane in Salem

Me in Salem

Cameron   Nora

Yanko and Sandy in Italy

Mark and Sandy

Leo's Great Uncle Jack

CHAPTER 4

After our return from Hawaii, life went back to normal—at least for a while. I had joined a couple of babysitting co-ops in Bend because this had worked well in Salem. It helped me get acquainted with other young mothers and offered our boys playmates. The mothers got together every month or so for meetings, which we brought our kids to. The co-ops worked on a point system. We would trade a point for an hour of sitting. When Byron started first grade at Kenwood School (several blocks from our home but within walking distance), it was somewhat traumatic for me. He had gone to kindergarten a few hours a week previously, but his starting first grade was different. I'm not sure how he felt about it. The first day, I packed him a lunch, and Leo dropped him off on his way to work. I cried after they left. I walked down there to pick him up after school with Cameron in the stroller, and we walked home together. Cameron was three years old. All this became a regular routine.

Leo and I started to develop a social circle, mostly around lawyers he worked with. And we continued to get together fairly frequently with old law school friends. We usually planned reunions at resorts in Central Oregon—Sunriver Resort, Black Butte Ranch, or Inn of the Seventh Mountain. By this time, every couple had at least one child, and some were working on their second. These get-togethers often included cross-country skiing, fishing, swimming, sleigh rides, and bike riding. Also, there was golf for the men and shopping for the women. And there were also OTLA (Oregon Trial Lawyers Association) weekends. These were often raucous events that included a lot of partying. When the guys were in classes, we girls hung out with the kids.

Dad's flight from Hawaii to Chicago to tend to his mother marked the beginning of the end for my grandparents. They had celebrated their golden wedding anniversary on October 10, 1975. Francesco had since been diagnosed with cancer, and so it was expected he would go before Francesca. But that was not the case. Jean sent a picture of Francesca a year or so before she died, and I didn't recognize her. They planned a trip to Bend in the summer of 1980 for Doug's wedding in spite of their failing health. On June 8, we were ready to go out the door at home, then drive to Portland to pick them up at the airport when Dad got the call that Gram-ma had dropped dead in the bathroom off the guest bedroom while getting ready for the trip. Sandy remembers Dad standing in the front of the kitchen stove after the call—his head bowed and hands holding on, with silent tears streaming down his face. She was seventy-nine years old. I guess it wasn't a bad way to go. Mom and Dad flew back for the funeral but discouraged us kids from going back, and I had little kids and no money. Francesca's death left my grandfather, whose cancer was progressing and had metastasized, all alone.

Sandy remembers our grandparents' last visit to Bend in 1978. We were all aware of Francesco's frail appearance. But what really sticks in her mind was a view of Francesca's sorrowful face through the guest house window. Francesca rarely cried, unlike her husband. Sandy went to the front door where Francesca greeted her, still with her mournful face and tears running down her cheeks. She told Sandy that if she could just make Francesco better she would never again be unkind to him. She knew better than anyone how much he was suffering. It was difficult for Sandy to visit them. She still cries when she recalls the whole scene.

Doug and Diane married on August 23, 1980. Our side of the family traveled down to Medford, where Diane's parents lived, and we all stayed in the same motel—a Travelodge with rooms surrounding a pool. Sandy was recently separated from her husband, so she had a room of her own. The groomsmen and maids of honor also had rooms at the Travelodge, including one of Doug's best friends. After the rehearsal dinner, we planned to head back to the motel. One of the kids was getting over a cold, and Leo was coming down with it. But before we left, Doug's friend told Leo he was going to go out with some of the other wedding party and invited Leo to come along, but Leo begged off because of his cold. He told Leo he was planning to party. Little did Leo know it would be with Sandy. In the morning, I stepped out of my room for a bit of fresh air and saw her sneaking out of Doug's friend's room. I wasn't the only one either. Doug wasn't a happy camper. He didn't like it either when he turned up with a cold on his honeymoon. I always thought that Sandy succumbed to the guy's charms that night because of her recent divorce. I found out later on that they were already in the middle of a relationship with each other (before the wedding incident) that had begun months earlier. He was attending college in Eugene, where she was working. He had brought up the topic of Sandy to Doug earlier on and Doug confided that he thought Sandy seemed smitten with him, and so he took the bait.

Dad started getting calls from his sister Jean in a panic. She described their father having poor care in the hospital and then his being discharged to his home. Dad sent Mom to help out. Francesco didn't want to go back to the hospital, but after Mom got there, she was sure that was where he belonged. He was delirious, having flashbacks from the war that he was reliving. His pain was poorly controlled and severe. He became incontinent of bowel and bladder. Mom reported back to Dad, who called the hospital. I'm sure his temper influenced the staff to readmit Francesco. Dad fired the doctor tending to his dad and enlisted another who helped get the pain under control. Mom told me after the fact that Francesco worried about soiling himself in the hospital bed. She told him that there was a bucket under the bed to address that problem, and so he stopped his worry about letting it go. I still wonder about Dad not going back himself. He was working, that's true, but it seems there was more to it. Was it too difficult to see his father in such a condition? Was it too difficult to say good-bye? A few years before, I had stopped by to see my folks unannounced. They were in front of the television and a movie about dying parents was playing. I pulled up a chair to have a brief chat with them, but Dad yelled at me to be quiet. I left abruptly and drove home crying. I was stopped by a policeman. I must have been driving erratically. I explained my circumstances, and he was kind. He escorted me home to make sure I got there safely. I reflected on my father's behavior and figured that it had to do with his parents' frailty and his identifying with the program. But I was still hurt by his outburst.

Francesco died in the hospital on February 6, 1981 at the age of eighty-two. When Francesco died, this time, Dad paid for all of us to fly back to attend his funeral. It was kind of fun to all be on the plane together. We had to wait at PDX for our connecting flight, and during that time, we kids decided to go into the bar for a drink, but Nora was only fourteen. So we told the hostess that she was a midget. We were surprised when the hostess led all of us to a table and even more surprised when they served Nora! After we landed in Chicago, it was good to see our cousins and other relatives. In the Chicago area, funerals are a big thing. Not like in Oregon. Wakes last two or three days and the family there is responsible for greeting friends of the family and other mourners. Then there is a funeral mass, a visit to the cemetery, and then a gathering at the home. Jean went berserk at her father's casket. That's another thing I've noticed about funerals. Protestants seem more staid and somber. In my experience, Catholics are full of dramatic shows of emotion and fits of wailing. I had trepidation about approaching my grandfather's casket. I had heard from my mother and other relatives of his suffering before his death and imagined what he might look like. But I was relieved and comforted by his appearance. He appeared to be serene. He was still handsome in spite of what he had been through. And he still had his full thick head of hair. He seemed to have gone to a kinder place—even if it would only be six feet under. After the funeral, we all gathered at Jean and Jack's. There was lots of food that friends and family provided. We sat around in the living room and watched old movies of better times. Seeing Francesca and Francesco moving about and talking to others made it seem as if they were still with us. We reminisced about the old days. On our way home, I sat with Nora on the plane. I ordered a Bloody Mary, as did the rest of us who were of age. I'm not sure what Nora ordered. She hit the side of my fold-down table and the drink spilled all over my lap. A stewardess came by with salt and soda water, but it didn't really help much. I had to laugh about the accident but it was uncomfortable for the rest of the flight.

Leo and I decided to try for another baby. I had always liked the energy of three kids in the household during my growing up years. (Nora didn't factor in here because I was nearly out of the house by the time she was born). It took a few months, but she was conceived, and I enjoyed this pregnancy. I loved pregnant sex and felt healthy and happy as I had with my previous pregnancies. I remember a party at Leo's office when I was about six months along. Leo told me to watch out for one of the guests—notorious for his attraction to pregnant women. He spotted me right off and came running. He was even open about his opinion that pregnant women are beautiful. He flattered me and paid me much attention the entire evening.

I hadn't had a best friend since Mary R. died when we were eighteen. Leo had developed a friendship with Joe, an insurance adjuster in town. They had become acquainted while working on personal injury cases together. Leo came home from work one day and said he thought I would like his friend's wife. He met her while visiting their home one night after work. We decided to invite them over, and this is when I met Jan. I knew right away that I liked her. We became fast friends. Jan and Joe had three daughters, just a little older than our kids. In fact, I had seen Jan a few years earlier at the nursery school co-op where both my son Cameron and Jan's youngest daughter attended. For some reason, we never worked the same day, so as far as I recall, I didn't meet her then and only saw her coming and going. The second half of that school year, I begged off the workdays because I was getting ready to have my baby.

Leo and Joe started hunting and fishing together, and it became a custom for the four of us to go out on Friday nights to a downtown nightspot. During the week, Jan and I would get together for lunch, go to a thrift shop, or go see a movie. I got to know her better. She was four years older than me. She had polio as a child and spent much of her childhood and adolescence in and out of hospitals. Her parents divorced when she was ten, and after that, her father was not as accessible to her as he had been. Her maternal grandmother blamed Jan's father for her having contracted polio. He had taken the four-year-old Jan out in a boat in a nearby lake to go fishing—contaminated water being a potential risk factor. Moreover, her paternal grandmother wouldn't accept her son's marriage. To her, it meant abandonment. She said as much in a suicide note and took her life. All this seemed to have eroded her parents' marriage. Jan was left with her mother and maternal grandmother who were often abrasive and harsh, and she missed her mild-mannered father whom she took after. Like Mary R., she bore physical manifestations of her illness. I, on the other hand, held mine on the inside. Maybe only an astute observer might guess. It seemed our childhood angst, although different, helped form our close bond.

On January 26, 1982—four days after my own birthday—I gave birth to a baby girl. Everything went well. When we inspected our baby, she had black hair like her older brother. Her eyes were a dark smoky blue. She was pretty and healthy. We named her Laura Marie. She was just what I wanted.

The first week or so after we brought Laura home from the hospital, I decided to walk down to the bank while Byron was at Kenwood School and Cam was in nursery school. Leo had dropped them off on his way to work. I bundled up and started out on the approximately thirteen-minute walk to the bank and then stood in a relatively long line for a teller. This is when I remembered that I had another child and that she was home alone. I dashed out of the bank and ran home as fast as I could. When I entered the front door, I ran up our flight of stairs to the bedrooms and found her asleep in her crib. How could I have forgotten that she was a part of our family now? Because now I was an addled mother of three—that's how.

In order to stave off anxiety and despair during this postpartum period (the other two were worse), I'd get all three kids in one of the old-fashioned buggies and head out for long walks with them. Byron got in first, then Cam between his legs, and then Laura in front of Cam. I had inherited the pram from Leo's sister Gwen whose three children had outgrown it. We became famous around town because people would see us all over the place. Sometimes Byron wanted to get out and walk along beside me because he was the eldest and could handle the exertion.

During this period, our friend Tom P. came to visit. He had some sort of legal training in the area. Leo, Tom, I, and the kids went down to DeJola's Restaurant for dinner. Leo and I started arguing about something regarding his youngest sister, and Tom took his side. I got so angry I got up and walked back home. Laura was an infant, in a baby seat under the table, and so there was nothing for them to do but hurry up and finish their dinner and then drive back home with the kids. As they drove by me walking briskly toward home, Tom asked Leo if they should offer me a ride. Leo took a good look and said he didn't think that was a good idea. A few minutes later, I walked in the door. Leo and I proceeded to the second floor where our argument resumed. Poor Tom could hear it all down in the living room.

A month or so later, my uncle Norbert and aunt Lois came to visit from Illinois. Mom and Dad drove up to Portland to pick them up from the airport and then to The Tivolli Garden for dinner. Leo and I left the boys with Frances and drove up with Laura to meet everyone at the restaurant. I was looking forward to the evening in the Italian restaurant with my relatives. We put Laura under our table in her baby seat as was usual this time in her life. But as soon as we got there, she started crying and carrying on. During the entire meal, Leo and I had to take turns walking her outside in front of the restaurant windows, waving at the others at our table as they enjoyed their meals. When we'd have our turn back at the table, we had to shovel our food down as fast as we could. During this splendid meal, Leo pointed out to me the couple who had been giving us dirty looks and complaining to us about Laura in spite of the fact that we had made valiant efforts to spare other restaurant patrons from Laura's wailing. Leo confided in me that he knew the guy, a lawyer who he was familiar with because of legal conferences they had both attended, and that the woman he was with was not his wife.

My sister-in-law, Diane, was expecting her first child, so I told her I'd give her a baby shower. Doug and Diane's baby would be born nine months to the day after Laura was born. We teased them that their visit to see Laura in the hospital must have resulted in this coincidence. Anyway, I started out with my plans for the shower. Mom said she would help during the evening it was to occur. In the meantime, we had purchased a yellow lab puppy (Chet) for Cam, thinking that the pet would reduce his angst about having a new sibling. What really happened was that he was now jealous of both Laura and Chet. On the day of the shower, Chet got out of our fenced backyard. I feared he would be run over by a car on the nearby busy thoroughfare a few blocks away from our home. So I set out with the kids to look for him. We knocked on doors, scoured the neighborhood, and searched far and wide for what seemed like forever. But I had to get back to the house before guests started showing up. I managed for a while, greeting guests and getting the smorgasbord assembled and served, but then I just disintegrated. I got in my car and left without even telling anyone. My mother was the one who had to take over for me, and later on, she let me know how she felt about that. I can't blame her, but that's what a postpartum brain can do. After a few more days of searching for our puppy, we found him after knocking on doors of a nearby apartment complex on the busy street I have mentioned. A guy opened the door. I told him about our lost pet, and he pointed to Chet in his living room. He said the dog had just wandered into the courtyard, and so he had adopted him. He gave our dog back, but I took him back to the breeder. A puppy and a new baby were just too much to handle.

After Sandy's return to Oregon, she confided in me about having irresistible attraction to certain men—often leading to brief intense encounters. I had already come to recognize something similar in myself. It started out with recognizing obsessions about things. Before we left Salem for Bend, I went to see Saturday Night Fever with John Travolta. I went crazy over it. I think the family dynamics seemed similar to my own experiences as a child while I was in Chicago and even later in Oregon. And then there was the music, dancing, and the raw sexuality that was mesmerizing. The Bee Gees had always been my favorite group since high school anyway because the melodious sound and poetic lyrics and the disco stuff they did for the movie was incredible. I went to see the movie over and over until it got to be joke in our household.

A little later on, I went to see the movie The Blue Lagoon. It was based on a book with the same title written by Henry De Vere Stacpoole in 1908. I saw it for the first time by myself and couldn't get enough of it. I'd walk downtown in the evenings to watch it over and over. My preoccupation with the movie seemed to be related to the sexual content and the symbolism— the unencumbered relationship that develops between the two who find themselves on a deserted island after a shipwreck where there is little interference as they mature and fall in love. The two are first cousins. The boy's father took his niece in after her parents' deaths. There's much religious symbolism, both in their old world and in the new, just lurking beneath the surface. The ship's galley cook, Paddy, lands on shore with the children and recognizes evidence of dangerous inhabitants on the island that he cautions the youngsters about. He also forbids them to eat a certain red berry prolific on the island—a thinly disguised symbol of the biblical forbidden fruit. Paddy soon dies, and his decomposing body is found by the children. They are perplexed by the sight but figure things out by recognizing the skeletal remains that resemble their own anatomy. They also have to figure out much more for themselves as time goes by, including changes related to puberty. The couple eventually has a child but have no idea how all this occurred.[29] I didn't really understand my attraction to the movie at the time, but now it seems evident—my resistance to sexual taboos of the Catholic church, my belief in the purity of love in absence of social convention, and my recent fascination with Hawaii, a paradise all its own. The album Guilty by Barry Gibb and Barbra Streisand came out

---

[29] "The Blue Lagoon (1980 film)," Wikipedia, The Free Encyclopedia, http://en.wikipedia.org/wiki/The_Blue_Lagoon_ (1980_film).

too and had a similar effect on me.[30] I played it over and over until everyone in my household except me was sick of it. It was the same with Lionel Richie's music.

After Laura got a little older, I decided I needed a break. Nursing and the toddler stage requires a mother to be available at all times. I chose a return to Kauai and the Coco Palms—this time, on my own. Leo agreed to take care of the kids during my absence with the help of his mother. Kauai was just as I had remembered it. The weather was perfect and the island was lush—a perfect place to relax. I found my favorite quaint little restaurant at the resort for breakfast, and this was where I met Mario. I was attracted to him right off and the feeling must have been mutual. I slipped off my wedding ring under the table in hopes that he hadn't spotted it yet and hid it in my change purse. The next day, he invited me to take a walk on the beach, and I took him up on the offer. We went back to the resort and to his room, and the next thing I knew, we were in bed together. What was I thinking? What was I doing, and what was wrong with me? But these questions fell on my own deaf ears and later on didn't prevent me from carrying on with my deception. The pull was just too irresistible. It took ahold of me.

---

[30]   "Guilty (Barbra Streisand album)," Wikipedia, The Free Encyclopedia, http://en. wikipedia.org/wiki/Guilty_Barbra_Streisand_album.

Mario was indefatigable when it came to lovemaking. He aimed to please, and his attentive perception of me led him to know what I wanted. The secretiveness of our tryst was also part of the allure. So was my proclivity for lovemaking in situations where we might get caught. I have wondered whether my first sexual encounter in the underpass as a child might have had precedential influence over me. Mario reveled in my sensuality (just the opposite of the nuns in school), which was liberating. I was hooked and intoxicated with emotion. I continued to push the treachery of it all out of mind.

Mario showed me how to work through the waves. The sea was warm and salty, and we bobbed around the surface while we observed the sea life below us. On one occasion, I was out on my own, and he came up behind me, pulled my swimsuit bottom off, and made love to me in the ocean water. I had my snorkel on and bellowed through it. The breeze carried the sound to shore. When we started back on the dirt trail toward our car, a beautiful middle-aged Hawaiian woman smiled at us and laughed. She told us she knew what we had been up to down there. One time, we went for a swim in the early morning. I got to see my first turtle, which swam right by me. The night before we left, we sat in front of the ocean and watched the sunset. The time there had been idyllic.

After I got home, I decided to take scuba lessons. My classes started out in the pool to learn rudimentary skills and moved on to three open water dives to get certified. The first two were in local lakes. My instructor, Phil, and other students gathered at the lake. I got down to about forty feet and my regulator malfunctioned. I was getting no air, but I knew that I couldn't ascend too quickly or I would get the bends. I was afraid but slowly made my ascent and was glad to get to the surface for a breath of air. The last and most difficult dive was in Newport, Oregon, and was in open water. The next morning, we all went out for the ocean dive. Some students dropped out during dives after they discovered they were uncomfortable in the cold dark water, which often offered little visibility. I have to admit that this last dive was challenging. The most difficult maneuver was to get into and then break out of a heavy current. It took strenuous swimming and effort, but I passed and got my certificate. As time went by, my proficiency in the water would come in handy.

My cousin Ken attended Oregon State University. He had always been fascinated with the West Coast ever since he and his family visited from Chicago while he was still living at home. They had traveled over to the coast as part of their trip to Oregon. This may have been when Ken developed a love for Oregon, especially the beautiful Oregon coastline which may have influenced his choice in colleges. He also had a sense of adventure that his other family members seemed to lack, and going across the country to attend school seemed to satisfy his spirit. During our college years, he, Leo, and I often got together since we were only an hour or so away at Willamette. Ken had always been like a second brother to me. He and I were exactly six months apart in age—he the elder. Mom had suffered a miscarriage before I was conceived and was devastated about it. Her loss was magnified by the fact that her brother Norbert and his wife, Lois (Ken's parents), were expecting a child (Ken) too. Mom confided in me years later that she felt jealous of Lois, and that it was difficult to be around Lois's expanding abdomen. But Mom became pregnant again fairly soon with me. Ken and I spent much time together in our early years. He started courting and later married his wife, Kathy, and she led to our becoming a foursome when they visited Leo and me. When I was pregnant with Laura, Ken called to inform us that he and Kathy were also expecting a baby about a month after I was due. When we got word that the baby arrived a few months early due to birth complications, I felt sad and worried. Kathy had suffered from abruptio placentae—the baby boy was very premature. When they visited us in Bend a few years later, I was shocked at the child's condition. But Kathy was trained and had worked with special needs children, and both she and Ken were diligent in finding every possible avenue to help Chris. The next time they came to Oregon, the change was dramatic. Chris went on to attend college with some of the highest math scores on his GRE in the state of Illinois. He went on to graduate school. He plays and coaches wheelchair basketball.

When Laura was three, she was hit by a car. I went a few blocks away to have my hair cut and called to let Leo know. He said he would come right home. In the meantime, I asked Byron to keep an eye on his siblings until their dad got home. Leo was planning to pick them up and take them to the store with him, and Byron, Cameron, and Laura were to wait on the front porch for him. But Leo got a call at the last minute and was detained at work. Laura saw some friends across the street and darted off. On her way back across, there was a Volkswagen coming down our street. A squirrel ran in front of the Volkswagen, and the driver slowed down to avoid hitting it, but she didn't see Laura as she ran into the street. She hit Laura who flew up into the air and landed on her back. Our neighbor Don (who lived behind us-in our backyard really) was a paramedic and summoned by Byron. He checked her out and called 911. As I walked around the block, I saw the fire truck and ambulance. I lost it. Leo had arrived from work minutes earlier. Byron, especially, was traumatized. He felt responsible, but I knew I was the one who was at fault. The EMTs put her little body into the ambulance on a stretcher. We followed it to the hospital. She looked so little on the examining table. There was a patch of her hair that had been scraped off. She had blood in her urine, and she walked with a limp for about a month. She reminded me of Walter Brennan on the TV show The Real McCoys from the 1950s. Other than that, she seemed fine. Her kidneys had to be checked because of the blood, but she fully recovered. I thought about the little squirrel friend I had at my grandparents' home when I was about the same age. But this time, Laura's squirrel had missed being hit. It was Laura who was hit by a car, but she too had survived. I heard from neighbors how distressed the driver had been. By the time I arrived, she was gone. I sent a bouquet of flowers to her the next day with a note saying thank you that she had managed to avoid a more serious or even fatal accident.

Laura was a stem-winder in general, though. She referred to herself as "Fween Lolo" (Queen Laura), and she was definitely in charge most of the time. She was always climbing, falling off of ledges, etc. Trips to the ER became embarrassing. She also had a great curiosity. We lived in the old two-story home that had been Leo's parents'. At the front door was a staircase that traveled to the second story with bedrooms and a bath. Leo had remodeled the upstairs master bedroom, and there was a window from the staircase looking into the bedroom. One night, we were making love, and both of us felt we were being watched at about the same time. We looked over at the window, and there was Laura's face peering in at us. When she saw us, her little head disappeared. When we got over to the staircase, she was out of sight. It was frightening to see what she must have climbed to be able to get to the window. She would also get up in the morning in her little nightgown at age three and make pancakes for us. She mixed the batter, plugged in the electric frying pan, and flipped the pancakes all by herself. Then she would present them to us on our meal tray, with syrup and butter on the side, while we were still in bed. She was feisty too. She was also about three when she kept coming back into our kitchen in her same little blue flannel nightgown after she'd been put in bed. Leo told her to go back to bed, but instead of turning around to head back upstairs, she ran full speed ahead into him with her fists flying. Leo just held her at arm's length, which made her all the madder. Then he redirected her back in the direction of her bedroom, but she attacked again. Her brothers were amazed by her gumption and found the whole scene astounding. After several attempts to beat up her dad without success, she finally gave up and went to bed. On another occasion, our neighbor Don was visiting in our kitchen—a frequent occurrence. The kids usually hung out with the adults until their bedtime, but Laura wasn't in the mood to go to bed while company was still around. Leo told her it was time for bed, and she begrudgingly trudged off. A few minutes later, though, she crept back downstairs and banged on our piano in the living room around the corner from the kitchen where we were sitting. Leo yelled for her to go back to bed. Well, she kept sneaking back downstairs over and over and pounding on the piano until Leo ran around into the living room and chased her up the stairs. She must have decided not to push her luck because that was the last time we saw her that night. When she got a little older, she liked to put pictures she drew up on the walls to surprise us—she got them up there with a big nail she'd hammer in to hold them up. Another time she "decorated" our Christmas tree all by herself. She got a bear-shaped bottle of honey and squirted the honey all over the tree and then threw handfuls of glitter at the tree. We never did get all the glitter off the ornaments (that were already on the tree) or the Oriental rug underneath.

CJ was softhearted. He loved animals of all sorts, but if one of them died, he was crushed. This led to his pet cemetery out next to our house off the alley. We had been to George R's home to visit—the man with polio who started the picnic group. George and his wife, Shirley, had a pond in their backyard with a big goldfish in it. CJ was so taken with the fish that George let him have it. CJ named the fish George R in honor of his benefactor. George required a large tank because of his size, and CJ was diligent in his care for his goldfish. One day Laura decided to treat the fish to some pink soda. The next day, there was a telltale pink tinge to the water, and George was floating belly up. He was the first member of the pet cemetery. We all had a funeral service out on the side of the house and CJ cried. Later on, he got another gold fish from the pet store, but it was small. This goldfish didn't last long either.

After he went to school one day, I noticed it belly up in the bowl too. I decided to get another one to replace it before CJ got home from school, but all they had at the pet store were the black kind of goldfish, so I purchased one that had a gold heart-shaped spot near its eye. When CJ got home from school, he saw the new fish and declared that it had metamorphosed into a black fish with a gold heart by shedding its skin. He decided to rename his miraculous fish Lovey because of the little heart on its head. He added that the heart indicated that his fish loved him. He believed all this until he was an adult when his brother finally told him the truth. Then the kids got a large turtle they named Aloysius after our parish priest. He lived in a large tank in our laundry room. He lasted about six years before he finally died. He was buried next to George R and Lovey. Wooden crosses and dried flowers marked the spots.

Doug Herland was one of Leo's best friends since grade school. Doug was born with osteogenesis imperfecta (brittle bone disease). He was born with a few broken bones—collarbone, left hip, and several ribs—and over the course of his life, there were many more broken bones. I remember seeing him when I first moved to Bend at the swimming pool where Sandy and I spent our first few summers. Swimming was one thing he was able to do. Leo and Doug were in the Boy Scouts together. Doug needed to do his fifty-mile hike in order to get his 50-Miler Award so Leo got up early each morning to accompany Doug during his hikes, and

Doug won his award. When he was a senior in high school, he was in a pool when someone jumped in on top of him. He found himself in a full body cast for six months after this mishap. During that summer, he spent all his time in a lawn chair that his parents moved him around in on its wheels. His mother wondered how he would get to school in his condition. Leo offered to drive him in his pickup truck. Leo and his dad fashioned a ramp to get Doug and the lawn chair in the pickup. The chair was secured with a rope tied to the bed on each corner, and they would head to the high school. After graduating high school, Doug attended Pacific Lutheran University and got involved in crew there. This led to his winning a bronze medal in the 1984 Olympics for his participation as a coxswain. He had to carry a four-pound bag of bird shot during the race because he didn't meet the minimum weight requirement without it. Doug visited our home often. The kids just loved him. He was good with them, and he was the same height as they were. This all seemed to induce a camaraderie between Doug and all the kids he met. He visited during the holidays the year he won the bronze medal and brought it over so the kids could see it. He let them hold it too. Cameron, in particular, was taken with Doug. He was his hero. Doug went on to make a career of rowing, in particular, for persons with disabilities. When Doug died in 1991, his mother called to let us know. Cameron was inconsolable. He was the one with the tender heart.

Life went on as usual at home. Our thirties were fun. We had a summer party every July or August with law school and Bend friends and family. The women prepared the evening meals and the guys golfed. My sister Sandy always came over from the valley to help out and attend the party. One year, we girls were home getting ready for the evening when I got a phone call. A woman named Ruth called to let me know she planned to attend but would be a little late because she had to drive from Salem. She asked if there was anything she needed to bring, and I told her no, we had it covered. After I got off the phone, I looked at my guest list and didn't see anyone named Ruth and didn't remember having sent out an invitation to anyone by that name either. I asked everyone present and no one knew who Ruth might be. We decided that someone who was invited may have told her to come. When the guys returned I asked them about it, but they didn't have any answers either. So we carried on with the party and waited to see if Ruth materialized. She never did. When Sandy returned to her home after the weekend, she noticed that her apartment appeared to have been broken into. She noted that the oven door was open and a half-cooked steak lay on a broiler pan. Her bedroom chest had been relocated to the living room, and all her jewelry had been linked together and displayed inside the open chest. Some of her clothing was folded in the chest while others were missing, and so were her glasses and a pair of shoes. There was her invitation to our party lying open next to her phone. She called me in a panic and said she suspected she knew who Ruth was and that she had inhabited her apartment while she was gone. She stayed at her boyfriend's house that night. They called the police. A few days later, the police spotted Ruth, a very tall woman, wearing Sandy's blue glasses, her shoes, and several layers of her clothing. Ruth was sent back to the mental hospital, and Sandy got her things back.

Being married and raising three kids, there was never a dull moment. One day I decided to make a lemon meringue pie from scratch. I made the crust first and then mixed the ingredients for the filling, which included freshly squeezed lemon juice. I used my eggbeater to whip up the concoction, and the fragrance that wafted in the air led me to put my nose near the bowl to get a better scent. While doing so, my hair fell next to the beaters, and the next thing I knew, one of them wound into my hair up to my scalp with the batter flying all over me. Luckily, I was able to push the stop button before any real damage was done. Just about that time, the doorbell rang, and so I ran to the front door with the beater hanging off my head and batter all over the place. It was a UPS worker with a package. He smiled, and I explained my predicament and then retreated to the kitchen with the package and proceeded to extract the beater and clean up the mess.

One time, I had to do some errands while the kids were home. There was some sort of appointment I was supposed to get to. I was driving a mustard-yellow Suburban at the time. The kids all piled in the backseat, and for some reason, the automatic door opener was back there with the kids. They always argued about who could work it. Just about the time I started to back out of the garage one of the kids started pushing the button. The garage door started going up and down, and so I told them to knock it off. I thought the garage door was up as I started backing out, but the door descended again and I backed into it. I got out of the car to inspect the damage. The garage door didn't look so good, but I left it as it was and drove off to where we all had to go. Another time, my car was being serviced, so I borrowed Leo's older-styled Mercedes—a car he was smitten with. The car was in the garage when we all piled in. Byron forgot something in the house, so he ran back in. He returned to the car but forgot to close the back door. I was distracted with the commotion in the back, so I backed out of the garage, and before I knew it, the car door was bent in the opposite direction it was supposed to be. I couldn't get it closed. I called Leo at work, frantic that I couldn't get the door closed. He and a couple of his friends showed up. He pried the car door back with a crowbar, forced the door closed and tied it in place so that we could leave. I felt chagrined, but they were all amused in spite of the condition of the car door. Leo sold his car not too long after this incident. We all missed the old girl.

After Mom turned Catholic, she became almost fanatical. This may have led to her decision to travel to Israel. Some of the Catholic priests in Central Oregon were arranging a group trip. She asked Dad about going, but he told her he had no interest, so she went without him. I'm not sure why he didn't want to go. She raved about her journey after her return and started planning for a return trip. This time, she would take Sandy with her.

Holidays and vacations were a highlight. Our parents went all out during holidays, and we gathered at their home for extravagant meals. At Christmastime, there was a pile of gifts under the tree. Mom always made spiked eggnog. Dad made the kids wait until after the meal to open presents. He would announce that waiting would enhance the experience, but I don't think the kids thought so. Sometime in December, Mom and Dad took all the adult children and spouses to Portland for a holiday weekend. Our rooms and meals were paid for. We each got three hundred dollars to shop with during the day and met up for dinner in one of the downtown restaurants. There were also vacations to the ocean. The kids were included in these excursions—Byron, Cameron, Laura, and Doug and Diane's daughter, Andrea (nine months to the day younger than Laura), and my sister Nora (who still lived at home and was only seven years older than Byron). We often spent Thanksgiving or Christmas in our favorite spot, and each family got their own apartment for themselves. The beach weekends continued on after the boys were married and had families of their own.

Dad and Mom would also take the kids. Sometimes Dad took Byron and/or Cameron to Portland. He was still just a kid himself, so they always had fun with him. They'd stop in at the trick store on Burnside and got to pick out items there—disappearing ink, fake vomit, trick cards, Halloween masks, and tricks where nails go through coins and pennies through rubber. Then they'd have dinner at the Brasserie Montmartre on SW Park Avenue in Downtown Portland. The restaurant has recently reopened after years of laying barren but doesn't have some of the features that drew Dad to take the boys there. In the old days, there were paper tablecloths that patrons were encouraged to draw pictures on with crayons that were also provided. There were contests, and the best ones were framed and displayed on the walls of the restaurant. Prizes were given out. The establishment also featured a magician who would travel from table to table and perform his magic tricks. Sometimes the boys would bring their own tricks and demonstrate them to the magician. Dad would put his fake mustache on them and sneak them into beer garden fairs on the river. Then he'd let them drive his Porsche back from Portland. (I didn't discover this until it was too late to object). Mom took the boys for a weekend at the Inn of the Seventh Mountain Resort while Dad was on one of his hunting trips. The weather wasn't good enough for the pool or other outdoor activities, so she took them to see Pee-wee's Big Adventure at the theater. They were thrilled and became avid fans after that. After seeing the movie, they had to see Pee-wee's Playhouse every Saturday morning. Their grandmother Frances made them a Pee-wee Halloween costume, and they learned how to imitate their hero's voice and every gesture.

We all had intimate relationships with the cars in our family, but those relationships weren't always so good. This went back all the way to Dad's jalopies in Illinois, the black V W Beetle we drove across the country in, and Doug's G. B. Soap Box Derby car. We always had names for each one. Dad bought a white station wagon when I was in high school, and we named that car the White Whale. It was practically indestructible. For instance, I was getting ready to drive it up to Seattle when I started college there. I took it down to the Robo-Wash a few days before I was scheduled to leave. I drove the car in and sat inside while the mechanical washer rode around the car on a track (similar to a train track). I started daydreaming about something or other as the water pummeled the exterior of the White Whale. Just about that time, there was a loud explosion, and the car ran into the robo-washer and threw it off its track with water spraying every which way. I looked back in the rearview mirror and saw the car that had run into me and pushed my car into the robo-washer. There was an old guy looking perplexed inside. He finally got out of his car. He hadn't seen me or the White Whale as he drove in for his wash. Earlier on (after Sandy drove the White Whale over the A&W root beer stand post) Dad had covered the resulting damage with yellow and orange flowered contact paper-and that's the way it stayed. But this time, the old girl needed a lot more attention to get her going again, but she did get me back up to Seattle for school, and lasted a while after that.

Leo and especially his brother Daren always liked to find a bargain as far as cars went. I wasn't always convinced that their purchases were all that great, but they thought so. Leo came home one day with a brown pickup truck for Byron after he decided he needed transportation to high school and back. I don't think Byron was too impressed, but he'd head out in the morning and try to get the pickup to start. Laura, Cam, and I could see him out the window. The truck would turn over again and again until finally, one morning, he got out and headed inside with a look that could kill. Laura and Cam ran for cover as Byron shouted obscenities about his truck and threw inanimate objects about the living room. After that morning, he named the truck The Brown Turd, and then that's what everyone called it. Byron inherited Dad's and my temper in general. After he started college, he was working on his computer to get certain classes that he wanted to take but it just wasn't cooperating, so he threw it out his dorm room window on the second floor. He called to vent about his frustration, and I commended him on his solution for the problem.

Dave and Sandy: Sandy's job in Eugene ended with budget cuts, and she found a job in Salem. She was lonely there, so she started going down to a nearby Denny's restaurant after work for a meal or just coffee and read books in a booth there for a few hours every evening. This is where she met Dave who was the manager there. I went to visit her one weekend and noticed a hickey on her neck, and then she introduced me to Dave, who I figured was the one who put it there. They moved to their newly purchased acreage near Lyons, a one-horse town outside of Salem. Dave had discovered the property before its purchase. The previous owner had gone to the bank for a loan to start up a resort on the same property. He described his plans to the loan officer, who granted the loan so that he could start his project. The land had been a dense forest, but the new owner clear-cut much of his new property and used a bulldozer to create a man- made lake for his "resort." Then he went ahead to build five houses around the lake. At some point, the loan officer decided to head over and check on the project. He was shocked at what he saw. There were five peculiar structures surrounding a humungous cavern in the ground that was half full with water. Soon, the bank initiated a foreclosure. Dave and

Sandy were looking for some property and came across this one and decided the price was right.

When Leo and I visited for the first time, they showed us around. One building looked like a barn with stalls that appeared to have been used like separate rooms for its inhabitants. They were piled high with garbage, including syringes, dirty baby diapers, and heaps of dirty old clothing that had been left behind. Another of the structures was built partly around a tree and held up by stilts underneath. The rooms had crooked floors that sagged and waved—difficult to navigate and gave a feeling of being in a boat on the ocean during a storm. In one of the rooms, there was a one-way mirror on the exterior wall of a room with a hot tub, presumably to be used to peer in at unsuspecting bathers. There was also a bathroom with a toilet. A pipe from the toilet jutted outside the structure, and its sewage ran directly into the lake. Sandy discovered that there had been a very curious bunch of inhabitants living there before the foreclosure and that the previous owner had hard feelings about having his resort taken away from him before he had a chance to realize his dream of running a full-blown resort and raking in the cash. So Sandy felt uncomfortable being out there on her own, expecting that a visit from the previous owner and/or his cronies might occur. A while after they were married, they had a reception at Dave's parents' home in Portland. When we went up for the celebration, someone asked Dave how he had found their place. Leo and Dave's dad were sitting in on the conversation, and Leo said, "What I want to know is why you found it?" Sandy said that Dave's father thought the line was so funny he repeated it over and over until the day he died, much to Dave's chagrin. Sandy and Dave worked to demolish all but the most functional of the five structures and continued to live there for the next five or six years.

Dave started driving truck, and Sandy went to truck driving school. When she finished her course, they started driving as a duo on cross- country routes or sometimes the West Coast routes going north and south. They both liked the work. There was a bunk in the back of the cab where they could take turns with naps. I found it interesting that Sandy was able to manage this job because she had a history of losing her way with even familiar travel from the valley back to Bend. She might take a wrong turn on the freeway and call hours later to let us know that she was in Timbuktu. I guess Dave's presence must have acted as a compass for Sandy on their dual excursions. They had one particularly scary event in NYC during their on-the-road years. A drop-off point for their shipment was a place called Hunts Point Market in the Bronx—an off-load wholesale market with barbed concertina wire obstacle fencing. On this particular night, they had a load of oranges in the back to off-load. But as they drove through, they noticed that something seemed amiss in the back of the trailer, so Dave got out to inspect and noticed that the back doors seemed to have been tampered with. In those days, they were to find out the place was corrupt, teeming with criminals whose intentions were to off-load the trucks themselves and take off with the loot. But oranges weren't high on their list, so after they inspected the trailer's contents, they left the produce alone. They were after more pricey items, like a trailer full of meat. These guys hung around as if they belonged there. Prostitutes were hanging around too, presumably to service the criminal element that ran the scams. Sandy recalled one fellow whom she found particularly repulsive. He commented on her strength as he observed her unloading the orange crates and remarked that he wished his old lady would have a try at this type of manual labor so that maybe she would lose the kid of his she was carrying. While Dave and Sandy continued with their work, their cab was gone through. And when they returned to it, their money, credit cards, and anything else of value were gone. A few cops suggested that in this neighborhood, they should just run stop lights in order not to get themselves into any more trouble. They warned that if a stop is made, break-ins were likely. The cops added that sometimes ether would be pumped into the cabs of the trucks from inside the trailer to knock out the drivers, making it easy to get off with what they wanted. Sandy and Dave had to find their way out of this hellhole and had to have money wired to them so that they could get back home.

On their north-to-south-and-back runs, they sometimes went down to Los Angeles. Sandy remembers heading into a truck stop down there where she ordered an ice cream. The young girl behind the counter asked her if she wanted a "cuppercone." Sandy, being a little on the dense side, asked "What?" The girl repeated herself—"cuppercone," "cuppercone," "cuppercone." Dave walked up beside Sandy and said, "She wants to know if you want a cup or a cone." In her own way of looking at it, the girl was unintelligible with her Valleyspeak.

They married on December 23, 1983 in Reno, Nevada, in one of those cheesy wedding chapels there. Sandy quit driving and worked at a local grocery store in Lyons. Dave started driving shorter truck routes. Sandy inherited a dog from a friend of hers. She was glad to have Sandy take the dog off her hands. Sandy noticed right off that the dog freaked out one day when Dave had his National Guard uniform on. This made her suspect that someone in the dog's past had been abusive to her, so they made sure Dave never wore his uniform in the dog's presence any longer. I asked Sandy to write a little something about her dog because I didn't think I could do the topic justice as she could. At first, she was hesitant to write for me. I asked her to write about other topics too, but she told me she was no writer. I suggested she just start writing and not worry about the end product. I told her it didn't have to be perfect and that I was sure she had the ability. She sent me the following:

"Winston—so named because she looked like a Winston-Lab-Scotty mix—coal black with wispy mustache, huge canines and penetrating eyes. Lovable and neurotic, she wouldn't let you out of her sight for even a minute. Should have called her Shadow the way she followed you from room to room. You couldn't sit down without her head ending up in your lap—adoring eyes staring up at you. Nothing ever loved me like that dog. It was discomforting. I had to go to town without her, so I went into the bedroom, closed the door behind me and then climbed out the window. Dirty trick I suppose, but once I left her alone in the car and she demolished the interior—put those canines to work & bit huge holes in the dash, reduced the visors to mere fringe and even severed the seat belts. Anyway, she sat by that bedroom door patiently waiting my exit when I returned home through the front door. Befuddled, she looked at me, then at the closed door and back at me. Then [she] trotted over to resume her watchful place at my side. The last time I ditched her to run to town she got loose and tried to follow. As I was coming home I saw a black form on the side of the road and thought— 'Oh, please don't let that be her'. Of course, all prayers are answered, just not the way we wish. She looked like she was sleeping, warm and limp. I picked her up and blood flowed out of her mouth and down the front of my shirt. I looked down the road in both directions hoping someone, anyone would stop and help me, but I was alone with my dead friend. I carried her home and buried her." Soon after, she called and related her story to me. She wept, her voice quavery, and I didn't know how to provide solace for her loss other than to just listen.

There were a few other times I had calls from Sandy when she was truly beside herself. The first time was in 1973. She was going to college at Oregon State and in a relationship with Mark. But on this night, for some reason, she was alone. They had recently seen the movie The Exorcist. She was petrified to stay by herself, so I stayed on the phone with her for a few hours. It made me decide never to see the movie, and I haven't.

After Dave and Sandy sold their acreage, they moved to a few different homes in Albany, Oregon. Sandy experienced some unusual happenings in both places. In the first, a small fixer-upper, she would sense a young woman crying at the kitchen nook. She later discovered that earlier on in the house's history, a newly wed woman had lost her husband during the time they lived in the home. In their next home (on the Albany historic registry) there were other peculiar happenings. Dave and Sandy loved the house and refurbished and decorated it in concert with its era. But the house, too, seemed to have other occupants other than Dave and Sandy. Dave would ask Sandy why she kept unlatching the windows after he had latched them all before bedtime, but she denied doing so. They always wound up unlatched, no matter what. The toilet tended to run at night too, and when Sandy got up to fix it, the chain would be found in some unlikely condition in the tank-tied in knots or a bow, for instance. Their dog would scamper back up the stairs of the basement whenever they took her down there and cry at the top of the stairs until they came back up. She refused to stay down there. One neighbor told Sandy that he had considered purchasing the house at one point, but that the basement had made him uncomfortable. The house carried signs of a child's prior existence in the place-low hooks for coats and jackets, crayon drawings on the walls, glitter set in paint on the kitchen-nook table, and a child's playhouse outside-a replica of the larger house, with working lights and a door bell. But the most frightening things occurred later on. Dave was working late one night and Sandy alone in her upstairs bedroom. She had not fallen asleep yet when she clearly heard people roaming on the main floor and was sure she was being robbed. It sounded like the downstairs was being ransacked. She was so frightened that she had thoughts of exiting her second story window to escape her intruders if they should proceed to the second floor-- for there was no phone upstairs. The next morning she expected signs of a burglary but the house was all in order as it had been before she went to bed. Not long after, Sandy and Dave hired a painter while they would be out of town.

When they returned, to their surprise, she found paint cans open and dried out, a roller in its pan with dried paint, and the kitchen door wide open. The painter had been using the basement to mix his paint, etc. Sandy was perplexed by the scene. The painter called to apologize profusely. He explained that he felt so terrified down there that he fled without thought about how he had left the place and too fearful to return to close the door and clean up. He didn't want to come back to retrieve his things and refused to finish the job.

Another time when she called, it was about her dying mother-in- law whom she was caring for. She described to me the pitiful state the woman was in and her brave battle to remain on earth as long as possible. (Sandy said she couldn't comprehend her wanting to remain living in such a condition). Her father-in-law had a total breakdown one evening— brandishing a shotgun when Dave and Sandy planned to leave for a needed break. He was so worn-out and afraid to be alone with his wife. Sandy agreed to write a little something about her mother-in-law and her dying ordeal:

"Ethyl was a true farmer's daughter—she lived in a cornfield surrounded by a mud brown fence. She had an easy sociable personality and an even temperament, seeming cheerful even when she was angry. The mother of five, she lived in the same 'bless this mess' house for years, always adding on but never improving. It became the local gathering place when the kids were still young. Everyone met at Ethyl's, and most just dropped by unannounced, her high-pitched singsong voice ever calling out 'Ahoy' to welcome her endless stream of visitors. Ethyl plain old had fun, and during one of her "hen parties" the women were having such a good time her young son (Dave) decided then and there that, by golly, he was going to grow up to be a housewife too. Just after her fifth child was born, she was struck with polycystic kidney disease. She had one of the first successful transplants in Oregon. Antirejection drugs caused her naturally slender face to become round as a pumpkin and damaged her joints, leaving her with a stiff-legged teetering gait, always bend right angle at the waist to garden or retrieve toys. Her skin became thin as tissue paper, and a mere bump would send her to the emergency room for stitches. She adjusted well to all the physical changes and refused to let them affect her life in general, so she went on to host dozens of holidays, birthdays, showers, and hen parties. But a sort of curse seemed to come along with her happiness. Ethyl was diagnosed with ovarian cancer, and she deteriorated rapidly after the initial chemotherapy treatments failed. Every day she became weaker and more dependent until she was completely bedridden. Her body became rigid and bloated, able to bend only at the elbows. Bile oozed from a feeding tube incision in her throat that grew ever larger due to necrosis. Each night you'd think 'she can't possibly survive 'til morning,' but she did, day after day after day after day. During the twilight periods of morphine-induced sleep, she had terrifying hallucinations—once seeing god-knows-what climbing out of a nonexistent opening in the wall. She was screaming and pointing to an area under a side table, desperate for us to see. We frantically moved furniture aside and slapped the solid wall just as desperate to prove to her no opening was there. But you can't reason with the irrational, and relief only came when the morphine once again took hold and allowed her to sleep. We all stood around helplessly watching as the focus of one vivacious woman's goal to make everyone around her happy turned to our goal to simply make her comfortable. The house closed its eyes and went to sleep the day Ethyl died. After all, its heart was broken."

"That first year, her husband Tom put down kitchen tile, a necessity Ethyl had, for years, failed to convince him of, and we kept up her flower gardens. These things, I suppose, were in tribute to the spirit that still lingered. Twenty years later, Tom was gone, the house was torn down, weeds and grass overtook the gardens, but Ethyl's hardy cyclamen had survived and spread throughout the nearly three-acre lot. It has bloomed beautifully every spring and fall over the years. Neighbors and family members have taken home the flat potato-like bulbs to plant in their own yards to bloom and to celebrate the memory of a truly lovely lady."

After some years on the road, Dave and Sandy decided to try something else. Dave went back to school and got a degree in chemistry and business. They went to work for a paint company, and eventually, they owned one. After that, Dave decided to try for a position as an administrator of a nursing home. He had some firsthand medical experience because he had been a paramedic during the Vietnam War and flew the wounded to medical facilities via helicopter. He landed a job in Spokane and turned the place around. This led to transfers to other facilities in need of attention, which really appealed to him because he liked the challenge, and they both liked seeing different parts of the country.

In the summer of 1984, we met Law School friends at Black Butte Ranch for a long weekend. We left the kids with Leo's mom this time. Susie brought her infant, their second child, because she was nursing. DUB was playing at the lodge's lounge above the restaurant. DUB was a Buddy Holly imitator who looked just like the real thing. He sang his songs too, and in between, he asked the audience trivia questions. Leo had a photographic memory and was able to answer just about every trivia question there was. He'd rattle off answer after answer so fast that no one else in the audience had a chance. The more answers he got, the more difficult DUB got with his questions.

That same weekend, while the guys were golfing, we girls decided to check out a little shop that was near our condo. After we got in the store, we started through some of the merchandise. It didn't take too long to realize that we didn't see a clerk in the store but figured that she might be in the back with the inventory. We called back there, but nobody materialized. So we continued looking around, expecting a clerk to appear anytime. One of us cruised back behind the counter to look at something, which set off a loud deafening alarm. We ran out of the store to get away from the noise but also because we started to think maybe we shouldn't have been there in the first place. We ran across the street and hid behind some trees. Just about that time, three or four police cars with their own sirens blaring pulled up and surrounded the shop. They got out of their cars with their weapons in hand and entered the shop. This is about the time we hightailed it out of there. They never did see us. The next day, we went back and noticed the hours of operation on the front door. The day before, we had been there shortly after the place had closed. We talked to the clerk and told her what had happened, and she said someone must have forgotten to lock up before they left.

The OTLA weekends at the Sunriver Resort always started out with a wine tasting gathering outside on the first evening. These evenings were always lively. The theme for 1986 was fifties, so we all dressed up for the dance the following night in fifties garb. The guys rolled cigarette boxes in their T-shirt sleeves, stuck zip lighters in their watch pockets, and slicked their hair back. The girls wore saddle shoes, bobby socks, and pleated or circle skirts.

We chewed gum and blew bubbles. The fifties music at the dance was great, and I got to do swing dancing. The best was dancing to "La Bamba" with Leo and our friend Bobby. Getaways usually included charades or Trivial Pursuit games. I didn't really care, so the team that got me was at a disadvantage. Usually, it was the guys against the girls, and the guys always won.

OTLA weekends included dances and theme parties—roaring twenties, fifties, tropical, Western, etc. Some weekends included lip sync contests, and I have to say that Tom, Susie, Leo, and I were pretty good. "Leader of the Pack" was our first theme song. The guys wore leather jackets, rolled jeans, and slicked back hair. They had cigarettes hanging off their lips. Leo rode a tricycle for the final act, ripping around the stage, singing the final refrain, crashing and slumping on the floor in a death grip, his arm extending up to rev his motor for the last time. We girls were the doo-wop backup singers. We wore poodle skirts, saddle shoes, and ponytails. After our "Leader of the Pack" appearance, we were approached by event planners to go out on the road with our act. Next, there was the tropical theme where we lip-synched Jan & Dean's "Honolulu Lulu." We always spent the whole three-day weekend devising elaborate costumes and rehearsing our skits. This one involved a trip into town to hunt for costume props. Sue and I drove in, while the guys went to their meetings. We came back with yellow star-shaped sunglasses to mimic the line in the song about Lulu having "stars in her eyes." We also found a long black wig, a grass skirt, and a coconut that we fashioned into a coconut bra. Leo donned the outfit. He gyrated around the stage in his drag getup accompanied by Tom on the ukulele. Sue and I did a synchronized hula in bathing suits. After his performance, one of the kids in the audience asked Leo whether he was a boy or a girl.

The next year, we did Patsy Cline's version of "Crazy" for the Western theme. Sue and I wore mustaches, cowgirl shirts, string ties, jean skirts, cowboy hats, and Groucho Marx glasses. We rode stick horses. The guys had stuffed brassieres they wore under their cowboy shirts paired with jeans and curly wigs. (Susie and I had to shop for the humongous brassieres a few days before). Leo sang Patsy Cline's part. "Patsy" started out singing along with her partner but slowly began to lose it on stage and wound up in a straitjacket forced on him by Tom. Our group name was "The Jugs." We always won. During these weekends, the kids always had a Monopoly game. They created handles for one another and themselves—Byron was Big Bucks Byron, Cameron was Cool Cash Cameron, Bob was Big Business Bob, and Laura was Little Loser Laura. She didn't mind being called a loser because she was just glad to be included. They decided that John was too young to play, so he was unhappy about being excluded.

Leo was the youngest of seven, as I've said, and three of his siblings were girls. They used their little brother as a dance partner to practice their dance moves at home before hitting the dance floors. Leo became proficient in swing and other fifties dance styles. I often went a little wild on the dance floor myself, although I hadn't had the advantage of older siblings who might have provided me with a partner as a child. But I figured it out anyway. Leo was my first dance partner in high school. By the time we were adults, we could really cut a rug, and we would often clear the dance floor, and then the crowd around us would cheer us on.

Leo had always been tolerant of my quirky sexual nature. He usually seemed unfazed by my escapades. (It was all about breaking social convention—so there, Sister B!) For instance, he never objected when I decided to wear provocative clothing in public. In fact, he had promoted a seductive style of dressing for me from the get-go. On one occasion, we were off to meet friends at a downtown bar and restaurant for our usual Friday night outing. I decided I would wear a see-through black blouse and modeled it before we left. Leo asked, "You're going to wear that?" and I said yes I was. After we got there, the bar was rather dark, so it wasn't overtly obvious that my blouse was see-through. However, some guys finally realized that it was as the evening wore on. Leo was aware of this but seemed rather amused by my brazenness. When we drove over to the valley together, we liked to make love in the car as he drove. Or we would pull off the road and finish up in the woods. The bottom line—he wasn't a prude.

Mario was like-minded about encouraging my disinhibition. While we were in Hawaii, we'd hike in some secluded tropical forest trails and make love. The object was not to get caught, but once, that did happen. The other hiking couple retreated down the trail. Later, we would make love under a blanket during our night flight back from our second trip together. That was tricky.

Leo discovered my fling. When he arrived home that night, it wasn't good. He waited until the kids were in bed to confront me. I lied at first, fearful of what might happen if I told the truth, but I don't think he believed me for a minute. He ranted and raved, argued and cajoled on and on into the night. It wasn't a lot of fun, that's for sure.

In the morning, he took the boys to school and went to work. It was terrible after the night before. Laura was home with me when Dad showed up at the door. He would occasionally stop by for a morning visit, so this was just one of those days. He knew right away that something was wrong. The first thing he asked was if Leo was having an affair. I said no, it was the other way around. Dad uttered the platitude "You shouldn't ever shit in your own nest." I cried and thought "look who's talking." Dad softened with my tears. He was always someone I could confide in. After all, we were a lot alike. The night Leo confronted me was not the last. He wore me down until I finally admitted to everything. Leo expected that I would either leave him or stay and give up Mario, but I didn't do either. I told him that he had the option of leaving me, but he didn't do that either. So things stayed this way for a while. We'd start arguing after the kids went to bed, and I can only guess how much they heard. I have always felt a loyalty to Leo in spite of everything else. Maybe it was partly because I had known him most of my life and that he has always been steadfast— one of the things I liked about him. But nothing was going to change my mind yet about Mario—at least not for a while. Some of it was because I'd been talked out of seeing college guy by Leo when I was an adolescent, and Dad's dictates while I was growing up also played a part. I had always succumbed to them. The other part was that it all signified a type of independence for me. And then there was the chemistry that was hard to ignore. But maintaining any kind of relationship with Mario had one very distinct disadvantage—guilt. So my relationship with him also suffered. I felt some reservations even before everything came out. And now if I was to carry on with him, it was with Leo's knowledge.

Mario brought up our traveling to Tahiti. He was unaware of what I was dealing with at home. I had great reservations about going now but forged ahead with plans for the trip. I finally approached the subject with Leo, who didn't object. Maybe he thought that, in time, I would get it out of my system and everything would get back to normal. Leo told me he meant to make changes in our marriage to ensure a more stable union. But I didn't trust his proclamations. What about how things had changed between us right after I moved to Salem to attend Willamette? And of course, he didn't trust me any longer either.

I met Mario in Moorea for what was to be our swan song trip. The place was breathtaking. Remote in a way that Hawaii wasn't. For a while, I was able to forget my guilt, surrounded by such beauty. The dinner that evening was from an underground oven—mostly indigenous plant stuff with no seasoning. I couldn't eat much due to exhaustion from the long flight, my emotional state, and maybe also the blandness of the food. We had our own bungalow looking out over the lagoon. French and English were spoken there as well as the native tongue. The staff was easygoing, very friendly, and gregarious. The surroundings were hypnotic, and I succumbed to Mario's ardor. Everything in sight was erotic. We picked fruit off the trees and found little grocery shops with very little to offer. We often went to the restaurant, so we got to know the staff there. One very large and beautiful middle-aged Tahitian woman laughed when she greeted us at our table one day. She looked at me and told me that she had never known a woman like me before. I wasn't sure what she meant, but we figured it out the next morning when we heard staff raking fallen palm fronds from around our bungalow while we made love inside. We discovered that they did this every morning so that they could listen in.

I got into a sexual fog during our time on Moorea, but this hadn't been the first time. We made love morning, noon, and all night long and with little sustenance in between. His kisses were like life-giving electricity— forceful but, at the same time, like a sweet caress, a sweet moment that defined life itself. One morning, I got up at dawn and went for a swim on my own. The water was quiet and the light subtle from above. All of a sudden, at a distance, I saw a large creature with water wings and a sharp tail that whipped around its body as it glided along. The creature began dancing with me underwater. When I moved in one direction, it moved with me, and then when I moved in another, it followed. At first, I was frightened but then the creature seemed only playful. I didn't even have a name for my friend until I later described him to Mario, who said I had seen a stingray. During the day, we explored other sea life together as we had in Hawaii, but the innocence of our time in Hawaii was not found in Moorea.

We made an acquaintance with four young Australian girls and also a young Latin couple. The girls were wild to say the least. They were also funny. They complained about Australian men and suggested that they might think about a visit to the States to find a better bunch than what they had to choose from at home. One day they showed up at our bungalow with mopeds and invited us to come along to explore the island. I said I wasn't interested, so they drove off without us. Several hours later, they returned, worse for wear. Each of their bikes had held two riders and one set crashed and burned. One of the girls was limping badly, and both were banged up in general. They had attempted to get medical attention, but there was only a small station at the other end of the island that didn't offer much. They stayed on three or four days longer and then flew back home. We exchanged addresses before they left, and after I got home, I received a letter from one of them. She explained that her injured mate had an embolism on their way home in the plane and had to be evacuated upon landing and rushed to the hospital. Luckily, she recovered.

The last big event was our flatboat excursion. Mario booked it for the day. There were a lot of resort guests on the boat from all over the world. An older couple that we had made acquaintance with earlier on was among the group. Frank was the husband's name. On the way over, we were able to have dance lessons. I loved the way the Tahitians moved, and I did my best to imitate them. I felt I did pretty well in comparison with the other guests but, of course, nothing like the Tahitians who had such dance in their souls. The staff on board put their nets out to catch fish for when we would get to our destination at another part of the lagoon. The fish were roasted over a fire after our arrival and accompanied with other picnic-type indigenous foods. But before we ate, we were invited to take our snorkels and explore the wonders underwater. Frank let me know that he wasn't much of a swimmer but willing to try. I liked him. He was an Italian man of about my father's age. I mistook his accent for one from New York, but he told me that he was from San Francisco. Maybe his Italian neighborhood had produced a similar accent. We took off into the water together. It was OK to swim topless there. I had found the experience exhilarating. Right after we arrived on the island, Mario had untied my bikini top and thrown it on the sand, and I had been swimming thus for the entire stay. In fact, the atmosphere on the island was just very relaxed in general.

I hadn't taken Frank's concern about his lack of swimming ability too seriously until I saw him drifting further out to sea. He had met with a current and had no idea what to do. I swam after him, and when I caught up, I told him I would try to help him get back to shore. He panicked but started to relax as I grabbed ahold of him. I recalled my lifesaving skills from my high school years. Mom had nearly drowned in her adulthood and had never learned to swim, so she made us kids take all and every form of water safety. I also benefited from my experience getting out of currents in my scuba classes. Frank commented on how pleasant it was for him to have me hauling him in while I was topless. We made it back to shore in time for our picnic meal. Mario and I sat on the beach to eat over in a semiprivate spot away from the rest. I glanced over to my right and noticed a very attractive young couple having coitus. They were knee-deep in the water, nude, and facing each other. They seemed not to have even noticed us or at least not cared. It is one of the most erotic things I'd ever seen. I pointed them out to Mario, who was equally impressed. There was plenty of red wine available for the picnic, and we drank plenty. On our return ride back to the resort, Mario and I wept with emotion. I think we both knew our end was in sight. The wine led both of us having a desperate feeling to have to pee. There were no accommodations on the flatboat, so we decided to jump ship. The staff became alarmed and tried to coax us to return to the boat but we said we'd just swim in the rest of the way, so that's what we did- maybe lucky a shark didn't get us!

After my return home, I was physically and emotionally exhausted. I was also very brown and thin. Leo welcomed me home and seemed aware of my fragile state. But Mom had arranged for us to travel to Los Angeles together months earlier. When she told me about the trip she was planning, I hadn't wanted to mention my Tahiti trip, so ours was only a few days after my return home. That's one thing that Mom was assertive about. If she made arrangements for travel with one of her kids, she was in charge of the trip and expected us to go along with it, no questions asked. So I got on a plane with her, and off we went. It turned out that we were in flight during a big earthquake in LA and had to circle around for a few hours before we could land. When we got there, the temperature was in the nineties. We stayed at Century Plaza, on one of the top floors. James Woods walked right past us in the ABC Entertainment Center right across the street from Century Plaza Hotel. This was where Harry's Bar was located—fashioned after the famous restaurant in Florence, Italy, with the same name. This is also where Dad had developed his friendship with one of the waiters there, Bruno, a Slovenian like himself. We went sightseeing. That first night in the hotel, I was wakened by the sensation that our room was swaying, and it was. I glanced at the clock and it was 4:00 a.m. on the dot. Then the room started shaking with a pounding noise. Mom sat straight up in bed and asked me why I had put a quarter in the bed slot. We had noticed that evening that it had a vibrating feature. Before I had a chance to answer her, she ran to the open window. I followed her, fearing she would fall off the ledge as the building was still shaking. There were several people down below in the pool. The pool had developed ocean-like waves as the swimmers leapt out of the water and ran every which way. I'm not sure if Mom ever really realized that night what had occurred. She seemed to have remained in a dream state. The next morning, we discussed the events of the night before and headed down to the lobby for breakfast. There were lines of people checking out of the hotel with plans to leave LA immediately. But Mom had no intention of considering that. We were here to vacation. We got through the rest of our stay without further incident and back home unscathed.

Dad sent Leo and me to the Catholic Church auction because he and Mom were going to be out of town. Dad loved auctions. He wrote out instructions in the auction book about what to bid for and for how much and gave us a blank check to pay for purchases. He especially was interested in a Disneyland trip he said he would give us for the kids if we could get the vacation for a reasonable price. And we did. This trip turned out to be only weeks after I returned from Tahiti and LA. So off we went at the beginning of November to Disneyland with the kids. The boys loved it. It wasn't crowded at the park that time of year, so they could get off their ride and get right back on again. Laura was only five and afraid of a lot of the rides. Leo took her on It's a Small World over and over. I was responsible for going on some rides with the boys that Leo had no interest in—the scary ones. I didn't particularly like some of them either, though. The first ride I took Laura on was the Matterhorn Bobsleds ride. This was a big mistake. I had to hold on to her for dear life, convinced that she would fly out of the sled. The centrifugal force pushed me up against her such that I was squishing her, but I couldn't help from doing so. Leo and the boys stood below and laughed at my screaming distress. Laura actually seemed unfazed on this particular ride—the one that was the scariest for me.

The boys and I tried out the brand new ride—Star Tours. It was loads of fun. I made the mistake of talking Laura into trying it, so Leo and Laura joined us for the next "tour." The ride was named after the Star Wars movie and was devised with use of military-grade flight simulators accompanied by a space travel film. A programmer used a joystick to synchronize the movement of the simulator with the apparent movement on screen.[31] The result was a very realistic-seeming flight through space—so realistic to Laura that she got angry enough to slug me in the arm right after the ride was over for having talked her into it. I was surprised by her reaction because during the ride, she had sat quietly beside me. I thought she was having a good time.

We all started out to do the Haunted Mansion but as soon as Laura got inside the elevator and heard the scary voice, she ran out and wouldn't go back in. So we took turns so the rest of us could see it. She didn't like Mr. Toad's Wild Ride either. It was the steam at the end that scared her. So it was back to It's a Small World for Laura.

---

[31] "Star Tours," *Wikipedia, The Free Encyclopedia*, http://en.wikipedia.org/wiki/ Star_Tours.

On the last night, we got the kids pizza in their hotel room and went out for dinner at the Wharf Bar at the Disneyland Hotel property. We had seen the bar and Sgt. Preston's Yukon Saloon and Dance Hall on our way back from the park one afternoon. We ran into an air traffic controller and his wife at the Wharf Bar, and they invited us to accompany them to the Review—a show that includes Sgt. Preston, the Royal Canadian Mountie who plays the keyboard in the band, Klondike Kate, dance hall girls, and numerous Disney characters, all part of the lineup.[32] I happened to be wearing a short flared jean skirt and cowgirl shirt that was conducive for hanging out in a saloon and for dancing. One of the Disney characters led me out onto the dance floor. After that, I became a dancing fool with Leo for a partner. It was a wild night. When we got home, we checked on the kids who had an adjoining room. Then we went to our room and made crazy love. Leo couldn't account for my mood, but I had some idea where it was all coming from—the aftershock of Tahiti and the indecision about how I should proceed in my life.

Cameron decided he wanted to live at Disneyland. He had big plans for how we would all relocate to this magical place. His dad would get a job at Disneyland, and we would find schools for them to transfer to. But we left and went home anyway, much to

[32] Frank Messina, "Sgt. Preston's Yukon Saloon Is the Goofiest Bar on Earth," Los Angeles Times, June 6, 1991, http://articles.latimes.com/1991-06-06/ news/ol-137_1_preston-s-yukon-saloon.

Cameron's dismay. When I got back to Bend, I knew that I needed to end it with Mario—but it wasn't easy.

There were some strange things that happened in my twenties and thirties that supported my belief that people are nuts. The first of these events happened in my twenties. I was shopping at the Highway 97 Safeway in Bend. I left my basket in the aisle to look for an item, and when I got back, I grabbed on to the cart's handle. I noticed right away that my hands were burning and that there was some slimy substance on the handle. I ran to an employee who took me to the employees' back room and washed my hands with soap in the big sink there. He asked me if I needed to go to the ER and would arrange that if necessary. I told him no, that I thought I would be OK. Then we went to examine the cart. That's when I noticed that the groceries inside the cart were covered with the same stuff. At first, my helper suggested that some caustic bottle of something must have fallen off the shelf, but there was no evidence of that—no bottles of that sort were even on the shelves of the aisle where my cart remained. He had to admit that he was perplexed. I suggested that someone had intentionally poured the stuff on the cart handle and the groceries. He said that he couldn't really argue with that. He had me fill out an incident report and helped me discard the tampered-with items in my cart and accompanied me as we replaced the items. He said that if I changed my mind about getting medical attention, the store would be responsible for any cost. I thanked him for all his assistance. He was very kind.

The next weird thing that happened involved my kids. They were all home from school one afternoon. The phone rang and a man on the other end said that he was conducting a survey. He started asking me all sorts of questions. Initially, the questions seemed benign then became more personal, such as what the household income was. I should have stopped right there but I answered him. He asked about the shoe sizes of my kids, who he already knew the names and ages of per the information I had provided him. He asked me to measure their feet because a gift for my participating in the survey was that shoes fitting each of the kids would be mailed to us. So again, I did what he asked—measured their feet and reported to the interviewer. Then he asked me to have them turn around, bend over, drop their drawers, and then administer rectal exams. I hung up as fast as I could. I couldn't believe I had suckered for such a scheme. The whole incident left me shaking. The kids asked what was up, but I didn't dare tell them. I did tell Leo that night, though. Not long after, I was talking to my sister-in-law Barb about the weird phone call. She told me that she had a similar experience with an obscene phone caller. The story goes as follows: Her husband, one of Leo's brothers, was out of town, and Barb was home alone one evening. The phone rang and a male voice on the other end said hello. Barb asked, "Is that you,

Larry (Barb's son) and he answered yes. She told the caller that he sounded different than usual, and he replied that he had a cold. They continued with a seemingly normal conversation until the caller told her that he had sexual feelings for her. Coming from who she believed was her son, she was shocked. The caller went on to describe what he felt like doing to her. That's when she hung up. But she still believed the caller was Larry, which made matters worse. So she called her son and confronted him. He was irritated with the call and told his mother that he hadn't called, and he didn't know what she was talking about. She also called her husband who was in his hotel room out of town. She told him she was frightened to stay alone. I guess she was starting to consider the possibility that it really wasn't her son who had been on the phone. Her story led us to a discussion about how it is difficult to process events that are so out of the ordinary. We tend to try to make sense of them by bringing them back to the status quo. Neither of us expected weirdness at first. I guess both of us were just gullible. (I was voted the most gullible student in my high school class. Yes, this was, in fact, a category for our Senior Awards Ceremony). That may be why she believed it was her son. After all, that is what she was told. And that seemed odd enough, but maybe not as odd as a stranger making such a call.

The third event involved Laura. She was about six years old. I ran to the Payless Drug on Highway 97 next to what was then

Wagner's Grocery. It was dusk. At the time, I drove the mustard-yellow Suburban. We ran into the drugstore to purchase some items. The plan was to return home and get dinner started. When I got back to the car and opened the door, I noticed something on the seat. It looked like someone had blown their nose there. It didn't take long for me to figure out what it really was. Laura asked what was up. I told her to stay put and found some old newspapers in the back of the Suburban. I put a bunch over the stuff and got her into the passenger seat. I drove home. I never used to lock my car doors on such occasions, but after that, I did. I told Leo, who said I should have called the police at the store. He did call, and two policemen came over. I told them what happened, and they confirmed what was on the seat. The next day, I spotted a red pubic hair on the floor of the car. So now I knew the pervert had red hair. Nothing more came of it other than my fear that the guy may have followed me home and might know where I lived.

The fourth event was at Wagner's Grocery. This time, I drove over with Laura to get some items and parked on the side parking area. Just about that time, a kid about twelve years of age rode his bike by us, as a woman in the car next to us opened her car door right into him. He ran into it, and he and the bike crashed. The woman proceeded to get out of her car, screaming and yelling at the kid that he had damaged her car door and started kicking his bike as he lay beside it. I went over to see if the kid was all right.

He seemed a little shaken but no worse for wear other than a few scuffs, but he did seem distressed by his attacker. I went over to the woman and tried to calm her down. Unfortunately, I happened to touch her arm and then she got really angry and went after me. After I got home, I called the police, but they had already heard from her, and she had told a very different story than mine. The policeman said the woman had shown him bruises she said I had caused. I told the cop that if there were bruises, they were self-inflicted. The policeman said that she planned on pressing charges against me. I talked to Leo about it that evening and I told Laura the next day after she got out of school that I thought we should drive around our neighborhood and try to locate the kid. I knew he would be a good witness on my behalf, but the odds of spotting him seemed unlikely—but what did I have to lose? So we just started driving around. We were out on Eighth Street, a few blocks from our house, when I spotted a kid riding his bike on the side of the road—the same road I used to ride on with my horse Lady. I said to Laura, "Doesn't that look like him?" And she agreed it did, so we followed the kid into a cul-de-sac. I had concerns that if it wasn't him, he might think I was weird or something. Anyway, we drove in near where he got off his bike. I rolled down the window and said, "Were you the one in the Wagner's parking lot?" and he said yes. I asked if I could talk to his mom, and he went and got her. She agreed to contact the police and the DA's office on my behalf, and I never heard another word about the incident. I still remember the kid's sweet disposition and face. I saw him around a few times after the day I spoke with him and his mother and have wondered how his life has proceeded.

Nora did the spring semester of her junior year (1988) in college in Italy. She went to school in Siena with a group from OSU. In early July, after school let out and before her return home, she and a few friends did some traveling—this included a trip to see Yanko in Slovenija. As was usual, the journey there was sketchy, but they finally arrived in the rural area where our relatives dwell. Nora only planned to be there a few days but discovered that Yanko had planned a pilgrimage to Poland for himself and his parishioners to see Pope John Paul II, so he invited the girls to join them. They all boarded a rickety old bus, and off they went. Yanko and his entourage were at the very back of the crowd who had gathered for the event. Nora described the event as exhilarating. The pope spoke to the throngs in Polish, so Nora didn't know what was being said. The people who did understand responded with exuberance.

After Nora returned to Oregon, it was only a few days before Dad's retirement party—July 22, 1988. His partners, their wives, friends, and family gathered for the celebration. I sat among my family. The event was sad for me. I stood when asked to make some sort of salutation, but all I could do was blubber. Underneath, I think I knew it was the beginning of the end for him. And yet, with Dad's retirement, there were some good times left for Mom and Dad. They traveled more extensively with each other and with old friends. They were still living the high life and would describe extravagant trips where they often met celebrities and other influential people. They went on a world cruise on the Queen Elizabeth 2 twice, and on one of them, they became acquainted with Dick Clark of American Bandstand and his wife. While they were at the Taj Mahal in India, in a nearby restaurant, Dick introduced Mom and Dad to Indian beer and giant cashews there that Dad raved about for years. It was about this time of his life that he started to dig through stuff at rummage sales and thrift stores for old clothes to take on his trips. This way, he could pack light, travel with ease, and just leave behind these items after they were worn. It was also about this time that he started telling people he was older than he really was, and the disparity between his real age and stated age grew the older he got. This, he explained, led to others complimenting him on how young he looked for his (fake) age.

My frequent flyer miles during the mid to late eighties left me with air miles to use up. Leo and I decided to travel to San Francisco in September 1988. Joe and Jan had a coupon book that offered fifty percent off some hotels there that they didn't plan to use, so they offered them to us. We decided on the Hotel Union Square, and we were able to book the Dashiell Hammett Suite.

This is where the author and his mistress, Lillian Hellman, may have conducted most of their love affair and where he did a lot of his writing. Hammett wrote detective novels and short stories, including The Maltese Falcon and The Thin Man.[33] We were surprised to see what the suite was like. It was very small, quaint, and remained in the style of his era. It wasn't like a hotel room at all and lent itself to a feeling that the author was still present. There was a large patio with tables and lounge chairs off the suite that looked out over the city. A wooden fence enclosed the area. We had checked in with the name of our friends because the coupon had their surname attached to it, and there had been no problem in getting checked into the hotel that way. One warm afternoon, we decided to hang out on the patio. We assumed it was private, so we decided to sunbathe nude in the lounge chairs. We also took nude photos of each other, one of me looking out over the city and another glancing back over my shoulder to smile for the camera. We got a call from the front desk letting us know that the patio was shared by other rooms that had access to it. Apparently, other guests had complained. We were asked not to continue on as we had been. When they called, they addressed us by our friends' surname, so when we got back home, we let them know that they had a bad reputation at the Union Square. They weren't too wor-

---

[33] "Hotel Union Square," *Wikipedia, The Free Encyclopedia,* http://en.w ikipedia. org/wiki/Hotel_Union_Square.

ried, though, because Jan said they didn't have plans to travel there anyway. We took a trip out to Alcatraz on a breezy cold day. We had to purchase San Francisco sweatshirts for the ride because we hadn't anticipated cold weather. Before our boat trip, we wondered why there were so many sweatshirts for sale in the novelty shops but figured it out pretty fast. We also tried out the local restaurants.

Since I was a child, I had curiosity about my grandparents' homeland and culture. I adored my grandmother, and her stories had fueled my interest in her world. So had the Slovenians who frequented my grandparents' home and neighborhood as a child. My aunt Jean and uncle Jack had already been over to Slovenija. Aunt Jean, who had refused to speak Slovene as a child in their home, had become interested in learning the language. She traveled to Chicago to take lessons from a Slovenian Catholic priest there. She never had the fluency that Dad maintained, though. She made attempts to get Dad to go with them. I felt an obligation of some sort to travel there myself. After all, my grandparents had always meant to go back but never did. Now that they were gone, maybe I could do that for them. I started a vacation savings account and told Dad that I thought we should go. He said that Jean was working on him too and agreed to think about it. Dad had already made plans to take us kids and our spouses to Coronado in San Diego in May 1989. The three couples met Mom, Dad, and Nora down there. Nora was twenty-one and about to return to college. Every morning was foggy, but it would lift around two in the afternoon. The Del Coronado was from a different century. I was intrigued by it. And Marilyn Monroe had done Some Like It Hot there. The hotel featured photographs of the filming and the history of the hotel. The beach in front of the hotel seemed to happen in slow motion. It was as though the place was caught in an earlier era, but right around it was massively built up with buildings, nonstop traffic, and noise. Somehow the Del seemed impervious. Sandy and I explored the hotel. She said it reminded her of our maternal grandparents' house—the scent, décor, etc. This made sense to me because it did resemble our grandparents' home. Mom and Dad took us out to some fancy restaurants while we were there. The tables were full of our family, and we were boisterous as usual. In spite of this vacation, Dad made plans with Jean, Jack, and Yanko (in Slovenija) for us to travel there in late summer.

It was difficult to leave my family for such a long trip. At least a month seemed long at the time. Dad and I flew to Chicago for a few days to visit relatives and meet up with Jack and Jean who would fly over with us. While I was there, I walked around Elmhurst to my old haunts. My mom's parents' home (the one my grandfather had built) was gone, and in its place was a grocery store parking lot. I also walked over to the Marquardt mansion (where we had so many Christmas Eve events). It had been converted to an office building, but the owners had maintained some of its integrity. My cousins Greg and Jeff and Greg's girlfriend lived at our grandparents' home. I stopped one evening to see the house and talked to Greg at the side door. I also set out from Jack and Jean's to try to find my old school. I still remembered the way, but when I got to where I thought the school should be, there was only a playground. There was a middle-aged woman with her granddaughter there. I asked about Roosevelt School, and she informed me that it had recently been torn down and a new bigger school was built several blocks away. All that remained of my old school was the playground. On my way home, I came upon the underpass, which I had avoided on my walk to the old school location by crossing the busy street above ground. But this time I decided to take the underground route. I headed down the familiar steps and held on to the side railings. When I got inside the underpass, I felt mildly uncomfortable. I stood in the spot where I had found myself years before, when I had felt unable to move at all. I thought it might seem a lot smaller or different or something, but it seemed surprisingly familiar, just as it had when I was a child.

The four of us flew out on Yugo Air. Shortly after takeoff, a few men with some sort of Eastern European accents, a good quantity of liquor under their belts and openly brandishing their liquor bottles, started to fight a few rows behind us. They really went after each other—punching each other and rolling around in the aisle right next to us. Jean couldn't help laughing in spite of herself. A few male stewards headed back and somehow broke up the fight and handcuffed each of the men and tied their legs together. One of the men seemed seriously injured, and an announcement came over the loudspeaker—"Is there a doctor on board?" Dad identified himself as such, and he was escorted to the injured men. He inspected them and told the staff that there really wasn't much he could do for these guys on the plane. So the two men were laid out in the back of the plane for the duration of the flight. I had never been in a plane where the seats were so close together and uncomfortable, but I suppose it was better than what those guys had to put up with. When we touched down several hours later, there was an announcement that passengers were to remain in their seats until further notice. From our windows a paddy wagon could be seen heading toward our plane. It stopped, and several officials got out and boarded. They traveled to the back of the plane, picked the two men up, and hauled them out to the paddy wagon and drove off. Then we were told we could start exiting the plane.

The first place we visited was Dubrovnik. Jack, Jean, and Dad settled into our hotel room to have a snack and a bottle of wine, but I wanted to explore—in particular, the Adriatic Sea. I couldn't wait to get my feet wet, lie on the warm sand on the beach, and take a long swim. I was surprised by the relaxed nature of then Yugoslavia. It was customary to swim nude or topless, depending on the body of water there. I also noticed that every shape, size, and age of person was represented on the beach. No one seemed to care whether or not they had a stunning body. Earlier, Jack had made disparaging remarks about how the beach inhabitants looked, but I thought it was great not to have to care. I left my swimsuit top behind and took in the sights and sounds on the beach. It didn't take very long before a tall, slim, dark-haired guy sauntered up and sat down next to me on the sand. He could speak pretty good English and told me he was a student at a university. He looked in his early twenties. I could tell he was flirting with me, but this surprised me. After all, I was thirty-eight. I told him so, but he said he didn't believe me. I also told him that I had a husband and three kids in the United States, but I'm not sure he believed that either or at least he didn't care. I figured he couldn't swim very well and decided to ditch him by going for a swim. I had been thinking about swimming to a little island offshore and explore it, but he told me that there were heavy and dangerous currents in that direction, so I decided to swim out to a large buoy instead. I swam hard and fast and settled on the far end of the buoy after I reached it. I sat on the ledge and looked out at the open water. I expected that my disappearance from the beach view would discourage my admirer. But a few minutes later, there he was in the water right next to me. He tried to coax me into the ocean water, promising me rapture. He said it would be heaven. I didn't think so. I remained on the buoy, and he pulled himself up next to me and pulled his dick out of his swimming trunks! It was huge. This had the opposite effect that he seemed to be hoping for. And he didn't have a pleasant scent, which put me off further. I explained that I feared pregnancy, which he seemed to understand. I jumped off the buoy and started back to shore, and he followed me all the way. When we got back on the beach, he implored me to meet him that evening. He kept pestering me as I strode along the beach toward the hotel. He promised to acquire some prophylactics before nightfall and showed me a place for us to meet. In order to be free of him, I agreed. I didn't say anything to my traveling companions right away, but a few days later on our tour bus, I told my aunt about the event on the beach. She thought it was hilarious and encouraged me to tell my dad who didn't think it was so funny, calling the guy an arse.

We traveled up the coast of then Yugoslavia, spending some time in a city called Split. I noticed there how cosmopolitan the place was. People of all ages, but especially adolescents and young adults, gathered in the city square to have conversation, smoke, hang out, visit a café, and horse around. The young girls held hands with affection and for protection. Musicians entertained the square's audience. The weather was balmy. The environment of the square was charming and exhilarating. As we traveled up the coast, Dad conversed with natives in his first language. Even in Dubrovnik, the southern part of Croatia, he was understood, and as we traveled further north, he was understood even more. When we got to Slovenija, he was understood the best but was told all the way along that he "spoke the old-fashioned way," telling us that the language had evolved since his parents had left their country. Having Dad with us was invaluable because he made it possible to communicate effectively. Without him, the experience would not have been as rich.

I found our trip exhausting from the start. The plane ride left me with little sleep, and after our arrival in Yugoslavia, the tours required us to be up before six in the morning and the days were jam-packed with travel. As I've said, I don't do well without sleep. Another difficulty while traveling with my companions was that they liked to have beer or wine with meals to avoid the water, which wasn't safe to drink. But drinking all day long didn't agree with me. I've always been a lightweight when it comes to alcohol. So I decided I'd stick with my favorite beverage—iced tea. I reasoned that since the ice was frozen, no harm would come to me. The bacteria that others had concerns about wouldn't be on my ice if I ordered it with a bottled drink or boiled tea. But that turned out to be an erroneous belief and I got an intestinal infection that was miserable for about a week of our trip. Luckily, Dad, being the doctor he was, always carried antibiotics and all other sorts of potentially beneficial medications during his travels. Before I felt the effects of the ice, though, we went to Plitvice Lakes National Park in Croatia.

As our tour bus entered the park, I became invigorated by the sight of the beautiful terrain, especially the crystal clear blue-green water of the lakes as we drove over a bridge that overlooked them. I decided and proclaimed that the first thing I would do after we got to our hotel was take a swim. Jack objected. He said that he doubted swimming was allowed in the lakes. I didn't respond to his discouraging words, but as soon as we checked into our hotel, I went down to the lobby to ask the personnel about swimming there. The girls at the front desk were delightful. Even in their youth, some of them had teeth missing. This was something I noticed was quite prevalent during our time in Yugoslavia. The girls were attractive to me anyway and were very helpful in directing me to the nearest beach. I trudged through the forest, not quite sure if I was going in the right direction, as they had given me directions in broken English, and I had no clue about their language other than a few words my grandmother had uttered when I was a child, and even these may not have translated from Slovenian to Croatian. But I found the lake and noticed that some of the sunbathers were nude, so I thought what the hell. I had packed my snorkel and mask, which provided me with much pleasure as I explored the clear cold water and its flora and fauna. I do mean cold because it was almost heart-stopping. I had learned to tolerate such temperatures when I had done my dives and stayed in the water as long as I could stand it. Unfortunately, as I was about to go back to the beach, I heard my name called and there were Jack, Jean, and Dad on the beach. I suspect that it was Jack who felt compelled to go looking for me, as Dad has always been very lax about feeling he had to keep track of anyone who traveled with him, but there they were, and I wasn't about to get out of the water until they left. They must have known that I was in there nude because my clothes were on the beach. But they just hung out there bullshitting with me, while I was freezing my ass off. I talked to them while I continued to swim around in the water until they finally left. When I got to the sand, I was shivering uncontrollably, so I lay down and let the sun warm my body. Then I returned to the hotel where they all gave me a hard time.

Mom and Dad had always been good to travel with. There was never much of an agenda, so traveling with my uncle's watchful eye was annoying to me. This made me all the more determined to do what I wanted. Thinking back on this trip, I was reeling with my determination to stick to ending things with Mario, but there was something missing because of it, and this opportunity seemed a good time to create a diversion. Italy would be the place where this would all play out, but back to Yugoslavia, plans were to meet up with Yanko at the Postojna Caves in Slovenija. We took the cave train ride of one of most famous caves in the world first and then waited for Yanko. As was with my sister Sandy and Yanko a few decades before, he didn't show up. So we hauled our luggage up a dusty dirt road from the caves until we found a bus stop and made our way to Yanko's rectory. He was delighted to see us, but we never really figured out why he hadn't come to fetch us. We stayed in his home during our stay on the second floor. The whole place had a distinctive odor that was pleasant, and we found out where it was coming from when he showed us a room with a large wooden vat that held hundreds of fermenting plums. It took up the whole room. The vat was covered with a tarp and had spigots on the bottom to collect the wine when it was ready. Milka was Yanko's housekeeper, a pleasant older woman who maintained the household. She didn't speak a word of English, so if one of us found ourselves in the kitchen with her in the morning without Yanko or Dad, all we could do was awkwardly smile at one another. Yanko did know some English. He mimicked Jean when she said certain words that he thought sounded funny—for example, the word "sandwich," which I have to admit did sound funny with Jean's Midwestern Chicago accent. She would say "Saaaahhnd witch," and Yanko would repeat it and laugh. Drinking there was no laughing matter, though. It was serious business. Yanko would pull out the plum wine with some fruits, meats, and breads to go with it. When it got really serious, it was the Slivovitz—a hard liquor that could remove enamel, made from plums. Then there was juniper gin made from the prevalent juniper trees in Slovenija—

even more potent. When my grandfather had first taken a plane to visit us in Oregon, he had commented on the juniper trees, which he said reminded him of the old country. There was no such tree in Illinois.

Yanko piled all of us into his little car, and off we went to visit all the relatives on my grandfather's side. We drove through the mountainous areas on narrow winding roads. I was petrified and complained openly of Yanko's treacherous driving. Dad defended him, explaining that he was a good driver, but coming from Dad, that meant nothing since he had a similar driving style that had made its way to America. I gripped the handlebars in the backseat and prayed I would return to the United States alive. The countryside was lush—grape vines and fig trees everywhere. Women who worked in the fields wore black dresses and babushkas. The farm equipment was very primitive by our standards. Most things were done by hand. Farm animals could be seen on the roads. There were no televisions, and if there were phones, they were also primitive. The people were poor but seemed happy.

Yanko told Jean, Jack, and Dad a story about a parishioner who came to see him one day. I only heard the story secondhand. The woman had come to see Yanko with her adolescent daughter who had turned up pregnant. The girl had tried to convince her mother that she had become pregnant by sitting on a toilet seat.

She explained to her mother that was the only possible explanation she could come up with. The mother wasn't convinced, so she had come to consult with Yanko, the parish priest, on the matter. Yanko suspected that his young handyman was the true culprit, not a toilet seat, and in fact, he was puttering around in Yanko's yard, looking guilty, during the conversation Yanko had with the disgruntled woman and her insipid daughter. To save the poor girl, Yanko told the mother that it was entirely possible that the girl had the unfortunate fate of being in her current state because of a toilet seat-saving the girl's virtuous reputation for her mother.

Everyplace we stopped, relatives would come out of their homes or fields to greet us with smiles. Then we would be invited in. They sat us down at the table and filled it with food and drink. They were a cheerful bunch who appeared to enjoy the simple pleasures in life. They lived off the land. I noticed that during mealtime, the women served the men and stood behind them while they ate, and then after the men were through, the women sat down and ate. This didn't go over well with Jean, who pulled a chair up to the table with the men and announced that she would be eating with them. That's how it's done in America, she had explained. I suppose that because she was a guest and everyone loved her gregarious and light personality, she got away with it. In fact, the other women, including me, followed suit. Dad traveled there several times after our trip together, and he told me that Jean seemed to have singlehandedly changed this custom because on future visits, the women sat with the men from the start. In the evenings after supper, entertainment included singing accompanied by handmade instruments, telling jokes and stories, and conversing in general. I didn't have the opportunity to enjoy all this as much as I would have liked because I was still suffering from my intestinal difficulties. But it was still entertaining, and the way we communicated was interesting. Someone would say something in Slovene and Dad would translate, then someone would say something in English and he would translate again. It made for lively evenings.

There were other cultural differences that I noticed. We dropped into a general store one afternoon with Yanko, and at the back of the store, there were pornographic magazines in plain view of anyone that would pass by, including children. The covers of the magazines had spread-eagle crotch shots of women. Yanko strolled by, a Catholic priest mind you, and chuckled. Jean ran over and covered his eyes and told him a priest shouldn't see such things, but he removed her hands from his face and laughed again. It was also interesting how, in general, bodily functions were out in the open. If any of the men had to pee they just turned their backs and went. Even Yanko, who stopped the car if he needed to go, opened the door, turned his back and peed. Nudity was no big deal for either sex. Nude beaches were common, and people of any age seemed to feel comfortable on them. We visited Yanko's parish church and others in the area. The influence the Second World War had on the country was represented in these churches. The stained glass windows depicted the devil with the face of Adolf Hitler. He and his army had ravished the area, and people there had not forgotten the atrocities. But there was also clear evidence of current political difficulties. Everywhere we went, there were soldiers with rifles marching up and down the streets and sidewalks. One day Yanko, Dad, Jean, Jack, and I went for lunch in a local tavern. The next thing I knew, Yanko was kicking me under the table and giving me dirty looks, suggesting that I shut up. I didn't get it, but I remained silent for the rest of our meal. When we got back in the car, he explained that it was unsafe to say certain things in public. I was still unsure what I had said, but it may have had to do with a comment I made about a picture of Tito on the tavern wall. Yanko also described recent incidents where his brethren priests in nearby parishes had disappeared in the middle of the night, never to be seen again. It would not be long before the war there broke out. Dad had planned to take Sandy the following year, but the whole country was secluded and no planes were allowed to fly in, so they went to Greece instead. Dad later explained that the Slovenians had anticipated a war and been secretly arming themselves. The Slovenians are known to be people who are fierce in protecting their homeland if necessary in spite of their size and relatively small population. Borders had changed many times over the years, and invaders had restricted the Slovenians' freedom and sometimes taken their people for slaves. But the little country finally obtained independence and, this time, would no longer be under Communist rule.

Yanko accompanied us to Italy. He drove us to the border town of Trieste, and I knew I was going to like this country after a very handsome young Italian in the border check-in box made eyes at me with a big smile on his face, which I still remember clearly. Dad had arranged another tour similar to the one in Yugoslavia, but the Italy trip was more relaxed. I still thought to myself that when, not if, I returned to Italy, I would be doing my traveling without the encumbrance of a tour. But as it was this time, I had to put up with it. Our tour bus wound around the country roads and city streets, always accompanied by the songs of Julio Iglesias. He was even bigger in Europe than in the United States. Our first destination was Venice. We took the mandatory gondola ride through the canal and visited the glassblowing establishment where Dad purchased an ornate flowered gold-and-emerald-green Venetian cup and saucer for me. It still sits on the bureau in my bedroom and reminds me of our travels through Italy together every time I see it. We also visited Pisa where we climbed the Leaning Tower. We had to make our way up a narrow, steep, winding staircase with a few small open windows on the way up. I'm afraid of heights, so I only got up to the lower summit. Jean and Dad traveled all the way to the very top. Next, we went to Florence and then Rome, the best place of all. Here, everywhere you looked, there were gorgeous men of all ages. At that time, Italian women were scarce. They must have been at home caring for children and running the household. But the men were free to roam the streets of the city. I found them gregarious, flirtatious, and charming. I brought a sexy short black dress with me that I wore in Rome. Dad (usually casual about such things) said that if I was going to wear the black dress, he wouldn't walk with me in the streets. I have wondered if Jack may have made some sort of comment to Dad. Jack watched me like a hawk and didn't want to let me out of sight. But I had my ways. Dad actually started out that day walking ahead of me, but when he noticed that I ignored his suggestion that I change what I was wearing, he gave up and walked along with me anyway. Men would come up alongside me and whisper Italian sweet nothings in my ear. At least that was what it seemed they must be.

One evening, we went to a restaurant, and our waiter was to die for. (He reminded me of Mario). I couldn't get him out of my mind. I fantasized about sneaking back to the restaurant after we had returned to our hotel, but I thought better of it. I have to admit that what probably stopped me from trying to meet up with the waiter was how exhausted I felt and knew that if I had spent the night in an adventure, I would have paid dearly the next day or two. I had a big fear of losing too much sleep because I knew what could happen to me if that happened. The next day, Jean and I got away together for a while, and she commented to me that it was the old Italians who paid me attention. But right after she said this, a young guy sauntered up to me and started courting me. Jean said, "Well, I guess it isn't just old Italians." She and Dad got to the point where they found the attention I was getting amusing. We had one Roman tour with a woman who was probably around sixty years of age. I still remember her face clearly, just as I do the young Italian man at the border in Trieste. She wore no makeup, was beautiful in every way possible—face, body, temperament, and spirit. She remains a role model for me in my older years in spite of the fact that I could never achieve her magnificence. My grandmother is my role model too. She didn't have the physical natural beauty of this Italian woman, but Francesca was all natural, earthy and real, and she had a good heart.

As the four of us traveled through Italy on the bus, we talked about family history. I learned a lot by listening to my dad and aunt. As I have mentioned, Jean told of Gypsy blood that ran in our family. We saw Gypsies during our travels through Yugoslavia and Italy. They held interest for me because I felt that maybe I may have been linked to them genetically. They were nomadic, colorful, poor, often thieves. I also felt akin to Italians. My grandmother looked Italian, acted Italian, and cooked Italian. Her language and her Slavic eyes were the exception. She had grown up only ten miles from the Yugoslav-Italian border, and the border in this area changed on a regular basis. My grandparents had immigrated as Italians. My niece Andrea, Doug's daughter, located a Luca Krkoc on the Internet. Andrea and Doug corresponded with him. He believed that he was related to our family. His had relocated to Croatia, but the family had lived in Slovenija earlier on. He also said that Krkocs had come from the areas near the border of Italy and Slovenija, in the towns of Ajdovscina and Gojace. In these places, he explained, "every second man is Krkoc" and "that [it is] a great looking place near [the] Italian border, near the sea." Luca added that during the time he visited Ajdovscina, he asked about the clan and was told that this family had actually lived earlier on in a little place near Verona, Italy.

There was an Irish couple traveling with us on the bus. The man became very ill, and suffered terrible back and abdominal pain. He sat in the back of the bus where there was a longer seat so he could lie down. Sometimes he would be doubled over with pain. Dad took a look at him and suspected he had kidney stones. He let the tour guide know that the gentleman needed medical care, so our tour was interrupted by visits to the hospitals in the cities we arrived in. Dad would accompany the man into the hospital. He knew some Italian and hoped to communicate to the hospital staff what he suspected. Unfortunately, the staff didn't seem to have the technology that Dad was used to in the States. So we went on to the next destination, and he would try again to get help for the Irishman. This went on for three or four days, and the man's condition seemed to be getting worse. Dad confided to me one evening in his room that he felt helpless about the man and that his condition could be life-threatening. He said that in the States, the stones could be pulverized with a simple procedure. Dad wept with frustration and concern for the man. The tour guide worked on finding a solution for the couple. It was decided to get them on a plane for Ireland where there might be better health care. But the problem was getting him on the plane because if it was discovered that he had a serious medical condition, the tour guide feared that they wouldn't let him board. So they suggested that he try to hide his distress until they were in the air. There would be no turning back if he successfully got off the ground. He and his wife did get aboard, and the plane took off, but we never knew what happened to him after that.

During our bus trip through Italy, there were sights that you wouldn't see in the States. I usually sat next to Dad on the bus rides. One day we witnessed an Italian on the side of the road with his pants around his ankles taking a crap. Dad was beside himself with laughter. I just thought to myself—Well, it's a practical thing to do. Later on, the bus was detained due to road construction. It took long enough that I needed to go too, so I left the bus and hiked over the road embankment to find a place to pee. I was surprised by the plethora of turds that lingered right off the side of the road. I certainly wasn't the first to use this spot. In the cities, the bathrooms were sometimes merely holes in the ground inside an outhouse- type construction. You just had to hunker down next to the hole and go. I was also surprised by the unisex bathrooms. You could be in one stall and a guy would be in the next taking a crap or using a urinal as you left a stall.

We went back to Slovenija before we flew home to say goodbye to relatives. We traveled to Ljubljana for our flight back to the States. By this time, the weather had changed from ninety degrees or hotter to cold. Fall was approaching. Before boarding our flight home, I decided to visit the bathroom in the airport. You never know what you're going to get in foreign bathrooms. They are all different. Well, I got into this one that had a stall door that went almost to the floor and a lock that made no sense to me at all. After using the bathroom, I couldn't get out, and no one was around. I yelled, but no one heard me. I began to imagine the plane leaving without me, so I started yelling louder. Finally, one of the airport staff heard me and tried to explain to me how to work the lock but with the language barrier, that didn't do me any good. They finally located Dad who was able to translate to me how to get out of there. My family had been wondering where I had gone, and the plane was about to take off. I was feeling a little homesick on the last part of the trip. I had tried to call home a few times, which was a nightmare. None of the phone booth phones worked at all, and if I had gotten through at all during the trip, the connection was bad, and it cost a fortune. This was a time before cell phones, and the part of Europe we had traveled in didn't have a telephone network as efficient as that in the United States. As we boarded the plane, I noticed a group of subdued women, all in black, with babushkas covering their heads. They reminded me of Francesca. I wondered why they might be traveling to America. Did they have relatives there? I marveled at their seeming out of place in the plane with the other passengers. I also wondered if this was how Francesca might have been after leaving her homeland and sailing off to a brand new country. But for me, it was good to be going home.

Baby Laura

Cam, Byron, Laura

In the Tub

Skeleton Byron

At the Ocean 1 (Byron)

At the Ocean 2 (Cameron)

At the Ocean 3

Audrey, Cam, Laura

Cam and Laura

Laura and Byron

Leo's Birthday 1

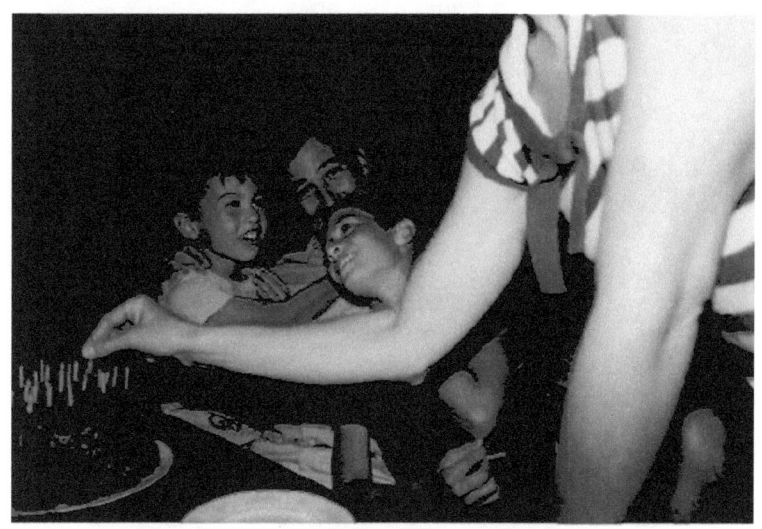

Leo's Birthday 2

Laura's Birthday

Nora and Me at Bike Races

Doug at Bike Race

Cam, Laura, Andrea

(Costumes for Bike Race)

Bent Moody

Family Christmas

Diane and Doug 1

Diane and Doug 2

Diane and Doug 3

Cam, Mom, Byron

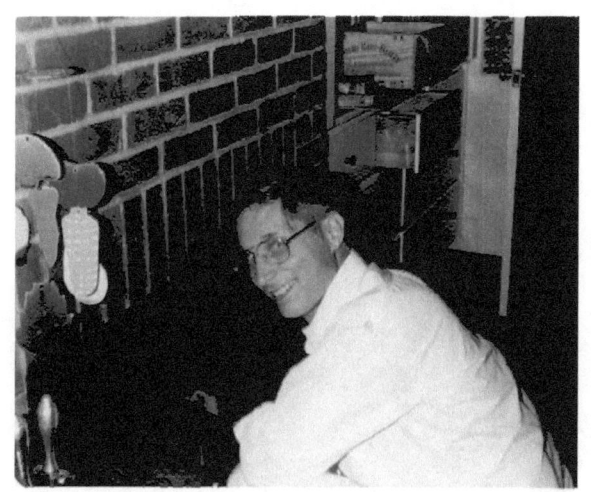

Dad

Cam

Laura

Disney Land (Nov. 87)

Cam- Peewee, Laura – Mummy

Leo and Dad

Byron, Laura, Cam

Roaring 20's 1

Roaring 20's 2

Roaring 20's 3

Leader of the Pack (Lip-sync)

Honolulu - lulu (Lip-sync) 1

Honolulu - lulu (Lip-sync) 2

Crazy-The Jugs

US and the Peachys 1

US and the Peachys 2

Sandy at our House

Dave and Sandy

In San Diego (June, 1989)

Jean and Yanko

Me and Dad in Slovenija (1989)

With Milka at Yanko's

Dad, Jean and Me in Italy

Yanko with the Pope

CHAPTER 5

My brother liked dangerous sports and fast cars. One of his passions had always been bike riding and racing. His wife, Diane, was also an enthusiast. Doug helped put on the Cascade Cycling Classic road race in Bend, which attracted world-class riders. He and a few of his friends raced along with them for several years. The races included long distance road races and criteriums, which happened in Downtown Bend. The criteriums attracted big crowds that lined the streets, and they were exciting to watch, especially for us in the family who would cheer Doug on. As the bicyclists flew around the street corners, they created a loud buzzing noise and appeared to be only a blur of colors as they passed by spectators because of the riders' great speed. Teammates worked together to help jockey one of their own to be able to pull ahead. Sometimes there were crashes. Doug asked me if I might sponsor some riders one summer. Leo and I were reluctant at first but eventually agreed, thinking that the kids would like having the experience. Doug had encouraged the boys to take up biking, and they were enthusiastic about it all. We felt we could accommodate three riders in our home and were lucky enough to have Canadian riders the first time—Brent Mudrey and Jill and Sharon something or other. At first, the boys were disappointed to have two female riders and only one guy, but they changed their minds pretty soon because all three riders were interesting and fun-loving. The Cascade Cycling Classic also offered races for kids of all ages. The boys raced in their categories, and so did Laura. She brought down her little red bike and helmet, which had been passed down from the boys, for her race. The bike and helmet remained on the sidelines with her, and when the adult categories began, Brent jumped on Laura's little bike, donned her helmet, and rode over to the starting line. The announcers were familiar with his clowning antics and introduced him as one of the racers gathering at the starting line—"Bent Moody". Bent's legs stuck out perpendicular to the bike, but that didn't stop him. He flew ahead of the other riders for a block or so until they took him over. We attended the road races too, packing lunches and waiting at the finish lines for the riders to pass it after long hot rides in the mountains.

The next year, we opened our home again to riders. We requested Canadians because of the good luck we had had with them the year before. This time there were three guys who were equally as fun as the first bunch. I spent time cooking up a storm for them because they burned up so many calories every day. They loved having good meals ready for them at the end of the day. They were young and adventurous, adopting a nomadic life for their passion of bike racing during the time they were in the racing circuit. One of these young men, Peter, invited us to visit in Vancouver, British Columbia. He said that his parents had a big three-story house and were used to company. I remembered my Vancouver visits during my Seattle U days and how fun that city was. So we planned to contact Peter about visiting the next summer for a family vacation to Canada but decided to get a hotel while in Vancouver. We arrived at Peter's home for dinner one evening. The other riders were there to greet us too. Included were an assortment of quirky folks who wandered in and out of the big rambling, cluttered, and comfortable home. There were bicycles, bike tools, and tires cluttering the entryway. Peter's mum and pop were the epitome of the English middle-aged couple. The dining room had a table with benches that seated a few dozen people if necessary. That evening, it was a full house. Dinner was casual to say the least. Peter's father sat at the head of the table. When someone wanted a potato or a loaf of bread at the far end, someone would yell out what they needed and the item flew across the expansive table and was caught in midair by the recipient. I also contacted a Chinese man by the name of Archie that Dad and I had traveled with through Croatia and Slovenija. He told us that he was a cab driver, but Dad told me later that he knew different—that he was wealthy and influential. Dad and Archie hit it off on the tour, and he gave both of us his phone number and said to call him if we were ever in Vancouver, so I did. I wasn't sure if the invitation would still stand or if he would even remember me, but he did and seemed pleased to hear from me. I told him I was traveling with my family, and he insisted on picking us up at our hotel. The next morning, a stretch limousine pulled up in the circular drive. Archie stepped out with a black suit and chauffeur's cap. He drove us up to his mansion on the hill and introduced us to his wife and one of his sons. Then he drove us all to a Chinese restaurant and ordered a feast. The kids loved it.

One evening we were all sitting around the kitchen table and somehow the topic of bike racing came up. Leo and I let the kids know that we thought we could do a hundred mile ride. After all, Doug did them all the time with his road bike. We only had mountain bikes, but figured we could take our time and make it in less than twelve hours. The kids said "no way" so we bet them a dinner at the best restaurant in town (Rosette) and they accepted. The next weekend we all barreled into our mustard colored Suburban to chart out the course-first to Redmond, on to Prineville, then Sisters, Tumalo and back to Bend. Then we set the date. It just so happened that we were hosting the Wednesday picnic on an August evening (before our ride the next morning) at a nearby park, but it rained and so the party had to move to our covered patio. The party didn't let up until after one a.m. and then I couldn't sleep for fear we would fail the next day. With little sleep, we woke at the crack of dawn to what would be a ninety-five degree day and my period started that morning too. But off we went with our kids as our support team. Byron drove the Suburban and the three kids made regular stops along the way to provide snacks and fluid. There were lots of bets made-mostly that we would fail-but Mom bet everyone she could find to bet that we would succeed and we did. Doug called that night surprised and delighted that we had done the hundred miles in a little over ten hours. He invited us up to celebrate with a hot tub. Mom is the one who really made out though. She earned 2,000 dollars on her bets that we would make it-some she made during the picnic at our house the night before the ride the next day. The kids complained and begrudgingly paid for our dinner out but I think that underneath they were proud of us.

Laura liked to spy on her big brothers, who were in their adolescence. Their friends would gather around the dining room table at our house and talk about sports, friends, school, and of course, sex. She often sat quietly under the table and got a lot of information that way. She also picked up a bugging device from our Western Union neighbor Fay—the one I worked for an entire thirty minutes. She attached it to our phone and started taping the boys' conversations, in particular Cameron's, with pubescent girls. One evening when the boys weren't around, she strolled into the kitchen where Leo and I were sitting around after dinner. She presented the device to us and informed us that it contained a conversation between Cameron and some girls he knew. We probably shouldn't have agreed to listen to it, but our curiosity got the best of us. It was shocking! Cameron mostly just listened to what the girls had to say and commented every so often. They described to him all sorts of things they might do for him. These were junior high girls, and I couldn't believe what I was hearing. After she left, Leo and I discussed what to do with this information. We decided not to say anything to Cameron. We feared what he might do to his little sister, and we also considered the manner in which we had obtained the information. One day, while Laura was out of the house, I found the gadget, and I got rid of it.

The boys started eating us out of house and home. I was at the grocery store every day to restock the cupboards, refrigerator, and freezer, but by the next day, everything was gone, so back to the store. Nothing ever went to waste. They were human bottomless-pit disposal units. When they got home from school, they'd search the kitchen for something to eat. Byron had a habit of taking a whole loaf of white bread, squishing it into a big bread ball, and downing it in a few gulps. One time, he couldn't find anything in the refrigerator that appealed to him other than some leftover bacon in the back. He decided to cook it up in a frying pan on the stove. When I got into the kitchen, he was downing the last piece. There was a rancid odor wafting in the kitchen air and I asked him what that was all about. He said he had just cooked up some bacon. I let him know that bacon had been back there for a while, lost in the back of the refrigerator, and he commented that he thought it tasted a little funky. But then he had eaten it all anyway. His excuse was that he was hungry. Dad and Mom loved to take the boys (and sometimes us too) to any all-you-can-eat spots available. They (or we all) would just watch the boys come back again and again with full plates, and the food would disappear real fast. Dad would say that he was glad he got his money's worth. Leo and I would take the kids to Skippers all-you-can-eat, along with their grandmother Frances because she liked to go there too. It was the same thing there. They ate seafood, coleslaw, and fries to their hearts' content.

Laura and her friend (about four years older than Laura) palled around together. They would head downtown and go to the drugstore where there were Playgirl magazines in the rack in the front of the store. They sneaked the Playgirl in between some teen magazine so that they could check out the naked guys. What one didn't think of, the other one did. One time, I took Laura, her friend, and the boys cross-country skiing. I was the only adult. They got the idea that they would take their skis off on top of a steep hill, let the skis fly down the hill, and retrieve them. This was supposed to keep them from having to ski down a hill that might have appeared scary to them. They did this before I came up on them from behind. The boys had skied ahead to wait for us at the shelter for lunch. Their skis flew down the hill and through the woods, out of sight. Now I had two kids with no way to ski out. I told them to stay put and skied ahead to find the boys, who were waiting for us at the shelter. Byron skied back to the girls and found a few of the skis, which had to be good enough. We slowly worked our way back to the car before dark.

Laura also went through a phase of stealing. One of these events occurred at Leo's office around Christmastime when I was cleaning. She spotted gifts in Leo's partner's office and sneaked one of them into her coat pocket. When she got home, she opened the package and kept the gift hidden. Leo's partner reported the gift missing the following Monday, so when he got home that night, we confronted Laura who surrendered the gift to us. She never could resist an unopened package. She would sneak down to the tree at night, open and then rewrap her gifts. The next morning, it was obvious what she had done because of her shoddy rewrap. The worst, though, was when I took her to a children's clothing store downtown. The store also had little toys, and she had asked about some little plastic dolls. I ignored the request, so she sneaked them into her pocket. A day or so later, I found them in her room and asked her about it. She admitted to taking them. I told her I would take her back down to the store where she would have to give them back. She got so distressed about having to do so that she disappeared. The whole family started looking for her with no luck. We even ran along the river near our house with concern that she might have run away and could have slipped into the water. This went on for a few hours. Finally, I heard a faint noise from our walk-in closet in our bedroom, and there she was, hunkered in the corner behind the clothing and stored boxes. I told her that she still had to go back to the store. She gave the trinkets back to the clerk, who thanked her, and never stole anything again as far as I know.

The boys were busy with their adolescent years, so sometimes I took Laura to Portland to visit Nora, who was working and living with a few roommates. We had fun on these trips. Nora was dating Todd. During one visit, the four of us went to the Brasserie Montmartre, where Dad often took the boys. I had never seen Laura like the way she was that night. I would have to say she was "on." She kept right up with the adult conversation and then some. She had always been precocious, but this went beyond. I suspect she had a crush on Todd. After dinner, we all went back to Nora's apartment. There was a full basement in the house with a television and a hide-a-bed couch. We pulled the couch out so that we could all fit and relax together while we watched our movie. Laura made some comments that were prurient and outlandish. It was hard not to laugh. It seems she picked up more from the conversations the boys and their friends had around the dining room table and the tapes that she recorded of Cameron's phone conversations than expected.

In July 1992, Mom planned a trip to Seattle for herself, Nora, Laura, and me. The four of us would be taking the train from Portland. After we boarded, there were delays, the air conditioning went south, and the toilets overflowed, so the ride wasn't real fun. But we all got there in one piece and checked into our hotel. The long weekend was meant for sightseeing, shopping, and eating out mostly. We headed over to Nordstrom for a big sale. It was so crowded (lines of shoppers at the check stands and frantic, mostly women, shoppers perusing the merchandise) we decided to move on. We took the new metro bus tunnel to get about town. The buses travel through narrow cylindrical dark underground tubes at high speed. If one were prone to claustrophobia, it might be something to avoid, but for me it was fun.

The high point of the trip, though, was our meal at a Japanese restaurant in one of the downtown hotels, but not the one we were staying in. The names of both escape me. Anyway, we all sat down in a private room where the table had hidden space for our legs so you didn't have to cross on a pillow Japanese style—much like the Bush Garden in Portland that we frequented with Mom and Dad as children. (I stumbled upon it recently in Portland, hadn't seen it in years, and discovered it had recently closed. It had been in operation since 1960, the year we moved to Oregon). A few women in traditional Japanese attire attended to us. They spoke little English, and we spoke no Japanese. The four of us looked over the menu. I spotted an unusual item that sounded interesting. I was always one for a new culinary experience, and so I pointed it out to my tablemates and then to the attendant who would be taking our order. She asked if I was sure I wanted to choose this item. That should have been a clue. She explained in her broken English that Americans usually shy away from this selection and that the dish required the whole table to order it. Nora was skeptical. "Are you sure we want to order this?" she asked me. "Well, yes," I answered. "Don't you want to experience something new and different?" She still wasn't convinced. As for Mom and Laura, they were neutral on the subject and went along with my suggestion. First there was the tabletop burner, then an assortment of bowls with a variety of vegetables and other ingredients—a plate of fish heads and other bony fish parts—and finally, the cauldron that the meal would be prepared in. Our attendant gestured to us that we were to toss the ingredients on the table into the liquid in the cauldron. We were left to our own devices to figure out how to proceed.

We started adding the bowls of food. The cauldron bubbled away. We expected our attendant to return with further instructions, but that never happened. By the time we decided to ladle our meals into our bowls, it had turned into mush. When Nora gets hungry she also gets grouchy. She just stared into the bowl with a fish eye staring back at her and looked glum. I tried to remain optimistic and made a jab at the stew but even I, who will eat just about anything, had a hard time with this stuff. Mom and Laura gave it a try too, with more humor than Nora had, but we all left most of our meals in their bowls. We decided we had let it simmer way too long, but Nora added that the fish heads would have done her in anyway. Mom had a fat bill to pay for the uneaten meal. After we returned to our hotel, we ordered some room service and called it a day. The next morning, we returned home.

My marriage seemed more on track, but something was unleashed during my affair. Now I continued to feel a restlessness and longing for adventure. This played out in my developing obsessions with certain men. One was an employee at a gas station where I had my car filled and serviced. Nothing came of this. I suspect he may have thought I was peculiar, and this is what probably put a damper on my crush. I wasn't overt about my emotions, but it seemed he was onto me. Next, I developed a crush on a younger acquaintance of Dad's, the seductive sort who came onto me in the first place. I went so far as to send him a love letter but only signed my first name. When I ran into him one day, I brought the letter up. He said he thought it was from a nurse at the hospital with the same name who had sent it. He explained that he was not in a position to have a relationship with me and explained why. He did have a good reason, whether or not that was really why he turned me down. Now I had never up to this point been assertive as far as men went. I was the demure type who waited to be courted. But with Mario's influence and his being out of my life, things changed. Was it just that he had opened up a world to me that I wasn't willing to abandon? In fact, I'm not sure I was capable of going back, even if I had tried. It seemed out of my control.

Byron was about ready to leave home, and the other two were growing up. I began to anticipate an empty nest and decided to plan ahead. We took Byron up to college in early September 1992. It was similar to when he had started first grade. It was emotional for me and Leo, and we cried all the way home after we left him there. To us, he looked lost as we drove off. Cameron and Laura sat in the backseat and didn't seem too fazed.

It became difficult to make our house payments after an addition was added and taxes increased, so we decided to put the house up for sale and find a new place. The big house on First Street had been Leo's parents' after they purchased it in the early sixties—the house Leo had grown up in between the ages of eleven and eighteen and where he and his family had gathered for a number of years after. It was difficult to move not only for sentimental reasons but also because after we purchased the home from Leo's mother, we had accumulated a lot of stuff that had to be moved or gotten rid of. It took a year and a half to sell, and when it finally did, we found a ranch home in Northeast Bend, not far from the house I had grown up in. In some respect, the move turned out to be a positive one, especially for me. I never really felt like the old house was mine. It always seemed to belong to Leo's parents. The previous owners of our new home had been a couple with a family, and the wife had died of cancer, so the widower was eager to sell. Our new home seemed to reflect some of the turmoil that must have occurred in the house with the woman's death and that also seemed to have passed on to us with our own brand of turmoil after our move in on April 1, 1993.

Nora and Todd married in Portland on April 17, only a few weeks after our move. We drove up the night before to attend the rehearsal dinner on the River Queen. Sandy got a bad clam in her meal there, which forever left her repulsed by clams. The next morning, our car was brought out of the garage by a valet, and a city bus ran into it. Luckily, it was still able to get us to the church on time. The wedding was in a small Slavic Catholic church downtown, and the reception afterward was at the downtown Hilton. Byron came up from college with a tall pretty blonde coed. The next morning, we all gathered for breakfast. It was Sandy's fortieth birthday, and she grumbled about turning forty.

Jan and I met for lunch one afternoon in early summer. She told me that Joe had decided to accept a transfer down to Southern Oregon, so they would be moving at the end of the summer. I couldn't believe it. She was distraught, and so was I. The move happened in spite of how either of us felt, but I decided I wanted to visit as soon as possible, so Leo, Laura, and I drove down at the end of the summer. They had settled in Jacksonville, a quaint little tourist town near Medford and Ashland. The Britt Festival was housed there-an outdoor stadium on a hill where music concerts are held in the warm weather months. I loved the area. The summers were hot and humid. Their Victorian replica home was surrounded by fields and pastures, and there were miles of roads out in the countryside where I could ride my bicycle during our visits. The little town of Jacksonville had weekend markets and novelty shops on Main Street. We'd poke around in them. I discovered CDs in one of the stores there that had alternative music. You could listen to the selections with headphones and I was hooked. I always loved Latin, African, Cuban, Gypsy, and Caribbean music more than any other, but now I had a source for purchases. The music moved me beyond description. I wondered if there was some truth to my aunt Jean's declaration that there may be Gypsy blood that runs in our veins.

I decided to try to get into graduate school in Portland for a master's degree in social work at Portland State University (PSU), if they would have me. In the meantime, I enrolled at Central Oregon Community College (COCC) in Bend and took a few pertinent classes, as I hadn't been in school for years. The prospect of the enrollment process was frightening, especially thinking about taking the GREs. I have never been a good test taker, and anxiety seems to play a big part in my difficulty. I think back to my years at home when Dad was so intent on my academic proficiency and his impatience with my shortcomings. I found volunteer work in the community to help improve my credentials for acceptance. I went up to PSU to discuss my application process with the dean of students, who told me not to bother. She explained that there were lines of people waiting to get into graduate school in this area who had years of experience in the field, but I decided I had nothing to lose in applying. In regard to taking the GREs, I contacted the school and asked about avoiding them if possible due to the years it had been since graduating. I had a very good GPA from undergraduate school, and they had liked my letter of intent that was required in the enrollment process, so they let me off the hook. It was such a great relief not to have to worry about the test. To my amazement, I was accepted. Byron would be going back to OSU for his second year, and I would be starting at PSU. Laura was the one who didn't like the idea of my academic pursuit. She had complained about my studying while I was taking classes at COCC. She was ten. I worried about what effect all this might have on our family, but Leo encouraged me and was supportive. He said he would look after our home while I was at school. This was also about the time that Leo decided to quit practicing law. He had grown tired of it. He had always liked to work with his hands, whether this was artwork or woodwork. His father had mentored him in his adolescence to learn how to build just about anything, and I also believe he had a knack for it in the first place. So it wasn't a difficult transition for him to give up law and start his own construction business. In fact, he loved it, and it afforded him a new lease on life.

I had to go up to Portland State for an orientation. I asked Cam and Laura if they wanted to come up with me. I said it could be a little vacation. They hung out on campus while I attended my meeting. While I was there, I kept hearing a name mentioned that was familiar to me. In fact, I thought it was quite a coincidence that the administrator of the social work program had the same name as one of my best friends from junior high and high school. The woman never materialized. It was mentioned that she was, for some reason, unavailable for the orientation. After it was over, I met the kids in the student union building, and we walked about campus. Then we explored the city and went to a movie. I went to get a big bucket of popcorn to share and Pepsis for each of us in a cardboard holder. I sat down and handed Laura the popcorn, which she immediately dropped on the floor. Then I distributed the Pepsis, which they both spilled too. Now we were down to only one Pepsi. They asked me for a new bucket of popcorn and more Pepsi. I had no cash left, and neither did they, so we had to share mine. I had driven up in my Ford pickup, and so we headed back out of town the next day. I got us completely lost. We drove around the Portland metropolitan area for what seemed like an eternity. Cam got so frustrated that he insisted on taking charge of the wheel, but I didn't have much faith in his driving skills either, so I continued on. On our way back, I kept thinking about Janet—my friend with the same name as the woman administrator at the university. Could they be one and the same? I decided (when I finally got home) to call her. I had her number somewhere. She answered the phone, and I told her about my visit to Portland and my plans to start school in the fall. She laughed and told me another story. She and a colleague had been walking on campus the day before. Janet (Putt) commented to her colleague that she had just seen a woman who looked just like a friend she had gone to school with years ago. She never really considered the possibility it might have really been me. Now we knew we would be seeing each other soon. She offered to help out anytime I needed it—her door would always be open, she said. And it was.

I was to start school the end of September, but an event that happened a few weeks before almost led me to give up the idea. Cameron was starting his sophomore year in high school. I had dropped him off initially and noticed that some of the students were jumping in the back of pickups of their friends after school to get rides home. I cautioned Cameron not to ever try this, that it was dangerous. One day he decided to get a ride home from a friend, and there were also a couple of girls who wanted rides too. Cameron offered to get in back of the guy's pickup so the girls could ride in front with the driver. Another of their friends jumped in the back with Cameron. Leo happened to be home around the time that school was let out. He answered the call from the hospital and was told that our son had been in an accident and to come right away. It just didn't seem real. I had to ask again what the call was about. The drive to the hospital seemed endless, but after we arrived, it was worse. The driver, a friend of Cameron's that we knew and liked, and the other persons involved in the accident were in the waiting room, looking chagrined. We were led back to the ER, and there he was. He yelled to his dad as best he could "Don't let Mom in here." He knew I didn't handle such things very well. But I did go in, and he had covered the lower half of his face with a towel so that I couldn't make out the extent of the damage right away.

We were instructed to take him a few blocks away to an oral surgeon who would work to put him back together as best he could. On the car ride there, I got an unwanted look at him in the backseat. The skin on his chin was hanging down by his neck, and he was having trouble talking. This was because he had lost several teeth and part of his jaw bone. I felt hysterical. After he was in with the doctor, Leo and I traipsed back and forth in the parking lot. The waiting seemed endless. Our regular dentist and his wife happened to be walking by and saw us. The dentist came over to say hello and asked what we were doing there in the parking lot. After we explained, he said he would go in and see how things were progressing. When he came back out, he told us that Cameron had a very serious injury, and he didn't know how successful the repair would be. He added that there had been nerve damage to his face in addition to the other injuries, and he might have a droopy face on that side. That's not what I needed to hear right then. After the doctor left, I really lost it. Leo was angry that he had told us all this. But the oral surgeon finally came out and said that the surgery had gone well, but that there would be others. He added that he felt he had successfully addressed the nerve damage and expected there would be a good result in that regard. We took him home. He remained in a great deal of pain, and he had a scar on his chin and several teeth missing on the bottom. I couldn't believe that they didn't keep him in the hospital for a while. I was so frightened about it all. He got himself to look at himself in the mirror and was stoic about it, but I could tell it was hard for him. He told me he was sorry. "I screwed up, Mom," he said to me. But I had my own guilt going on too. He had wanted me to drive him to and from school because he didn't like taking the bus. I did for the first week or two, but after that, I told him he could either take the bus or walk home. That's how it had been for me when I was growing up. I still wish I had agreed.

I couldn't sleep that night because I knew he was suffering so, and I felt ill-equipped to be helpful. I didn't know what to do other than give him his pain meds when scheduled. I felt sick to my stomach and couldn't eat or sleep for days. It was difficult to see him that way. In fact, he was a stout fellow before the accident, but because he had a few years before the surgeries were over and he had functional teeth again, he had trouble eating all that time and lost a lot of weight. I don't think he ever grew as he would have. His high school sports were over. I knew from how his friend, who had driven, appeared in the hospital that he was having a hard time and feeling responsible. I called him a few weeks after the accident and talked to him. I wanted to let him know I knew he hadn't intended any harm.

Cameron had to have bone grafts to build up his jaw first. Then he had to go without his dentures while his jaw healed. This was in preparation for placing implants to attach teeth to. Then there were gum grafts. When other students asked him about his appearance, he told them that he used too much chew and cautioned them against it. The whole process took about two and a half years. I didn't think about it right away, but after some reflection, I wondered about my extreme reaction to Cam's injuries. I think that it all brought back my own oral assault as a child. And this would not be the last experience that would bring the event back to me in catastrophic form.

I decided to at least give school a try. When Cameron had one of his surgeries, I took time off from school, or Leo tended to him. In some respect, life went back to the old routine other than my being away for four days of the week and home for three. I decided that in order to have time with my family on the three days at home, I would take advantage of the other four and cram in as much as I could. I took the Greyhound bus up and back every week. I got to know the bus drivers, who often let me on for free or at least half price because I traveled every week. I decided on the three-year school option instead of the two to give me more time at home. I studied, read, and wrote papers on the bus and until bedtime on my school days. During the first year, I stayed with another student from Bend part of the week and slept on her couch, and part of the week with my sister Nora. One day I was studying in the Student Union. A sultry, seductive and enticing African American gentleman asked if he could join me. I said yes. He was hard to resist. As time went by, he asked for my phone number and I gave it to him. When I got back to my roommate's apartment, she let me have it. She was so angry that I had given out her phone number [the fellow had called on me], she kicked me out, so I had to move to a dorm room as small as a prison cell on the freshman male dorm floor. Why they put me there is beyond me. Loud music and cavorting in the hallway went on all night long. My room had a view of an apartment across the way, and I would see all sorts of goings-on from my window. My sister Nora lived in Portland too. She was newly married by then and working for a CPA firm. Her husband, Todd, was working as a chemical engineer. I stayed with them one night of the week while I was in Portland. Todd would pick me up from school, and we'd all go to some restaurant and then to their house. Nora had only been two years old when I left for college. Now we were spending time together as adults and getting to know each other.

But I was anxious and seriously depressed during these school years. I literally trembled with fear the first month or so in my classes. I was sure I would fail. My depression may have been partly due to Cameron's condition, but it was also grueling and lonely at school. People were nice, but most of my time was spent alone studying, going to class and traveling back and forth. The third year was especially hard. I had intense classes that focused on self—difficult aspects of self—and it was understood you would have to share with others. Being brought up to hide things from others, this was difficult for me. And some of what I was reading led to insight about myself that wasn't particularly easy to accept. I did begin to understand myself better, though. All this led to what I would describe as a breakdown. In spite of all this, I carried on.

During the second year of school, I had a practicum at the Veteran's Outpatient Clinic in Portland. I worked on a multidisciplinary team of psychiatrists, psychologists, clinical social workers, nurses, and physicians. Everyone was nice and helpful. I also liked the population I was able to work with—mostly males with schizophrenia, bipolar disorder, or posttraumatic stress disorder. I got to run groups, make home visits, and be a part of the group treatment team. My supervisor seemed to have faith in me, which was probably the most important aspect of my training there. A social worker named Louie Altig was particularly helpful. He took me out on his home visits to show me the ropes.

The flood in our new house happened first. It was Thanksgiving 1994. We had all gone out to breakfast in the morning, and when we returned, we were up to our knees in water. The washing machine pipe had frozen and broken. Water had filled the whole back—half of the house. Our kitchen and bathroom linoleum had been the nearly indestructible kind that I grew up with, but the water rendered it useless. We had to replace it with the crummy cheap stuff that they sell nowadays, so I mourned the loss of my old linoleum.

In January, Dad offered to take me up to Portland rather than have me take the bus. He said he wanted to see my dorm room and campus, and we could visit on the way and have lunch at the summit's Huckleberry Inn, where they served homemade pie. Then he planned to spend a few days at the condo in Vancouver and meet up with Nora, Todd, and Mom in Portland. I had agreed to this plan the day before. That morning, however, Leo and I drove down for our usual breakfast at Hans Bakery before heading to the bus depot, but the car slid off the road on the way there and ran into a curb. This concerned me because Leo was a good driver and had never even had a small fender bender. I assumed that since the roads seemed treacherous in town, they would be worse on the pass. So when we returned home, I called Dad and suggested that we postpone our adventure for another week. But he seemed disappointed and determined to go and assured me that he could get us over safely. Against my better judgment, I agreed to go. We started across the pass. It was a beautiful sunny day with snow banks along the sides of the highway and packed snow and ice on the asphalt. We were having a good time as we started up toward the summit—about a fifteen- or twenty-minute drive to the restaurant—looking forward to lunch there, when the car spun out of control. It weaved back and forth across lanes, and luckily for us, no other cars happened to be on that stretch of road. But we veered off the road, down a steep embankment, through the forest, and directly into a large tree trunk that stopped us cold. I looked over at Dad, and he had blood all over his face. I couldn't feel my legs and my back hurt. Seeing Dad like that created the same sort of emotion that I had experienced when I saw Cameron in the hospital after his accident. Dad started calling himself a fool for having taken us on this drive. I felt bad for him. Luckily, a man from Bend with a car radio saw us leave the highway. He trudged through the snow to see how we were doing and called 911. He helped us get as comfortable as possible and told us help was on the way. It seemed to take forever for the ambulance to arrive. We were transported to Providence in Portland, where Dad had to have facial surgery. I was lucky to have only a bad strain in my back and bruises where the seat belt had been. I wasn't paralyzed but in a great deal of pain. I called Leo to let him know what happened. I intended to stay for the rest of the week to attend my classes and go back on the bus as scheduled. This wasn't a very good idea, though. At the time, I hadn't anticipated the extent of damage the accident had caused me. Dad dropped me off at my dorm room without ever seeing it as he had intended. He didn't miss much, though. He headed up to his condo in Vancouver to recuperate.

The next day, I could barely get out of bed. I had to ask other students to carry my books for me. I went over to Nora's for the rest of my week in Portland. She gave me frozen pea bags to hold on my back. I got through the week and headed down to Union

Station to catch my bus back to Bend. While I was waiting, I struck up a conversation with another traveler who said he had just got out of prison that day. He explained that he was heading home to Redmond (about fifteen miles west of Bend) after having served his time and was looking forward to going home. He told me all about his jail time experiences. We got so carried away in conversation that we didn't notice the bus had left until a man tapped me on the shoulder and asked if I was on my way to Bend. I said yes, and he informed me that the bus had just pulled out of the terminal. I ran to try to stop it, but it was too late. My companion and I pondered why the guy had waited until the bus left to let us know. I had been so anxious to get home after the hard week in Portland that I felt like crying. My companion told me he was let out of jail with no money, and that he would have to wait in the terminal until the next bus arrived at 5:00 a.m. I gave him enough money for a meal. Then I had to figure out what to do with myself.

I remembered that Dad said he and Mom would be staying at the Hilton for a few nights before heading back to Bend, and they planned on meeting Todd and Nora there for dinner one of those nights. I called the hotel to see if they were checked in there, and they were. I asked for their room, and Mom answered. I told her about missing the bus, and she invited me up and said she would get a room for me for the night and that I could join everyone for dinner. Then I could catch the bus for home the next day. I called Leo again about missing my bus and spending the night in Portland. When I got to their room, Todd and Nora were there too. I hadn't seen Dad since he dropped me off at my dorm three days earlier. He looked terrible—his face swollen and stitched and his eyes blackened. I related my story to the group—how another traveler who just got out of prison and I had been so engrossed in conversation that we had missed our bus, and that I had given him money so he could eat a meal before getting on the bus the next morning. Dad got really angry and called me an idiot for giving money to my mate at the Union Station. I guess I was feeling pretty fragile after the long week with the accident and all. I felt hurt that he would yell at me. I told everyone that I didn't feel like having dinner after all and headed for my room. Mom called after I got there and tried to convince me to come to dinner, but I said I didn't want to. Then she said to call for room service, so I did. I got up in the morning and left again for Union Station. This time, I caught the bus home.

Sometimes Laura would travel on the bus and stay with me, while I attended my classes for the week during her school breaks. On one of those weeks, there was an ice storm that pretty much stopped all commerce in the Portland area. The streets and sidewalks were like an ice rink. We tried to make our way down to the bus station on foot because the city buses were out of operation. We had our luggage with us and had to hold on to each other to maintain our footing. We inched our way down as best we could. It was treacherous. The sights were beautiful, though. All the trees were covered with frost, creating a winter wonderland. We weren't sure the bus across the mountain would be running, but it was. It seemed better equipped than the Portland transit because the climate is usually milder on the coast side of the state and the mountain was expected to have considerable snow and ice in the winter months.

During spring break, I had a whole week at home to relax—or so I had hoped. The weather was nice, and CJ and Laura decided to take a walk in our neighborhood. Leo and I remained at home after our dinner. It was a warm evening. The two of them didn't get more than a block away from home when a group of guys and one girl pulled up along the curb and barreled out of their car. They jumped in front of Cam and Laura and started harassing them, making sexual comments to Laura. Her brother told her to make a run for it, and that's what she did. When she was out of sight, they pushed Cam down onto the street and started kicking him. The worst thing was that one of them kicked him in the mouth. Cam didn't know these kids other than he had seen one or two of them at school. Laura sneaked home and told us what was happening. I got on the phone with the police, but Leo got his shotgun out. Luckily, the police were at the door in minutes before Leo had a chance to leave with a gun. About this time, Cam returned home and told us and the police what happened. He and Laura described the attackers and the car they had driven up in as best they could.

A few days later, Laura and I were driving past a house a few doors down from ours when she recognized the car. I was livid and stopped right there and went to the house where the car was parked. A middle-aged woman came to the door. I asked if she knew whose car was in front of her house, and she said it was her son's. I told her what had happened a few nights earlier and added that CJ had just had oral surgery and had been kicked in the face. She said she was sorry to hear this but was sure her son and his friends had nothing to do with it. She beckoned her son to the door. He stood there in front of me with a smirk on his face and blew cigarette smoke in my face as he denied knowing anything about it. But I knew different. I don't think I have ever been so angry. All this time, Laura sat in the car. I went right back home and called the police again. They said they would make a visit to the house. Two policemen came back in the evening and asked to speak again to CJ and Laura. They wanted to know if they would be able to identify and describe the assailants, but neither of them said they could be sure because it had been dark and that it had happened so fast. I think they felt intimidated. So that was that. However, CJ found out for sure who they were after one of them bragged to other students at school about the event. One of CJ's friends suggested they take care of things themselves. I got wind of this plan and cautioned them against retaliation. Whether or not anything of this nature occurred, I don't know.

A month or so later Cam traveled to Canada with friends from his in Young Life youth group. The plan was to stay for a week or so hiking in the mountains. We got a call from him a few days before he was to return home letting us know that his teeth had fallen out. He sounded distressed and asked if I could arrange for him to be seen as soon as possible after he could get back home. When he did, the doctor felt that the trauma from the attack a month earlier was responsible for his teeth coming out. This meant more dental work.

Byron dropped out of school at OSU in the spring of 1995 for "a break." He said he wanted to spend some time at the coast and went up to the northernmost stretch near Cannon Beach and Seaside. He camped out on the beach and found a job at a pizza joint. He also found a woman that he decided to move in with. Leo and I went up to see him in May 1995 after Leo picked me up from school to move me home for the summer. We met Angie for the first time. She was exotic-looking and brazen. Later on, after we were on our way back home, I told Leo that Byron was smitten with Angie and vice versa, but he didn't believe me at first. Maybe not until he and Angie had moved to Portland where

Byron decided he would transfer to Portland State for college, but especially after Angie turned up pregnant.

While they were still at the beach, Byron called us in August to let us know that they were living in their car and needed money to rent an apartment in Portland, so we sent money, and they moved. Dad knew Byron was living there, so when he and Mom went up to Portland, he would call and invite Byron and "his friend" out to dinner, but Byron always had an excuse. Dad called me one day and asked if Byron had a male partner. He thought this might explain Byron's reluctance to show up for a dinner out, anticipating that his grandparents might disapprove. But I told Dad that Byron was with a woman. Byron had always been a private person, and I suspect he just wasn't ready to open up to his extended family about Angie. When I traveled up to Portland every week by bus, I would walk up from Union Station to the PSU campus. During my third year in school, Byron was working at another pizza place in Portland right off Broadway. I would walk right by it on my way up to campus and frequently stopped by to see him and sometimes invite him to dinner. We usually ate at Pazzo. On one particular day, he offered to walk me up to the PSU campus. On our way up, he announced that I was going to be a grandmother. I was speechless at first. I made an attempt to remain calm and finally asked what he planned to do, and he said they would wait for the baby to be born. As soon as he left, I called Leo. "Holy crap" is what he had to say.

Byron has an uncanny resemblance to the actor Gael Garcia Bernal, not only in appearance and stature but also in voice, manner, demeanor, and expressions, and both men's eyes having the deep, intense, and sometimes troubled quality. They both emanate a soulfulness. This may be one of the reasons I have to see every movie the actor is in. It is as though I'm witnessing my own son on screen.

Laura went up with me to school again right before spring break. Mom and Dad were staying at their condo in Vancouver, and Dad offered to pick us up from school so that we could visit for the night, have dinner out with them, and then he would take us back downtown the next day. Then Laura's and my plans were to spend an extra day in Portland and get on the bus for home. All went well with this plan until the morning he would drop us off downtown. I told him we wanted to visit Powell's Books first thing, so that was where Dad agreed to take us. Mom and Dad were getting ready to move to a riverfront condo. This was more of Mom's idea than Dad's. She had fallen in love with the place, and he agreed to sell the one they were in and buy the other. I always liked the first better, but they didn't consult with me. Dad asked me to put a couple of things in the back of his Ford Bronco for him because he was planning to drop some things off at the new place on his way back. So that's what I did. When he went out a few minutes later, he opened the hatchback and some of the things I had loaded in there fell out. I didn't think that should be a big deal, but for Dad it was. He started yelling at the top of his lungs. Some passersby called out to me, asking if I was all right. It must have seemed to them that they were witnessing a domestic violence situation. I called back to them that I was all right, but in fact, I wasn't. I wasn't physically harmed, of course, but emotionally, I was. His red hot temper had struck again. I got so angry that I went back into the condo and told Mom that Dad was an ass and explained to her what had happened. I added that "nothing was ever good enough for him." She tried to calm me down, but that didn't really work. I got into the passenger seat of the car, and Laura got in the back. I remained silent as Dad rattled on about this and that as we drove toward Portland. At some point, he asked if anything was wrong, and I verbally blasted him. Things came out that may have been bottled up for years. He responded by saying it was no big deal. I told him that it wasn't a big deal for him because he wasn't the one being yelled at. I remained silent until we got to Powell's. Then he pulled over and parked. As Laura and I got out of the car, so did Dad. He ran up and hugged me, weeping and holding on to me. He said he was sorry, and I hugged him back. This event was to change our relationship forever. He never yelled at me again. Mom told me later on that he continued to fret about it all and remained remorseful. I don't think he ever really realized how his angry outbursts affected others. For months afterward, every time I saw him, he brought up the event and apologized again. I would tell him it was all right. He told my sister Sandy, after all this had taken place, that when he was growing up, his mother yelled at him all the time but that it never bothered him. Maybe he's more thick-skinned than I am, or maybe he just couldn't admit that he had been hurt by her, but then he used to mention that she was difficult to have for a mother while he was growing up.

In July 1995 Leo came home for lunch and started to parboil some ribs on the stove to prepare for barbecuing at dinnertime. As Laura and I headed out to do some errands, I reminded Leo to turn off the stove before he headed back to work. A few hours later, we returned home. I drove into the driveway, and Laura jumped out ahead of me and ran in through the family room door. She came running back out with a horrified look on her face. My first thought was that she had seen Leo lying on the floor—a heart attack, maybe. But no—she described a terrible stench and a smoke-filled house. In the meantime, Cam had come in the back door after school a few minutes earlier and discovered the fire. He put a wet towel over his face, opened all the windows, and called the fire department. He had discovered the burning and smoking pot of ribs on the stove, took a pot holder, picked up the pot, and threw it on the back lawn. There was a scorched spot there for a few years after. The three of us sat on the back porch. The odor was putrid and the smoke was dense inside the house. We sat out there until Leo pulled up in the back driveway, home from work. Later, he said his first thought upon the scene, as the smoke billowed out of the open door and windows, was "What have they done now?" I ran out to his car and said "What about the ribs?" That's when he figured it out. I was pissed. After inspecting the house, he commented that it smelled like someone had napalmed a pig farm, and he was right.

We had to live in Leo's camp trailer in our backyard for the rest of the summer while our house was being refurbished. Luckily, we had insurance, because every article of clothing had to be sent to the cleaners, all the furniture and carpets had to be professionally cleaned, the walls had to be repainted, the cupboards and closets had to be emptied and cleaned, etc. Insurance paid us to do as much of the work as we agreed to do—so much for a relaxing summer before my third year of school.

Mom decided to send me, Laura, Diane, and Andrea to Disneyland in September 1995, right before my last year at school would begin. She arranged for us to stay at the Disneyland Hotel, purchased our plane tickets, and gave us all ample spending money for the vacation. Laura was thirteen and Andrea was twelve.

Remembering Laura's first trip to Disneyland, I hoped this time would be more pleasant for her. This time, she had a blast. I suspect that Mom arranged this trip so that Laura and Andrea could really take advantage of the park. The girls tried out all the rides that Laura had been afraid of when she was five—all but the Haunted Mansion, which was closed for repairs. The four of us had dinner at the Blue Bayou Restaurant in the French Quarter after our ride on the Pirates of the Caribbean. We sat at our table under the fake night sky listening to the fake crickets and watching the fake fireflies flit about us—the atmosphere so seemingly real that Laura blurted out "We really are outside, aren't we? " We all laughed because the same shooting star kept going by. We had to point this out to her before she was convinced that our surroundings were make-believe, much like the rest of the park.

The night before the four of us left, we went down to the park at dusk. It was to be the last evening when the park would be open until midnight, so there were throngs of people and special events in store. On Main Street, it became so crowded that the four of us were carried along as if the mass of people was an ocean wave heading to shore with a force that couldn't be contained. Diane became panicky, unable to navigate on her own, and finally grabbed on to Andrea, and they were able to force their way sideways, out of the mass of people. Diane shouted to Laura and me that they were heading back to the hotel. This left me and Laura to explore the park at night further after the crowd on Main Street dispersed. First, we headed down by the Matterhorn roller coaster at the entrance, where a crowd was gathering and where it seemed nothing was happening. But there appeared to be an empty spot where the ground started opening up and a stage surfaced from underground as the band Ace of Base performed on stage. Recordings I had heard of them before didn't do them justice. Their performance was electrifying. Two men and two women comprised the group. One of the women, a little dynamo with a big voice and energy, grabbed my attention. I felt euphoric. Her energy was contagious. People in the crowd couldn't help but dance wildly to the music being played in front of them, and since Laura and I were without male companions, we danced alongside everyone else. After their performance, the stage started its descent and disappeared as quickly as it had appeared from underground. It was as if they had never been there.

To top off the evening, we decided to head over for the light show on the river. I wasn't expecting the extravagant event that occurred that night. There appeared to be two battleships at war on the river. All this must have been orchestrated by projecting a movie film over the water and the night sky at different angles, which made the scene three-dimensional and hard to believe the battle wasn't really happening right in front of us. Midnight was marked by fireworks lighting the night sky above the battlefield.

We took the monorail back to the hotel and called it a day. The next morning, the four of us took one last trip to the park before our flight back home, and I was delighted to see that the Haunted Mansion had just opened back up that morning and was back in operation. So we all accompanied Laura for her first trip through.

For my third year practicum, I asked if I could be placed in Bend rather than in Portland so that I could spend more time with my family. The biggest reason that the school agreed was that they were considering a distance learning program for Bend, and if I had a successful practicum there, they would have some of their work in starting the program already done. It also helped to have my high school friend Janet (Putt) as one of the administrators at PSU. I visited her occasionally while attending school when I had the time. She and her best friend from high school had both adopted their two girls, but I suspected that Janet might have finally gotten pregnant. She had a protruding abdomen. But I knew better than to ask. She seemed a little old to have kids at forty-three but not unbelievable. It turned out that she had a kidney disease, and her friend Susie had decided to be a donor for her. Janet confided this to me during one of my visits to her office. The transplant turned out to be a success and further strengthened their friendship.

The Bend practicum was approved, and it was my responsibility to find a placement. I contacted the social work department at the hospital, and they agreed to have me. Unfortunately, the placement was a disaster. I dreaded going to the hospital. I nearly dropped out but didn't want to have to do a whole other year somewhere else, so I stuck it out. The whole nine months, my arms and legs were numb from anxiety. I attended the mental health treatment team on the second floor of the hospital and met Dr. Hyde, a psychiatrist who loved to teach. He was from London and had a dry British humor. He offered to have me go on his rounds at the hospital. Dr. Hyde had a private practice but also worked part time at Deschutes County Mental Health, so after I got a job there, I had the pleasure of working with him for several years before his death. When I met with him for consultation, he often had great Indian curry lunches that he had prepared. I would comment about how good they smelled, and then he would bring me some the next time I was in. He continued to offer learning opportunities for colleagues by arranging supervisory treatment team meetings on his lunch hours. I missed him after he was gone.

One thing I did at the hospital practicum was to attend a multidisciplinary community treatment team that gathered there. It addressed issues with children and young adolescents. I sat in on the day-long sessions to observe. The first one I attended, I sat across the conference table from a very attractive psychologist. It was love at first sight for me. His voice was deep and soft—soothing, I would have to say. He had the most beautiful face I had ever seen—with kind and rather sad eyes, a strong Roman nose, and full sensual lips. His body was muscular with broad shoulders. I detected an East Coast accent, which I adore. There seemed to be an introverted shyness and sensuality about him. He was obviously Italian—my favorite. But that wasn't all. I observed how he addressed the treatment group when he was expected to put his two cents in. He was unassuming, humble, and seemed a little self-conscious and uncomfortable being in the spotlight. There was no hint of judgment in his comments, as I noticed with some of the other presenters—only compassion. I knew he was out of my league, but that didn't stop me. Now I had never been a pursuer before, other than my few furtive attempts with the gas station attendant and the flirtatious acquaintance of Dad's. I don't know what got into me, but I went full steam ahead. Maybe it was because I suspected he was attracted to me too.

I look back and wonder about all that had happened in the past few years that had been so stressful—school, Cameron's accident, my accident with Dad, the terrible practicum at the hospital—and if all this had, in part, to do with my developing obsession. After all, when I feel in love, everything else doesn't matter so much. I made sure that on the days of the treatment sessions, I wore discreetly seductive clothing, and I felt seductive when I talked to him at breaks. He flirted back. But when he discovered that I was married, he backed off. I went to see him one day and told him how I felt. He said, "You're married," and I said, "Who cares?" He laughed at that but remained steadfast in his position. My failure to win him over was a great blow, and I became even more obsessed, but I didn't want to make him angry or not honor his position. This made me think about him all the more. I could hardly wait until the next time I would see him again.

The treatment sessions at the hospital were on Mondays. I had gone up to school one wintery week and a violent storm hit the mountains with torrential rain. The pass flooded almost immediately. When I got down to Union Station about 4:00 p.m. to catch the bus home, I was told that the buses weren't going to be running because of the storm. I feared I might be stranded in Portland for the weekend, meaning I would miss the Monday session at the hospital. I wasn't about to do that, so I went into action. I left the bus station and walked to the nearest hotel and explained that I had to get out of town. The clerk at the desk let me use the phone, and I called the airport, which was being bombarded with frantic travelers. I booked a flight back to Bend over the phone and took a shuttle from the hotel to the airport. The ride was invigorating. It was jam-packed with other people trying to get out of town too. The situation created camaraderie among the travelers. When we reached the airport, there was a mad dash to get to the ticket counter, but by that time, most of the flights were booked. I had my ticket already paid for, so I was able to secure it. I got on the plane, and when I got back to Bend, I found out that it was the last plane out of the airport for the next few days. The next day, everyone at the hospital was surprised to see me there. I was so glad to have made it back so that I could sit across the conference table from my crush and make furtive glances in his direction.

Back at school, I went a little crazy. I felt so frustrated about my unrequited feelings that I started doing foolish things. There was a Mexican man who took classes at the college. He was born in Mexico and still a citizen of that country. He started following me around campus. I really wasn't attracted to him other than the fact that he spoke Spanish and had a collection of records that were wonderful. He even had some of Jose Feliciano when he was six years old, singing in Spanish. I started hanging out with him. He would take me to parties where I was the only non-Spanish-speaking person there. And when I'm in a situation where everyone else is speaking something I don't understand, it does something to me. Just like when I was a little kid under my grandparents' kitchen table. The parties were wild, with dancing and Latin music. We started having sex. I felt ashamed of having had a dalliance with him, someone I didn't really like-and I was married, for god's sake. But before I broke it off, he had encouraged me to call him when I was home in Bend. So I would head down to Café Paradiso, where there were pay phones, and call him. While on one of these calls, Dad walked out of the men's bathroom and picked up on my conversation. I didn't notice him until it was too late. I hung up and Dad called me out on my shenanigans. He always seemed to show up when I least expected it and at the most inopportune times.

It wasn't long after this that Dad called to see if I would like to go mushroom hunting with him. He said he had found a good spot near my house, so I said yes. He picked me up and we drove down to the nearby field. He had his paper bags, and we went through the field picking our mushrooms. As we were loading them in the back of his car, he stopped and told me about his sister Jean. He explained that she was having an affair with some guy, and this had motivated her husband to insist on driving her everywhere—to her work at Marshall Field's in Chicago, to her beauty shop and doctor appointments, etc. Dad said that he had chastised her, but it hadn't done any good. Of course, he already knew about my track record and his own. At this point in his life, it seemed he had developed regrets about his own infidelity and other behavior that he considered unsavory and hoped to spare his sister the same regrets. What he said next stuck with me. He described the four of us—himself, me, his cousin Emil, and Jean—as being like black people, and this was because of our being Slovenian. I realized that in spite of his having traveled to Slovenija and the experience having been a positive one for him, that he still hung on to his own negative opinion of himself and his ethnicity. The word "pariah" came to mind. I too had sometimes felt as he did. Maybe I looked like everyone else, but inside, I didn't feel it. But I felt bad for him, and I wondered if my awareness of all this encouraged some kind of rebellion on my part. Our conversation brought to mind another that I had with Dad about his sister years earlier. He told me that Jean had been in love with an Italian fellow during her high school years. He said that Francesca had disapproved of the relationship and had badgered Jean to end it until she finally acquiesced. Dad also admitted that he too had played a part in sabotaging the relationship and seemed a little guilty about it. The community of Slovenian ladies then stepped in as matchmakers to help find Jean a suitable mate. It made me wonder if all this may have played a part in Jean's affair. Over the years, I gathered this much from the few conversations Dad and I had on the topic of infidelity. It seemed to be a theme that ran through his side of the family—at least with the first and second natural-born citizens in America.

A few months after extricating myself from my most recent liaison, I was on my way home on the bus from Madras heading to Prineville before Bend. The travel had been slow that night, and I was eager to get home. The bus driver suggested that I wait for another bus coming up from California that would be taking a direct route to Bend. I decided to do that, so I got off the bus and waited for the other. It was cold and dark that night. I called

Leo to let him know I would be late. When the bus arrived, it was almost totally full with Mexican men and a few women who were heading up for jobs in the orchards. I found a seat next to one of the men who was sitting next to the window. I could hear quiet conversations in Spanish. There was something womb-like inside the bus—somewhat like the ride in the shuttle to the airport earlier on. As the bus rounded corners, my seatmate would be pushed up against me, and I didn't resist the contact. I could hear his subtle heavy breathing, which aroused me, and the Spanish language all around that sounded like music to my ears. Not understanding a word that was uttered, I pressed closer to him. He breathed harder, and I felt between his legs. Then he returned the favor. We had to remain quiet so as not to arouse suspicion among the other travelers. I'm not sure if we succeeded. Afterward, he remained close to me. No words were ever spoken. When we arrived in Bend, I felt sad and glanced over at him as the bus drove off to northern parts. I called Leo, and he came to pick me up. I told him about my ride and what had happened. After we got home, he said my story had aroused him, and he made passionate love to me. He later added that my tryst was foolish and could have been dangerous, but I never felt threatened in any way by the man in the bus, only sentimental.

Since I was just hanging around a lot at the hospital with not much to do, I asked if I could do a research project with Deschutes

County Mental Health (DCMH). I was taking a class on homelessness, and I proposed that I spend time in DCMH's residential treatment facility to explore how they handled homelessness and how prevalent it was in their population. I was given the go-ahead by my practicum supervisor on this idea. I suspect she was tired of having me around.

I also attended treatment team meetings at the main clinic site. Here is where I met the four social workers who pretty much ran the clinic at the time. It was exciting to be there, and the atmosphere was friendly. There seemed to be a focus on how to provide good service to clients. Tim was one of the four, and he ran the geriatric program. Gordon was another, and he ran the residential program. Tim told me that, at some point, he would welcome me to his team part time as one of his team members was out on medical leave for an unknown length of time. After I submitted my research project to Gordon, he also said he would keep me posted about potential job opportunities at the county. I had worked very hard on my research project, which was difficult in the last semester of my studies because I had anticipated being able to slide out of school without undue effort in the last semester. After graduation, I was still anxious about finding work in spite of the potential prospects at the county. I heard from Gordon first that a position at the residential facility had opened up, so I applied for it. I got the job, which started on October 1, at the five-bed residential treatment facility where I had done my research, and I worked twelve-hour shifts on Fridays, Saturdays, and Sundays. It was a difficult but challenging job. The residents were often suicidal, psychotic, or manic and didn't always get along. I prepared meals, did group and individual sessions, and supervised outings and other activities. I was it as far as staff on those days. If a crisis occurred, I either called DCMH backup or 911. And there were frequent crises. Later on, I split my time between the geriatric and the residential work, but at some point, I had to choose one because each team needed more of my hours. I decided on the geriatric team.

Cameron started college at Oregon State University in September 1996, right before I started my first job at the county. After Cam's accident, Leo fought the insurance company held by the driver, and Cam was awarded a good settlement. He had a cash award and would also receive $1,000 a year for life. Some of the money would also pay for tuition for his college education, and the rest went into a bank account. Looking back, a trust fund for him would have been a better idea because he started really going through it. We didn't know it until it was too late. First an expensive guitar, then extravagant gifts and vacations for a girlfriend he had met at college who was eager to be spoiled by him. But things really got out of hand when Cam decided to do an exchange program in Mexico in the fall of 1998. He became a party animal, and a significant amount of money disappeared down there. He made a surprise visit home on Christmas eve, able to speak fluent Spanish. I was so glad to see him walk in the door because this would have been the first Christmas with a member of our family missing if he hadn't returned from Mexico. He started at COCC for the next two terms and then frequented the International Café to keep up with his Spanish. This is where he met a lot of Spanish-speaking people—among them was Evelyn, a Guatemalan foreign exchange student, whom he started dating. She was a spitfire who livened up our home. She was living with a host family in town but spent most of her time at our house.

Both of the boys did rock climbing and volunteered for search and rescue-not something I was real excited about, but they liked it. Cameron even did an audition for a French beer commercial that included a rock climbing scene to be filmed at the famous Smith Rock outside of Redmond, Oregon. He got the part and was paid three thousand dollars for a few days of work. He got a copy of the commercial and it was hysterical. I guess it aired only in Europe. After he retrieved a rock climber's body off some cliff in a search and rescue mission and started dating his wife-to-be, he lost interest in the sport.

I started stopping by to see John, the psychologist I met at the hospital treatment team sessions. I was met with various responses from him. Sometimes he was friendly, and other times he seemed indifferent about my drop-in visits. Secretly, I was obsessed with him, and this obsession surpassed any other I had ever experienced. His scent drove me wild, so did his easy and sensual manner and his bedroom eyes. But I still kept my feelings under wraps. I didn't want to freak him out. I simply fantasized about him day and night and called his business number in the evenings just to hear his voice. For me, it was all-consuming.

Byron and Angie had our first grandchild on October 31, 1996, in Portland, one month after I started my job. We drove up to see the baby. They were living in an apartment above a French restaurant on Burnside. We rang for them in the entryway of the apartment building, and Byron walked down the stairs with his bundle of joy in his arms. Sage McKenzie (after the river) was simply gorgeous, with raven hair, full lips, big brown eyes, and a tawny complexion. Angie had come from a family of thirteen. She was the youngest of eleven children. There's Native American heritage in her family, and she is the one of all the kids that looked it. Her older siblings would tease her when she was little, telling her that she was adopted and was an Eskimo. She believed all this for a long time. Sage resembled her mother, but there was also some of Byron thrown in—his coarse black hair, high cheekbones, and more angular features. Angie's parents divorced and not long after, her father died. Her older siblings were leaving home, so it was Angie and her mother who became nomadic during Angie's childhood. Angie's mom had the measles while carrying one of her sons, so he was born severely impaired. Her mom tried to take care of the boy at home until he became too difficult to manage. He was institutionalized. Angie always cried when speaking of this brother. She and her mother visited him whenever they could and gave him gifts that a child would enjoy, even though he was a grown man. She called me when he died and wept over the phone.

Angie rescued a Labrador that she spotted on the highway while she and Byron were still living at the coast. She named him Jack. Jack had been mistreated by a previous owner—this was obvious because of his opinion of most human males. Jack lived with them when Sage was born. Byron was still working at the pizza joint, and Angie was waitressing at a nearby restaurant. I suspect that before Sage's birth, her parents were doing some serious partying, which may have continued on in some moderation after Sage's birth. Byron came to work late one too many times and got fired. He called his dad for a loan. Before their move to Portland from the coast, he had also called his dad asking for money to get an apartment in Portland, because, he explained, they had been living in their car. This time, Leo insisted that he would help by moving them to Bend, where they would live with us until they could save enough to get back out on their own. Neither Angie nor I was happy about this arrangement, but that's what happened anyway. They moved in with us in April 1997.

Sage was a good baby with a pleasant temperament. She loved all sorts of food, even hot and spicy. Jack, on the other hand, could be difficult. When a male friend would show up at the back door, he behaved like he was ready to tear the guy from limb to limb. He'd lunge at the door and growl. Byron and Jack seemed to have a mutual dislike for each other but usually managed to avoid each other too. One exception was when Leo had gone hunting with his buddies one weekend. Byron, Angie, Sage, Laura, and I were left behind. Our house wasn't all that big to accommodate the extras, and Byron and Angie had their frequent spats. I got along with Jack OK, as he didn't really have problems with women, but he seemed a little squirrely to me in general, so I didn't entirely trust him around Sage, and neither did Byron. Sage was toddling about under the dining room table one evening after dinner, which, for some reason, seemed to agitate Jack, and he growled at her and looked ready to attack. Byron took action, grabbed Sage, and pummeled Jack. Then Angie went after Byron. Laura and I stood by and watched. Byron, from our perspective, acted out of fear for his little daughter and to protect her. Jack did seem to learn a lesson because after this incident, Byron seemed to have established dominance over Jack, and so did Leo, who didn't put up with Jack's aggression either. It seemed the combination of Angie's devotion to him and the men's thwarting his aggression resulted in Jack's turning into a pretty good dog. He became tolerant of male visitors and became gentle with Sage. He remained fiercely protective of Angie.

Angie can be thoughtful, funny, generous, and affectionate, but she can also be hell on wheels. She is uninhibited, earthy, and always speaks her mind. Leo's mother, a Southern Baptist who had mellowed some over the years, came over for dinner one evening. Angie described her and Byron's courtship at the beach after dinner—how they had cavorted in the ocean nude when they first met and how she had marveled at his impressive anatomy. The rest of us couldn't believe our ears. Frances just sat there without any obvious reaction whatsoever. Maybe she didn't hear the comment. Angie has a sensual, feminine, and motherly aura too. When she hugs you, it feels as if you're enveloped by a soft warm pillow. She loves to find the perfect gift for family and friends and goes to great lengths to find it. She has an artistic bent expressed in her cooking, her home decorating, her style of dress, and her work.

Laura and I stopped by Mom and Dad's one afternoon, and they told us about their vacation in Beverly Hills, where they had stayed at The Beverly Hilton. Dad explained that they had first gone down there three or four years earlier in January for a break from the Central Oregon winter weather and had discovered that the weekend they had chosen was when the Golden Globes would be held at the hotel. It had taken them the first year to figure out how to navigate the terrain in order to get front row seats to see the celebrities arrive and give interviews. They spoke of who they had seen on their most recent visit. Among them, there was mention of John Travolta, and that's all it took to spark fifteen-year-old Laura's interest. She told her grandfather what she would give to see such a heartthrob. He said he would see what he could do. And before we knew it, he had booked hotel reservations and flights for January 1998 for the four of us. The first day we were there, Dad had an agenda, which included a visit to a Jewish delicatessen where a whole roasted chicken was one of the menu items. He raved about the last time he and Mom had eaten there, and so off we went. As was often the case, if such a visit didn't measure up to his recollection, Dad would be disappointed and explain that the meal or whatever didn't compare to his previous experience. This was the case with the chicken dish, which he explained was not of the same proportion as it had been before. We went from there to do some shopping and see the sights. The four of us stopped at the corner of Wilshire Boulevard, and Dad, being the inattentive person he often was, stepped right out in front of a fast-moving car. Laura was standing next to him and, in a flash, grabbed his arm and jerked him back off the street as the car flew past us all. Now Dad was aware of what he had done and exclaimed that Laura had saved his life and limb, and I think he was right.

Back at the hotel, Dad introduced us to the routine as far as getting the limited number of tickets required to get into the grandstands the next day. He explained that the staff there would act dumb and pretend they knew nothing about the tickets. I decided to inquire at the front desk anyway, but sure enough, they looked at me like I was crazy. Dad told me and Laura to set our alarm for five thirty in the morning and then go down to the lobby and scout it out. The next morning, Laura and I did what we were told. She remembers wearing a neon green sweater that morning, being flirtatious, and striking up a conversation with a cute security guard there who described himself to her as a black Irish-Italian. He clued us in on where to get in line. There was a couple milling around in the lobby too. The four of us got in line together. We were the only people there for about an hour before others started showing up, Mom and Dad included. They joined us in line after they had a leisurely breakfast but brought us something to eat while we remained in line. If someone had to go to the bathroom, the other three of us saved our spot.

After our long wait for our tickets, we finally got them and moved outside to the bleachers. We got front row seats and waited for the celebrities to walk down the red carpet and do interviews for the televised coverage. I didn't know who some of the people parading in front of us were but Laura seemed to. I commented to her about a woman in a long tight-fitting gown who I suggested had the most amazing behind I had ever seen. Laura informed me that the woman was Jennifer Lopez. Michael J. Fox was one of the celebrities who drifted by too. This time, I commented to my family that he didn't look OK. He hadn't made public his difficulty with Parkinson's yet, at least as far as I knew, but only a few months after the awards, it did become public knowledge. That year, John Travolta wasn't one of the people up for an award, so Laura didn't get to see him after all, but all the other excitement seemed to make up the difference.

The day before, Laura and I had decided to explore the hotel. We took the elevator up to the top floor, where we discovered a banquet room being prepared for a party, presumably a post-awards bash. We continued to explore the hotel to get the lay of the land. After the awards, Dad suggested we head down to the lobby where the winners were on display to give autographs and accept congratulations. I didn't know some of the younger celebrities, and Laura didn't know some of the older ones. She became excited about meeting Matt Damon and Ben Affleck, whom we stood right next to across from the area cordoned off with velvet ropes that divided the celebrities from the common folk like us. I didn't even know who they were, but Laura did. They were pleasant, and it seems their award-winning hit Good Will Hunting is what brought them lasting fame. Burt Reynolds was also in the lineup. Laura was excited to see him too and even asked for his autograph.

She handed him her pad of paper and pen, he held on to it for a minute and handed it back unsigned. Oh well. There were just scads of famous people around. We had a glance at Brooke Shields and Faye Dunaway in the lobby. When people started to disperse, we went for the elevators, but they were jam-packed with people and lines waiting in front of the doors. We wanted to get to our room and finally discovered a hidden elevator with no one around, so we got in, and it took us up to our floor. Having discovered this elevator, I got an idea. I told Laura "Let's get all dressed up and see about crashing the party." Laura wasn't sure about this idea but went along with it.

We headed back to the obscure elevator and pushed the button for the top. We were amazed when the elevator doors opened because no one seemed to notice us being there, and the banquet room we had seen the day before was full of people and lots of food and drink with a view of the whole city. Now I had to recall Laura a few years back when we had spent time with Todd and Nora and Laura had been so "on" during our night out at the Brasserie in Portland. This evening, she would be even more so. She flitted about yukking it up with this and that famous person. The first was Calista Flockhart, another person I was unfamiliar with, but Laura was a fan. I watched while the two of them acted like old friends on a couch next to where I sat. The spread was impressive, and so we got in line. Laura whispered to me that Kelsey Grammer from

Frasier was right next to me, working on the shrimp. She had to tell me who he was too. (Years later, I started renting Frasier episodes and understood why he and the show was such a hit—I still love to watch it). People I did recognize were Armand Assante, Gary Sinise, and Jon Voight. I admired Armand Assante from a distance. Gary Sinise was a different matter. I caught his intense eyes that followed me around the room. I told Laura I was going to visit the bathroom, and when I came back, she was chatting it up with him, but I kept my distance. I started fantasizing about a rendezvous with him but was also feeling shy and a little intimidated. Or was I imagining his interest? The party started revving up. There was a band starting up on the balcony outside and dancing ensued.

As Laura and I stood around chatting, a short middle-aged man introduced himself to us as one of the producers or writers of a soap opera we were both familiar with. I had begun watching it shortly after its inception in 1972, when Byron was an infant, and I would nurse him (not for very long) and then bottle-feed him in front of the television during the show. I followed the show for quite a while after that too. This gave us some common ground for discussion with the producer, writer, or whatever he was. He seemed to want to know who we were and hinted that he suspected Laura might be a young starlet or that we might be related to Merv Griffin, who had a suite on the top floor of the hotel and who was mentioned had recently purchased the hotel. I decided to remain vague in regard to our companion's inquiries and let him imagine what he would about us. He even invited us to a party he was planning for the following month and described all the influential people that would be attending. This is when Laura informed him that we wouldn't be around and that we, in fact, lived in Bend, Oregon, where she was a freshman in high school. This is about the time he stormed off flinging insults in the air at us. I asked Laura why she blew our cover. She didn't really have an answer for me, but I suspect she was sometimes irritated with my bent for deception. As for me, I would have played along with it all for the duration. I figured that since our identities had been discovered by at least one of the guests there, we might meet with some hostility from others who might discover who we really were. But I wanted to check out the dance floor first, fantasizing yet again about Gary Sinise. Before I had a chance to see if anything with anyone might happen, I decided we had better get out of there. We'd been found out for one thing, and I was afraid I might do something I would regret for another. After we got to our room, we called Mom and Dad to tell them about our evening. I felt like a chip off the old block. Later on, Laura and I were kept awake by carryings-on in the next room. Neither of us said anything until it seemed to go on forever. I finally asked her, "Do you hear that?" She laughed. We wondered if it might be a prostitute faking it or if the guy really was that long winded. The next morning, we hung around the door to the room but we never saw who had occupied it the night before. Dad took us out for a brunch the next morning before we would head back to Oregon, so we had a chance to fill Mom and Dad in on the particulars of our eventful evening the night before.

Byron did factory work and some construction with his dad while they lived with us, which seemed to have prompted him to go back to school. Before he moved to the coast, he had less than one year to go to get his bachelor's degree. His temporary move to the coast seemed to have thwarted his plan to finish up, so he started over at the community college in Bend for an associate's degree in design. After they moved into an apartment in the spring of 1998, they had spent fifteen months with us to save enough to get their own place. But before they left, I overheard a conversation between the two of them in the kitchen about another pregnancy. Mya Skye was born (a few months after their move) on September 22, 1998 in the hospital in Redmond, about a twenty-minute drive from Bend. Leo and I drove up to visit the parents and the new baby. She had almond-shaped black eyes and high cheekbones, which reflected her Slavic and Native American genes.

In the fall of 1998, Cam transferred to Southern Oregon University (SOU) in Ashland, Oregon. This was where he would meet the woman he would marry. She was born in China, and her family had immigrated to America when she was six years of age. Her name was Min Yi Su. Cam brought her home to meet us, and we fell in love with her. She was spirited, bright, exotic, and full of fun. She had grown up in New York City's Chinatown on Mulberry Street. Her mother, Ya Ying, worked long hours sewing in the sweatshops. Her father, Guang Hui, commuted to Atlantic City for work as a money counter in the casinos. He had been a banker and a scholar in China until Communism took over. His father had been imprisoned for years to "reprogram" him and was only released in his old age—a broken man. While her parents worked long hours, Min Yi looked after her little brother, Ben, and found work on the sets of Real Time with Bill Maher and Baywatch while in high school. Baywatch landed her in Hawaii for a while for shooting there. She also took college classes at NYU before graduating high school. She then attended Hunter College, where students were expected to participate in an exchange program in their junior year. She decided on an exchange at SOU for a semester. This is when she and Cam met. She returned to Hunter to finish up and graduate and then returned to Ashland.

Dad went hunting with some doctor friends in October. While he was gone, his best friend Joe's sister, Joanie, called. She talked to Mom about her brother's poor condition and his having been admitted to hospital. Mom tried to reach Dad without any luck.

Joe died on October 2, 1998. When Dad got home the next day, he called Joanie. She let him know that Joe had died. Joanie told me that he sobbed and sobbed and told her he would never come back to Elmhurst again. She said to him that of course he would, for there were still others for him to see there. But he never did. I happened to drop by at Mom and Dad's house a few days later. They were in front of the television in the family room—the same place they had been years earlier when Dad was fretting about his own parents' poor health. He told me that a part of him died along with Joe, and I do believe that he never really got over it. Joanie told me that people in their family would affectionately call Dad a "mula"—loosely translated a "brat." She also told of the time when Dad and Joe were adolescents. Dad told Joe he wanted to go across the street and sock some guy. Joe asked him why he'd want to do that, and Dad had told him it was because he just felt like it. So Dad did just that and then ran back over across the street where Joe was. The kid didn't want to have to take Joe on, so he let it go. Joanie also told of a gift Dad sent Joe once. It was a box of rocks from Oregon that she described as looking like any ordinary kind of rocks. But Joanie found them one day under Joe's bed and brought them downstairs. When Joe saw them, he asked what they were doing there. She told him she planned on getting rid of them, but Joe told her to put them back where they belonged. Even after Joe died, Joanie kept the box of rocks. It turned out that these rocks were collected in Central Oregon by astronauts who visited the area to train for their moon landing. I'm not sure how Dad came across them, and Joanie's story about the rocks was news to me. Joanie also reminisced about Dad's frequenting a coffee shop on York Street in Elmhurst every time he visited. This is where the old gang would gather—Joe and all the rest. Their paths had all gone in very different directions, but none of that interfered with their lifelong friendships.

Cam continued on with school, and he and Min Yi married in 2000, the same time that Laura graduated from high school. The summer was busy. Laura, Angie, and I worked on the wedding that was to occur in Bend—the wedding at Shevlin Park and the reception in our backyard. Min Yi's parents, brother, and friends traveled across the country to attend. Her family stayed about a week before the wedding. One evening, her father (Guang Hui) made stir-fry for us on our back deck. He set the wok out on the floorboards, hunkered down, added the ingredients, and served up a fine meal. Ya Ying walked around and around our yard, amazed by the space around our house. She borrowed one of our bikes to explore the neighborhood. Ben was sullen, I suspect unhappy about losing his big sister to her groom. Min Yi put up the right number of red lanterns on our back deck for good luck.

The wedding at Shevlin Park was accompanied by a grove of breeze- blown birch trees and the melodious voice of Bill Keale, a Hawaiian with long flowing black hair who sang, among other songs, "Hawaiian Wedding Song." (Bill and his wife have since bought and live in the home I grew up in on Ninth Street). Sage (Byron and Angie's daughter) and Elizabeth (Todd and Nora's daughter) were flower girls. Our friend Tom from law school days married the couple. Leo's mother, then ninety years old, was one of the guests. At the reception, the bride and groom were required to kneel before their grandparents and then their parents as a sign of respect, the eldest first, and recite their feelings of honor for their elders. Another ritual involved the groom tying a blindfold over the bride's eyes, and then she had to attempt to work an egg up one side of the groom's pant leg and then down the other without letting it break. Leo's mother was seated right in front of them and, in spite of her Baptist upbringing, laughed until tears streamed down her face. Cameron couldn't help breaking up either, especially when Min Yi got to his crotch. Dad commented that this Chinese ritual was the best form of foreplay for newlyweds he had ever come across. Family danced and partied on into the night to what turned out to be a mediocre high-priced disc jockey. They left for Camp Sherman on the Metolius and then on to Mexico.

I continued to daydream about having my own place and more independence. My restlessness had already led me into an affair, and now that Byron and Cameron were out of the house and Laura would be leaving for college soon, my daydream began to seem more realistic. I talked to Leo about it all and even added that I wasn't sure I wanted to be married. But my Catholic upbringing held me back from seriously considering a divorce. Also, our lives were intertwined so deeply that it seemed hard to imagine any way out. We had shared a long history, since high school, in fact—family, friends, children, and now two grandchildren. It was a dilemma for sure. I decided to look for a place of my own anyway. One Sunday morning, Leo and I were returning from a breakfast out when I ran across the perfect place. I couldn't wait to call my realtor who agreed to meet me at the house right away. I fell in love with it. There was an old garage behind the house that would be perfect for an office/guest house. It just needed to be renovated. That very day, I went over to sign the papers, and it was pretty much a done deal. I moved in.

I began to visit John again. It was all about his kind and sensitive nature and his sense of humor. He was someone I needed in my life and knew could help mend me. I don't think he understood me (nor did I) but that he did recognize my desperation. I hoped he would acquiesce at some point, but I had to be patient. It had never been just sex for me. It always went beyond the physical. In the right circumstances, it was turbulent and transcendent and, in the end, would bring on convulsions and weeping—every fiber of my being rejoicing in a complete union with the other.

Laura and Byron at Christmas

Me (and Laura as Elvis)

Laura as Elvis

Byron and Date at Prom

Leo and Me

Family Christmas Photo

Angie, Byron and Sage

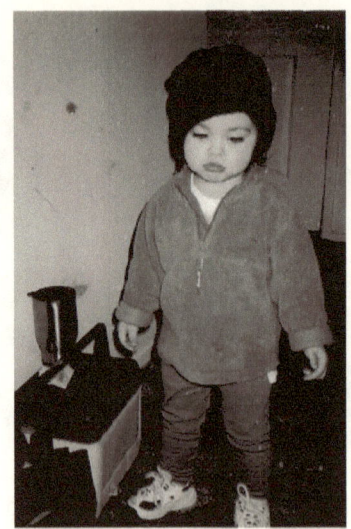

Sage

Cam

CHAPTER 6

Mom and Dad moved from our home on Ninth Street in 2000. They had already purchased a condo in Vancouver, Washington after Dad's retirement and they would drive back and forth between Bend and Vancouver routinely. Dad initially thought about a place in Reno, but Mom didn't want to be that far from family, so they both agreed on Vancouver. Dad had preferred the Reno idea because of the warmer weather there. Vancouver turned out to have cloudy and rainy weather that negatively affected his mood. But the place, Indian Hills, was beautiful. They lived on the edge of farmland with fruit trees, fields, and livestock out their windows. Dad liked to walk to the mall, which was only five minutes away. There were also a lot of restaurants within walking distance, and Portland was right across the river. They would invite us kids to visit, and it was fun. Now they would be selling the Ninth Street house and buying another condo in Bend on the river right across from Pioneer Park and within walking distance from downtown. Things seemed to go OK for a while there, but this didn't last. Mom hinted that she had talked Dad into retirement because "the job was becoming too difficult for him." And his malpractice insurance costs prohibited him from working part time. He did regularly head to the hospital cafeteria and hang out with his doctor buddies, though. He also had another group of friends who met for coffee or lunch at various local restaurants. But Dad started looking frail. Mom expressed concerns about his memory. But they were still making the frequent drives up to Vancouver and back. Mom started chain-smoking, and if we went by in the evenings, she often appeared to be inebriated. Dad had quit drinking for the most part and appeared to have silent concern about her drinking. At the same time, she goaded him into driving about to purchase her cigarettes and bottles of wine. He reluctantly acquiesced. His concern seemed to turn into irritated disgust. None of this seemed to matter to her, though. When we went out for dinners with them, Mom would slur in her speech and was unable to walk out of the place without assistance. She began objecting to Dad leaving the condo without her.

Dad encouraged her to go out to lunch with me, but she would always come up with some excuse. She didn't even want him to go out with me, but on one occasion, he was able to get away. We walked to Hans. We sat at a table by the window. Hans had always been one of his haunts. He had been one of their first customers when the place opened. This is where he would head down in the mornings on his days off from Ninth Street, have coffee and a pastry, and read his paper. But this time, he sat across from me with tears running down his face. He wept. The fact that others were in the restaurant with us didn't seem to faze him. This time, he would tell me that Mom had wakened him at the condo in Vancouver and told him good-bye. That she told him she had taken a bottle of pills. Then he told of walking her up and down all night long and pouring coffee down her throat. She had survived. I didn't dare ask why he hadn't taken her to the ER. What good would that do now? It was so sad seeing him like that. I didn't even know what to say other than the fact that all of us had concerns about Mom's emotional state. He also told me about her binge drinking. He called her a binge alcoholic. He seemed to feel helpless in this area too and described how when he wanted to go for a walk, she accused him of seeing other women. Dad explained that after his prostate cancer treatment, that was the end of his sex life and, consequently, the end of Mom's too. He added that he would tell her how ridiculous her accusations were, but she would persist anyway. I think this is the first time I suggested that he think about a retirement facility. After all, this was right up my geriatric professional alley, and I felt that the structure might resolve some of their problems. I don't think Dad was ready to hear this. Not yet anyway.

During the summer before Laura left for college, we had fun. She seemed in love with life. There may have been some sort of ephemeral love affair going on with her at the time, I'm not sure, but she was in a romantic mood. She'd come home from work and put on Dean Martin. Then she'd pick cherries from our tree, pit them, and make delicious pies as she wore her apron, rolled out her dough with a rolling pin, and sang along with Dean's love songs. I got home from work one day and she had them all lined up in the kitchen. It was a perfect summer day. I sat down on the deck outside, and she served me a slice. It was still warm from the oven. I've never tasted anything better. The piece of pie was so good I had another. Then I suggested we walk over and deliver one of the pies to a friend. So we started out. (We often took walks at dusk and sometimes we'd have "wine and walks"—filling a couple of cups with wine and sipping on them as we went. We had even longer walks on the weekends when we would walk two or three hours at a stretch). But this wasn't that far, and just before we got there, I knew I was in trouble. I told Laura that I better head back home right away. The two pieces of pie had hit. I didn't get very far before I told her I couldn't make it home. She pointed out a vacant lot between two houses, but the street was a main thoroughfare. I ran for the lot anyway, got my pants down around my ankles, and there was an explosion of light green foam that formed a pile on the ground beneath me. Laura approached but was disgusted by the sight and the smell. The pie was still in the plastic bag, and I had thoughts of proceeding on to deliver it, but Laura pointed out that the light green foam had found its way to the bag carrying the pie, to my hands, and to my pants, so we went back home.

Laura started college at Portland State in September 2000. She even stayed in the same dorm I did during graduate school. Looking back, this may not have been the best choice in schools for her. Portland State is a city campus with a lot of commuters, so not as focused on the social aspect of college life as some other Oregon campuses. I'm not sure to this day how much of an influence I was in her choice of colleges. The dormitory seemed to carry with it an atmosphere of gloom that she and her cohorts soon inherited. In no time, Laura was feeling morose and wanting to leave. If the truth be known, I also think she was homesick. In spite of Leo's and my differences, Laura had always been a homebody to some extent and liked hanging around with us. And I also suspect she wanted to keep an eye on what would happen next as far as our relationship was concerned. Before returning home, though, she decided to transfer to Eugene, where a high school friend was attending university. She enrolled and moved in with her old friend, but this only lasted one term, and then she was back in Bend. This time, she waited until fall to enroll at the community college.

Leo talked about us going on a tropical vacation when we turned fifty, and so he arranged for a stay in Jamaica during April

2001, so I went. We had talked about a divorce, but Leo would come up with all sorts of reasons for not going through with it. One was that he would lose the health insurance from my county job. At first, I thought maybe this would work out. I could just stay married and live my life the way I wanted, but it turned out to not be as simple as that. The vacation would be cheaper if the Funjet broker could choose one of the six resorts they managed for us. This was explained by the travel agent. Leo came home and asked me if I was game, understanding that there was a chance we could end up at one of the two Hedonism Resorts on the island. I said sure. When our package was mailed to us, sure enough, we were booked for Hedonism II. I remembered Dad years earlier talking about the place. He had heard of it while he and Mom traveled to Jamaica with Doug, Diane, and Sandy during the early eighties. Dad even toyed with the idea of planning a family vacation there, but I think Mom put the nix on Dad's plan, presumably after hearing what all went on down there. I knew the place had a reputation, but I didn't expect what it turned out to be.

After our long flight into Montego Bay, I expected the bus ride from the airport to be a half-hour tops, but it didn't turn out that way. The bus ride to Negril was more like two hours long over bumpy narrow dirt roads that were packed full of travelers. Our bus went down the road at top speed, and so did the oncoming and passing traffic. Our bus driver weaved around every vehicle in his way, slicing through traffic here and there, often nearly running off the road or hitting a passing vehicle. What made it all the scarier was seeing the dead bodies tossed over on the side of the road—human roadkill, so to speak. Occasionally, the driver made a stop or slowed down to avoid road construction or livestock crossing the road, and this was when the ganja man would show up. He would stroll by the bus's open windows and stick a bunch of the stuff through saying "ganja?" Leo had been warned by the travel agent to avoid purchase of ganja in Jamaica because sometimes the ganja man could make a few extra bucks by turning his customer in to the authorities. Then the tourist would land in jail and have to pay a steep fine to get out. So we avoided any purchases of this sort.

When we finally got to the resort, we checked in and were escorted to our room off the ocean. We drew the blinds and fell asleep for a few hours. When we woke, the sun was setting, and it was dinnertime, so we headed to the open-air pavilion that included a buffet and entertainment. The room was filled with people from all over the world—the wildest, a group from Australia. The emcee goaded the crowd into participating in all sorts of lascivious behavior, and there were plenty of willing participants. The rest of us stood by as couples feigned various forms of copulation. Wild dancing ensued. There was one particularly lewd Australian woman wearing little other than a G-string and a skimpy bra dancing next to us. Leo decided to refer to her as skanky. In the midst of all this, there was an announcement that there would be a scavenger hunt. Teams of volunteers formed, but we decided that this game might be too dangerous to participate in, so we remained with some other more timid guests on the sidelines. The emcee announced the items that needed to be brought up to the stage. That night, I was wearing a black cotton knit spaghetti strap dress and flip-flops, and that was it. The attractive female emcee looked straight at me when she announced that the next item to be searched for was a black dress. There was a mad dash in my direction, and the first person to get to me was a middle-aged guy who pleaded with me for my dress, and the crowd chanted that I should give it up. So in one swift move, I pulled the dress over my head and handed it to the guy. He raced up on stage with it, and the crowd cheered him on. I don't think any of the audience expected me to be completely nude. Leo was across the room from me because the women and men had been separated for the hunt. Later, he told me he knew I would do what I did. After I got my dress back we decided to head back to our room before anything else could happen. When we got back, he said, "What have I got us into?" I said, "I don't know."

The next morning, we stepped outside our door, and there was a nude couple standing right in front of us. They shared pleasantries with us and seemed nonchalant about their state of affairs, so we took their lead and decided to head to the beach sans clothing. It didn't take long to feel comfortable because everyone else on the nude side of the beach (there was also a prude side in front of the pavilion) was the same way. I had been on nude beaches before but not of this magnitude—nude bodies of all shapes and sizes as far as one could see. There were drink machines everywhere too. All you had to do was stick your glass up to a spout and you had a choice of a strawberry daiquiri or a piña colada. There was also a full bar for anything else you might want or to just hang out at. There was one skinny mustachioed fellow who hung at the bar about 24/7 and was never seen in a sober state. All this made the crowd all the more uninhibited. We decided that we better be careful in this atmosphere lest we get into real trouble. After our visit to the beach, we headed over to the pavilion for breakfast. This is when the staff would announce all the activities available for the day, and they were quite persuasive about guests signing up for them. I wasn't about to do so, but it took some stamina to avoid the pressure. Instead, we decided to head back to the nude beach and just read and swim. But on the way, a very attractive woman tried to lure me into her tent for a shave. She suggested that I needed one. I just shook my head and moved on. The beach was a disappointment for me because I loved to have access to the open waters. The resort's beaches that I came across had barriers at each end of the property so that you could only walk or swim in the confines of the resort's property. There were also limits to how far out to sea you could go because there were barriers in that direction as well. If you left your resort, you had to check in and out. The whole property was fenced off. In spite of all this, I decided to go for a swim as far out as possible. When I got out near the barrier, an old ganja man paddled up in his little boat next to me and offered me some ganja. I smiled but declined his offer and decided it was time to head back into shore.

That night, we explored the resort action, which I have to say was rather frightening. As we strolled along, we could see and hear orgies going on in the lit-up rooms with their open blinds—all manner of cavorting going on there. Then there were the hot tubs at one end of the resort. We stopped by because other guests said that this was where the action was. When we got there, it turned out to be the wrong kind of action. There's no way I would have gotten into that water with those people. We figured out a way to steer clear of potentially kinky circumstances, but they tended to crop up anyway. For instance, we tried out the disco one evening. It was underwater, and you could see into the swimming pool while you danced. There were the usual Australian party animals present and one particularly intoxicated woman who peed all over the floor right next to us. We carefully moved to another section of the dance floor.

Each morning at breakfast, there was a great buffet. There were tropical fruits I had never seen or eaten before, and they were delicious. I still have never come across them anywhere else and have wondered if they exist in places other than Jamaica. We made reservations for the dining room a few nights for a more romantic evening than the buffet offered. The dining room fare was authentic Jamaican food that many of the guests shied away from. This made it all the better to eat there because there was never a raucous crowd to contend with. Another positive aspect of the stay was the entertainment in the pavilion that occurred during random times throughout the day. One afternoon, we happened upon a show that included a contortionist who was able to fit himself into a box not much bigger than a shoe box. Well, maybe a little bigger, but not much. It was hard to believe. A dance troupe followed him. There was a group of men and women who took control of the stage. There was a frenetic and erotic quality to their dance that I have never experienced before or since. It was mesmerizing to witness. When the dancers broke into couples, they imitated wild copulation that seemed to work the audience into a frenzy. You would have to be dead not to have been aroused. We met some other guests who were mainly from the East Coast, especially New York and its boroughs. One couple was fairly conservative compared to many of the folks there, and the wife would only swim on the prude side until the last few days when her husband talked her into going to the nude beach, where she took her top off but not her bottoms. In general, there were a lot of men looking for anything they could get their hands on, and even if a woman was with someone, that didn't matter much. They'd ask anyway. Leo and I managed to avoid all this type of frivolity during our stay. Even if I had the urge to roam there, and I didn't, it seemed too dangerous a game they were all playing.

We got up at four in the morning on the day we left for the airport. I had dreaded the return bus ride to the airport the night before, but this ride would turn out to be much different. It was still dark when we boarded the bus, and at this time of day, there was almost no traffic at all. The bus driver took a leisurely ride down the road. There were children of all ages dressed for school in their parochial uniforms, waiting for their buses, in the dark, in front of their brightly colored shanties, to take them to school miles from their homes. It was a glimpse of the real life on the island. Leo had bought a painting from a local man on the beach a few days earlier that depicted the scene we witnessed on our bus ride back but in daylight and without the children at the bus stops. He carried his painting onto the plane to keep it safe, and it sits above his dining table to this day.

After our return home, I waited a while and then went to see John again. He was friendly. I heard through the grape vine that he was dating some woman, but there really wasn't much I could say to him about that. I was still married after all. When I asked him, he did admit that he was dating someone, but he said it was nothing serious. The lengthy stretches of time when I forced myself to stay away were torturous for me. It's difficult to put into words just how much I craved his presence—and still do. But I started to lose hope about having a future with him because I was unsure about his feelings for me. This may have contributed to what I think of now as my descent into crazy.

Cameron and Min Yi came home one weekend from Ashland and announced that she was pregnant. We were pleased with the news, albeit he was still in school and they were not really in the best situation to start a family. But that's the way it was. The baby boy was born on August 10, one day after his Uncle Byron's birthday on August 9. His parents named him Jing Wen. He resembled his mother with his black hair, eyes, and dark skin. Min Yi's mother came out from New York to help out, and we drove down to Ashland to see him. It's a Chinese tradition to make soup for the mother from the placenta to help her regain her strength. Ya Ying made this for her daughter. This was available for others to sample too, and I found it quite good.

A few months later on September 11, there would be the tragic attack in New York City. I was getting ready for work when we saw the news showing a plane crashing into the towers. We called Cam and Min Yi about her family who lived close by in Chinatown. The city was paralyzed. Her father was stranded in Atlantic City, where he worked. The city was in chaos, and it took time before she found out that her family was safe. The days and weeks after the attack, everyone everywhere seemed in shock. There were so many rumors about other potential attacks that no one seemed to know what to expect next. My friend Jan and I had already made plans for the following weekend to travel up to Portland for a holiday.

Sometimes we brought her girls and Laura along with us. We would get a suite somewhere downtown, and we would have fun. But this weekend, it was just the two of us. Dad had given me a coupon for the Marriot in Downtown Portland, although I usually stayed at the Hilton or, once in a while, the Vintage Plaza. With the attack, we didn't know for sure if we should still go, but we did. When we arrived in Portland, we went directly to the hotel to check in, and then we planned to relax and have dinner somewhere downtown. But the lobby was full of swarthy men, and I have to admit this made me nervous. We had a quick dinner (I don't even remember where) and went back to our room. We watched a little television and went to bed early. I was up all night, feeling claustrophobic, staring at the ceiling, and expecting the hotel to blow up any minute. When Jan and I went to breakfast the next day in the hotel restaurant, the swarthy men were there too. She admitted to me then that she hadn't slept the night before either.

It seemed like the whole country held a sense of trepidation for months. My own continued after my return from Portland. Laura and I had been planning a trip to Italy since she was fifteen. We started a savings account and added to it every chance we got. But now, when the time was finally coming to take our trip, I had concerns about traveling so soon after the 9/11 attacks. We decided to move ahead with our plans anyway, but again, I have to admit that it all made me a little nervous. I always told Laura that the way I thought we should do this trip was to plan it ourselves and even call to make reservations in Italy. We studied travel books until we came up with the desired itinerary. It would be Rome, then Naples, and finally Sicily. I was able to find phone numbers in the travel books to make our reservations. Laura was studying Italian in school and would help me out if necessary.

In December, I came home from work one evening. I had felt fine that day, but a while after getting home, it felt like a ton of bricks had landed on me. I still remember how this strange awful feeling came over me. I had to lie down on the couch. I was so sick by bedtime that I could barely move, and my temperature rose to 105 degrees. This is how things remained for three weeks. I moved into a spare bedroom and didn't leave it other than to cross the hallway to use the bathroom. I slept twenty out of twenty-four hours during a twenty-four hour period. I felt so bad that I couldn't read, watch television, or do anything whatsoever. Laura would bring me something to eat, but I didn't have much appetite. It felt surreal during my confinement. I remember drifting in and out of consciousness for days on end. I also remember thinking I might die, but I didn't really care. I almost hoped that's what would happen. The only thing that kept my temperature below 105 was taking aspirin every four hours. As soon as the four hours was up, my temp would go back up. I felt too ill to go anywhere, including a doctor's office. I missed weeks of work. Laura got the same bug but wasn't as ill as I had been. Even after I went back to work, I still felt weak and tired for a few months after the fact. My illness added to my trepidation about Laura's and my trip overseas. I think it made me feel even more vulnerable.

But the time came for us to leave. We started off on our grand adventure on July 10, 2002, Dad's birthday. I had been overseas before, but this was a first for Laura. The flight left us both exhausted by the time we landed in Rome. Then there was the cab ride to our hotel right in the middle of the city with its wall-to-wall traffic. We inched our way there in what seemed like an eternity. We had booked our stay at the Pensione Panda (near the Piazza di Spagna) on Via della Croce right off of Via del Corso. When we arrived at our hotel, the managers were pleasant and showed us to our room on the second story of an old building. We struggled up the narrow stairway with our humongous suitcases. The room was small, clean, modern, and dark. The bathroom included a bidet that we had to try out. There were two windows overlooking the city street below. Shutters at the windows could shut out the light and every bit of street noise that continued day and night. Our first afternoon in Rome was a ninety-plus- degree humid day, and the only option as far as cooling the room was a fan. We settled in and then decided not to go far for some dinner. We headed down our street below and found a restaurant two doors away. We ordered pasta dishes, salads, and glasses of wine. Laura left most of her meal on her plate. She explained that she was too hot and too tired to eat, but I wondered if there was more to it. I suspected she was suffering from culture shock as well. After we got back to our room, the heat felt stifling. I had had my problems with my ice cubes while in Slovenija with Dad, so I feared drinking water from the tap or any other potentially suspect source. It seemed too late to go traipsing about the city looking for water at this point, so we both made an attempt to get to sleep. We turned on our fan and directed its breeze over our beds. The sound of the fan lulled me to sleep, but I was abruptly awakened some time later on as I became aware that Laura was leering down at me over my bed. The fatigue, the heat, our small quarters, and nothing to drink had led Laura to have a full-blown panic attack. I promised her that we would go in search of water first thing in the morning, and that seemed to calm her down. Somehow we got through that first night in Rome, and the first thing we did in the morning was get dressed and find a vendor (there were many) that would offer bottled water. We bought as much as our arms would hold and stockpiled them in our room. Then we were off on our first day of sightseeing.

One of our guidebooks showed a walking tour of Rome, so we decided to try it. We only made about half of the walk that day, but if I ever go back, I intend to do the whole thing if it still existed. Anyway, we saw some interesting things on the tour. First thing, we stopped for lunch at a restaurant on a cliff that had outdoor seating. The buildings in this part of town were all pink with flower boxes at the windows. Our balcony had a yellow tarpaulin over the tables with green-and-white checkered tablecloths. It was a relaxing way to start off our day of exploration. After our meal, we came across number 6 on the walking tour—the Capuchin Crypt.

The Capuchin Crypt is made up of several small chapels below the church of Santa Maria della Conzecione dei Cappuccini and decorated with the dismembered remains of Capuchin friars. "There are six . . . rooms in the crypt"—among them—The Crypt of Skulls, Crypt of Pelvises, Crypt of Leg and Thigh Bones, and Crypt of Three Skeletons . . . A placard in five languages reads "What you are now we used to be: what we are now you will be" . . . [34] The brochure explained that this was all done to venerate

---

[34] "Capuchin Crypt," *Wikipedia, The Free Encyclopedia*, http://en.wikipedia.org/wiki/Capuchin_Crypt.

these friars who had tended to the church and to remind its visitors of the transiency of life on earth. The human bone decorations were incredibly ornate in five of the six rooms of the crypt. All this brought to mind the earthy and spiritual temperaments of the Italians, which was reminiscent of my experiences during my early years while growing up in my grandparents' home. After a few more visits to the numbered sights on our map, we decided to head back to our pensione and call it a day.

There was twenty-four hour entertainment right outside the windows of our pensione. A handsome Italian father of an adorable six- or seven- year-old son would arrive like clockwork to entertain the crowds on the street and the patrons above looking out over Via della Croce. The child entertained the spectators with a smile, his beautiful face, and his accordion while his protective father looked on. Laura and I gladly threw coins and bills out to him, as did many other of the spectators, and he would gather up all the donations after his performance. There were usually several amputees sitting along the sidewalks as we looked out our window too. Some of them just hung out there, while others held out cups for coins, hoping that passersby might contribute to their cause. I wondered if the plethora of these men had to do with something that might be in the local water or if it had more to do with the lifestyle in Italy that included spontaneity, insouciance, and a general focus on enjoying life— this including the wild driving style of the populace.

On one of the first evenings in Rome, it was hot and particularly humid, so we decided to watch a movie a few doors down from our pensione. As we entered the small theater, we welcomed the cool air. The movie was some sort of spaghetti western in Italian that didn't hold a lot of interest for either of us, but at least we had the opportunity to cool off.

On another day we headed to the Piazza Navona. I remembered having spent some time there earlier on with Dad, Jean, and Jack while the four of us had been in Rome. Dad had decided that wherever we ate that had tiramisu on the menu, we had to sample it so we could determine which restaurant offered the best of all. I also recalled on my earlier trip that Dad, Jean, Jack, and I had been in a crowd watching some sort of show in the street when a man pushed through the crowd in an attempt to grab someone's purse. He pushed right into me, but I held my purse tight, and so he wasn't able to grab on to it. I don't think he was successful in getting anyone's because I saw him exit the crowd without anything to show for it. Now here I was years later with my daughter. The place was entertaining with statues—actually people spray-painted white or green on stilts—that occasionally made subtle movements that seemed frightening because they had appeared to be made of marble at first. There were also vendors who had all manner of crap for sale. We settled on a bright green plastic gun that, when the trigger was pulled, let out a tommy-gun noise accompanied by flashing lights and colored bubbles that shot out of its pistol. This toy would prove to be significant in the days to come. We decided on Caffé Bernini for lunch and took a table outside. The weather was hot and sunny. Laura had thick black flowing hair and a cute little figure during the time we were traveling. She was a hit with the male waiters and other Italians just walking down the city streets. They flirted with and complimented her. She had been dating a guy who was older before our trip, and he had pretty much dumped her right before our vacation. She had ideas of marriage and babies with this guy, but he seemed to be a confirmed bachelor to me and something of a cad. It also seemed that the attention she was getting here would be good for her. The waiters asked to be photographed with her, and one suggested meeting up with her later, which she cleverly ignored. Before we left, I ordered us a tiramisu to share with her for my old times' sake.

Later in the day, a couple of swarthy Italians struck up a conversation with us and invited us to join them in their Italian version of a siesta. We laughed at the invitation but declined their offer. One thing I noticed about the Italian men on this trip and during my earlier visit was that if they proposition you and you decline, they remain jovial and friendly. I suspect they just try again with the next woman they take a liking to. I also noticed that there were more women out and about in the city streets of Rome than I remembered while on my trip with Dad twelve years earlier. Before, it had been mostly men who gathered on the city streets. It seemed that women had gained a measure of independence.

One afternoon, we decided to go shopping. Some of the shops were so different than here in the States. Crazy, I will have to say, or at least that was our impression. In the one we visited, the front of the store had clothing for guys and gals with dressing rooms several rows deep behind the store's front. The dressing rooms were a free for all. They were separated by flimsy curtains that customers just swept aside, and they would run through the rows of curtained off spaces until they found one they could fit in—this meant being semi-nude or in all stages of undress while guys and girls trudged past us on their way to the next available spot, or they just settled in with us. No one seemed too concerned about it. In fact, it seemed that everyone had a good time with it all. There were so many people trying on and taking off clothing in each section that you could barely move. We each found something to purchase just so that we had something to wear from this funny store.

On our last day in Rome, we had intended to visit Vatican City, but it turned out that we slept in too late and ran out of time. We had been in Rome for five days, and now we were headed to

Napoli. We got down to the train station, purchased our tickets, and waited. In the meantime, we noticed a young Asian woman looking distraught. She approached us and made an attempt to communicate with us, but we couldn't understand much other than the fact that she didn't know how to get to where she needed to go, and we understood this only by her demeanor rather than her spoken words. I led her over to a line of offices in the station with officials in each that I hoped would be able to direct her, but they seemed as bewildered as we had been. As Laura's and my train pulled out of the station toward our next destination, the poor woman was still running around frantically. We both wondered what would become of her.

Napoli was less touristy than Rome during the time we were there. The city also seemed less affluent. It was by far the most out of control place I have ever experienced. People, cars, and mopeds were everywhere. The cars and mopeds flew through narrow alleyways as pedestrians made way for them. The outdoor seating of the wall-to-wall restaurants was teeming with people. The women who rode their mopeds wore flashy clothing and high heels. The city was chaotic and alive.

We stayed in a fairly modern hotel compared to the place in Rome— Hotel Paradiso at Via Catullo 11 on Posillipo Hill. It hung high up on a cliff with a panoramic view of the city, its harbor, and Mount Vesuvius. The restaurant had an outdoor seating area with a breathtaking view. Laura and I had attempted to book a room at Le Fontane al Mare, a hotel by the sea that had been advertised as "luxury accommodations at a relatively low price . . . [with] balconies overlooking the sea."[35] I had called from Oregon and was told that the status of the hotel was up in the air. The Italian over the phone spoke enough English that we were able to communicate fairly well. He explained that the current location was in question and that either the place would need renovation or the hotel would be moved elsewhere. He explained that he didn't know just when this might occur. So I decided booking was too risky. Instead, we went to a travel agent and the Hotel Paradiso was recommended—a ways away from the water but with nice accommodations and safe.

To get down to Napoli, we took a short walk down a steep hill leading to a covered trolley station. The trolley car ran up and down on the same track and inside a tunnel with graffiti on its walls. The trolley lumbered up and down all day long and into the evening. Without it, we would have had a difficult time getting to the city as we had not yet realized that taking a cab was another alternative. We had read in one of our travel books that cab drivers charged exorbitant rates, so for the first few days in Napoli, we

[35] Best Western Hotel Paradiso, http://www.booking.com/hotel/it/paradise, html?aid=311088;label=hotel-80056-it-A/yili...10/25/13.

walked everywhere other than using the trolley to get down the cliff. It turned out that cab fares were cheap, and the cabbies were a riot. My initial plan was for us to have a meal at the waterfront for a view of the bay and then take a boat ride out to Capri, but after the trolley ride, we had to walk for a few hours to get into the heart of Napoli. Then we had to find a bank to make a money exchange. It turned out to be more complicated than we had anticipated. The bank was beautiful and monstrous. You had to take a ticket like one does in the DMV here in America. We sat on one of the many rows of benches next to a slight elderly woman wearing a hat and holding an umbrella at her side. She immediately struck up a conversation with Laura in Italian. It didn't seem to bother her that Laura didn't know too much of the language. Or maybe she just didn't notice that. Laura smiled, gestured, and threw in a word or two of Italian, which kept their conversation going for some time. She found the woman enchanting. All the while, I smiled over at them so as to join in as best I could. It took about an hour to have our number called and to be waited on for our exchange, and then we were off.

Laura became exhausted and irritated after what seemed like hours of walking. We still hadn't reached our destination and still hadn't had anything to eat. She stopped in front of the next restaurant we walked by and announced that we would be eating in it. We were greeted by a waiter who showed us to a table and took our order. Our meal had just arrived when a stretch limo pulled up in front of the restaurant. A slight older man with a shock of white hair, a bright yellow suit, white boots, and numerous chains around his neck stepped out of the limo. He was accompanied by two large mean-looking bodyguard types. The three barreled into our restaurant and walked right past us to the kitchen in the back. They had a short conversation with the staff, who looked uncomfortable. It seemed that they came to some sort of agreement with the restaurant staff, and then the trio headed back outside to their limo and disappeared as quickly as they had appeared. In spite of the fact that they were gone, Laura wanted to get as far away from the place as possible. We made an attempt to eat at least part of our meal and then high-tailed it out of there.

After we got down to the waterfront, I noticed the name Le Fontane al Mare on the front of a large stone building right on the water. I told Laura, "Look, it's the place we were thinking about staying in." So we went over to see it up close. There were a few workmen inside, and we asked them about the place, explaining that we had called months before about booking a room. One of the workers said that the hotel had been abandoned and that its future was still questionable. He invited us to explore. We walked up the stairs to the interior balcony with numerous doors to rooms that had once been for guests. The place looked like an abandoned castle of stone, barren and cold. It was difficult to imagine that it had ever been a desirable place to stay. We agreed that we were lucky that we had not wound up there—at least in its present state.

We did some more sightseeing and started back in the direction of the interior of the city and closer to our hotel. By this time, it was about four o'clock when the city really started to come alive. The crowds on the street were wall to wall. The atmosphere was utterly chaotic. The restaurants were boundless. We perused the variety of restaurants surrounding us, but this was about the time that Laura said she had had enough and that she wanted to go back to the relative peaceful environment of the hotel restaurant. The crowds became so thick that it was difficult to navigate down the streets and sidewalks. Again, as in Rome, Laura became panicky, so we found a group of cabs, picked one, and headed back to the hotel. When it came time to pay for the ride, we were pleasantly surprised at how cheap it was. After that, we had no reservations about using this mode of transportation.

The next day, we headed back out. For the most part, we just liked to stroll around the city and see what we would run into. As we walked along, a guy sidled up next to us and started a conversation. He spoke English, but he had an accent. I wasn't sure at first if he was Italian or not. He had lighter hair and a lighter complexion than most of the residents in Napoli, but his face also resembled other of the Italians there. He introduced himself as Pietro and continued to follow us around the city. He offered to provide us with a tour, and so we took him up on it. It was obvious from the start that he was taken with Laura. This was the beginning of an unpredictable courtship between the two of them. Laura interacted with Pietro with a youthful capriciousness, and he interacted with her with flirtation and ardor. I found their banter humorous, sweet, and entertaining. He called her "Lauw-raa."

Pietro's voice was deep and hoarse like gravel. This complimented his broken English and somehow reminded me of my grandfather's voice. He even had a somewhat similar look and manner to him. As Pietro walked alongside us, he confided in us about his personal life, sometimes only providing clues about his travails. He told of his year or two in London, where he had picked up some of the English language. He had been forced to leave Italy because a member of the mafia had put a contract out on him. He explained that he had tried to help a friend of his who was being harassed by the mob, and they took offense to this. Word got back to him that if they caught up to him, the plan was to shoot him in the legs. He added that from that point on, he had decided to mind his own business. He remained in London until he felt it was safe to return home. While he was there, he complained that the Londoners had made fun of his broken English. He remained somewhat sensitive about this topic. I suggested that the Londoners were likely to do no better than he if they were in Italy. I have to admit, though, that as time went by, it was sometimes difficult not to giggle at some of the things he would say because of his limited knowledge of the language. Laura and I weren't trying to make fun of him, but his expressions were too funny not to laugh at. After his return to Italy, he resumed his work as a mason. He lived in the second story of his parents' home and was going on thirty when we met him. He went on to describe himself as a mama's boy. My memory of the expression he used to describe himself was "a mamacita," but I have only been able to find the Italian word "mammone," which seems to define the meaning in Italian. So I don't know. Anyway, he described what being one of these entailed—a young man remains in his parents' home where his mother continues to take care of him. He has only the semblance of being a full-grown man and is afforded time to carouse and chase women. Even if he marries, he might still remain on the second story of his parents' home and move his bride in-this was what occurred with my own parents when they married. Pietro hinted about "an angel" that had broken his heart and that Laura reminded him of "his angel." I wondered who this angel was.

First thing he took us to was the Castel dell'Ovo. Pietro described the legend of the castle—"the Roman poet Virgil (who had the reputation in medieval times as a great sorcerer) put a magical egg into the foundations to support the fortifications. If something had broken the egg, the castle [would be] destroyed."[36] The three of us explored the castle, looked out over the precipice, and searched for the egg, as the Neapolitans do. While in Rome, Laura and I had come across weddings and funerals everywhere we went, and Napoli was no different. As we wandered around the city with Pietro, weddings were happening everywhere we looked, and we all commented on the humor of it. We also ran into a funeral in progress—an ancient Italian woman dressed in all black, wailing and pounding her chest as she looked down into the casket of her loved one.

Another place we visited that day was Galleria Umberto I, a marble- and-glass ancestor of the modern [day] shopping center with its high glass dome roof. It was a beautiful and monstrous place.[37] We roamed around in there looking in different shops, but the most memorable part of the visit was the young woman we came upon, dressed all in white, her head covered with a hijab. She had a face that looked as though it had been chiseled from fine marble with expressionless ice-blue eyes. An aura of the ethereal emanated from her. It looked as though her hardships had defeated her. A small child stood next to her with the same face and eyes. The mother held out a cup for us without uttering a

[36] "Castel dell'Ovo," Wikipedia, The Free Encyclopedia, http://en.wikipedia.org/wiki/Castel_dell'Ovo, 10 /11/2013.

[37] Fodor's Up Close, 2nd ed. (Random House, Inc., 2000), 354.

sound. Pietro cautioned us not to give the beggar anything, but we couldn't help but put a generous amount of cash into her cup. Later, he explained that catering to beggars was discouraged in his country but that he understood why we had given her the money. Laura and I had become aware of other non- Italian residents in Italy who stole, sold their wares to tourists in the cities' piazzas, or begged on the streets. These people seemed to be tolerated but not appreciated. This also went for the dogs in the cities we visited. They were usually underweight and wandered through the streets, begging for food or hanging around garbage cans behind restaurants to scavenge what they could. It didn't seem that any of them lived with people. I remembered my grandmother having an aversion to animals in the house. She said that when she grew up in her home, there were dirt floors and that, often, livestock shared the space with the family, so she had no use for domestic animals other than their providing a meal. When Dad, Jean, Jack and I were in Slovenija, Yanko took us to Francesca's home. It was small, made of rough stone, with a fenced family cemetery consisting of ancient tomb stones and crosses. He told us the house was over three hundred years old. The experience left me with a new sort of connection with my grandmother and our generational history.

After Pietro dropped us off at our hotel at the end of the day, he suggested we make plans with him to accompany us to Capri and to the best spot in Napoli for pizza Margherita during our stay, but that never happened. He gave Laura his cell phone number for her to call, but that wasn't what she had in mind. The next morning, in spite of my protestations, she let me know that this trip was for us to spend time together and that she had no intention of including Pietro in any more of our vacation. In the meantime, I copied the number down for myself, just in case. I had been under the impression that she was somewhat smitten with him as I was sure he was with her. For now, Laura and I were off on our own for another day in the city.

As we walked along near the waterfront, we chanced upon Palazzo Reale (Royal Palace) and decided to purchase tickets. We had to wait a while to get them, but it was worth the wait. The grounds around the palace were serene and impressive—they lent a sort of Central-Park-in- New-York-City feel. Inside, the palace was spectacular—opulence beyond belief. Now Laura was in a particularly gregarious mood that day. She had her camera, and in spite of the signs warning against taking pictures, she hoped to sneak in a few. We wandered around in the expansive palace in awe, as we usually shied away from tours. However, a handsome middle- aged Italian man with white hair approached us and introduced himself. He had a name tag and was one of the guides for the palace. He had overheard Laura talking about taking pictures, and he explained the reason for the rule but offered to look the other way if she didn't get too carried away with her camera.

She discarded the idea of taking photos, explaining that she didn't want to damage any aspect of the grand palace. He offered to provide us with a personal tour. We followed him around from one room to the next, and he described, with great pride, the history of the castle and of Napoli. Earlier on, Laura and I had noticed a sort of outdoor garden balcony, and we had decided to go out and take a better look, but there was a sign at the door stating "no admittance." We asked our guide about the reason. He explained that renovations were in progress, and there was concern about the safety for both the guests and the garden itself, but he offered to provide us admittance to the garden with his supervision. Laura was thrilled to have access to this special and lovely spot. He spent a couple of hours with us, and upon the end of our tour with him, he told us that Neapolitans are often not rich in terms of wealth but rather in terms of life. "Our life here is rich," he explained, and I understood what he was talking about.

On our last day in Napoli, we finally made it down to the waterfront for a meal at Zi Teresa. We got down to the pier too early for dinner, but the waiters who were setting up for the evening showed us around and booked us a table for later on. In the meantime, we headed down the pier behind the restaurant and found a little bar there. After perusing the bar menu, we decided on ordering something neither of us was familiar with—a red martini. When they were brought to our table, the drinks looked like a rufescent splendor. They tasted like heaven itself, so we both ordered another. We tried to ask the bartender about the drink's secret ingredient(s), but something got lost in translation. This experience began a search for the secret and for other sources of this extraordinary elixir as our vacation progressed.

We headed back to Zi Teresa and were shown to our outdoor table. It was a glorious evening. Our three waiters were flirtatious and entertaining. They each reminded us of members of our family at home. We ordered dish after dish of Italian specialties. Near the end of our meal, I roamed into the interior of the restaurant, where the toilets were. In Italy, you never know what you're going to get—a hole in the ground or unisex bathrooms where a guy might be in the next stall. The toilets and stall doors are all unique. Sometimes it was impossible to figure out how to get out of the stall. This particular toilet took the cake. When I pushed the button to flush, the seat began to undulate as it moved around in a circular fashion, disappearing behind the tank and then reappearing on the other side. The seat looked as though it were made of rubber and making waves. All this action was, presumably, to sanitize the seat as it moved around out of sight and returned into view again. I told Laura to check it out.

After our meal and visit to the peculiar bathroom, we headed out of the restaurant and into the crisp night air. There were numerous cabs lined up in front of Zi Teresa, and we hailed one. Laura and I had put away two red martinis and shared a bottle of wine at dinner, so we were both feeling our oats. Laura, in particular, was in one of her gregarious moods, and for some reason, this and the alcohol brought on a barrage of fluent Italian from her lips. The young Italian cabbie was cute and friendly. He and she began to banter back and forth in his native tongue, and she would translate for me here and there during their conversation. He spent most of his time looking back at us as he drove down the city streets, occasionally looking ahead out the front window of the cab to see where he was going. We were all laughing as we drove along toward our hotel, but before we got there, he invited us to a nearby tavern and suggested that we meet him after his night shift was over. We may have taken him up on the offer, but we explained that we had a plane to catch in the morning. He accepted our excuse, continued to laugh and converse with us, and then drove off waving after he let us off in front of our hotel.

The next morning we woke up bright and early and begrudgingly to catch our plane to Sicily. We packed and took another cab to the airport then sat and waited. Something didn't seem quite right after we'd been there a while, and we kept hearing that flights were being canceled or delayed. We had arrived at the airport early to make sure we wouldn't miss our flight, and now it was going on three hours waiting. Finally, there was an announcement in

Italian from the loudspeakers, and a flurry of agitation and shouting ensued. The whole place was full of angry Italian men rushing about and shaking their fists. It was chaos. Laura was able to decipher what was happening with her broken Italian—not as good as the night before—and gleaned that there was an airline strike, and no planes would be in service in the foreseeable future. Long lines of customers formed in front of the ticket counter to complain, get a refund, or just be angry. We sat there on the bench and wondered what to do next. We had reservations in Scopello in Sicily for the next five days and nights. All of a sudden, I came up with a plan—to call Pietro and see if he would agree to take us down there. Laura wasn't all that enthused about the idea, but she didn't really have any better ideas either. Even at that, she remained hesitant about making the call but finally agreed to give it a try. She rang for Pietro, and he answered right away. She explained our predicament, and he said he would be over to the airport in no time and to wait outside in front. We retrieved our baggage and headed out to wait for him. I started getting anxious about whether he would really show up or not, but about that time, there he was. He had left his work abruptly with some sort of excuse. After he parked his car, he opened his backseat and stuck paint cans, tools of his trade, tarps, and then our baggage in the hatchback. Laura got in the passenger seat, and I crawled in the back, and we were off.

We started down the coastline, through countryside and farmland. Pietro turned the radio knobs to find some music for our road trip, but all there was on the channels were not-very-good Italian pop songs. Laura and I had brought a small carry case of disks, and I handed him one from the backseat—Center Stage from the movie with the same name. It had an assortment of songs from the movie sung by different artists. It was the perfect music for our high-speed travel. I sat in the backseat, content, with the windows rolled down to get at the breeze that blew in from outside. I have to say that during our drive south, I had never felt as happy and carefree in my life before or since. I asked for one song in particular, "First Kiss," to be played over and over—a manifestation of my obsessive tendencies. Now that we were on our way with Pietro, Laura relaxed and became flirtatious with him again, as she had been the first day we met him. It seemed that she was also caught up in the adventure of it all. Pietro drove like a maniac, just like most of the Italians on the road. He would take a wrong turn and then whip around in the middle of the road to get back on track, never mind the other vehicles in his way. But none of this bothered me. I was in my own euphoric space.

We traveled down to the southern tip of the mainland to Villa San Giovanni in Calabria, where there was ferry service to Sicily. The trouble was that there seemed to be nowhere to park Pietro's car, so he just drove down a hill to an empty field and left it there.

Then we had to hike up the steep hill that we all kept slipping off until we finally got to the ferry landing. We purchased tickets and then stepped onto the ferry. There were a bunch of Italian attendants who were more than happy to assist Laura and me with our luggage. They spoke to us in Italian as if we could understand them. They were sweet and gentlemanly. We nodded and smiled at them to try to communicate our appreciation. This was the first time of many that I would notice the difference between the Italians living in Rome and those living south. In Napoli, the men had been swarthier than in Rome. In (or near) Sicily, they were shorter, darker, and seemed less familiar with foreign travelers, and for that reason, I think they also seemed more enamored with us.

The ferry moved leisurely along until we arrived in Messina. By this time, it was late and dark, and we were in no condition to try to get to Scopello. Besides that, the only way there was by train, and none were running until the next morning, so we would be staying in Messina for the night. I found a phone to call the bed and breakfast hosts to let them know that our arrival would be delayed and that there would be an extra guest if they could accommodate us. Then we decided to find a place to eat. Without Pietro along, our travel along the dark forbidding streets would have been frightening. His swagger suggested that he felt comfortable in this milieu. He led us to a small restaurant that was, luckily, still open. We were the only ones in the place. We ordered spaghetti and a bottle of wine to split between the three of us. The plates of spaghetti were only three dollars each, and the bottle of wine cost the same, yet it was the best meal I had the entire time we were in Italy. After our meal, we weren't sure where to find a place to stay. I had my travel books, and both mentioned the two hotels near the train station that were reasonably priced but cautioned the reader to beware of the walk. The two were close together—Hotel Touring and Hotel Mirage. I remember passing by both of them, but I can't remember which one we stayed in. Pietro checked us in. After we got to the room, he told us that the hotelkeeper thought he was mafia because he had checked in with two women in one room. This, he explained, was common practice among gangsters. We decided that Pietro would have one bed, and Laura and I would share the other two that stood closer together. The room was big and had a large bathroom. I had brought along a sarong for my travel, and Pietro was curious about this garment that he had seen me take out of my suitcase. He picked it up off our bed and Laura offered to demonstrate how it worked. He held his arms up above his head and smiled as she wrapped it around his waist, sarong style. This became a source of amusement and joking. He quickly went into the bathroom, and Laura followed, closing the door behind her. They were together in there for a while. I could hear laughing and giggling. That same night, after they emerged from the bathroom, flushed and smiling, Pietro developed a hoarse cough and some respiratory distress. He was convinced that he was coming down with a cold. The next morning, I expressed my concerns to Laura in confidence about his becoming ill, but she told me she suspected that his symptoms were related more to lovesickness than to a bug. As time went by, I became convinced that she was right.

The next morning, we headed down to the train station and bought our tickets. The train was charming—something you'd see in a 1920s, 1930s, or 1940s film. Laura and I seemed to be the only tourists in the train, other than Pietro, but at least he spoke fluent Italian. There were mostly short and swarthy men, who were shy but friendly, on the train. They smiled at us a lot. The atmosphere was right up my alley—being surrounded by men and a beautiful language that, for the most part, I couldn't understand. It was reminiscent of my bus ride with the Mexicans on my trip home from Portland a few years earlier. The scenery was beautiful as we peered out the window. Many of them were left open to let in the breeze because there was no air conditioning on this antique train. The clickety-clack of the train over the tracks felt hypnotic. After we arrived in Palermo, we took a taxi to the airport, where our rental car was waiting. We had arranged for the car when we thought we would be flying into Sicily. We took off for Scopello and our hostel a day late from our expected arrival. On the way, Pietro made a short stop to call home. This became a frequent occurrence—bogus explanations to his mother for his absence from home and work.

After we arrived at the hostel, the proprietress greeted us. I asked if they had been able to provide a room to accommodate the three of us. The proprietress said she had but seemed a little annoyed by the request and Pietro's presence. The proprietor looked as though he had some sort of neurological condition. He walked with a peculiar gait and had some difficulty with his speech. In spite of this, he grabbed Laura's and my baggage and attempted to drag one at a time up the steep narrow set of stairs leading to the second floor where our room was. Due to his difficulty with the first bag, I suggested that I could get mine on my own, but he ignored the offer and proceeded to drag the second up the flight of stairs. Our room was big with a small bed at the back of the room and two near the windows looking out over the front of the hostel. The proprietress delegated the back bed for Pietro and the other two for Laura and me. She also provided a screen to partition off Pietro's side of the room, explaining that this would provide everyone privacy. We settled in.

The dining room on the ground floor had a stiff and formal atmosphere. The other guests had an aristocratic air. People in the dining room ate without much conversation between them at all. Pietro ignored all this, and the three of us carried on as we would have in a livelier atmosphere that was usual in Italy. There was energy among the three of us that drew attention from the others, which I might describe as disapproving. One female guest, however, seemed amused and commented that she wished she was having as much fun as we seemed to be having and wondered about what sort of arrangement the three of us had going on. All this seemed to goad Laura all the more. I had seen her "on" before, but this seemed to be an all-time high of teasing flirtatiousness, clever banter, and sexual innuendo. I have wished that I had written or recorded the gist of some of these conversations, but at the time, I was all too in-the-moment to think of such a thing. Breakfast and dinner were served at the same time each day and, basically, the same meal for each. The food was plain—indigenous whole fish and vegetables, a small salad, and dessert. There was no resemblance to Italian cuisine. After a few of these meals and while away from the hostel, Pietro would complain about the food and would insist on finding "a good meal" elsewhere.

Whether or not he had been in Sicily before, I don't know, but he seemed to know his way around. For the time we were there, Pietro was our lead. His Italian was certainly a plus in the realm of tour guides. One day he had taken us to a local beach. The beach was crowded with Italians of all sizes, shapes, and ages. We sat on the sand and took in the sights. A middle-aged Italian man walked down the beach carrying a mobile rack of beach wares. It was immense and difficult to determine how he was able carry the contraption, which held hats, purses, sunglasses, beach balls, toys, and snorkeling gear. I decided to make a purchase and ran down the beach to catch up with him. I found a cute tan weaved straw sun hat with brown trim and flowers attached at the brim. It offered good shade for the rest of our trip.

It was a hot day at the beach, and after we packed up our stuff, we found a restaurant a few miles away. There was an assortment of selections in a case, and you had to point at one to order. All the food looked delicious but also heavy, and on such a hot day, I would have preferred a lighter fare. The staff invited us to find a table outside, where they would bring out our meals. When they were served, the plates were piled as high as mountains with pasta. It tasted good, but Laura and I could only put a dent in it due to the ninety-plus-degree temperature and humidity. There was an open field behind our table, and we had thoughts of dumping our leftovers out there but thought better of it because we might get caught doing it. When it was time to leave, I went inside to pay the bill. I stood at the counter where we had ordered, but no one acknowledged my presence. I finally asked Pietro to assist me in paying the bill. After a short conversation with the proprietor, Pietro told me that he was unwilling to accept my payment. I had insulted him after his seeing our close-to-full plates come back to the kitchen. Pietro said there was nothing to be done to turn things around, so we left without paying. I felt terrible for unintentionally insulting the establishment's proprietor and wished we had thrown the extra pasta into the field after all.

On another day we took a day-long hike along the mountainous coastline. We were traveling by foot high above the ocean, and the trail was up on a cliff. We could look down and see the open ocean and coves where bathers gathered. To get down to a cove required a steep descent. We had walked along for a few hours before we chose one that looked inviting. There weren't many people, and it had a sandy beach. We ate our picnic lunch. Laura and Pietro decided to take a swim, while I remained on the beach relaxing in the hot sun. I watched them together out in the sea. They looked like sweet young lovers kissing, hugging, bobbing up and down in the waves, and smiling and waving back at me on shore. It seemed Pietro saw me as a protective motherly chaperone, looking out for her daughter. A role he seemed to respect.

One morning while Pietro was still sleeping behind his screen, Laura loaded our gun with bubble water, sneaked across the room, and blasted him with the tommy-gun noise, flashing lights, and bubbles. He grabbed the gun away from her, chased her over to our side of the room, and attacked her with bubbles. We were all laughing. After that, any chance one of us got to surprise the other with a sneak attack, that's what would happen. The noise, the bubbles, and the light show the gun provided are difficult to describe. It just made you want to laugh. Our moods altered somewhat a few minutes later, though, when Pietro read to us and translated an article in the newspaper that had been left in front of our door that morning. The article reported a serious train wreck that had occurred the day before. Many of the passengers had perished in the wreck and others had been injured. It was the same train that we had taken to Palermo only a few days earlier.

That same day, we told him we wanted to see the Capuchin Catacombs. Min Yi had traveled with her mother to Italy a few years earlier and told Laura and me that it was a must-see if we got as far in our travels as Sicily. So we headed out. As soon as we arrived in the parking lot, a couple of tough-looking guys approached our car. One of them knocked on the window of the driver's seat where Pietro was sitting. Pietro stepped out of the car with a worried look on his face. We remained inside and watched as the three of them walked a short distance away. It was scary. A few minutes later he returned and explained that they were mafia who had extorted money from him in order for our car or us not to be harmed. He assured us that they would not bother us again, but I wasn't completely convinced. After that episode, we headed to the catacombs. The building was light stone-colored stucco. The catacombs themselves were partially underground with rounded open-air windows to let in the fresh air from outside. The friars who greeted us were serene and friendly. They briefly described the history of the place—bodies of over eight thousand deceased inhabitants of the area, gathered over three and a half centuries, found their resting place here. Family members had carefully dressed their loved ones in their finest. Bodies were lined up against walls in various forms of decomposition in the massive chambers in order to venerate their memory. We were told that the climate in the area allowed the bodies to remain remarkably intact. There were numerous categories of rooms—soldiers, virgins, children, etc. The most remarkable, though, was that of a very young female child who had died during the First World War. There was a room for her all to herself. She lay on an altar wearing a white dress and holding a bouquet of flowers. She was lovely, perfectly preserved, and looked as if she was only sleeping. If she had gotten up off the altar, I wouldn't have been that surprised. Laura and I walked from room to room, taking it all in. Pietro, on the other hand, remained uncharacteristically quiet. Finally, he told us that all this was fake, but we assured him that it wasn't. I think that, for him, the final straw was seeing the little girl so perfectly preserved and hearing from us that all these clothed corpses were real. He told us he would wait for us outside and left abruptly.

We spent some time in Palermo later that day, mostly walking the streets of this ancient and seemingly rough city. Apartment buildings were literally falling apart and often decorated with clothes drying on lines outside their windows. It was particularly hot that day, so we stopped for some gelato from a vendor on the street and ate our treat on the street curb as it melted down our hands and fingers. The three of us did some sightseeing too that afternoon, mostly old cathedrals. It would be our last day in Sicily, so for me, at least, there was a sense of trepidation mixed in with content. When we got back to Scopello, Laura and I took a walk together because Pietro said he had something he needed to do. He was rather secretive about it. So Laura and I went for a walk on our own. We looked through some of the little shops in the town and ran into a charming elderly Italian shopkeeper. Laura was in a particularly gregarious mood that afternoon, and the two of them hit it off. They talked about the charm of Sicily. We told him that we would be leaving his little town in the morning for home. He said that he had something for us to take home and handed us each a huge bouquet of oregano tied together with a ribbon. Its aroma was exceptional. We offered to pay him for the gift, but he said that it was, in fact, a gift. He then explained to us that this oregano was the finest in all of Italy. Later on, when we showed our bouquets to Pietro, he explained that everyone in Italy insists that their oregano, and many other foods, wines, spices, etc. are superior to all others. He added that his own mother would have argued with the shop owner about her garden oregano being better than his. Laura and I were still thrilled with our gift of oregano but wondered how we would get it home on the plane (but later, there was no problem with it. They let us carry our bouquets on board, and we just held it or set it next to us). Then we asked Pietro what he had been up to. He announced that he had gone gift shopping for us. He presented Laura with a pair of earrings. He told her that the stones that made up the earrings were the color of her eyes, which he adored. She still has them.

Pietro was not about to spend our last evening in Sicily eating at our hostel, so we searched for a place in Scopello that served red martinis. Laura and I had told Pietro all about the ones we had discovered in Napoli. We found a restaurant with tables outdoors. The cocktail waitress was an attractive and sensual woman with a knack for playful banter that she and Pietro carried on in Italian. She cocked her head with a look of skepticism as we tried to describe the kind of drink we were after. She finally guessed that the secret ingredient in the martinis was red vermouth and said she would see what the bartender could come up with. She left to discuss all this with the bartender and came back shortly with three red drinks. They were OK, and we appreciated her efforts, but they just weren't the same as the originals. After a few of these drinks, we moved on to dinner—a real Italian meal that we let Pietro order for us. Pietro had told us, since we'd been with him, that the custom in Italy was to take a walk after a meal "for good digestion," so this was what we did after every meal. He also always made sure that he walked next to the street on the sidewalks to separate us from the street. This, he had explained, was to protect females from attack, mud splashed from tires, etc. We all found ourselves repositioning ourselves on almost every occasion to make sure this custom was adhered to.

That evening, Pietro wanted to take Laura out. They were both in good spirits when they left. I relaxed in our room, alone for the evening, in reverie about the romantic evening I expected they would have. The night was particularly beautiful, stars in the sky, in the small town that had few artificial sources of light. There was a hint of a thunderstorm that threatened to erupt, eliciting an aura of electricity in the air. There was a great din from crickets and other creatures in this rural setting. Donkeys in the fields were settling down for the night. The moon was full. All this only intensified my sadness about having to leave the island in the morning. I'm not sure just what occurred that night between the two of them. But I do know that a few days later, Laura told me that I had not seen another side of Pietro that she had seen that night. She also confided that she too had recognized the disparity in her feelings about him, and that during the last night they had spent together in Scopello, she had been very aware of a cosmic energy that had surrounded the two of them that night.

The next morning, it was still dark when we were awakened by the alarm. The three of us dressed hurriedly. As Pietro drove us to the airport, the sun was just coming up. There was a stillness in the air. The rest of the island was still sleeping. I remember being concerned that after he would drop us off, his car, left in Messina, would have been stolen or confiscated. He told me not to worry about that, but I did anyway. After we got to the airport, he held Laura in an embrace for the longest time, and he sobbed as he let go of her. I felt the same. As we boarded the plane, I was afraid to look back. But after we were in our seats, he waved good-bye from outside our window. And then we were gone. The plane was in the air, and I just fell apart there sitting next to Laura. I wept like I never had before. It was because I might never see Pietro again; because my relationship with Mario had ended; because my grandparents had left this part of the world, their families and their culture, never to return; because I felt there was not much hope as far as having anything with John at home—John, who I felt akin to, who had such a gentle soul, and who I was in love with—because I had made a mess of my marriage to a man I knew still loved me in spite of it all; and because I had recently become aware of the beginnings of my father's demise. I couldn't stop myself. I wept most of the way home until there were no tears left.

After we got home, I could think of nothing other than Pietro. I was still under the delusion that Laura would somehow come to her senses and realize that she felt the same way he did about her. I began calling him. I'm not sure who first brought up the idea of his coming to visit, but that's what happened. As our telephone conversations continued, I became aware that he was talking as though he wasn't just in it for a vacation but meant to remain in America if things were to work out as he hoped. He said as much to his family. He mentioned that he had purchased a suitcase that would accommodate all that he planned to need for such a pursuit. I let Laura and Leo know that he would be visiting. I don't think either of them was that excited about it, but I felt that after he arrived, all would be well. Laura and I drove up to the airport on September 19. The plane was late. I got concerned about his having missed his flight or worse. But the arrival of his flight was announced, and I waited impatiently for him. He finally emerged into sight from the crowd exiting the plane, one of the last. He looked tired, with a day's growth of beard and his hair disheveled. We all embraced. Then we went over to the baggage pickup. As the conveyor belt began to move, we waited for his luggage to come into view. When he recognized his bag, he grabbed ahold of the handle. It would have been impossible to miss, as it was the largest piece of luggage I had ever seen. I couldn't believe that he had been allowed to check it in in the first place. When we laughed at the size of it, he seemed a little irritated and explained again that he was hoping for at least a lengthy visit, if not a permanent one, and wanted to bring with him all that he would need. He hauled it out to our car. It was late, so we spent the first night in Portland at the Ramada.

The next day, we took a trip to Downtown Portland for lunch and a movie. We also visited the immigration building that was near Union Station to get information about his getting a visa for work. That evening, Nora, Todd, and their kids met us for dinner at Pazzo downtown, which got Pietro's approval as far as Italian cuisine was concerned. (Although he was a mason by trade, he had aspirations to own a restaurant of his own at some point. He was an excellent cook, who had watched and imitated his mother in the kitchen during his growing-up years). That night after dinner, we stayed at Nora's house. Laura and I slept on the hide-a-bed in the basement, Pietro in an upstairs spare bedroom.

The next morning, September 21, the three of us drove up to Seaside. It was a beautiful summer day with fall approaching. We had lunch at the Shilo Inn and sat on the beach. There was a mist in the air that day, and over in the distance down the beach to our right, there was a wedding ceremony being conducted right there on the sand in front of the waves— the couple in their wedding attire; the priest, minister, or rabbi in front of them; and the family members behind. The event looked ethereal with the mist and the ocean sunlight. The distance from us made the wedding party seem to move in slow motion. We all laughed remembering the many weddings we had witnessed everywhere we went in Italy. And now here was another in the most unexpected of circumstances. We wondered if it was a sign. Even Laura commented sentimentally about it. Pietro asked her if she might want a wedding of her own (he called it a wed-ning). He added that if that is what she wanted, he would acquiesce. That day in Seaside, Pietro courted Laura as he had in Italy, only it seemed more desperate and assertive than before. She continued to vacillate in her emotions about him. Sometimes she reciprocated his affection, while at other times she was downright mean to him. I suspect that, on some level, she was irritated with me for cooking up this whole scheme to have him visit. But Laura wasn't about to put up with any of it. One thing that really bugged her was that he would tell us that males can never be friends with a female. I disagreed with this opinion of his but had some idea why he thought that way—sex always getting in the way, of course. Laura, on the other hand, was downright offended by his remarks along this line, and I believe it made her wary of him, or at least just annoyed. They would argue the point to no avail.

We drove back down from Seaside and stayed another night at Nora's. In the morning, as I was getting dressed, Nora came down to visit before we would be leaving. It was just the two of us. I broke down again, in a similar manner to what occurred on the plane back from Sicily. I told Nora that I felt in love with Pietro. I was surprised that came out of my mouth, but it did. Up until that point I don't think I realized it. Maybe the Seaside trip had made it clear to me just how irritated Laura was with Pietro in general and with me for having arranged his visit. Any hopes I had for them to have a future together were pretty much dashed. Nora held me and tried to comfort me. I think she too was surprised by my confession and by my emotional state. I told her through my tears just how absurd I felt my sentiments were and that I hoped to assuage them.

The next day, we drove over the mountain. I had expected he might enjoy the scenery, but he seemed oblivious to it. On some level, I wondered if he was already feeling a sense of hopelessness about things working out as he had hoped. I also wondered if he was also feeling some homesickness. He frequently compared his current surroundings in America unfavorably with his in Italy. This made sense to me, as I tended to feel the same way about the two, but for Laura, it was an additional irritation. She felt pride in her homeland and wanted him to appreciate it. After we got back to Bend, this disparity became even more exaggerated.

When Pietro arrived in Bend, he presented us with gifts he brought from Italy. He had red vermouth for us so we could make our own red martinis and Italian delicacies, including jars of melanzana that his mother had made. He also grilled some peppers and eggplant and made some of his own melanzana for us the first evening he was with us and cooked meals for us, which were delicious. The cultural differences between Pietro and Laura were great. For me, it was different—a welcome change of pace and something I felt familiar with. His manner was endearing to me, but Laura began to criticize and imitate his manner of dress and his Italian swagger and posturing behind his back. What made matters worse was that he had spent some time in a tavern downtown where some of the guys there were wearing cowboy hats, so he purchased one for himself. He seemed to think that the hat was the epitome of Central Oregon. In a way, it is—it's just that it didn't seem to fit the rest of him, but he seemed taken with it and wore it all the time. I didn't fail to recognize that Dad and Pietro shared the same fascination with cowboy gear. What is that all about anyway?

The whole situation went from bad to worse. Laura began avoiding him, spending time with her friends and not including him in her social circle. She made a point of letting him know that she didn't have time for him, and this was carried out at one point when a date showed up at the house to take her out. He was furious but remained behind to have dinner with me and then left. He walked downtown to one of the local pubs and met up with some of his newfound mates. It just so happened that earlier on that evening, he had also met up with some young women, one of them whom he hit on. He stuck out in Bend, so there was no doubting who this girl was talking about when she told her friends at school about him the next day. One of the girls was Laura. All this didn't fare too well for him, and from that point on, he was pretty much on his own as far as Laura was concerned.

I started spending more time with Pietro. In spite of his falling out with Laura, Pietro considered staying on for a while if he could get a visa for work, but this was easier said than done. I tried to help him with the paperwork, but there was so much more to it. One evening, the two of us were just talking. I felt so sad that I wept. I wanted to explain things to him—how I felt about him and why. He tried to comfort me, holding my hand, caressing my hair. But I didn't even know why I was so drawn to him at the time. Now I do. He was the epitome of all that Dad had tried to squelch in himself, the part that I loved the most, and I transferred that love to Pietro.

Things changed. We would go out for lunch or dinner and a drink— once to the October Festival downtown. I went to talk to John. He didn't say much.

Mom and Dad took us all out for dinner on October 3. We all had a good time. They liked Pietro, and Mom told me later that she thought he was handsome. Doug and Diane had Pietro over for dinner on October 7. Cameron and Byron met him too. I wanted my whole family to get to know him. It seemed to me that he would bring our family back to its origins.

The next day, Pietro and I took the Breeze up to Portland. I got two rooms at the airport Ramada. I expected it might be the last time I would ever see him, so I was prepared to make the most of the time I had left. At first, I felt giddy and had high hopes about our evening together, but this was also mixed with melancholy about Pietro's upcoming departure in the morning. I began to feel ridiculous about my infatuation with him but, at the same time, wanted to recapture the affection between us. I felt an emotional connection that still seems beyond description—maybe recognition of some sort of kinship of our psyches. Or was it all one sided? I don't know.

The next morning, we took the hotel shuttle to the airport. Pietro wore his cowboy hat and carried his monstrous suitcase. I still wasn't sure what his destination would be. He was vague about it. He had suggested that he might check out the southern part of the country—I think maybe Dallas, Texas. I worried about what kind of reception he might get there and how much trouble he might get into if he didn't just go home, but I kept my concern to myself.

We got to the airport a little late, and it was crowded. We stood in line to check his bag and get his ticket. Some fellow behind us asked him if he had someone stuffed in his suitcase for a free passage—in reference to its size. It really did look big enough to stuff someone in. I smiled, but Pietro wasn't amused by the comment, and he scowled at the fellow. I suspect he knew he was being made fun of. When we got to the ticket counter, the first thing the attendant said was that the suitcase looked over regulation size. She inspected it further, and we were told that, in fact, it was too big to check. I offered that Pietro had been able to check it on his way over here, but she said that regulations in Italy must be different. I said, "Well, what are we supposed to do then?" Time was getting tight as far as his getting his flight, and he still had to go through inspection. The attendant shuffled through a box behind the counter of abandoned empty luggage. She found a few duffle bags and helped us stuff his things inside them. What didn't fit we threw in a nearby garbage disposal. He checked one duffel bag and the other would be his carry-on. Then we headed to security. He asked me what he should do with his suitcase, and I said I would take it home with me. He made a hasty departure and then disappeared into the crowd. I waited until his plane took off to be sure he got off the ground. Then I headed over to the shuttle landing to catch the Breeze back to Bend. During my ride home, I thought about Pietro—petulant, temperamental, unpredictable, volatile, spontaneous, playful, and funny. I wondered where he was headed. I hoped he would stay safe.

When I returned home, I had his suitcase. I decided to use it for storage, and I still have it. Things sort of went back to normal, but Laura was still pissed at me. We went for a drive together one afternoon shortly after my return home. We talked about a lot of things, including Pietro.

My relationships with Laura, Leo, and John changed after Pietro's visit. Pietro seemed to have been some sort of catalyst. Laura became more independent. I saw her less. She tried to reconnect with her old boyfriend. She called and asked about visiting him. He had moved to Eastern Oregon, so she drove over to see what might come of it. Shortly after she arrived, another female friend of his showed up too. It didn't take too long for her to figure out that he wasn't that interested any longer, so she left. After that, she dated a few guys, but none of them amounted to much. She attended school at the community college and worked. I began to wonder if I even knew my own daughter anymore. I did know that our adventures with Pietro most likely had something to do with the change. I made a more concerted effort to get a divorce, but this wasn't received well by Leo.

I went to see John after my return. I told him that Laura was mad at me, and he said he didn't blame her. I agreed. I told him all about my time in Italy and about the time when Pietro was here. Again, he mostly just listened. That's what I like about him the most. He's mild-mannered, level-headed, and isn't quick to judge.

I wasn't supposed to have any kind of relationship with John according to the church. Being a Catholic, you're not allowed to get a divorce unless you accept a life of loneliness and celibacy afterward. Technically, in the eyes of the church, you're still married but just not cohabiting when you separate from your spouse even if you get a legal divorce. A sexual relationship with another person is forbidden, including a marriage to someone else, because, technically, you're still married—even John, who had divorced and hadn't been with his wife for years. (This may have contributed to my reluctance about getting a divorce in the first place—in the eyes of the church, I would still be married anyway). The other option is to petition for an annulment, which requires sworn statements by both parties why the marriage really wasn't a marriage. If the reasons seem sufficient to the priest or bishop who reviews the case, then the marriage is deemed null and void—as if it had never happened. Sandy had grappled with this dilemma years earlier. When she left Mark in DC a little over a year after their marriage, she moved into a place with a girlfriend and then moved back to Oregon. She lived in the guest house behind Mom and Dad's for a few months and then found a job in Eugene and moved there. Eventually, she left for another job in Salem. She would go down to the Denny's restaurant near her little cottage, drink coffee, and read in a booth there in the evenings. This is where she met Dave. He was a divorcee who managed the place. This all led to a romance. When Mom became aware of Sandy's relationship with Dave, she suggested that Sandy petition for an annulment, but Sandy would have none of it. She told Mom that she felt her marriage to Mark had been real and valid (in spite of its short duration), and she didn't intend to suggest it wasn't. I suspect Mom was hoping Sandy would have a clean slate so that she was open to have a Catholic wedding to Dave, a good Catholic boy himself.

Dave moved into one of the row of cottages a few doors down from Sandy's. Pretty soon she was spending most of her time at his place. Dave rigged the phone so that when it rang for Sandy at her place, it switched over to his. This was to prevent Mom from finding out about their arrangement. But this didn't work very long because the phone made clicking noises when it transferred the call, and Mom got suspicious. She told Sandy what she suspected, and Sandy didn't deny it. This resulted in some sort of argument. Sandy called me about what happened.

This brings to mind a similar incident, years earlier, involving Sandy. It was during my junior year at Willamette. I was living with Leo and his roommate for part of the first semester. As far as Mom and Dad were concerned, I was still living in the dorm. We had come back from Christmas break in Bend, and Sandy had ridden with us as far as Salem. We dropped her off at the bus depot for her ride up to Portland and then on to her campus at the University of

Portland. She was supposed to call Mom when she got there, but she forgot. So about midnight, Mom tried to get ahold of me, and when that failed, she called Leo. He answered. Mom asked if I was there, so he put me on the line. She asked what I was doing there so late, and I said we were studying. This couldn't have been further from the truth. Mom panicked about Sandy, so I said I'd call the dorm. It turned out that Mom had asked another girl at Sandy's dorm about her. The girl told Mom that Sandy wasn't back yet, but the girl thought Mom was talking about the other Sandy in the dorm. In fact, our Sandy had been asleep in her bed for some time. When I called, somehow it became clear on the other end that we were inquiring about Sandy K. and I was put on the line with her. I told her about Mom's call and she said sorry. She called Mom to let her know what had happened and to reassure her that she was safe. Dad had always made comments to Sandy and me during our college years about how foolish kids were who came right out and let their parents know that they were shacking up with someone. "How dumb can those kids be?" he would exclaim. This was a strong hint not to do so, and I think this was mostly to prevent Mom from finding out, not him, so we tried to heed his advice.

But I'll get back to Dave and Sandy. I offered to intervene (something I've tried to avoid since this sorry incident) and called Mom. She went on and on about the whole thing and said that she was planning to disown Sandy and write her out of her will. I suggested to Mom that she sounded just like what some of her family had been like to her when she married Dad. That's when she hung up on me. Mom was never like this. She wasn't the yelling type. When she got really mad, her usual response was to use the silent treatment. Mostly, this involved Dad. Sometimes, depending on the degree of mad, it would last for days. But all this with Sandy had riled her. I think it must have brought up all the anguish that was caused by her own family—her having broken her family's rules and now her unknowingly imitating her family's response to her rebellion.

The next morning, she was at our door. Leo let her in. She walked into the kitchen and apologized. She said she hadn't slept all night. She cried and hugged me. She said that she would never bring up the topic again, and she didn't. But she did start calling me, usually in the evenings, sometimes inebriated, imploring me to go back to the church. Mom knew that Sandy and I were not regular mass goers, if we went at all. It all made me recall years earlier when Dad had explained to us that Mom would be taking instruction to become a Catholic. He went on to explain that too much of his heritage had been lost with his parents' leaving their homeland, and so he wouldn't be giving up his Catholicism. So it was left to Mom, who was willing to sacrifice her own, and then our family would be united forever in one faith. Now Dad was a spiritual man, but I'd have to say he wasn't really devoutly religious.

He regularly dropped off to sleep during mass. It was more a cultural identity he was holding on to, and I got this. I had inherited this from him. Mom, on the other hand, had transgressed against her own family by marrying Dad in the first place. She had already displeased her clan and had suffered for it. Did she really have much more to lose by conversion? And then there was the streak of rebel in her. It all seemed to catch up with her, though, especially after her two oldest children didn't seem to appreciate her sacrifice. Speaking for myself, I'd been exposed to the whole religious controversy from early on. I had grown tired of the subject. And as I got older (with exposure to all sorts of different ideas or even just on a soulful level), I didn't often agree with some of the rigid (I thought) dictates of the church. I was still drawn to the spirituality of the Catholic Church, though, and it is part of my heritage, so I remained conflicted about the subject too. Mom dug right into Catholicism from the start. She became devout, rarely missing a day without attending mass. Why wouldn't she expect me and Sandy to hold up Dad's part of the bargain?

Sandy and Dave moved to a farm in Lyons and finally decided to get married. Sandy said this was mostly because she thought if they bought a house together, it would be more difficult to hide the fact that they were living together without the benefit of marriage. They went to one of those cheesy chapels in Reno on December 23, 1983. Later on, they had a wedding reception at Dave's parents' home. Mom, Dad, Leo, I, and the kids went. We met all of Dave's family. It went well. Dave's mom made a Mexican feast. I had never had cilantro before, but I liked it. It was served as a condiment. The guys hung out in the den and watched the fight between Mike Tyson and Buster Douglas.

I felt about the same as Sandy about annulments. How could I have ever said that my marriage hadn't been real after thirty plus years, raising three kids together, and now having grandkids? I felt conflicted about a divorce too, so I stayed in limbo for a while, but I knew I wanted out. I don't think I really made decisions for myself early on in my life. I had never lived on my own other than the few months in an apartment right before I got married, and even then, part of that time I had a roommate. For a lot of my life, I had lived with relatives. I'm not saying this didn't have some merit, but I was ready for a place of my own. After I bought my house, I loved it—the quiet. I decorated the house with sentimental things, having always collected mementos, clothing, photos, etc. attached to special events.

Cameron graduated from Southern Oregon University in June 2003. We all went down for the graduation. That night, we went to his favorite restaurant in Ashland for a celebratory dinner. After dinner, Byron went out to his car and found that he had left his key in the ignition and the doors were locked. Angie went ballistic. We called for a locksmith, who said it would be at least an hour before they could get to him. We agreed to drive Angie and the girls to their motel, while Byron waited to get into his car. It all sort of put a damper on the evening. The next day, we all poked around Ashland and came upon an open-air restaurant that was housing a Mexican wedding. The band was playing lively music, and everyone was dancing and having a good time. It reminded me of our own wedding. We headed in and started dancing with the guests. I just couldn't resist the music. I expected that would be all there was to it, but the bride and groom and their guests made us feel comfortable, and they invited all of us to stick around, so we did.

Cameron, Min Yi, and Jing moved to Hawaii shortly after graduation and lived there for a year. I went to visit them in February 2004. Min Yi booked a place for me at the Moana Hotel. She had been able to get this stay for me at a greatly reduced rate because she was a resident there and because she was a New Yorker who knew how to get things done. The catch was that I had to be her to get the room. The hotel staff seemed a little suspicious but let it slide. The room was small (one of the originals, as additional rooms added to the hotel later on offered more luxurious accommodations) and looked out over the sea and the courtyard with its huge banyan tree. The tree was planted in 1904, only a few years after the hotel's inception. The hotel itself and the grounds around it are palatial in appearance, the first built on Waikiki Beach. Moana

(Hawaiian name for ocean or open sea) is an expansive Hawaiian gothic beauty. [38] The front of the hotel facing the street is surrounded by palm trees. A large porch holds rows of rocking chairs where patrons of the hotel can sit and watch the traffic and pedestrians pass by.

Jing was only two and Min Yi was pregnant with her second child. Cameron had admired the Moana since his move to Honolulu. He, Min Yi, and Jing had gone for occasional lunches there, but now with my staying at the hotel, we all had access to the pool too. After I checked in, they came over. We sat by the pool and had drinks. Jing sat at the table like a grown-up. He pulled his imaginary invisible puppy out of his coat pocket and set him down gently on the table in front of me. "Do you want to hold him?" he asked. "OK," I said. He had the puppy jump through an imaginary hoop, eat out of his dog dish, etc. Then he decided to put him back in his pocket for a nap and that was the last time I "saw" him. My gift to him that day was a snorkel and a mask. Jing was afraid to use them at first, but I got him to jump as I stood in the pool to catch him. Before long, he wanted to try this over and over, and he'd look beneath the water with his mask. He couldn't get enough of it.

---

[38] "Moana Hotel," Wikipedia, The Free Encyclopedia, http://en.wikipedia.org/wiki/Moana_Hotel.

The next day, we all decided to go to Chinatown. Instead of taking the bus, we walked, but this turned out to be an all-day excursion. When we finally got there, we were just in time for dim sum. Min Yi found a restaurant to her liking. Carts of specialties were brought around to our table. She helped us decide what to choose. Jing put a toothpick from the table in his mouth and insisted he was smoking. His mother told him that if he wanted to smoke, he would have to go outside because smoking was prohibited in the restaurant. She expected this would deter him from the pretend habit, but he proceeded to the entrance and stood outside with his toothpick, taking pretend puffs off it. When he was done with his "cigarette," he joined us at the table to finish his meal. Afterward, we went to the Chinese market. It was impressive, with all sorts of exotic fruits, vegetables, live lobsters, and other sea life for sale, and all manner of Chinese delicacies. There was a platform nearby used for martial arts demonstrations. Jing got up on the stage with his Asian martial arts attire and put on a show for us and anyone else that might be walking by. The walk back to the hotel left us tired and with sore feet, but it had been worth it.

The next few days, there were typhoon-force winds. Inside the hotel, the fixed pane windows were sealed with tape to prevent breakage. The double doors at either end of the lobby were left open to allow the wind to blow right through. The long sheers on the floor-length windows floated around in the air as the wind whistled through the lobby. This was a good time to inspect the place further. A staircase from the lobby led to the balcony above. On the walls of the balcony were historic photographs of Oahu. They portrayed a simpler life where its native people belonged to the earth. They looked out from the photographs, beautiful and proud. After the storm subsided, the beach had disappeared. All that was left were rocks and dark pebbles and the water was right up to the abutment of the hotel. But the next morning the water had abated and white sand had reappeared. It held hints as to how the beach had been revived—grader truck marks. The staff explained that the hotel had reserves of sand for such occasions, and the sand was brought in by truckloads so that the guests would have the beautiful beach that existed before the storm.

The last day I was there, I asked Cam and his family where they wanted to go for dinner, and they chose the Moana Restaurant. There was still a chill in the air and some threatening clouds hanging about—left over from the storm the day before—but we decided on the veranda anyway. It stretched from the patio out to the sea. We arrived early, and there weren't any full tables outside at all. The waiter told us he would take us to the best table in the place—the furthest out on the veranda. We ordered the five-course meal all around. It was one of the most memorable and leisurely meals I had ever experienced. After our meal, and while we were served our dessert in this serene setting, we watched the sun set over the water.

From Oahu, I took an island hopper flight to my treasured Kauai. I was able to find a condo right across the road from the dilapidated Coco Palms. In fact, the old Seashell Snack Bar across the road from the main Coco Palms property was right below my window. There was an ocean view from my second floor balcony window, and I could almost see all of us frolicking in the waves as Dad demonstrated the art of body surfing years earlier. But the shoreline had changed. Maybe it was the time of year that made the difference, I don't know. The beach then had been broad and open, with gentle waves and a safe feel. Now it felt rather ominous. The fine vanilla-colored sand had been replaced by coarse dark sand. There was a sharp drop-off replacing the previous long gradual decline of the shoreline. The waters were turbulent. I decided to head down anyway and was contemplating taking a swim for old times' sake when a local approached and cautioned me not to go into the water. He explained that because of the season and conditions, it was treacherous. He ambled down the beach, and after he got out of view, I considered ignoring his warning but thought better of it and settled for a brief walk down the coastline. I got back to my condo and found a tape player with some tapes sitting next to it. I put one in, which had an interesting cover, to play. The music was mesmerizing, and I couldn't help but dance around inside. I played the tape often during my few days in Kauai. I wrote down the name of the artist (an Italian) Fabio Massimo Lazzari with an address in Rome. I tried to find the recording on the Internet after my return home with no luck.

The weather remained gloomy and rather cold on the island during my stay. The main purpose of my visit to Kauai had been to explore the fate of the Coco Palms after Hurricane Iniki that almost blew it off the map in September 1992. On my second day on the island, I decided to walk across what was now a busy highway and investigate. There was a high chain-link fence surrounding the property with "keep out" signs posted here and there, but I could see through to what had become an overgrown jungle that had taken over the remains of the resort. It appeared ethereal and even more beautiful than when it had been in full bloom. My being kept out by the fence made me all the more determined to get inside to see it up close. I walked around the periphery of the property, which included the famous coconut grove behind the hotel. This is where I discovered that there was an open chain-link double gate, so I just went through it. I didn't see anyone around at first. After getting inside, I felt a sense of calm and mystery. The earth there seemed spiritual, mystical. I explored the lobby with its broken and missing stained glass windows and with the jungle infringing on its prior purpose. The glass cases with artifacts were still there. I could still picture in my mind the first time I had set foot in the lobby, delighted that I would be staying in this beautiful setting. I had been twenty-eight in 1979. The three swimming pools were still there, but now they were without pool water, only collected rain water, debris, and palm leaf fronds existed on their floors. The pig pit was still intact. So were the other structures, only now their windows were broken or had a smoky gray tinge to them. The grounds were difficult to navigate due to the fallen and overgrown vegetation that wrapped itself around the other. The moat still existed too. Its water flowed through the jungle as before. The coconut grove still stood but was now overgrown with fronds and debris forming a carpet over the earth. I finally noticed a few grounds workers off in the distance. They may have noticed me too, but I wasn't sure. At any rate, they didn't acknowledge me one way or the other. I stayed on exploring until dusk and then worked my way back toward the open gate, but now it wasn't open any longer. It was closed and there were heavy chains fastening the two parts together. I knew there was no way to exit here. It was starting to drizzle, and the sun was setting. I walked to the front of the property, exploring for some other form of escape but found none. It seemed the entire property was fenced in, and so was I. I finally found a gap between the earth and the fence near the highway. I could see cars going by. I hunkered down and crawled out under the fence and into the mud, but that was OK because I was now free and had only a few steps to travel to get to my condo.

The next day, I decided to take a drive, and as I passed the "Coco Palms" sign that still remained, I noticed that the double-chained gate at the front of the property was open, and there were people inside. I stopped the car and could see that among the crowd was a tall middle- aged Hawaiian man. I ran over and approached him. I asked about what appeared to be a tour going on, and he acknowledged that is what it was. I told him that I had stayed as a guest at the hotel twice. He then invited me to come along. I offered to pay for the tour, but he declined my offer. It was so exciting to be hearing all about the history of the place, some of which I already knew. I offered my own two cents to the guide and the crowd during the tour. They seemed to appreciate my telling of my own experiences while I had been there. The guide spoke of prior attempts to reconstruct the resort and the controversy that was attached to it. I had kept track of some of this over the Internet and had finally come to the realization that this might not happen. Originally, there was a plan to bring the resort as close as possible to its original state. But this would be expensive. And there was disagreement among different factions about how this would be accomplished. Insurance and benefactors also played a part. The most recent was in 2001. There were investors ready to work on the project when the attack on the World Trade Center occurred in New York, on September 11, 2001. This was where the investment funds were to come from, but the attack changed all that. September 11 is the same date, although nine years earlier, that Hurricane Iniki crushed Kauai.

Before leaving for home, I had to take the flatboat ride up the Wailua River and hike to the Fern Grotto for old times' sake. I also took a walk to the Poliahu Heiau—a sacred ground on the cliff of the Wailua River— which emanates a mystical aura. I hoped I would be able to carry some of the spirit of the place home with me. I thought about earlier visits, people I shared experiences with here, and felt the passing of time with some melancholy.

Cameron, Min Yi, and Jing returned to the mainland before the new baby boy was born. They named him Clayton. He was born on July 30, Leo's birthday. Clayton looked a lot like Cameron did as a baby. They moved to Springfield, Oregon. Another baby boy (Burion) followed on September 22, 2007—the same birthdate as that of his cousin Mya and his great-great-grandmother Nora. Cam started work with an artist in Eugene who makes lamps. Cam became his protégé. The lamps are shipped all over the world. Min Yi worked for a magazine. Both of them also taught martial arts, yoga, and such in various community settings. Cam writes poetry. Min Yi is a doula. They grew their own vegetables and raised chickens. They volunteered at their kids' school. Now they have moved to San Francisco for new careers.

Leo and I decided to do our own divorce. We filled out the paperwork together and took it down to the courthouse. It cost each of us less than three hundred dollars to file. There really were no arguments about our belongings. The divorce was something I wanted, but that didn't make it easy. For a while, I stayed away. The kids came for Christmas to his house the first year. After that, I was invited to be a part of the holiday, but it was awkward at first. The idea was to be able to spend time together as a family for the holidays. As time went by, the kids didn't come around as much. In fact, my whole family and our longtime mutual friends all seemed shaken by our divorce. It wasn't my intention to hurt my family, but I know I did.

I started spending time with John. I'd go to his place on the weekends. Sometimes we'd go out of town for quiet weekends together. Sometimes we'd just cook a meal at his house, rent a movie, and relax. He had taken up golf a few years earlier and loved it. I didn't have any interest in the game, but he'd invite me to go out with him and walk the course. It was fun and relaxing. He was easy to be around. That's how it was after all the time I had dreamt about it being like this.

Once, John went to Boston for training and to see his family. He asked me to stay with his dog, Heidi. She had a difficult time getting used to me being around, as she had John all to herself for a number of years. She used to get in between us on the couch to keep me away from him. When I was alone with her while he was gone, it was a nightmare. I think she missed him, and my being there seemed to be a reminder that he was gone. She had been somewhat used to a middle-aged woman who had looked after her in the past when John was away. When I was staying with Heidi, she would squeal and wriggle out of my arms if I tried to pick her up to take her outside. When I tried to take her upstairs with me to bed, she stood in the corner of the entryway with her head down and ignored me. I finally had to leave her downstairs and check on her throughout the night to make sure she was all right. Even after John's return, it took time before she finally seemed resigned to my existence in the house.

John was raised in a large Italian Catholic family. His father had been a physician, developing a calling to the profession as a child after witnessing his older brother's fall to his death from the roof of the family's tenement building on Second and Houston in New York City's Little Italy. The two boys had been playing together on the roof, possibly the safest-seeming place to do so in their environment. John's father was the only son left in the family after the accident—his other siblings were all girls. John's maternal widowed grandmother had supported her large family by running a boarding house in the city. Only six of her twelve children survived into adulthood. John's father's family didn't approve of the union between his parents, so there was bad blood from the start, especially after John's father left his new wife with his parents to finish up his medical training, and during that time, his father had forced her to have an abortion. When she got away from them, she went on to produce seven offspring—a seemingly just retaliation. John was the third son born to the couple. After that, a daughter was born with Down syndrome, then another son, another daughter, and finally one more son. John was devoted to his sister, Rosemary. Home movies show them out in the water in front of their lake summer cottage, his patient attention to her as he helped her float over the waves. John and his eldest brother, Pascal, were both sent to boarding school at about the age of fourteen because of poor performance in the public school. John went from there to the seminary to study for the priesthood, left a few years later, attended college, and married at age twenty-six. He took a state job, went back to school, divorced at age thirty-three, and then continued with his schooling for a doctorate. He found his way to Bend for his first job. After his divorce, he dated but never remarried. His divorce had been painful, and I suspect he shared with me the notion of everlasting marital ties as a Catholic. His ex-wife called him occasionally and even visited once after his move to Bend, but he said it wasn't the same. I mention all this to point out the similarities in our upbringings—similarities that I think contributed to our mutual attraction to each other. Of course, I knew none of this from the get-go. It was all subterranean in nature. Dad was the one person I confided in about my relationship with John. I had taken him to a doctor's appointment one afternoon, and afterward, we stopped by at my house. I showed him a picture of John, and he commented that he was "a good looking man." Dad didn't seem judgmental about my relationship. He was matter-of-fact, as usual.

Laura decided to travel to Europe with her friend Kara during the summer of 2005. I hoped that she would reconnect with Pietro while she was in Italy. She told me she had called him before her departure to let him know when she would be in Napoli. He told her he was excited about her visiting. The two girls traveled all through Europe over a two-month period—first London, then Amsterdam, Germany, Switzerland, Italy, Greece, and plans for Spain. I didn't know it at the time, but Laura took out school loans to pay for the trip. During their time in Switzerland, she took a liking to a guy there and had a brief affair with him. Then the two girls left, traveled on, and landed in Napoli. After she and Kara arrived, Laura left word for Pietro. He began calling nonstop while the girls were out and about. He introduced himself to the hostel keeper as Laura's "cousin." The keeper let the girls know that Laura's "cousin" kept calling for her. This annoyed Laura, and so she didn't return his calls and left without seeing him at all. I have wondered if Laura thought about resuming a relationship with Pietro. I have also wondered if she ever really had any intention of seeing him in the first place. Was she just trying to please or appease me with an intention to reconnect with him? Or was it that his amorous and impetuous nature (reflected by the incessant phone calls) merely reminded her of what had always annoyed her about him? Even if they had met, I suspect that their differences would have all come back to her anyway.

Laura told Kara that she wanted to return to Switzerland to resume the relationship with her newfound friend. This left Kara to go on to Spain on her own or go back to Switzerland with Laura. Kara returned with Laura, but after a few days, feeling like a third wheel, she went on to Spain but didn't fare well there on her own. Being a solo female in that country presented problems in terms of men seeing her as available. Later on, the two met up in another part of Italy and traveled together again, but Kara had hard feelings, and the rest of their trip was strained. It just so happened that upon Laura's return home, John and I were headed back east to visit his family. We stayed at the Ramada the night before our flight, and Laura had just arrived back and was also booked at the Ramada. She visited us in our room that night and told us about her adventures. She took the Breeze back to Bend the next morning.

This was our first trip together to Connecticut. John's brother Paul picked us up at the airport the evening we arrived in Hartford and drove us to their oldest brother's farm, where we stayed the night and borrowed a car for the extent of our stay. The next morning, we drove out to the lake cottage. The first time we drove into the dense jungle surrounding Coventry Lake on one of its primitive dirt roads, flashbacks of my childhood emerged. There were the near tropical scents, the vegetation, the cricket's and frog's song, and the mystery of the sun-impeded light. As we drove toward the cottage, John reminisced about childhood memories of his own that flooded his brain. He pointed out this and that cottage, explaining the history of the inhabitants that had once occupied them. Now almost all had been vacated by their previous owners and replaced by people who were strangers to John. But the two places on either side of his family's cottage still had people he knew. His longtime neighbor, Phyllis, came over to greet us and supplied information about the goings-on in the neighborhood during John's absence. On the other side of the cottage, his family's nemesis remained. It seemed he didn't like the commotion of John's family over the years and went so far as to create a barricade that extended out into the lake, permanently disfiguring the lake's shoreline. He dumped load after load of dirt out into the lake and covered his jetty with shrubbery and trees. John's mother was a fiery little Italian woman who had often tossed curse words over in his direction, and he had tossed them right back at her. Over the years, the battle between this man and John's family had been reduced to silent contempt.

The first time we stayed, I was enchanted by the cottage. The front door led to an entryway with a nonfunctional laundry room on the left and a furnace on the right. The kitchen was beyond the entry. It was fashioned in the forties and fifties style—rustic with dark wood paneling and printed vinyl wallpaper. To the left was the dining room that extended out to a living room area with a large stone fireplace. A scattering of John's mother's artwork decorated the walls. A bust she had done of her husband stood on a side table in the dining room. In front of the living room was a screened sun porch with ill-fitting windows that John's father had commissioned a friend of his to install. There was a matching set upstairs in the bedroom that faced the water. The living room had a steep flight of stairs that led to the bedrooms and a small bath on the second floor. A claw-foot tub had a curtain to allow for showering. John and his ex-wife had hung flowered paper years earlier that still decorated the walls of the bathroom. It had begun to curl on the edges. The upstairs seemed like a womb to me. I had never slept so well anywhere as I did there. At night, there was no external noise other than the cricket's and frog's song. The air was humid and hot. The bedrooms were dark with the assistance of old-fashioned cloth pull blinds. The bedroom John slept in faced the front of the house. The walls were decorated with religious pictures, one of the Virgin Mary with her immaculate heart. I usually started out there with him but wound up in the middle bedroom because of his tossing, turning, and snoring. It had no external windows at all. This room was piled high with family mementos—old clothing hung in the closet and stuffed in bureau drawers, piles of record albums from the forties through the eighties, an old baby crib full of old lampshades and other stuff. In front of the middle bedroom was a sleeping porch. It had screened windows, two twin beds with book cases at the heads, and a crucifix in between them on the wall with photos of John's two younger brothers and a framed child's artwork. A large walk-in closet to the right was piled high with old furniture, clothing, books, etc. Squirrels and bats had inhabited the room for some time, and there was evidence of their presence in the closet—torn insulation hanging from the walls and dung scattered about on the contents of the closet. At night, you could hear the critters scampering and flying about. It was as if the house remained a shrine in veneration of the history of its family.

I loved going through the old photo albums under the side tables in the living room. Every nook and cranny held objects from the family's past, and I felt akin to these things too because of my familiarity with many of them from my own childhood. It all told a story of his family and the era. I know that the cottage brought

John back to earlier times in his life, not only the summers spent there since he was six years of age, when his family purchased the place, but also the summers during his adulthood. He had spent time living in the cottage with his ex-wife toward the end of their marriage and after she left him. He remained there for a winter while he continued with his studies. This time seemed to have been sad and lonely for him. I could see it in the expression on his face in photos taken during this time. No photos of his ex-wife remained in the albums. So there were all sorts of memories attached to the place, and I felt that they were all easily felt while inhabiting the cottage.

Then there was the lake itself. The water was perfect, and this was really the best time I ever had in any body of water. Central Oregon lakes are almost always too cold even in the summer months. Ocean swimming often has the somber influence of the frigid water, hard waves, and dark depths. But Coventry Lake is serene with a perfect water temperature, a beautiful jungle surrounding it, and underwater wonders to explore—fish and lush vegetation.

I met John's family during our first trip back, a little at a time. The first evening there, we joined Paul and his wife, Julie; Joe and his wife, Dee; and Pascal at Dimitri's for dinner, a few miles from the cottage. (Pascal's wife had recently died of cancer). I loved the evening at the restaurant with everyone. It reminded me of my earliest childhood memories at my grandparents'. There is just a different feel between the West Coast and the more ethnic areas, like the East Coast and Chicago. I didn't realize how much I had missed it until that night.

On the weekends, the family gathered at the cottage, and for them, it was like old times. They reminisced about the summers spent there as children and adolescents. The brothers swam and horsed around together. John and Paul are fanatics about golf. John invited me to go along with them, but we found that if you don't actually golf on Connecticut courses, you're not welcome. In Oregon, I walk the courses with John all the time, and it doesn't matter if I don't swing a club. So John and Paul took off as much as possible on their own. I liked the time to myself, though. I could read, relax, and take a long swim with my snorkel and mask, exploring the sights below the surface. Sometimes the women came out to join me.

One of the best things about our trips back was the nostalgic quality of the East Coast. Old buildings weren't usually so thoughtlessly torn down. Traditions remained intact. We visited antique stores with old-fashioned candy counters that held items I hadn't come across since childhood—Chuckles, Squirrels, Mary Janes, etc.—and real diners, drive-in movies, and old-fashioned ice cream parlors (my favorite Shady Glen). It's like going back in time.

Toward the end of our first trip back, John's brother Joe encouraged John to visit his mother. His dad had died of a heart attack at the age of sixty-one. After his death, John's mother, Angela, and Rosemary spent summers in Coventry and winters in Florida until it became apparent that Angela was becoming confused and forgetful. The family took them back to Connecticut, and before long, Rosemary started her life in foster homes. She seemed content with the change. The day we were to visit his mother, John became distracted, making excuses about going at all. On our way there, he stopped at various attractions alongside the road. I remained silent about these stops but thought to myself that he was avoiding the visit. Finally, we pulled into the parking lot of the nursing home. As we approached the building, he seemed anxious but spotted his mother through the window of the dining room. "That's her," he told me when he recognized her. We were escorted to her table where the residents were having a lunch. The escort suggested we move to a sunroom for more privacy. They brought her lunch with her. The three of us sat at the table, and John made attempts to converse with his mother. She simply smiled back at us with a steady gaze. An aide suggested that John feed his mother the rest of her meal, and so he took a place next to her at the table, and I remained across from them. As he spoon-fed her, tears ran down his face. He stood up, shook his hand as if to dismiss the whole scene, and walked away from the table to gather his composure. Then he resumed his task with what appeared to me was a heavy heart. This was to be his last visit with her. She died the following April when he would find himself flying back for her funeral. Family told of their mother's last hours. Rosemary was brought to her mother's deathbed. Just as her mother took her last breath, Rosemary said, "She's gone."

After we left the nursing home, John told me that he didn't think she remembered him, but I was sure she did. She had such a look of pleasure on her face as she gazed at her son with her big smile and bright eyes. She was lovely, really—a strong Italian face and thick salt-and-pepper hair. She seemed to acknowledge my presence too with a steady gaze and smile. I felt that she recognized there was some sort of connection between John and me. We also visited Rosemary over the years. She needed to be forewarned of a visit or she wouldn't be happy to see you. An unplanned visit put her off her schedule. These visits became more and more difficult as time went on for John too, as she deteriorated. I had come to expect his procrastination about visiting, and during our visits, there were his dismissive hand gesture and tears, sometimes leaving the room as he had with his mother to gain his composure, and his sometimes futile attempts to communicate with her. We always brought presents—a coloring book, crayons, a child's toy.

With earlier visits, she seemed pleased with her gifts, but as time went by, gifts were met with disinterest.

After Laura returned from Europe, she went back to school and work. I still didn't see as much of her. She started dating a guy she knew from high school—someone she had run into right before she left on her trip. He was working at a health food store. Her romance with him was frightening in that both of them dove into it with great abandon, and the crazy lifestyle they created together lasted way too long in my mind. They began cavorting about town together. I suspect others wondered what it was all about too. Their eccentricities seemed to emanate from one to the other. The two also seemed to pick up pointers from Cam and Min Yi, who adhered to a Bohemian lifestyle. But what could I expect?

Mom continued to be tormented with her childhood (and other) memories—in particular, her difficult relationship with her mother. Mother's Day seemed to induce a preoccupation with her mother, and this is when I felt even Dad was unable to reach her. The upcoming date motivated her to let each of her children know that she no longer wanted us to celebrate Mother's Day on her behalf—no cards, flowers, or gifts. Each of us responded differently initially. Sandy decided to respect this dictate. Doug said he didn't care what she had to say about it, that it was ridiculous, and so he continued to send a card, bring by a bouquet of flowers, etc. Nora and I weren't sure what to do, so we waited a year and then decided to ignore Mom's instructions too. After a while, we all observed the holiday, and Mom seemed to have forgotten all about her objections to it. I thought about my relationship with my own daughter. It had seemed idyllic until our fateful trip to Italy together—something broken—difficult to mend. But Mom was unable to let go of her angst regarding her mother. She couldn't escape her demons, which led to depression, drinking, and inertia. I can't help but think that she took Dad down with her. He tried to help her, but nothing helped. He was too loyal to ever escape their emotional downward spiral.

Things started getting worse with Mom and Dad. Dad had developed a significant tremor. He stuttered and stammered over his words. He seemed to forget. He had never been good with gadgetry, but now working the microwave even seemed too much for him. Doug started getting almost daily calls for him to come reset the television remotes. Both Mom and Dad looked more slovenly. They had both always been careful about their appearance. Mom had always been a good housekeeper too, but now the place seemed rather unkempt. We kids wondered about what they were eating. Sometimes there were clues—piles of empty pizza boxes in the entryway, garbage with old Chinese takeout containers, a recycle bin with empty wine and beer bottles out in the garage. We started bringing food over, either already prepared or easy to prepare, but these items were often later discovered in the garbage along with the Chinese containers. Mom's increasing smoking habit was downright irritating, not to mention dangerous. We often found her in her terry cloth bathrobe with numerous burn holes in it. They also showed up on the carpet around her chair. Things in the apartment started showing up broken—a lamp, dishware, etc. Then the calls started—from tenants in the adjoining apartments, concerned friends and neighbors, the police. Dad was becoming a menace on the highways and byways. Dents started appearing on their car. He had never been a good driver in the first place, but now this was another matter.

The scariest thing of all was that they continued to drive back and forth from one condo to the next. When they were in Vancouver, we had no idea what they were up to. Nora was in Portland across the river from them, though, so she would drop in often to check in on them. She noted that Dad often wandered around in the more unsavory areas of the city and she told of nightmares involving Dad unconscious in a ditch somewhere. This wasn't all that unlikely to happen because he was always in the habit of carrying around his large bundles of cash wherever he went. In his younger years, it was hidden away in a billfold, but now it would protrude from a pocket he would stuff it into. Sandy told of a visit she made to Vancouver during this period. She and Dad talked in the living room while Mom sneaked beers out of the refrigerator, ran into the bedroom to drink them, and then came back for more. But Mom didn't get anything over on Dad or Sandy. They could see the reflection of the whole scene in the window they sat in front of, the mischievous look on Mom's face and all. Dad just shrugged and raised his eyebrows at Sandy to indicate that he was aware of it all. At this point, he seemed resigned.

All of us decided to have a talk with Mom and Dad. Dad had a plan. One of us four kids would move in and be their caretaker, but there were no volunteers. The prospect of trying to reason with them in order to make such a plan successful seemed unlikely. They would be in charge, and that meant certain disaster for all. So Doug and I suggested other options. Before they had become non compos mentis, they had both voiced their intentions of living in an assisted-living facility and even had a place picked out. But now it was different. Dad became angrier as everyone declined his offer. Then he resorted to bribery and threats. This didn't work for him either. But something had to happen because their living situation was becoming more alarming with each passing day. Dad finally agreed to a place that Doug picked out. The place they had talked about earlier on wasn't available. The place was nice, and there was nothing wrong with it, but there were "old people there" with walkers, hearing aids, etc. According to Dad, he just didn't belong in a place like that. With Mom, it was different. She seemed OK with the social aspect of the place, going down for meals and such.

The problem with her here was pretty much the same as it had been in their own place. She wanted to smoke and drink to her heart's content, and this simply wasn't allowed on her terms, which meant any time, any place, and as much as she wanted. Mom was also becoming unhinged. Maybe it was some sort of realization what path the both of them were on, which meant they were losing control of their lives. She "escaped" from the assisted-living facility one morning in her bathrobe after announcing that she had a plan to drown herself. There were no bodies of water close by, which suggested that she may have thought she was still at their condo, which was a riverfront property. The staff took notice of this. I did too because it made me recall what Dad had told me about Mom's suicide attempt in Vancouver and comments she had made about drowning herself while they were still in the Bend condo. I have to admit, I felt I understood her despair. Both of their worlds were falling apart, and she didn't know how to handle it. Dad had always been more practical. He would just continue to rail against the establishment and figure out ways around the rules.

Not long after Mom's attempted escape, we got a call from the people at the assisted-living facility saying that our parents were gone. Somehow Dad had arranged for a move back to their condo. I'm quite sure he had talked his doctor friend into arranging it all, but then there were also reports that Dad was seen driving back and forth between the assisted- living facility and the condo with his car full of stuff. They had been in assisted living less than six months. Things got even worse after their return. Other condo members began calling more regularly with concerns and complaints. Mom was seen running out into the driveway with her bathrobe on fire. She had thrown the burning garment in the snow and retreated back into their apartment. It was also reported that she was smoking on her deck and throwing the cigarette butts over the railing, so they landed on her neighbors' decks below. They had politely discussed this with her and her response had been to do it all the more. She also started putting the butts out in the neighbor's flower pots in the front shared courtyard. They all had realistic concerns about the whole place burning to the ground. As for Dad, he took to making purchases from catalogs and magazines to amuse himself. He ordered all sorts of trifles and stuff and usually used his purchases as gifts for others. It was a strange assortment of things he bought. As an example, he gave me a statue of a cat with wire whiskers and a wobbly head. When the great-grandkids came by to visit, he always had something for them. He always did like toys and purchasing things for others, but now these gifts were perplexing to the recipients, or at least just met with disinterest. For me, it was sad but endearing, and I tried to display expressions of my appreciation and gratitude no matter what the gift was.

Since Doug and I were the two living in town, it was up to us to discuss the car issue with them. It didn't go well. I tried to find out through the DMV whether or not Dad had a valid driver's license, but that information was not forthcoming. I expressed my concern but was told there wasn't much that could be done until something, such as an accident, occurred. I decided to enlist one of my coworkers to go out and do a home visit. He was able to do a mental status exam and then contact the DMV for information about Dad's driving status. He found out that Dad was driving with a suspended license. Doug called Dad's insurance and then went over to take the car. This didn't fare well for him. Doug tried to explain that Dad didn't have a license any longer, and so the car had to go. Mom had given up driving on her own after a few fender benders. Now they were without wheels. Mom went into a rage as Doug drove off with the car, and Dad wasn't too happy either.

After the car was gone, they resorted to walks to nearby restaurants or taverns for food and drink. The place most frequented by them was Joker's in the old Elks Lodge building downtown. They only had to walk a few blocks down an alley to get there but often didn't leave the place until it was late and dark. Mom, in particular, would be in a bad state and had frequent falls on her way home. She complained of broken ribs and fingers on a few occasions but didn't say how these accidents had occurred. Dad often showed evidence of falls too, with bruising over various parts of his body. On more than one occasion, the police had to escort them home, and this was about the time we started getting calls from them. Dad started talking about going back to their condo in Vancouver. But now he had no way to get there. He asked us all for a ride, but we came up with excuses because we didn't trust them on their own up there. But Dad remained determined to get there one way or another. One day he walked down to his bank and tried to withdraw a bunch of cash. Dad had intended to use some of the money to get a cab ride from Bend to Vancouver, Washington, and have the rest for spending money up there. The bank teller called Doug, whose name was on the account as Dad's conservator. Doug was told what Dad was up to. He was put on the phone with Dad and gave him some flimsy excuse why he couldn't take out that much cash. Dad never was able to figure out how to get back to his Vancouver condo, but that didn't stop him from trying or from bringing up the topic from time to time.

Mom and Dad were still ordering takeout. One place they often called was a Chinese place with delivery service. One evening after they had their meal, Mom called me and reported that Min Yi and Jing had visited, wandered about their apartment, and then stolen some hundred dollar bills. They had called the police who came over and took a report. I went over. I explained that Min Yi and Jing were in Springfield and hadn't been in Bend at all for a while. Dad sat in his easy chair and looked at me with chagrin. He said, "I told her that it wasn't them," but Mom persisted with her story. In fact, this story resurfaced for months afterward until, I think, even Dad started to believe it. Dad had become very protective of his money and insisted on having large amounts of cash at his disposal. In spite of his mental state, he still managed to find his way to the bank. Then he would withdraw hundreds of dollars in cash and stuff the bills in his pockets for his walk back home. He had, since his early years, been a shrewd investor and was determined to continue to manage his portfolio. He became suspicious of Doug whom he had, in a more lucid state, appointed as his conservator. He began to think that Doug was mismanaging his affairs, so he insisted on inspecting his financial reports. This was difficult because Dad became convinced that his assets were greater than what existed. For instance, he received a Publishers Clearing House notice with a million dollar check included and called to let us all know that he had just got a million dollars in the mail. No amount of discussion could convince him otherwise.

Our next move was to suggest in-home care. First, a few young women came in for an interview and to explain what services were available to them. Mom and Dad were polite but, after they left, said they didn't want them to be hanging around. I could understand it. How could they do what they wanted with those people in their way? Not long after, Doug told me he was heading over there to check on them, and I said I'd walk over too. We got there about the same time. Dad was quiet and sitting in the living room. He pointed to the bedroom. Doug and I headed in, and what we found was shocking. Mom looked dead. Her wig was off, her face sunken and pale. But after we shook her and called her name, she started to come to. It seemed that in addition to some sort of medical condition, the two of them had had a disagreement about something. We called EMTs, who checked her out but didn't find anything seriously wrong with her. This, we decided, called for some sort of action. Again, we encouraged in-home care, but this time, we arranged for two guys to come over to give their pitch. We sat in too. The guys showed us all a tamper-proof pill dispenser, which could dispense their pills safely. A bell chimed at the appropriate time, and all they had to do was push a button and the pills would come out. It seemed simple enough, but then I had become aware of the extent of Mom and Dad's limitations, so I had my doubts from the start. I kept my thoughts to myself. They also offered a few hours of assistance for errands, meal preparation, cleaning, etc. Didn't this sound great? Mom and Dad didn't look very enthused but reluctantly agreed. A week later, I got a call from Dad, yelling at me on the phone to "get that G—Damn machine and those people out of here." I called and told them not to come back. The next day, Doug and I went over to take the pill dispenser out of the apartment. We had been given a key to get into it. When we got it back to Doug's house, we were supposed to take the almost-one-month's supply of pills out and return it to the agency. Mom and Dad had only had the machine a week, but almost all the pills were gone! We told the agency staff about what we had discovered, but they had no explanation for the missing pills because the dispenser was supposed to have been tamper-proof.

I started to keep a journal about happenings. We kids were afraid to try to get guardianship too soon because Dad, in spite of his dementia, was still shrewd in some ways. A court battle might be disastrous. I contacted their physician about our concerns. We talked to Mom and Dad again, and they finally agreed to another try at assisted living. This time, it was the place they had talked about years earlier, and I told Dad that some of his doctor friends resided there. Unfortunately, the only apartment available was on the second floor, all the way down a long hallway. It didn't take Dad long to discover a door next to their apartment that led outside. The exit door was hidden from view by large trees and shrubbery. Dad simply crept down the stairs, propped the door open with some small object, and headed to Costco for cigarettes and booze. Then he'd sneak his contraband back into the apartment. Mom drank and smoked up a storm. She was warned, but to no avail. One day I walked in unexpectedly and saw her out on the deck trying to extinguish her cigarette. She was caught red-handed. She knew it, and boy was she angry. I didn't say anything about having seen what I saw, but she started yelling at me anyway. From guilt, I presume. I quietly mentioned that smoking was prohibited and could result in their being evicted or that with the oxygen some of the residents used, there was the potential to blow the place up, but she didn't care about that. I'm not even sure she heard me.

Not long after, Doug and I were asked to attend a care meeting, where all this was brought up, resulting in a plan. She would have to come to the front desk, and an attendant would escort her outside for her break. The trouble was that she was there in front of the desk making a pest of herself all day long and getting angry if she had to wait. If I stopped by to visit, the first thing she asked was for me the take her out for a smoke. On one occasion, I sat with her on a bench outside the front door. She reminisced about her father—the memory of him with his pipe throughout most of their lives. She intimated that this was the reason she loved to smoke— because it brought her closer to the memory of her father. In addition, Dad was still sneaking out, and now he was getting lost some of the time. The police would bring him back. Dad's doctor friend took him on outings and bought Dad what Mom wanted, so the problem wasn't resolved. Not that this wasn't enough. One of the aides saw a red spot on Mom's leg. She was taken to the doctor, who discovered that she had an MRSA infection, which could potentially result in an amputation or even death. The first course of action was to place a PICC line for antibiotic treatment. Mom didn't understand what it was for, so she would pull it out. I had to go back in with her for the port to be replaced. This required the technician to make another incision in her arm. Mom winced a bit but was stoic during the procedure. I, on the other hand, found it all revolting. After her return to the assisted-living facility, she required very frequent checks to make sure she wasn't messing with the line. The treatment went on for several weeks but was finally successful. This was when we finally decided it was time to file for a joint guardianship. Doug and I hoped that we could avoid a court battle. We were told that Mom and Dad would be advised by a court visitor of their right to contest a guardianship. Fortunately, they were unable to manage the process, but they were able to express their anger about what we had done.

In the spring of 2006, John and I had our second visit together back east. This time, we visited in May to attend one of John's nephews' wedding. I dragged John out onto the dance floor at the reception, and everyone was surprised to see him out there. Rosemary was there too, and her brothers joked around with her. We all danced with her too. She had a sense of humor. If she noticed that one of her brothers tripped, she would always say "Did you have a nice trip?" Then she'd laugh. Sometimes they'd trip on purpose just to hear her say it again. Then she might say "Bravo, encore," and they would trip all over again. Rosemary couldn't pronounce her Rs, so when she told her brother Paul a story, he would mimic her and say "Oh weally" with the accent on the first syllable, and she would say "Yes, weally" back at him.

Pascal had begun dating a woman that none of the family had met yet. Her name was Bonnie. I guess because we didn't live there, he felt more comfortable having us meet her, so he arranged for the four of us to go out for dinner. He also suggested we stop by to see his daughter who worked at a tavern near the lake. She was working that day, so we stopped by for lunch. That same evening, the four of us drove out to Evergreen Walk where the restaurant was. Bonnie was a social worker in private practice who was outspoken, but I liked her anyway. She was interesting to talk to. Something with the lunch earlier on wasn't right because before long (even before his evening meal), John knew something was wrong with his digestive system, as he kept having to get up during our meal for the bathroom. He struggled on our drive back to his brother's place. We stayed up with him for a few hours because he looked so miserable. I was a little worried. I could hear him up several times in the night, and his malaise lingered a few days longer.

Pascal also planned a trip for the four of us to go to New York City. He got on the web and booked rooms for us in the theater district at the Mayfair hotel. John drove the four of us to the Bronx where their two spinster aunts lived—two of their Dad's sisters who had remained in the family home after their parents' deaths. The plan was to park the car there and then take the bus into Manhattan. We walked to the bus stop a few blocks away. The bus ride into the city took forever. We traipsed about the hot and humid city streets with our luggage, looking for our hotel. It was a small old building with a rickety elevator. Everyone at the front desk was friendly but didn't speak much English. Our rooms were clean but tiny. We found cheap tickets and went to Spamalot (I'm not much for the Broadway scene), ate at Katz Delicatessen, and went back to the aunts. They prepared an Italian feast. We ate in the basement, where it was cool and there was a dining table. John hadn't been to the house since he was a child. We inspected the place. For him, it brought back so many childhood memories. He said nothing much had changed. For me, it was reminiscent of my grandparents' home. On our drive back in the middle of the night, Pascal told family stories that none of the rest of the family seemed to be aware of. He is the eldest and seven years older than his closest sibling, which may account for the difference. This excursion also led me to memories of my first exposure to New York City when I was sixteen, and it reinforced my determination to return. After I was back in Bend, I realized I had left my purple raincoat of many years in the hotel closet. I called, and the woman on the other end and I had some difficulty communicating, but we were patient with each other, and the coat was mailed back to me. All I had to do was pay in advance for the UPS fee.

In the summer of 2006, we kids decided to have an eightieth birthday party for Dad. This was because his dear sister in Illinois might never see him again. (None of this was considered for Mom because there was no way her only brother would consider traveling across the country). Jean, Jack, Cindy, and her husband, Gary, all flew out. Sandy, Dave, Nora, Todd, and the kids also drove over. The party was at Doug's house. He went to pick Mom and Dad up at the assisted-living facility, but they were in their room, settled in for the night. This kind of thing occurred regularly. Doug would invite them to dinner once a week at his house, drive to get them, and they would have forgotten or just didn't want to go and would refuse. But this time, Doug insisted because everyone was waiting for the man of the hour. Dad sat out on the patio next to Jean. It was a warm and pleasant evening with a view of the whole city at sunset. By this time, Dad was having some difficulty with his speech, which would in no time be reduced to occasional one-word responses. I don't think Jean was prepared for the drastic change she saw in Dad, but she laughed her usual laugh, and they seemed to enjoy each other's company. In the meantime, Mom was going nuts inside the house. I suspect she'd had a few before she even got to the party. Now she was wandering around inside the house, searching for half-drunk glasses of wine or what have you and slugging them down. We had resorted to providing her with nonalcoholic wine for such occasions, but now she was getting to the real thing. Sandy went inside to check things out and was horrified to find Mom sitting on a couch and banging her head repeatedly on the wall behind her. She described her as looking like someone possessed. Then there was the slide and home movie show. Doug had assembled the slide projector, slides, and old movies. Everyone was gathering in the living room for the show, but Mom continued to wander about, looking for more half-empty glasses or beer bottles in the refrigerator. Doug told her to come sit down for the show. She told him that she had seen them a thousand times before and had no interest in seeing them again. Then the only thing to do was to make the glasses and anything in the refrigerator disappear and get Mom back to their apartment.

During Dad's birthday party and while everyone congregated on the deck, Cindy and I remained alone together in the kitchen. This was the first time in years I had the opportunity to really talk to my cousin. She brought up the incident that occurred while we were living with them. She remembered the police coming to the house to question me while she, Sandy, and her brother Greg hid behind the living room couch. I confided in her about what had occurred in the underpass—things I hadn't told the police. It seemed that I wasn't the only one affected by the event that occurred at my aunt's house so many years ago. So were the rest—my mother, my cousins, my sister, and probably even the rest of our household.

I spent time with Jean, Jack, Cindy, and Gary during the next few days they were in Bend. Jack had just had a second knee replacement, which hadn't turned out as well as the first. Jean was well but said she had a cough and was hoarse. She wondered if she was coming down with a cold or allergic to something in the air. We spoke of old times. It would be the last time I would see her alive.

Laura announced that she was pregnant. It didn't come as much of a surprise. Nicoli Francesco was born on September 13, 2006. Laura and Jake were still living their Bohemian lifestyle. They were living in what I will have to say were hovels, and when a particular place didn't seem to be working out any longer for whatever reason, they just moved on, sometimes to Jake's parents' home and sometimes into their van. They even moved in with Cam, Min Yi, and the boys at one point, but that didn't last very long. Laura has always relished a mess. This went back to her childhood and only got worse as she got older. She and her brothers never produced a made bed but piled up layers of miscellaneous blankets on top of their bedsheets and crawled into the pile for their night's sleep. But the boys never came close to Laura in her love of a jumble. She had found a perfect match in Jake. He could keep up with her in the jumble department and then some. Visiting their home was pure chaos and something that's hard for me because of my need for orderliness in my surroundings to compensate for the chaos that lives inside my head. Jake had a serious head injury from a bike racing accident during his adolescence. In fact, he had ridden in the same riding club as Doug. Early on in his and Laura's relationship, he found employment in establishments that sometimes required his ability to run a cash register. I remember being his customer on occasion and marveling at his confusion in operating the register or providing the proper change. I wasn't sure if it was the brain injury—or was it more his and Laura's love haze that had to do with it? Jake is artistic, and painting is his real passion. Other than her family, Laura's passion has been her writing.

Jake's dad's side of the family are of Polish and Scandinavian descent. His surname Norris was originally Norske. His dad, Walt, came from a family of eight children. Jake's grandfather was known to be a difficult person to get along with. Mom and Dad knew the grandparents, having been devout Catholics too and attending mass regularly. Grandpa Norris owned and ran the Hobby Haven on Bond and Minnesota. Bend kids congregated there in the old days. Three of the eight children developed multiple sclerosis in their adult years. One daughter took vows to be a nun but left the vocation later on. All the kids attended St. Francis School with us. After all the kids left home, Jake's grandmother left her marriage behind, moved to Portland, and started a new life for herself, including the procurement of a boyfriend. Jake's mother Liz's side of the family is of mixed descent. The whole family—Liz, Walt, Jake, his sister Hallie, and Liz's parents (Norm and Nancy) are a gregarious, magnanimous, and lighthearted bunch.

The third visit John and I made back east was in 2007. Our flight came into Hartford late—too late to pick up our rental car. I suggested we stay at the Sheraton near the airport, which is connected to the terminal. This would allow us a good night's sleep before figuring out what to do the next morning. There didn't really seem to be much of a choice in the matter. The man behind the desk was snooty and the cost was exorbitant, but it was still worth it. When we picked up our car the next morning, instead of heading to the lake, we drove to Pascal's. The cottage had plumbing problems, so we stayed with Pascal this time. He and Bonnie were on and off again. This summer was particularly hot and humid, just the way I like it, so it was difficult not to be right on the lake and able to get up in the mornings and just head out to the water as usual. One day while John and his brother Paul went golfing, I asked him to drop me off at the lake. I had the place all to myself and swam or read on and off all day long, but not having a functioning toilet was a big problem that required drastic measures to get along all day there.

Later on in the week, John and Pascal worked on digging a deep hole in the front yard to start the process of fixing the plumbing, but the place still wasn't ready to be inhabited that summer, so we spent more time sightseeing. Mark Twain's home near Hartford was fun. We also included a trip to Evergreen Walk and a meal there at Burtons Grill and an evening date at the Mansfield

Drive-In. And family get-togethers were always some of the best part of our vacation.

During the summer of 2008, Doug and I got called in for a meeting at Mom and Dad's assisted-living facility. We were told they were being evicted and they explained why. We enlisted Nora to come over and help out. We found a place that was locked and especially for people with dementia. They would get so worked up about packing and moving that we all decided we just wouldn't tell them about the move. It was the week between both their birthdays—July 10 and July 18. Nora and I said we had a surprise for them—a day out to celebrate with a lunch, a movie, and then to my house for cake and ice cream. In the meantime, Doug and Nora communicated by cell phone to orchestrate the move. Doug sat outside the assisted-living facility with the moving van, and she called to let Doug know that the coast was clear after we got Mom and Dad safely into the car. As we drove off with them, I glanced back and could see Doug and the movers heading up the back stairs (the stairs Dad had used to smuggle booze and cigarettes in for Mom). Off we went to start our fun-filled day. Everything actually went pretty well other than Dad's meltdown in the movie theater because he couldn't see the screen after someone took a seat in front of him. We had to move to satisfy him. Nora and I got more and more nervous as the day wore on. Doug called to let us know that it was taking longer than expected to get all their stuff set up in the new apartment. Doug had decided it would seem less traumatic for them if everything was in its place. He finally called and gave us the go ahead to bring them over. Nora and I were in the front seat of the car and they were in the back. One of us said that we had a surprise for them. We had found a brand new better place for them to live. We both expected this news wouldn't go over well, but they didn't really say much. We drove into the circular drive. We were met at the front door by Doug and the staff and some of the residents. Then we were shown to their room, which looked lived in and orderly. Dad looked around the room and said "This is better." And that was it. The staff at this place knew what they were doing. Medication management was one of the things that turned things around. They really did need something to tone down their anxiety, depression, and agitation. And as the weeks went by, things improved but not to say there still weren't problems.

Mom and Dad had created a sanctuary in the back yard of our Ninth Street home. There were numerous kinds of bird feeders, nuts and other food for squirrels and such. In their later years, they really enjoyed watching the critters, especially Mom. After they moved into their new digs, we kids put bird feeders outside their window. Later on we added another contraption to a tree branch- one with a spring and a stake to attach a corn cob to. When a squirrel jumped on it, the spring caused a bouncing motion as the squirrel ate the corn cob. This entertained them both, especially

Mom. The most peculiar thing was that near her end she started seeing tigers and bears go after the corn cob too.

John's and my fourth visit to the East Coast was in 2008, just after Mom and Dad's move. We had a rocky start for this vacation. John's friend Bob was in the middle of doing a remodel for John's office. Bob and John had to empty out the whole office before we left to drive to Portland, and so we didn't even get out of town until about 7:00 p.m. We hadn't eaten, so we stopped at Madaline's Grill in Redmond for dinner. The food is good there, but when it's crowded, the wait can be on the long side. Usually, this didn't matter, but we still had most of the drive ahead of us. By the time we got back on the road, it was dark. As we approached the metropolitan area of Portland a few hours later, we took a wrong turn off the freeway. This hadn't been the first time. We found ourselves out somewhere in the industrial part of the city and then into Vancouver, Washington, across the river from Portland. I pointed out Mom and Dad's condo to John. We finally made our way back toward Portland after stops at service stations for directions and got to the hotel near midnight. We had to be up by five for our flight. When we got to the airport, there was some discussion at the check-in counter about John not having a seat after all, but luckily, that got ironed out, and we finally boarded our plane.

During our stay this time, we went to New York ourselves. We drove to New Haven to catch the train into Grand Central Station. We found a reasonably priced hotel in SoHo, The Gem, which just so happened to be right across the street from John's dad's tenement, where his dad grew up in—the one where his dad's brother fell from the roof to his death. We could see the green stucco building surrounded by a lush fenced garden from our hotel window. It had a pharmacy on the street front and was still an apartment building but upscale. We also discovered Little Italy. It reminded me so of the real Italy. These first few years, we hadn't discovered yet that the streets really come alive on Friday nights when traffic was barricaded. That would come later. I had asked Min Yi for her mother's phone number and address before we left. John and I found her apartment building on Mulberry Street in Chinatown as we were walking down from the Gem to Little Italy the first evening there. I called her the next day, and she invited us over. She would meet us after work. As we approached her building, I called her to let her know we were near. I spotted her across the street, smiling and waving as she ran up to greet us. We walked back with her to her place. There was a high heavy door to the apartment building. Inside, there was a narrow stairway, and the walk up numerous flights was exhausting. She just sprinted up. I was about to see the home where my daughter-in-law had grown up since the age of six. The place was clean but cluttered. It would have to have been because it was so small. She had her adolescent son and relatives from China staying with her. They all sat with us around the kitchen table. The bathtub was in the kitchen. Ya Ying spoke broken English, but I did OK in understanding her most of the time. Her relatives just smiled at us. She invited us to dinner. John and I were the only Caucasians in the place. She also invited us to go out dancing with her the following night, but John wasn't into it.

The next day, we headed uptown to explore Rockefeller Center, Times Square, and Central Park. On our way to Central Park, we came across an upscale high-rise with an extravagant antique store on the ground floor-Trump Tower. The window displays caught our eyes. They were so impressive, and John was interested in seeing if there might be something there to add to what would be his newly remodeled office upon our return home. There were signs in the store windows saying the place was closed, but we could see merchants inside. They saw us too and opened their doors to us, explaining that the store was technically closed for an inventory, but they would make an exception and let us in. There were beautiful things in there. John asked if they shipped items and was told they did. In fact, they said they were loading a van in the back headed for the West Coast that very moment. The merchant suggested that we better act fast if we were going to be able to get our purchases on board. They started following us around the floor.

There was something about these guys that made me uneasy—so uneasy that I thought about fleeing, but John was discussing items of his interest with one of them. To pass the time, I took a look at some rugs in a separate rug showcase, one in particular, beautiful with rich colors. Dad had been a collector of oriental rugs, so I knew something about them myself. When one of them noticed that I seemed to have taken an interest in the colorful rug, he was all over it. He explained how exquisite it was and that the price was a steal. I said that although I loved the rug, I had a very small place that wouldn't accommodate such a purchase, but he persisted in his sales pitch. All of them in the store had an aggressive edge to them that made it difficult to argue. But finally, he gave up on the one rug and steered me to a smaller one, not really to my liking. The next thing I knew, I was pulling out my credit card. John had just agreed to a sizable order himself.

After we got out of the store, I told John I thought we'd been had. He had a friend in Bend who grew up in the Bronx. He would often tease and call us rubes, and John and I had to admit he was probably right. We discussed his friend's opinion as we walked away from the antique store. (The incident reminded me of Laura's and my run-in with the mafia in Napoli). After our return home, we finally got a few items that we had paid for, but the big ticket item of John's never arrived. He called the store and was given the runaround. One excuse was that the delivery van had been in an accident, the contents destroyed en route, but nothing was said about a refund. A few years later (John and I still irritated by the whole thing), we happened upon the place on our way to Central Park. We decided to go in and see what would happen. John explained how he had never received his merchandise and wasn't compensated for it and just so happened to have the receipt in his wallet. The guy looked up the transaction and then just looked back at him with a blank stare and shrugged his shoulders. He had no intention of making it right. They were a bunch of crooks, good at intimidation, and I was glad for the second time to be exiting the place.

We also wanted to find The Loeb Boathouse that day after seeing Big and Carrie fall into the lake on the television show Sex and the City. The two had been on rocky ground before their meeting there and Carrie had promised her friend Miranda not to let Big kiss her no matter what because that might make Carrie vulnerable to Big again. He had broken her heart already on numerous occasions. But when they met at the Boathouse, Big was his old charming self, and when he leaned in to kiss her, she averted her face and lost her balance. Big tried to grab her, and they both fell in the water, where the tension was broken. I had been a big fan of the show ever since Byron suggested I check it out. This was while I secretly pined away over John. After I started watching it, I realized how similar in appearance and manner John was to Big. I told my girlfriend in confidence about my crush on John and how Big reminded me of him. She was familiar with the show too. I still remember seeing the last episode when Big's name was finally revealed as John. My girlfriend got on the phone with me while the show was still playing, and we laughed about the coincidence. I had since told John about my notion about his and Big's similarities. We started watching the show together, and I think he saw what I meant. So we had lunch at the Boathouse and looked out the window at the lake, Central Park, and the boats that went by. Before we'd left home, John heard from a few female friends of his that they had gone to NYC and spotted Chris Noth (Big) in his limousine. They were both fans and started jumping up and down and running toward the limo. Chris had the limo driver pull over, and he invited the girls in. He took them to his club, The Cutting Room, and showed them around. They were thrilled with his cordial manner, so when they returned to Bend, they told people all about it. John told me this story, so before we left for vacation, I looked the place up and found the address to The Cutting Room. We took a cab there. It was midweek, fairly early, and there weren't many people in the place. We ordered a drink and waited to see if Big would appear, but he didn't. By the next summer, the place had closed.

After my aunt Jean's return home from Dad's birthday party in 2006, it was discovered that she had lung cancer, but it wasn't discovered soon enough. At first, it had been diagnosed as reflux or something like that. We started talking on the phone. Her voice sounded weak and high. She would cry. She had lost her hair, she said. I think she knew she was dying. She kept her sense of humor, though, and we still laughed about the time we all lived together in Elmhurst and our adventures in Slovenija and Italy. Only months before, she had gotten word that Yanko had died in Slovenija. When we got word of her death, Sandy flew out from Spokane, and Doug and I from Portland. We met at O'Hare Field in Chicago. Doug got a rental car, and we started out toward the hotel. He wanted to impress us with how a GPS works and dialed in our destination. Siri's voice directed him over an express toll bridge where he spotted a camera at the last minute. We all laughed. He explained to us that the camera probably recorded his license plate, but it was too late to do anything about it. But nothing ever came of it. The next day, Doug and I waited in the lobby for Sandy. We finally called her room. She had slept through the alarm. We had to rush to the service. It was good to see so many relatives, some of them I hadn't seen since I was a child. There were many mourners, among them were Big Joe's sister, Joanie; Jean's Slovenian sister's society members; and many of the Slovenian community. She looked peaceful and beautiful in her coffin. After the funeral service, there was a big celebration at a local Italian restaurant. Jean had wanted polka music, so her family had a polka band playing during our meal.

Before we left Illinois, our cousin Ken and his wife, Kathy, took us on a tour. We visited the Marquardt house, which is now a business. I rang the doorbell and asked if we could take a look inside. The husband who owned the place was cordial and showed us around. They had kept the integrity of the mansion, except for the destruction of the alcove where the Christmas tree stood and Santa left his presents for us years ago. He explained that the owners next door insisted on it being taken down because of their own plans to expand their home. I wondered why the guy had agreed to such a demand. The owner's wife scowled at us, so we ignored her. I got to see our old house in Villa Park too. I recognized it even before we got up close to it. We went by Dad's alma mater, Elmhurst College, and other childhood landmarks. Jeff took us over to our grandparents' home, where I was born. Jeff's wife and children were living there. The last time I had seen the inside was when my grandparents still lived there. It felt just the same- except that the house Grampa first built next to their home had been torn down and replaced by a McMansion. Doug and I flew home on Halloween night of 2008. We had a great meal at the airport in San Francisco, and he called Diane to see how things were going because she was in charge of the Halloween party they had planned before Jean's death. After I got home, I had to tell Dad about his sister. He cried.

In the spring of 2009, Byron lost his job and house due to the recession. He had been designing high-scale homes in the area, but new construction just wasn't happening. He found a job in New York State. Early in the summer, we helped pack. Angie was in tears. She, of all the family, seemed the most interested in family. She was the one who loved holidays and any sort of family gathering. And how would they get Jack the dog (he was ailing), the rabbits, cat, and fish back east? It took until we were able to get her out of the house on some errand to get anything accomplished. She had just been running around in circles, fussing about what to take, what not to take, and what to do with what would be left behind. It turned out that Byron drove himself and the girls in the moving van, and Angie followed them out with the family car and all the animals in it. Even the fish tank sat in the backseat behind her. She had to plug it in when they stopped at motel rooms overnight. The cat had been sedated for the trip but had a bad reaction to the drug and went berserk inside the car. Angie had to pull over and let the cat outside until the sedative wore off before they could proceed. When they called to let me know that Jack had made it to Connecticut, I was surprised. I let them know that John and I would be flying to Connecticut in a few weeks (our fifth trip). We invited them to visit us at the lake. They would be driving over the last few days of our stay.

SENTIMENT; A MEMOIR

It became a custom to meet at Dimitri's Restaurant with John's family our first evening in Coventry. It was good to be back again. The next morning, John and Paul took off for golf, and I would have the lake to myself. I sat outside by the water and read. I kept my cell phone close by in case John needed to get ahold of me. The old-fashioned dial phone in the cottage had long since been disconnected but remained on the telephone stand in the dining room. I also expected I might hear from Laura, who was past due to deliver her second baby. I had expected to be in Bend when she delivered this baby, but she had run late, and I left on my vacation before she went into labor. This time she was determined to have a home birth, as she had hoped would happen the first time. When my cell phone rang that morning I half expected it to be her, but it was Leo. He could barely speak. His sobs on the phone breaking through his words, explaining that his mother had died in the night. He had been with her only a few hours earlier, and in fact, I had seen her a week or so before I left. His siblings had gathered. The next morning, the phone rang again. This time, it was Laura. She did have her baby at home in her birthing tub with her midwife, with Jake and Nico in attendance. Mom, Dad, Nico, and the baby were all doing fine. They named the baby Ori Jens.

We headed back to NYC midweek. (The weekends at the cottage were reserved for get-togethers with John's family). It was becoming a pleasant habit to stay at The Gem. It was so close to

Little Italy, Greenwich Village, and other nearby neighborhoods we liked to explore, and it took only minutes to take the subway uptown. On the first day, we hung out at Rockefeller Center and had a drink in the bar with a view of the plaza. We took a ride up the GE building and then headed toward Central Park. We loved to walk through Central Park and take in the sights when in NYC. This time, we happened upon the Tavern on the Green. John knew of it because he watched Live with Regis that starred Regis Philbin, who had mentioned dining there with friends for lunch. It was so quaint that I couldn't resist suggesting we eat there, and so we did. The dining room was extravagant with chandeliers and an opulent atmosphere. The colors were bright and light with vases of brightly colored flowers everywhere and floor-to-ceiling windows looking out on a lush garden. It was a very romantic setting. I discovered recently that the place closed for business only a few months after we were there. We had planned to visit again.

On the second day, I really wanted to go to Ellis Island, where John's grandparents and my grandfather had come upon entering this country. (Francesca had come through Boston Harbor). The weather was horrendous. I couldn't believe the throngs of people waiting in a torrential downpour to get tickets. I think John would have been content to forget the whole thing, but I was determined to go. I imagined what it must have been like for my grandparents—to be boarding their ship and heading to a new land and the weeks of living stuffed in its bowels—as we boarded the crowded ferryboat. I had hoped to be able to ask for help in getting more information about my relatives while there, but I never discovered where or how to go about doing this. The rooms, with the passports family had donated to what is now a museum, were impressive. They were displayed behind glass—thousands of them. I have my grandparents' passports. Dad gave them to me about ten years before his death. I cherish them but doubt anyone in my family would have any interest in them when I'm gone, so I've thought of donating them so that they have a permanent home among others who have immigrated to America.

Byron, Angie, and the girls arrived at the lake. Angie saw the charm in the cottage and inspected each room much like I did on my first encounter with the place. We all hung out in front of the lake, and the girls tried getting in the water, but they aren't fish like I am. None of my family, to this point, had met John other than Laura and Jake. It was difficult for me to say good-bye because I didn't know for sure when I would be seeing them again now that they were living on the East Coast. This would be our last year at John's family's cottage. It was going up for sale. Some of his family talked about buying it, but no one was firm about an offer. Others preferred to sell, and in the end, that is what happened.

Our Hotel Door in Rome

Our View Below in Rome

Laura in front of Fendi

My Big Luggage

Pietro Driving to Reggio de Calabria

On the Ferry to Sicily

Laura and Pietro at the Beach

Beach day

At the Beach

On the Beach

Silhouette   Bubbles

Laura and Pietro in the Ocean

Laura and Pietro in the Ocean

Laura and Pietro in Scopello

Our Last Evening in Scopello

Me in Scopello

Red Martinis

Minyi and Cam

Jing, Sage, Mya

Mya and Sage

Jing Wen

Angie, Sage, Byron, Mya (In the Snow)

Min Yi, Cam, Jing Wen (In Hawaii)

Minyi and Jing Wen

Jing Wen (2004)

Clayton (2004)

Clayton

Jing and Laura

Jake, Laura, Nico

Family Photo (2006)

Todd, Nora and the Girls

Sage, Angie, Byron, Mya on Vacation

Byron on Vacation

Byron and Angie on Vacation

Sage and Mya

CHAPTER 7

In 2010, we returned to Connecticut. We were able to rent a place on Coventry Lake around the bend from the family cottage, which had been sold over the past year. While we were there, we took the canoe out and paddled over to the old place. It looked as though it was occupied by a new family. There were paddle boats, lawn chairs, life preservers and such scattered about on the sand in front of the cottage. Everyone in John's family who visited the lake that year made the same canoe ride over to inspect their old home. Now it had a new generation of inhabitants. The old had only memories and a view from their canoe. But during the week while many of the cottages are vacant, I swam with my snorkel and mask over to the old place. No one was around, so I walked out of the water and onto the beach, then up to the house. I peered into the windows of the screened deck. It had been remodelled but maintained the general appearance that I remembered, except that the ill-fitting windows John's father's friend had put in had been replaced with new ones that looked as though they were more functional. I went around the exterior and looked through the rest of the windows.

The whole place had a fresh new appearance but remained rustic and quaint. I felt glad that it still felt familiar and seemed to have caring recipients of its comforts.

This time, we didn't go to New York but instead planned a trip over to Candlewood Lake in the western part of the state. John and I made plans to visit Byron, Angie, and the girls at their home toward the end of our vacation. On our way there, we took a detour to Torrington. John wanted to show me the town he had lived and worked in for seven years—most of his married life. He had been employed in a government job with vocational rehabilitation there. First, we took a walk downtown, and he pointed out the various points of interest. We went by his old work. The place was vacant and had broken windows here and there. We did manage to find a restaurant that was open. He remembered this place too. We happened to be its only customers, but the food was pretty good. The whole place gave me the impression of a ghost town. Many of the stores and businesses were vacant, and the ones that were in operation seemed out of date. The Yankee Pedlar Inn is an old hotel in the town, built in 1891. It is known for being haunted. John remembered this place well too. We decided to give it a look-see. The lobby included an old-fashioned barbershop down one of the main floor corridors. The air had a faint hint of mold. There was a rather peculiar man at the front desk who quoted prices for a night's stay—twenty-four dollars. The lobby was right out of any of the turn- of-the-century establishments of its kind. It didn't look as though much had changed since its inception, at least not the original part of the hotel. Another newer section had been added, but we didn't have much interest in that part of the building. Anyway, I told John it would be fun to stay there sometime in the future. I grabbed a business card from the front desk, and we were off.

John asked me if I minded if we tried to find the house he and his wife had bought and lived in during the seven years they were there. Since he couldn't remember the exact address, we drove around the old neighborhood. A street sign looked familiar, and so he parked the car and we walked around until he recognized the street name he had lived on. He was visibly excited about his discovery. When he spotted the house at the end of the street, we noticed that there was a woman out in the front yard tending to her garden. As we approached, he said he felt weird about walking by with her there, but we continued to walk toward the house anyway. As we approached, we could tell the woman was Italian, and she seemed friendly, so John let her know that he had once lived there. She seemed surprised as he provided more details and told him that it was she and her husband who had purchased the home from him and his wife. At first she sized me up, looked quizzical, and then assumed I was John's wife, but we both told her otherwise. She invited us in and introduced us to her husband, who was equally friendly. As we went through the place, John reminisced about his old home. He described what had changed and what was unchanged. Of course, they already knew how the house had been and what had been done since. Everyone told their own brand of history with the place. John asked about a couple who had been his neighbors years earlier. A tragic story was told. John's old neighbor and his wife had been out on the highway for a ride when another man in the next lane had a cardiac event. The ailing man's wife tried to take control of the car, but her husband's foot was jammed in place on the gas pedal. The car careened out of control and crashed into John's ex-neighbors' car. His wife died. Her husband (John's ex-neighbor) stayed in their home alone for a few years, remarried, and then moved on. We discovered before the end of our visit that both John and the current owner loved to golf, and the couple invited us to visit again so that the two men could enjoy a golf game together.

We drove out of Torrington and on to Danbury and Candlewood Lake, where we visited Byron and his family at their rented home for a few hours, took a hike around the lake, and then went out for dinner at a local restaurant of their choosing. We laughed about Dwight from the television show The Office. The girls loved the show, and they had sat next to the actor, his wife, and toddler on a flight back from Disneyland a few years earlier. They had been too shy to speak to him then. The girls entertained John by repeating

Dwight's quips, some of which were emblazoned on some of the T-shirts they owned. The following morning, Angie called suggesting we meet for breakfast before our departure. They paid for the meal, and we made tentative plans to get together again the following year.

After we got back to Coventry, we decided to drive over to Newport, Rhode Island. This was only a day trip, so there was really more driving than anything else, but we did take the ocean cliff walk to the Vanderbilt mansion and explored it before heading back to the lake.

Before we left for the East Coast that year, I had noticed something was different about my stools, but I didn't pay it any mind, even though way in the back of my mind, there was the warning I'd heard about the importance of reporting such things to one's doctor. But then Dad had dealt with diverticulosis later on in his life. He had described to me how his stools appeared different than before. I still remember Mom breaking down in their kitchen on Ninth Street one afternoon when I dropped by to visit. This was before he had been diagnosed. She confided that the doctors had found blood in Dad's stool, and she feared the worst. She broke down sobbing as she related this to me. I had never seen my mother so distraught in all my life, and it distressed me to see her so. But the worst news didn't materialize. It wasn't cancer but diverticulosis, irritating to deal with but not usually life-threatening. I figured that was where I was headed. I had noticed the stool change that Dad had described, but I hadn't noticed blood until a week or so before John and I left. It was just a dab on the toilet paper, but I decided to keep an eye on it to see what might develop. After we got to the cottage, I started to notice that the dabs were becoming more frequent, so I called to make an appointment with my doctor before leaving Connecticut for home. All this brought to mind recurrent night terrors I'd had over the years, some pertaining to this topic. Some were so gruesome that I could never describe them to others even when they asked. Putting the visions into words might traumatize my listeners or even me. So I kept quiet about them. One of my more benign recurrent nightmares had to do with shit. I would go to the toilet and flush, but instead of the stuff going down it came up like vomit from one's stomach. It ran down the sides of the toilet, all over the floor. I would make frantic efforts to stop the flow or clean it all up, but that only made matters worse. I found myself covered in shit too. This dream was to become prophetic, and I started to ponder the connection that might exist between our dreams and what we perceive as reality. In fact, my dreams have taken on a new dimension. I have become more aware of their objective nature—dreams that seem to have a source other than my brain—a quality that has challenged my previous belief about them.

After my return home I went to see my doctor. She was new to me. I had recently lost my doctor of many years to his retirement and found a younger doctor that I really liked. But after a few years with him, he left town, so I had to go searching for yet another. I was referred to a female physician that seemed OK. This was only the second time I had seen her. She checked out my ass. This was to become a regular routine over the next several months. The verdict was hemorrhoids. I was relieved but skeptical. I had occasional bouts since my pregnancies, but this just seemed different. But I did what I was told—warm baths and Metamucil. This only seemed to make matters worse. I returned after a few weeks. I was becoming alarmed because the bleeding was getting worse, and I had a low-grade fever, which I pointed out during my examination. The diagnosis remained the same, however, and I was told to just continue on the same regime.

After a few more visits, I was referred to a gastroenterologist. He looked up my ass too and said he couldn't determine anything, so he referred me to a surgeon in the same building. I liked this guy. He had a sense of humor and was straightforward. He took a look, but this time the surgeon said he could see something that concerned him. He just wasn't sure what it was. He told me that either he or the gastroenterologist would contact me to schedule a colonoscopy. Oh no! I had one after years of my gynecologist (the doctor I had seen since I was eighteen) dogged me to get one. The whole thing was no fun. But the worst part was afterward. I couldn't even keep water down for three days and nights. I finally called the office and was told that I had squirmed and moaned so much on the table that they just kept pumping more of the hypnotic into me. "You had a big dose," I was told. Finally, the nausea and vomiting subsided. Anyway, I wasn't all that excited about going through it again. I waited to hear from one of the doctors to schedule this second colonoscopy, but after three weeks, I still hadn't heard back. I finally called the surgeon's office and was told that the gastroenterologist would be doing the procedure. I waited another week and still nothing. By this time, I was getting frantic. Blood was pouring out my ass, and I was running to the toilet all day long. I called the gastroenterologist's office about scheduling but, again, didn't hear back. I finally called my relatively new gynecologist in tears—my old one had finally retired. She arranged for me to see another doctor. She told me to get the records from the other office right away and take it to the new doctor's office. I went in to the office and asked to fill out a release. I waited about half an hour and was handed my records. Then I went straight to the new doctor's office and handed the receptionist the papers. It didn't take long to hear from the office manager about my request for my records. I told her that I was moving on and why. She explained that she had called a few weeks earlier with messages for me to call to schedule an appointment, but she had not heard back from me.

I never heard any messages nor did my caller ID suggest that any of these supposed calls had occurred. She called me back again and said they would fit me in right away, so I didn't know what to do. I decided to go with the new doctor. It was a good decision.

John went with me to the hospital for my colonoscopy. My new doctor was aware of my trepidation about the procedure and assured me that he would do his best to make this time less traumatic. Indeed it was, but the news wasn't so good. He told me I had ulcerative colitis, an autoimmune disease and a form of inflammatory bowel disease. He started me out with suppositories, but I didn't respond well to this treatment. It was all the beginning of a few very unpleasant years, and the disease is difficult to predict. It has been life changing.

The next summer (2011), we returned to Connecticut, but before we left town, another matter had to be taken care of. John's dog Heidi had been failing for the past year or more. She became blind, deaf, and incontinent. She was now in the eighteenth year of her life. He struggled with her decline and talked about putting her down but couldn't really consider it until things got really bad. He finally decided he would arrange for a veterinarian to come to his home the morning of our departure. That would give him a few weeks away from home where he wouldn't have the constant reminder that she was gone. That morning, he was agitated before the vet's arrival. It reminded me of how he was when faced with visits to see his ailing mother and sister on our vacations to Connecticut. But finally, the knock came on the door, and he let the woman in. She briefly described the procedure that would take place. John wanted to hold his beloved pet in his arms while the shot was administered. I sat next to him on the couch as the vet did her work. First, a sedative was given and next came the shot. Heidi shuddered slightly and then grew limp. John wept and continued to hold her until the vet gently took the body out of his arms. She expressed her condolences and then was gone. The ride up to Portland was quiet and somber.

I was still struggling with my disease and had lost over twenty pounds. I had concerns about making the flights back and forth, but in spite of all this, I decided to try to go. The first night there, we stayed at Paul and Julie's house. Paul had just purchased a dog, much to Julie's chagrin. John and I stayed in an upstairs room that had been the bedroom of two of their four boys. In the morning, I got up to take a shower in the bathroom down the hall. When I got back to the bedroom, the dog was eating my suppositories. He had retrieved them from my suitcase on the floor. I panicked, not only because of the potential harm to the dog but also because my suppositories were essential in having any semblance of control over my annoying symptoms over the course of our vacation. Paul called the vet, and the dog was OK. I had to get ahold of my pharmacy in Oregon to arrange to replace the eaten medicine.

We left for New York on a Thursday, checked into The Gem, and headed right down to Little Italy. There are so many restaurants there that it's hard to choose. That first night, we decided on a place called Angelo's. We got a table in the front of the restaurant next to a table full of older Italian men who looked as though they could have come right out of The Godfather movies. They were boisterous, drank wine, and had a great time. If my memory serves me right, I also think they smoked cigars after their meal. The next evening, we would happen upon a Friday night celebration. The streets were blocked off. We usually eat on the early side, so we were able to get a good table. This time, we chose a place we had been before—Cafe Napoli. The restaurant was open-air, and we were seated in front, so we had a great view of passersby. There was a steady stream of people passing by all evening long that, by the end of the night, had turned into a throng. It was just like a big party down there. The energy and atmosphere were wonderful. The food was delicious, although I had annoying restrictions about what I could eat because of my problem. The next morning before our departure from NYC, we ate at what had become our only breakfast spot in the city—Pulino's Bar and Pizzeria. It was only a few blocks from The Gem. I always got the same thing for breakfast—a specialty of theirs, grilled grapefruit, and their Greek yogurt and fruit plate.

This year, we went to the Tenement Museum. I had read about it in one of my NYC guidebooks. There is an assortment of tours available. We decided on one that demonstrated how immigrants lived during the greatest influx of immigrants that came through Ellis Island. The buildings had been vacant and rundown for years but renovated to create the museum. The dwellings, however, remained essentially as they had been when inhabited by families. Each apartment had a story to tell, and in one an Italian family had inhabited, the recorded voice of one of the original inhabitants told her story. The experience was another that led me closer to my heritage.

The only good weather we had in 2011 was while we were in NYC. By the time we got back to Coventry, the weather had turned cold and rainy and remained so for the entire time we were there. Byron, Angie, and the girls came to visit. We had been in our rental cottage the past two years. When they came to visit, it was the first time they had seen it. Swimming and hanging out on our beach was out of the question, so we had to come up with something. We went over to Aero Diner in Willimantic for a fine breakfast and then to the Manchester Mall to shop. The rest of the time there was spent with John's family and a trip back to North Windham's East Brook Mall for a movie.

After we got home, John got me a little stuffed monkey. He's light brown with a tan muzzle and tail, two black beads for his eyes, a red bow around his neck, and a slim-lipped grin, which lends an impression of playfulness and mischief. Sometimes he's even naughty. His little body is pliable, so he can be arranged into all sorts of positions and postures. I named him George. He usually has a spot for himself on my night stand next to my bed, but he's full of adventure and fun, so John or I might find him just about anywhere in his house. At night, he might sneak downstairs, and we'll find him lounging in John's spot on the couch—legs crossed, one arm cocked behind his head in front of the television with a shit-eating grin. Other times he might greet one on the landing outside my bedroom first thing in the morning—all casual and cocky. He might explore my bathroom down the hall, grab a snack down in the kitchen when we least expect it, or just catch a nap on John's pillow—all cozy and comfortable. You just never know. I don't know what I'd do without George.

Laura was pregnant with her third baby. She and Jake decided to get married, so she called Leo about marrying them as he has a certificate to marry people. He had done just that for Byron and Angie years ago and a lot of others who asked him to marry them.

The date was set for December 21, 2011. At first, Laura just invited a couple who were her and Jake's friends to be their witnesses, but then she decided to invite me too. The ceremony was to be at their home. It was very informal to say the least. Leo and I got there about three in the afternoon. Laura was in the bathroom getting ready for the big event. She emerged wearing a white lace frock I had given her a while ago. She had flowers placed strategically in her hair, and a bouquet that matched her headgear stood on a pedestal for later. Jake was dressed in a white long-sleeved shirt and a black vest. The kids ran around the living room. Then the couple who would act as witnesses arrived. All of a sudden, Laura decided to invite Jake's parents and grandparents. She and Jake made hasty calls to each, asking them to come by the house as soon as possible but not explaining why. His mother and grandmother explained that they were at work but would see what they could do. Pretty soon the four of them trickled in. They may have noticed that everyone else was "dressed up," but still, nothing was said at first about the reason for the gathering. When the marriage intentions were finally revealed, they were thrilled. The ceremony was simple, short, and sweet, and the focus of the celebration was Laura and Jake's love for each other with family there to share in it. Nico didn't seem too happy about all the attention his parents were getting, so he misbehaved. Everyone ignored it. Ori played with his toys.

I had been working for the county since 1996. I started out, as I've mentioned, with a temporary job at the county's residential treatment facility. I got this job after I became acquainted with people from the county whom I met during my hospital practicum and while doing my research project at the county residential treatment facility. The director liked my thesis and offered me the job. In the meantime, he had me attend treatment team meetings at the mental health clinic where I met other team leaders. Tim was the head of the geriatric team, and his colleague was out on sick leave for an indeterminate period, so he offered me a part-time job too. For a while, I worked with both programs, but eventually, it was decided that I had to choose. I went with the geriatric program. The woman who had been on leave returned. She was a psychiatric nurse. The three of us were it for a while, but we grew to a team of five that worked well together. We also always had an assortment of interns passing through. Tim loved to take the role of educator and mentor. He had been so for me, and he encouraged all his team to take on this role as well, so we took these students under our wing. Our work was always interesting, challenging, fun, and never boring. There were many aspects of the job. We did evaluations, individual and family psychotherapy, consultation, group work, and crisis intervention. We worked with other community agencies and facilities that provided services or housed our population and with other departments in our own agency. We didn't just work with elderly people. We also worked with younger people who had some sort of physical disability, along with psychiatric issues. We all felt like we made a difference. In those days, it was fee-for-service. We wrote our chart notes by hand. The notes were simple and to the point. We spent most of our time serving the people in our community. Tim was known for having the best geriatric program in the state, and the county commissioners were aware of this, and they frequently received favorable feedback from recipients of our services. So we were allowed to carry on without too much interference. As time went by and managed care got an upstart in health care, things began to change. It was insidious in nature. Our work environment had become stressful and difficult around 2008. I speak of all this only to relate the change in our work environment as the downfall of our program and a detriment to the well-being of myself and my team members, not to mention the detriment to those we served.

Instead of the focus of our work being "client centered," (which meant forming a therapeutic connection with the client, listening to his or her goals and helping the client make changes he or she wanted) focus went to documentation of services and how to get them paid for. The format for all this changed almost daily. What was right one week was wrong the next, so lengthy training sessions were required to "retrain" us in the proper technique, which was soon again outdated. The jargon changed just as fast. A person we served went from client, to consumer, to individual. (I had noticed that with each change, the word to describe the person we were serving became longer and with more syllables so it would naturally take longer to type and, consequently, waste even more time. It also seemed that with each change, the description of the person suggested little or no personal relationship between the therapist and whatever it is they're called now). There were also ongoing threats about confidentiality leaks that we might be responsible for if we didn't go to outlandish lengths to avoid such mishaps, while at the same time, computerized records were touted as impervious to disclosure. The outcome of all these changes was simply that we spent most of our time in front of a computer dealing with minutiae and complicated documentation requirements, and almost no time doing anything productive. For me, the job became meaningless. The other more personal negative effect was a high degree of stress for all of us—so much so that our own health became compromised.

During this same time, my parents continued to be challenging. They remained at the facility for persons with dementia, but that didn't mean that problems still didn't arise on an almost daily basis. Dad became preoccupied with his financial status and became suspicious of Doug's part in managing his portfolio. He began to demand to see his monthly statements. Doug and I always made sure Dad had cash in hand even though this could potentially result in the money being stolen. It was a way to have him feel he still had some control of his life. Dad had always had a quick temper, which never abated. He would head down to the lobby every morning asking for his mail. When he didn't see what he wanted there, he sometimes became combative with the staff. The saddest aspect of Dad's decline, though, was witnessing the loss of almost every aspect of his independence. He lost his ability to speak, other than a few words that would find their way out. He started having frequent falls, which would produce telltale bruises and abrasions. His gait became shuffling and labored until he became immobile. I would witness his struggle as he fumbled to get his pants zipped and buttoned after a trip to the bathroom. The television became a constant source of frustration because he could never figure out how the controls worked and so he finally lost interest in it altogether. Then he lost control of his bladder and bowels and had to resort to diapers. He became dependent on staff to feed him, and when I visited, I would. Surprisingly, he didn't seem to be bothered by my feeding him. In fact, he seemed grateful and would smile at me between spoonfuls I'd offer him. Then there were the periods where he would lapse into unconscious states sometimes accompanied by twitching movements. This is when we would get calls from the facility wanting to know what we wanted to do about it. The first few times Doug took Dad to the emergency room at the hospital, a battery of tests were done. Nothing would come of all this, though. We were told that Dad's damaged brain was the cause of the periodic coma and seizure-like episodes and that nothing much could be done about it. At some point, Dad seemed to have resigned himself to his circumstances.

Mom was another matter. Initially, she remained obsessed with her cigarettes and booze—especially the cigarettes. The new facility wouldn't tolerate real cigarettes, and she was told this every time she asked for one. When Doug and I went to care meetings, this topic was brought up. The staff finally agreed to a trial of the smokeless cigarette. Doug was able to send away for a kit that contained two "fake" plastic cigarettes and cartridges, which produced varying degrees of vaporized nicotine. Mom begrudgingly accepted these substitutes but continued to try just about anything to get ahold of the real thing. She also began a habit of repeating the same phrase over and over. Every visit seemed to produce a different subject matter. It was as if she started on a thought and got stuck there. For instance, she might make a comment about a sweater I was wearing—"That's a pretty sweater. Where did you get it?" And that would be the extent of our conversation for the entire visit. Another thing that happened was a switch in the seating arrangement in their room. Dad had always sat closest to any of their apartment's entry and Mom behind him. When he still had the ability to talk, he remained the primary conversationalist. But now, they had switched places in both respects. She was now the person who greeted us from her seat near the entry, and she was the one who monopolized the conversation. At first, I thought the change may have come about to protect Dad from his increasing inability to communicate verbally, and that may be the case. However, I wondered if there was more to it—that maybe after all those years when Mom was in the background, now she had her chance in the limelight. This could be frustrating, though, because I felt that Dad deserved a chance to struggle to get out a few thoughts here and there. He would start out that way, but Mom either didn't want him to have the attention, or she simply couldn't tolerate having to wait for him to get it all out. She'd often cut him off, and then he would just shrug. I got to where I would ask Mom to give him time to form his thoughts into words and sometimes this worked, sometimes not. Another change in her was that she seemed to have lost her inhibitions and her ability to empathize. She had always been an anxious person, worried about others' travails, concerned for others' well-being. She wasn't mean in her evolving disinterest in others' feelings. It's just that it all seemed to go over her head. When I went to tell them about Dad's sister's death, Dad cried. Mom seemed oblivious. Mom had been modest too, but not anymore. At a moment's notice, she might lift her shirt to show someone how her ample breasts had fallen and think nothing of it.

The most blatant example of Mom's character change had to do with a male resident at the facility. He was an alpha male type. He'd strut around as if he was still a young buck. He liked women of all ages but steered clear of the men. If it was just me visiting Mom, he was always friendly. If Doug was there too, they'd both face off with each other like two strutting roosters. I felt sorry for the guy because he was younger than many of the other residents there and often acted like a caged animal—frequent attempts to escape, nonstop wandering and pacing about the place, a feisty attitude in general. He seemed to have retained a semblance of his prior self. With some of the other residents, it seemed difficult to imagine what they might have been like before their dementing illness. Some were even zombie-like. But I'll get back to Mom's "boyfriend"—he and Mom took a liking to each other. Dad had had his own day as the cock of the walk, but not any longer, and I think the guy recognized this. Dad maintained some gumption, though, and would get agitated and angry when the guy was around Mom. Mom seemed oblivious to all this, or at least pretended to be. While I was back east during one of my summer vacations, I got a call from the director, Patty. I had worked with her in the past professionally, and she was top-notch. She explained to me over the phone that she had some sensitive information for me that she felt obligated to share but said it could wait until my return if I didn't want to deal with it on my vacation. I told her to go ahead and let me have it. She explained that the relationship had gone further. They had been caught kissing in the hallways and caregivers had discovered them making out in Mom and Dad's room with Dad looking on. I asked how far things had gone with them, and she said she wasn't sure. The staff had resorted to locking Mom and Dad's room and keeping a closer eye on Mom's pursuer. After I returned to Bend, the whole thing seemed to be under control, but a similar incident occurred again, and Dad became so angry he somehow got out of the locked front door and two aides had to run alongside him for several blocks before they could convince him to return to the facility. He was fuming mad. This all took place after he had deteriorated physically to the point where he really wasn't able to walk at all. That's what adrenalin can do, I guess. I wondered about Mom's thing with this guy. She seemed to have lost her inhibition in general, but I also wondered if it was pay back for the few of Dad's amorous peccadillos from his past or if it was just that she missed having sex in general since Dad's prostate cancer. She had, in fact, confided in me one afternoon while I accompanied her on a cigarette break in the interior outdoor patio at the facility. Of course, the cigarette was electronic, and she complained about that in addition to the absence of physical intimacy in her life. I'm not sure at this point she was capable of recognizing that Dad was out of commission. Maybe she just felt neglected by him-or was she finally trying to establish some semblance of independence for herself? Dad had confided in me about his impotence with a hint of resentment toward Mom because she had suffered from cystitis for years, and now that they were no longer having sex, her cystitis had cleared. It seemed to me that he suspected she may have blamed him for her years of suffering with her condition, or maybe he just blamed himself. And then people of their generation didn't have the wherewithal to consider alternatives to intercourse, so any signs of physical affection had disappeared from their relationship.

There was always something new and different when we'd visit. One woman was capable of speaking plain and clear English, but at any point, this would be reduced to various forms of gibberish or even just plain loud repetitive noise—stutters, whoops, bellows, and shrieks that often carried a hint of hostility. The more with it, residents could be heard commenting with something like "There she goes again" and calmly distancing themselves. After hours carried its own brand of nutty. Some of the residents revved up and wandered about the halls and byways, looking for their rooms. It was usual for residents to claim another's as their own and move on in. Sometimes a resident would return to his or her room and find someone in his or her bed or on the toilet. One time, Nora visited after hours. There was one resident, a large grumpy old guy prone to aggressive behavior, who happened to be wandering down the hallway outside Mom and Dad's room as Nora was leaving. He started after her, shouting obscenities and shaking his fist as he followed her down the hallway. When Nora got as far as the locked door between the living room and the lobby, there was no one there to let her out. She had forgotten the code. She called Doug in a panic. He had to drive down to get her out.

Another problem that arose had to do with Mom and Dad's clothes. Each time we'd visit, we would discover a new assortment of clothing that we had never seen before. Or if I bought them some new item, the next thing I knew, it went missing. We were told to label all the clothes, but that never really made much difference except for relocating something that had disappeared from their room in the first place. We hired a caregiver, Debbie, whom I had become acquainted with while making home visits in my work. I thought she had a good way with her clients, and she was always able to manage with more challenging people. She started visiting Mom and Dad even when they were still in their own place. She had been the only one they would tolerate coming in. I think part of this had to do with Debbie presenting herself to them as just a friend who was willing to help out. After Mom and Dad were in the last place they would be, she was familiar to them, was an added support, and they enjoyed her company. Debbie would run interference for me too. I could tell her that one of Mom's new articles of clothing had gone missing, and she would search the whole building, usually retrieve it, and return it to its place. I was also constantly getting calls from the staff about underwear and socks. These items simply disappeared, never to be seen again. I'd go out and buy underpants, bras, and socks to restock Mom and Dad's supply, and they'd rapidly disappear again. Then I'd have to go out and buy a whole new set, and within a few weeks, I'd get yet another call.

One event with my parents during this time sticks in my mind. Mom wouldn't go anywhere unless Dad accompanied her. This mostly involved doctor's appointments. I dropped by one afternoon, and they were ready to go. I got them into the car—not an easy task—and we headed to the clinic. Mom had developed a great fear of contracting the flu and fretted about having to be in the clinic at all. We managed to get through the appointment without incident. The real difficulty emerged during our exit. Dad started panicking, saying, "I have to find a bathroom," and ran ahead of us willy-nilly. Mom chased after me, proclaiming that she wanted to get to the car because she would surely get the flu bug if she remained in the clinic's lobby. I suggested she stay put until I could get Dad to a bathroom. I ran after him around the corner, located a door with the appropriate bathroom sign, and he ran past me into it and locked the door behind him. I yelled through the door that I would check on Mom and return. I found her wandering about the lobby, still fretting about the flu. I escorted her out to the car. I didn't really feel comfortable leaving her there by herself, for I couldn't trust her to remain in the car. I didn't have much choice in the matter, though. I made her promise to stay put while I checked on Dad. I told her if she didn't, she would have to come back into the clinic with me. I alerted staff in the lobby of my predicament, asking them keep an eye on Mom out in the car. Then I ran back to check on Dad. I could hear him shuffling around in there from behind the locked door. He explained that he was in trouble, and I asked for him to open the door, but he wouldn't. I guessed what was probably occurring in there. I continued to run out to check on Mom in the car, and she did actually stay there. Then I told her I had to check on Dad again. This all went on for about an hour until I finally found a doctor who was walking by the bathroom door and explained my predicament to him. He talked to Dad through the door, and Dad finally said he thought he finally had things under control. Dad emerged a few minutes later, looking chagrined, and explained to me that he had to throw his underwear in the garbage. He had spent all that time trying to clean up after himself. (With my own gastric problems I could relate to Dad's embarrassment). We went out to the car where Mom was waiting and headed back to their place.

Dad developed a fascination with scissors. He took to cutting little vertical slices at the top of his socks. I couldn't figure this out for a while, but I decided they had become uncomfortable for him. He developed some edema in his legs, and he had taken care of the problem. Mom was having some accidents. She had developed problems with diarrhea. When this happened, her solution was to just throw her underwear in the garbage can or hide them in her bureau drawers. But then the staff called to report that now they were finding Mom's underwear in the garbage cut into little pieces. I'm still not sure what this was all about. I think it was Dad, not Mom, doing the underwear cutting, though. Was he just hiding the evidence for Mom? And if so, did the underwear have to be cut up rather than just disposed of? I've had thoughts that Dad may just have been entertained by cutting stuff up. I hoped it wasn't some deviant resentment of Mom that had surfaced. I do know that he had become quietly irritated with her at times—her rambling and repeating, their unrelenting togetherness, her having lost track of her sensitive disposition. He would communicate his irritation with facial expressions—rolling of his eyes, raised eyebrows, sly smiles. Well anyway, the scissors or any other sharp objects had to go. Unfortunately (and no one could ever figure out how Dad did it), the scissors always seemed to find their way back to the room. As I've said, he always was a cagey guy, and nothing ever changed that.

Mom was becoming more of a socialite too. Dad's company must have seemed lonely for her after he couldn't communicate, slept more and more, or just stared off into space. She still wanted him near her, but Dad's "new self" left her craving others' companionship. Staff and other residents found Mom pleasant to be around and she was rarely obnoxious by this time. She developed a close friendship with a very sweet old lady who was kind, friendly, and very down-to-earth-she wore her long thick gray hair pulled back in a ponytail (which accentuated her beautiful weathered face) and wore plaid shirts that reflected her blue collar background. The old lady was more cognitively functional than Mom, but she was able to communicate with Mom on Mom's level. They were affectionate toward each other and could be seen holding hands or just sitting and talking together. Some of Mom's ability for affection started to resurface, and she would be sure to tell us kids how much she loved us and Dad when we visited. She and Dad were crowned the king and queen of one of the facility holiday dances when Dad was still able to get around the dance floor a little. Everyone raved about what a cute couple they were, and this event seemed to have been a happy occasion for both of them. The environment at the facility, I will have to say, was that of kindness and tolerance. I have a special respect for professional caregivers who don't get paid much but work hard to make other people's lives more tolerable.

The difficulties of work and my parents' need for attention took a toll on me. My disease was only getting worse in spite of treatment. I was told that my condition is often difficult to treat successfully. I struggled for the next two years. Things got so bad. My disease was causing my body to attack itself—with ulcerative colitis, the body attacks the colon. After my colonoscopy, my doctor said that my condition was severe. The disease had produced ulcers that were causing severe diarrhea, weight loss, bleeding, general malaise, and pain. Other parts of the body can also be affected—eyes can also develop ulcers and compromise sight, internal organs can be attacked and render them impaired or useless. Blood literally ran out my ass. I was running to the bathroom up to twenty-five times a day. Sometimes it would feel like I had to go but nothing happened. Other times I couldn't get to the bathroom on time and had accidents. The pain felt like a dagger had been shoved up my ass, but this doesn't really describe properly how different this type of pain was from any other I had experienced in my life to this point. There was something sinister about it. I lost twenty-two pounds in all. This made working and tending to my ailing parents difficult to say the least. Everyone at work was so preoccupied with the changes going on and their own stress that I didn't really get much empathy from anyone there. They all had their own problems to deal with.

I decided to explore the possibility of retiring from the county. I felt a sense of panic at the thought of lost income and losing my medical insurance (which I was now entirely dependent on), but I felt that the stress I was under was contributing to my difficulty in getting into a remission, so I started visiting the county human resources department. The more I found out, the more I figured I could do it. I could take my Social Security benefit at sixty-two, and I would also have my county retirement benefit and continue with most of my medical benefit until age sixty-five if I paid in between five and six hundred dollars a month for the insurance. Plus, I had about two months of unused vacation time and an extra retirement account I hadn't known about that I could use until my Social Security kicked in. I might have to change my lifestyle a bit, but at this point, I didn't care. But in the meantime, I also found out I could apply for medical compensation. Not only had I been taking time off during the workday to attend to my own medical care, I had also been taking time off work to take Mom and Dad to medical appointments, to the hospital, or just to head over to the facility to deal with some sort of crisis that would crop up. Luckily, I was able to factor in time off to tend to myself and my parents when I applied for my health-related compensation. I just had to document the time away from the job to attend to my or their medical care. My last day on the job would be May 31, 2012. It was one of the best decisions of my life.

After my return from the East Coast the end of August 2011, Dad started to appear very frail. The staff at the facility recommended hospice care and we, his kids, all agreed it was a good idea. You never knew what to expect from one visit to the next. Sometimes he remained asleep in his recliner with his head hanging down on his chest. Sometimes drool slid down his jaw and neck from his half-opened mouth. I was never sure if his apparent sleeping state was just that or the more ominous coma state that was happening more often. The staff could usually tell the difference by whether they could rouse him or not. But sometimes I didn't feel like disturbing him no matter which of the states he was in. Other times, he would rouse, attempt a weak smile if he could muster it, and then drop off again. If he happened to be out in the dining room and was alert for any length of time, he still showed evidence of having an appetite and sometimes offered a weak smile then too. His dining room visits were getting scarce, and it didn't seem long before he was confined to the hospital bed that hospice brought in.

It didn't seem to me he could go on much longer in this condition, but he did. Mom talked more during this time. She wanted to be near Dad but, at the same time, seemed to have some sort of awareness that he was becoming unreachable. On the outside, though, she acted like he was perfectly fine. She talked to us as if he was still working and would explain that he took naps because he was tired from the long hours he put in.

Finally in April of 2012, the hospice nurse let us know that the end was in sight. She would lift the bed covers to inspect the condition of his feet, a tell-all to determine such things. I called Byron back east to ask if he wanted to fly back, and he did. I called Sandy in West Virginia and Nora in Portland. Both Sandy and

Dave would fly out too, but it would take time to arrange for these flights. I called Cameron. He and his middle son would drive over. In the meantime, the rest of us gathered around his bed—me, Nora, Doug, Diane, Andrea. Cam and Clay joined us. (Laura had given birth to her third son on April 4 and remained in her birthing bed. Jake had delivered their third child. In their own words: "We were having such a good time alone, we decided not to call the midwife after all.") We sat in chairs brought in by the staff. Joe, a young aide who had developed affection for Dad, sat with us. He had confided to me once that Dad seemed like a father to him. Joe had been with Dad over the past four years. He was so young to have such sad eyes, and I wondered what his story was. He was there for our family until the bitter end.

It took longer than I expected for Byron, Sandy, and Dave to get to Bend. It was days before they arrived. Dad hadn't eaten or had any fluids during all that time. He looked like a breathing corpse—his shriveled body, sunken eyes, hollow cheeks, sallow paper-thin skin. His eyes had a fixed cloudy crusted-over gaze. He was no longer capable of blinking. There seemed not to be enough moisture left in his body for that. They were like slits on his face—his eyeballs only partially visible, the right closest to us less visible than the other. His breathing became more and more shallow. His face remained directed toward the people around his bed though. The hospice nurse came in to check on him. She cautioned us to be mindful of what was said in the room, explaining that Dad was capable of hearing and understanding everything that was uttered. She added that even after a person is technically "gone," they are still aware of what is occurring around them. So we talked to him, told stories about the old days, and paid attention to what we said in front of him. All this time, Mom ignored the drama around her completely. We had been telling Dad to hang on because Sandy and Byron were on their way. Now I look back and wonder if this was for the best. But he did hang on-and I do believe he planned when he would succumb.

Sandy and Dave's flight had come into Portland, but they stayed an extra day before driving on to Bend because Dave's brother was near death himself. Byron called to say he had arrived at the Redmond airport. He had a layover and was hours later than his expected arrival. -Leo and I drove over to pick him up. It was so good to see him. We drove straight to the facility. Sandy and Dave arrived minutes after Byron, Leo and me. Byron stood in front of Dad, arms crossed and straight with his hands folded inward as Dad had always done while in repose. Byron spoke in a low soft voice and told Dad he loved him. Sandy and Dave seemed uncomfortable. Sandy finally approached and just stood there. I went up near the bed next to her. I suggested we sing the song "Pals and Buddies" that Dad had sung to us when we were little—"Pals and buddies, you and I. Pals and buddies 'til we die." It was hard to sing the song without breaking up, but we did it. Dad hadn't had a drop to drink in more than the ten days. The hospice nurse had explained that in a dying state, fluid leads to a feeling of suffocation and discomfort in the dying person. In spite of his dehydrated state, a tear fell from his right half-opened eye and ran down his cheek. Whether true or not, the tear indicated to me that Dad was moved by our song and that a part of him was sorry to be leaving us. Dad's breathing became more and more shallow and labored. It was more like panting, really—the kind a woman is taught to do or does instinctively during the last phases of childbirth.

Doug put the rosary our grandfather brought with him from the old country on Dad's chest. Dad was an only son and was given the rosary by his father, and then Dad had given his only son the rosary after his own father's death. Other than the newcomers to the room, we had been with Dad for days already, and we were expecting a long night ahead of us. (We should have known better). The staff offered us a meal there, but I think we all needed a little break from the whole scene. I know I did. Doug, Diane, and the pregnant Andrea went home for a bite. Byron went back to his dad's. The rest of us decided to go for a quick dinner and then return. I left first. I felt I needed to see John, so I asked if we could meet for a quick dinner at our favorite spot. I just needed a little of his calm presence in order to carry on. Sandy and Dave were ready to leave too, but Nora was afraid to desert Mom and Dad, so they stayed on for a while longer. Finally, Nora asked the staff to check in on Mom and Dad until our return. I met up with Sandy, Dave, and Nora as they were finishing their dinner. Then Nora and I started back in my car and Sandy and Dave in theirs.

In the meantime, Min Yi and the other two boys had arrived at Leo's house. Min Yi hadn't seen Dad yet, so she, Cam, and Clay headed over to the facility. Leo remained with Jing and Burion, who had no interest in going. After dinner, Nora and I stopped by my house on the way back, and I pulled into my driveway. I was going to go inside for something when the phone rang. It was Doug. He said that Dad was dead. Cam, Min Yi, and Clay had returned and told Leo what had happened. Leo called Doug because he couldn't get ahold of me or the others. We must not have heard our cell phones in the noisy restaurant. Anyway, Nora and I called Sandy. Then we all started back to the facility. On the way, the phone rang again. I have Bluetooth, so both of us could hear a voice on the other end telling us that Dad had died. Nora asked, "Who is this?" The voice replied, "Todd." We both started laughing. It may have been to release our tension, but it was also funny that Nora hadn't recognized her own husband's voice. He had heard the news from Doug and was still in Portland with the girls. It seemed the phone just kept on ringing until we got there.

Nora, Sandy, Dave, Doug, Diane, and I all arrived about the same time. I called Leo to invite him to come over too, but he wept and said he couldn't. Dad looked about the same as he had before we left other than the fact that he was no longer breathing and seemed restful rather than struggling. The staff had taken Mom for dinner while Cam, Min Yi, and Clay had been there with Dad, but now she was back and still didn't fathom what had happened. The rosary was missing, and it would take a while to discover what had become of it. We waited for the mortician to arrive. He is a friend of Doug's. He was very kind and helpful. We girls stayed with Mom in the dining room while Dad's body was prepared for its departure. Mom finally seemed to sense that something was going on. She became agitated. We told her the truth, but it just didn't stick. She would say "He's dead? That makes me sad." And then a minute later the thought was gone, but she still seemed to sense that something was amiss and so resorted to her calming measures—asking for a drink and a cigarette. The girls on duty accommodated her. Now it seemed that Mom was our main concern. Dad was where he had wanted to be for some time now. (I always felt that Dad had willed himself to live as long as he had for Mom). We talked about feeling we had abandoned him at the end and thankful that Cameron, Min Yi, and Clay had been there for him instead. They had sung to Dad. They had kissed his face and held his hand to their chests. They saw him take his last breath. It was Friday evening, the thirteenth of April.

Cameron wrote this poem within the next few days:

When Grandpa Died
I
With second son beside
knelt in awe
of life so thin
stretched round bone
his skin.
Patient ears,
chewing precious sounds
of sweet old stories
and confessions of
lessons learned
from times
when he, like me
took care to teach
so lovingly.
That young boy's voice
from heart words fell
"Hewo Gweat Gwampa,
I wuv you."
Tumbling they flew
in that sacred vault

under the ancient black rosary
that rose and fell
reminding me
of the last few grains
in a vast hour shaped glass
who's sand stands still
while the air
and such
continues to churn
and swirl
eternally
effected
by the crash
of the final
speck.

II
And after . . .
that defining silence
that gives our birth
and death context
like the moments
and final breath.
To swallow one last time
as air
escapes for keeps
and arms reach out

with babe like strength
we weep.
With death's shadow cast
i wondered how
i could feel your life.
And though I had
cried anticipation
i held the first
tear of mourning
on my thumb
and rather than
wipe it on my slacks
i took that holy drop
and crossed it on your brow.
Then seeing your
shoulders bare
i tucked you in
and placed your
golden ticker
in my breast coat
all to the blessing cry
of our merry,
Mary angel,
who knows miracles
and shows me
how to
and why.

III
And then days
of travel past
i passed through
doors of old
and dogma mask
for which i'm cold
was dropped to me
with your draped cask-
et displayed.
We sat
and stood
and knelt
and sat and stood
and knelt and sat,
and i loved
and mused
and cried
and loved and mused
and cried and loved.
And heard your life retold.
85 years in 85 words
with our boyhood
trappings like the wrappings
of those gifts
your hands and heart
passed on to me

creating and changing

my life

for-ever and ever.[39]

We decided to have the funeral for family and a few invited guests only. The days before Doug and Nora had picked out a suit for Dad. Sandy and I chose the flowers—white orchids, white calla lilies, and green hydrangea for the Easter season. Doug had long since ditched the coffin Dad had purchased and stored in his den for five of the years he and Mom had lived in their Bend condo. It was a plain wooden box without any padding inside. Doug had commented that when the time came, he didn't want to have to hear Dad rattling around inside as he was carried by the pallbearers down the church aisle. So he had ordered a hand-carved wooden casket fashioned by Trappist monks. This, at least, seemed to adhere to the idea Dad had of going out in a simple fashion and to me it was more beautiful than the metal sort. The white-and-green floral arrangement of the casket spray complimented the beautiful hand-carved casket. It lent the casket an earthy feel. There was a viewing of the body in the mortuary chapel along with recitation of the rosary the evening before. Dad's four children sat in front. I caressed Dad's forehead. It was ice cold. In spite of every effort the mortician had made, his face still held a hint of his last

---

[39] Cameron Joseph Parker, "When Grandpa Died," April 13, 2012 (Unpublished).

days of suffering. After that, we all congregated at Doug's house. Four of our cousins came from Chicago—Cindy (and her husband Gary), Greg, Jeff on Dad's side, and Ken on Mom's side. All of us kids who had lived in the house in Elmhurst together (at Aunt Jean and Uncle Jack's) had only all been in the same place at the same time as adults (now and at Jean's funeral) since we were kids.

The next day, there was a funeral mass at the church we had always attended in Bend and where family weddings, christenings, first communions, and confirmations had all taken place. It was also the church where I had been forbidden to sing in the choir as a child. I had asked Mom's personal caregiver to get Mom ready for the funeral. We had explained this to Mom the day before. We kids had questioned whether or not to include her in the service but finally decided we should at least try. The plan was for Debbie to go early and get her ready to go. Debbie had always had more luck with this sort of thing than I had. Mom would routinely refuse to get dressed for doctor's visits if I was the one taking her. But this time, Debbie called me saying that Mom was refusing her too.

I called Leo and asked if he would try to get Mom to the church, and he agreed. I knew if anyone had a chance of success with Mom, it would be him. Debbie was amazed that as soon as Leo arrived and suggested she get ready for church, she was cooperative and expressed her enthusiasm at his being her escort.

When they arrived, Mom was seated next to her kids in the front of the church. At some point, she questioned the reason for her being there. We told her that the mass was for Dad's funeral. She expressed her sadness as she had the evening he died and then forgot by the time the service was over. Debbie took Mom back to the facility. Then the rest of us drove to the cemetery. Dad had purchased a plot years ago with a place for the whole family. He had also had the gravestone engraved with his and Mom's names and a brief description of his life. Mom had not wanted anything about her added. Their children's name appeared on the back side with a salutation from us that Dad created—"from our loving children" and then our names. Only the dates of their deaths remained blank. After the cemetery, we gathered at a local banquet hall for a reception. In addition to family, a few friends attended. The next day, everyone departed. I would be alone with my grief.

In the days after Dad's funeral, I tried to spend more time with Mom. She seemed happy to see me. In fact, she was more affectionate than I had seen her in a long time. I wondered if the stress of Dad's decline and demise had weighed on her without her even being consciously aware of it. She had seemed preoccupied or just plain goofy most of the time. But now there were times when she asked about him. Where was he, she wanted to know. When I told her about his death she seemed surprised, then sad, and then asked where he was again. At some point, I decided it best to make something up. "Oh, he's around here somewhere." Maybe that was true. By June, she had developed pneumonia and was hospitalized. Doug called to let me know. When we visited, we didn't expect she would make it. She was very confused and frightened in the hospital. Doug and I were there with her when they had to help her onto a commode. She was weak, in pain from a knee that had bothered her for years, and now she was placed on the commode, with her backside exposed, where she was expected to crap right away. With Mom's audience, that seemed unlikely. So she was put back to bed. Antibiotics saved her for the time being, but she really never fully recovered. When she returned to her home, she had lost her mobility and bowel and bladder function. She remained in a weakened state, but she continued to appreciate visits from her kids and also seemed to enjoy the company of staff and other residents in her home. That would be how things would remain for a while. My condition worsened, I think my job and Dad's death had something to do with it. My gastroenterologist listened, and he decided to do another colonoscopy. All this was only a week or so after my retirement from the county and six weeks after Dad's death.

I tend to have difficulty with anesthetic medications and opiates. They often make me nauseous, paranoid, or even put me in some sort of altered state even after the medication's effects should have dissipated. John went with me to the hospital, but when I started to regain my conscious state in the recovery room, I found myself alone and sobbing uncontrollably. I had a keen sense of hearing and could make out conversations in the other cubicles around me—clear and distinct voices away from my eyesight. Nurses came running when they heard me. They explained that sometimes a reaction to the anesthesia will produce the effects that I was experiencing. The explanation didn't make my emotions feel any different, though. I had had experiences similar to this in the past but not quite so extreme. In childbirth, I had entered into what I will call an altered state of consciousness, and there were no medications involved because I had natural births. It also happened sometimes with intensely emotional lovemaking. Anyway, I could not stop the weeping no matter how I tried. It felt like my life was passing before me, as others have written about over the centuries. I don't mean just memories, though, but a reliving of past events coming in rapid succession. Emotions involved felt magnified to the nth degree. Intense emotions from my past came crashing down on me. This is also when it became clear to me that I wanted to write. I had always jotted down notations in my datebooks or on scraps of paper to help me remember what, to me, were important details of my life. I think I had always had thoughts about writing, but life had gotten in the way so far. Now I knew it was time.

By the time John was able to join me in the recovery room, the strange mental state had subsided. I had the notion that he had heard me weeping and asked him if he had. He said no. I tried to describe it all to him, but I'm not sure he got it. We had to wait what seemed like forever to see my doctor. I told John that I was afraid this was a bad sign. And sure enough, when my doctor came from behind the curtain separating us from the corridor, he told us that it was "pretty bad." He offered to show me pictures he had taken of my insides, but I passed. He let me know that I would need to start taking a biologic to treat my condition. I knew something about it already because I had had a few clients who had what I now had. Before this colonoscopy, I had been taking an oral tablet twice a day, suppositories twice a day, and two different kinds of enemas every day. Fitting the enemas in on my work days had been challenging. I had to go home and lie on my side for at least a half hour and try to hold the enema in. Sometimes I couldn't, and as I tried to get to the bathroom I would leave a trail of diarrhea and enema throughout the house and have to clean up after myself. I was also having frequent accidents at work and would have to race home to change my clothes. I resorted to large quantities of Kotex to reduce the fallout. I went through rolls and rolls of paper towels and boxes of baby wipes and toilet paper every week. Everything I ate went right through me until it seemed easier not to eat at all. I had finally applied for the medical compensation, which offered me some flexibility when I had to take time off work due to my illness. But even this wasn't enough to make work plausible after a while. I even looked into a clinic in Mexico that a woman I knew swore to me had cured her years ago, but my doctor had discouraged this route, citing there was little evidence that the clinic's methods were effective. He also explained that there are different kinds of colitis, and mine was not the type that any treatment offered in Mexico would be beneficial.

It took a while to get started on the biologic. My doctor went on vacation. I was supposed to hear back about an appointment for my first infusion, but I didn't. I was reluctant to call and make a nuisance of myself, but after a week or so, and finally out of desperation, I did. I was told that there was a holdup on authorization, and I would get a call back as soon as possible, but I never did. Every day was torturous, but I became resigned to waiting for my doctor to return. It just seemed it wouldn't be productive to try to call back beforehand. It just so happened that I had an appointment scheduled with him right after his return. The first thing he asked was how I was doing on the biologic. I explained that I hadn't had the treatment yet and explained why. The next day, I got a call and was told my infusion would be the following day. I had read some about this type of treatment. There were potentially serious side effects to consider, but I didn't feel I had much choice as my life hadn't seemed worth living much over the past year and a half.

The first time I went to "the infusion room," I was nervous. The place is on the second floor of the health clinic. The infusion room has a circle of big padded chairs with side tables attached. There's a nurse's desk that they work out of. They are a bunch of very nice people that tend to their patients. First, your vitals are taken to make sure you're well enough to have the infusion. Then you're given Tylenol and Benadryl in a little cup to ward off possible side effects. One of the nurses fixes up your concoction and an IV nurse administers the biologic or whatever else a patient needs for their particular problem. It feels a little like the old days on an airplane flight. You get treated with special kindness and consideration. Snacks are offered. A camaraderie develops among the patients that inhabit the big padded chairs for their two- to four-hour stretch. Some are there when you arrive and others come while you're already hooked up, so there's a steady turnover. The people always seem to be different, but still, during the course of one's stay, conversations breed familiarity. I have developed affection for the patients and nurses I have met there. After my first visit, I no longer felt afraid of the process. It took time, but I started to notice improvement in my condition and had some hope that my life might improve. I decided to take the whole summer off and just relax and try to get healthier. I had to work on slowing down because my job had been go, go, go. I spent more time with my mom.

John and I had been to Portland for a weekend earlier in the year. We had stayed at the Hilton downtown. As we were on our way back to our room the first day there, I saw a store with fifties vintage-looking clothing and just had to check it out. It was called Bettie Page after the 1950s pinup model. The clothing was right up my alley. John was amused by the assortment of women of all sizes, shapes, and ages stopping by who were enchanted with the merchandise. He sat and observed. Women would come out of their dressing rooms, spinning around in front of the mirrors provided in the store. Rarely did any of them leave empty handed, even me. One of the clerks mentioned the locations of their other stores, one of which was in NYC. So before John and I left for our annual trip back east, I looked up the store address on the Internet and wrote it down in my datebook. We went to NYC first this year. As we ascended from the subway and started toward The Gem Hotel, we were discussing our plans for the evening when I spotted the Bettie Page store a block away and across the street. John laughed at my perceptiveness. The store was literally only a block away from The Gem. The next morning, the first thing I did was visit the store, and I bought a dress I would wear for our Friday evening dinner in Little Italy. Then we were off to Manhattan and the American Museum of Natural History. Neither of us had been there since we were adolescents.

This year, we met Joan. She was Pascal's new girlfriend. Bonnie was out of the picture. Joan was an elementary teacher and very nice. She and a sister, also a teacher, had lived close to their parents all their lives. Their parents became ill early on, and the two took care of them until their deaths. After their parents died, the two sisters continued to live next door to each other. Neither had ever married, but this was to be in Joan's future with Pascal. Joan was included in family get-togethers at the various local Italian restaurants we frequented or at any one of the family's homes. Toward the end of the vacation, Byron, Angie, and the girls came to visit. Angie wanted to go to Newport in Rhode Island, so that's what we did. When we all got back, Paul and Julie met all of us at Dimitri's for dinner.

Before we left for home, John's brother Joe took John and I out to see Rosemary. Now she was in a nursing home, her care needs too much for the foster home. Rosemary had a roommate who was suspicious of the three of us from the start. Joe went through Rosemary's dresser drawer looking for some photographs he wanted to show all of us, but her roommate told him to leave the stuff alone and called out to alert the staff who tried to explain that Rosemary had family visiting. This didn't make much difference, though. The woman kept on hounding us. Rosemary had that not-good look that I had become too familiar with, and I thought to myself that this might be the last time John would be seeing his sister.

In September 2012, I started my writing. I had done what I told myself to do and that was to rest over the summer. It was starting to sink in that my county job was no longer a part of my life, and that was a great relief. I have stayed in touch with people I had worked with, though. I see them at my dance class or out and about. Our old team gets together occasionally. We have all moved on in some way or another.

After Mom's bout with pneumonia, she returned to the facility but never fully recovered. There was a drastic change in her. Now she was completely sedentary. Her legs just gave out on her. Before the pneumonia, she had limped around on the bad leg—the one she had injured years ago in her ski accident. Her old spinal injury—the one she got while washing windows in preparation for my wedding—came back to haunt her too. The doctors told her it was all wear and tear, and there wasn't much they could do about any of it. She remained stoic about the pain and inconvenience, though. With her incontinence, she was always aware that she needed to go but didn't have the strength or wherewithal to do anything about it. Sometimes she would become frantic and yell for someone to get her to the toilet, but it never seemed to be soon enough. Finally, she seemed to accept her fate. She would announce what was occurring below her belt and then just wait for someone to do something about it.

Mom was always happy to see me. This time with her may have been the most intimate that I ever had with her. She expressed her feelings more freely than she ever had. She was cordial most of the time. On bad days, she would say she didn't feel well. As time passed, she spoke less of Dad. However, when the time came that she seemed to anticipate her end, she mentioned him to caregivers. They would tell me that she told them she would be with "Bobby" soon enough. Sometimes she saw him or talked to him. She didn't tell me or her other kids any of this, though. I have wondered if she thought her mention of her demise might upset us. Maybe it was better to tell caregivers such things—people who might not be as sensitive to the topic. But as time marched on, Mom's brain appeared to have gone more adrift. She'd say things that made no sense at all. She often couldn't track a conversation. Other times, there was an agitation to her. It just seemed she was uncomfortable but couldn't explain why. For a long time, she had been shying away from most food. The only thing that appealed to her now was dessert, and after a while, that is all she would eat. No amount of encouragement would help. Other changes were insidious.

In April, I learned of the death of a St. Francis School chum, Arlie. He was the one I had a crush on in the sixth grade and whom I had horsed around with out on the playground. Over the years, I had run into him around town. He had married, raised a family, and was a schoolteacher. He had never left Bend other than to attend college. One of the last times I saw him was at a local restaurant in the Old Mill District. He was there with his ex-wife. There had been rumors about an affair that had contributed to a breakup but that, at some point, the two had reconciled and remained friends in spite of "the other." I didn't think much about this story other than that it sounded a little like my own. I wasn't even sure the rumor was true other than that they had divorced. Anyway, I attended the funeral. The church was full when I got there, with standing room only. There were many old St. Francis, Cascade Junior High, and Bend High cohorts there. Before the mass started, I found myself standing in the back of the church next to another St. Francis chum from my class. Tom and I stood at the back of the church and talked before the mass started. He told me that when he arrived at the church, ushers had tried to escort him up to the choir loft because of the overcrowded church. He said there was no way he was ever going back up there again, and he told the ushers so. The reason why, he explained, was that the nuns had never allowed him to sing in the choir way back when. He remembered Sister what's-her-name listening to the choir from the church nave downstairs during practice sessions on school days. Then she would ascend the stairs to the choir loft and point to the students she didn't think had good enough voices to sing, and Tom had been one of them. I was surprised by his revelation, and it was only after he described his memory that I remembered it that way too. All that had been saved in my mind previous to that point was that I had been the only one instructed to merely mouth the words to the song but not utter a tune.

The reception for Arlie was at McMenamins Old St. Francis Pub—the old St. Francis School. It was just like old times other than the fact that Arlie and others in our class were gone. A few weeks later, I was talking to a friend at my dance class about Arlie. She was a teacher who knew him well, and she told me that he had died of complications from ulcerative colitis—a form of liver failure that sometimes occurs. I told my friend that I suffered from the same disease. It all made me think how Arlie's and my lives had gone down some sort of parallel path without our ever being aware of it, even Tom, who had suffered the same humiliation in the church I had, and I didn't know of it until Arlie's funeral. It made me think how much of others' lives are kept from us.

Nora and I had planned our summer vacations. Nora was to visit Sandy in West Virginia with her three girls after school let out. They were to spend the first week or so with Dave and Sandy and take day trips to nearby historical sites. Then Todd would fly out to meet them, and they would head north to other destinations on their own. John and I had secured reservations for the East Coast trip again too. All this was done before Mom's frightening and sudden decline. Nora and I were on the phone almost daily to try to decide what to do. We also consulted with the hospice nurse who had also been with Dad. Even she was unsure but speculated that it would be weeks—whatever that meant. Doug encouraged us to go. He said he would hold down the fort. So we did, but our trepidation stayed along with us while we were away.

John and I went to NYC first. We spent our time in Little Italy and then at Central Park and the Metropolitan Museum of Art. This year, I had decided that the girls might like Torrington, with its haunted Yankee Pedlar. When John and I had asked about the cost a few years earlier, a night was only twenty-four dollars or so. Now it was up to the nineties. Sage and Mya explained that there had been a television show about the supernatural nature of the old hotel, and this had made the place more noteworthy and thus more expensive. The girls were into ghost stuff, so they thought the idea of a night there sounded fun. We all spent the night, and the next morning, they announced that they hadn't spotted any ghosts. I didn't either, but I'll have to say the place was still a little spooky. The next day, we all drove up to see the Norman Rockwell Museum, which was a big hit with everyone. The remainder of our trip was spent with John's family and at the lake. Before we left, John's brother Joe escorted us to the nursing home where their sister Rosemary had been for the past couple of years. This time, she looked even worse than the year before. It was difficult to engage her at all. She maintained a bewildered look throughout our visit. This time, when John said he didn't think she recognized her brothers, I think he might have been right. But with this visit, it seemed John was resigned to his sister's decline, and he made it through without as much distress as the year before. Now Rosemary was on hospice services, which led me to believe that we wouldn't be seeing her again.

One of the last things we did in Connecticut before we left for Oregon was to go to the drive-in. We had gone on previous trips but not for the past few. It was only a few miles from Coventry Lake, out in a field, and had three different screens, a playground for the kids, and an old-fashioned concession stand. The evening was balmy. We got there early to get a good spot, which allowed us to observe the activity all around us. People spread out blankets on the grass or sat on lawn chairs or in their open hatchback or pickup beds they had facing the screen. Some adolescents played Frisbee. Parents watched over their kids on the playground. There were pizzas and all other sorts of food all around. I went to the concession stand to purchase some drinks, and there were bottles of birch beer for sale. I bought a bottle for each of us and headed back to the car. John was thrilled with the find. He said he hadn't seen birch beer since he was a kid. It tasted great. We watched lines of cars heading toward the ticket booth as the sky dimmed and headlights were mostly all we saw of the line of cars. They kept coming until the entire field was full—cars facing whichever movie screen they had paid to see. It was a glorious evening and the movie was OK.

Nora and I arrived back in Oregon about the same time. We had succeeded in getting back without anything occurring with Mom. But when I got home, things didn't look so good. I called Nora, and she came right up to Bend from Medford. This was the beginning of a scenario very similar to what had occurred with Dad. I called Byron to let him know it was nearing the end, and he said he wanted to return to Bend when the time came. When Nora arrived, we both figured this was it. Mom looked terrible. But the next day, she rallied. She was alert, pleasant, and in fact, she looked like a different person altogether. So Nora went home. Things went on this way for a while. But it came to the point where there was little doubt that Mom wouldn't make it much longer.

Doug, Diane, and I went over to visit on Sunday, September 15, 2013. We took Mom into the Country Kitchen, a semiprivate dining room that the staff lets families use for more private visits. Doug often had trouble communicating with Mom anyway, but in her altered state, it was worse. When we visited, he usually talked about what he'd been up to, which didn't seem to interest her in the least. Or he would talk to whoever else happened to be around—

me, his wife, the staff, etc. I don't think he recognized that Mom picked up on this, but she did, and it irritated her. I understood Doug's difficulty with Mom, though. She had always tended to live within herself. But now that she was bonkers, it was even more difficult to carry on any kind of normal conversation with her. I tried my best to bring up the old days, take photo albums in and such. Sometimes this worked, and other times, she would get in a loop and repeat the same question over and over. I'd often changed up my answer to stave off boredom, and she never seemed to notice. Other times, she just wasn't interested in anything I had to offer. On this particular visit with her, Doug pulled out his smartphone and suggested he call her brother Norbert so they could chat. It was his birthday after all. But Mom said she didn't want to talk to Norbert. In fact, for some time now, she hadn't wanted to. We kids had speculated about this change. She had always adored Norbert. He made a habit of calling her every week since she and Dad had been in the facility, but Norbert had started complaining that no one ever picked up when he tried to call. If he did get through, Mom didn't say much. This complaint was heard from Sandy too. I think Mom not being able to see the person on the other end made a difference. It was as though she couldn't figure out how she could hear someone's voice without seeing them. Well, Doug called Norbert anyway. I think he thought this might be one of the last chances the two would have to talk to each other. Doug put Norbert on speaker phone and talked to him. Mom refused to take the phone so Doug handed it over to me. All the while, Mom looked unhappy and neglected and remained so the rest of the visit.

The next weekend, Doug begged off going. Cam and Jing had come from Eugene to see Mom. They were staying with Leo. I asked Leo if he wanted to visit, and he agreed to come along. I expected this might be one of the last times any of us would have the opportunity to see her. When we got there, Leo wheeled Mom into the Country Kitchen. I noticed right away that something wasn't right with her. She kept fiddling with her sweater, complaining that she couldn't button it properly. But the sweater didn't have buttons, and I told her so. That didn't stop her from continuing to try to button it, though. No amount of cajoling could distract her. Jing, who was twelve, just looked at Mom. I don't think he got it, and I also think he was somewhat perplexed by the whole experience. In the middle of all this, though, Mom gravitated to a conversation with Leo. I don't remember what they talked about, but Leo seemed to have a better rapport with Mom than any of her kids. Out of the blue, she asked him if he had one of those fancy new phones like Doug had. He said no. Then she said, "Well, good. No one will be talking to Norbert today then." I was surprised she even remembered the week before, and I sensed that she was holding on to some resentment about Doug's attempt to have her talk to her brother. I also became aware that she likely resented the attention Doug and I had paid her brother the week before. So this week, we all tried to think of ways to include her in our conversation. It wasn't easy, though. She continued to behave in an odd sort of agitated manner and remained fixated on her sweater. I noticed myself feeling irritated with her—an emotion I would come to regret. Cam tried to help her with her sweater too, but to no avail. He suggested that we get her another one, so I offered to go to her room and find one. I also asked her if she was cold, and she said she was, so when I went to her room to get another sweater, I grabbed a blanket too and made sure the sweater had buttons. When I got back, I replaced the button-less sweater with the button-full sweater, put the blanket over her legs, and buttoned the sweater for her. This didn't help much either, though. She continued to fiddle with the buttons, complaining that they were buttoned wrong. I started to suspect that she was having not only delusions but probable hallucinations as well. It didn't entirely dissipate my irritation, but underneath it all, I think there was dread. It was about all I could take of her, and so I wheeled her back to the dining room where she was fawned over by the staff and where she continued to fiddle with her sweater. They confided in me that this sort of thing had been going on for the past few days. This would be the last time I would see her in a lucid state.

It was September 29. Doug and I both got a call from the facility and the hospice nurse that Mom had taken another turn for the worse. Now she was in her bed and stayed there just as Dad had. Doug and I made the necessary calls, and family would come. Doug and I drove to the facility and sat with Mom all day. Diane and Andrea came and went. The rest were on their way. Nora arrived from Medford in the afternoon. Mom was really not responsive most of the time. Occasionally, she would open her eyes and look around. We heeded what her hospice nurse suggested and talked to her anyway. Doug and Diane didn't anticipate a quick end, so they had gone home for the night. I told Nora I was going to get something to eat and then return, as I had been there all day. I went to Leo's house to fill him in. He prepared a quick meal for me, but while I was having my dinner, Nora called and didn't sound good. She cried. I asked if I should come right back, and she said yes. She told me through sobs that she thought Mom was very near the end, and she was afraid to be there alone with her. I went right back, and when I saw Mom, I knew Nora was right. It was curious how similar Mom's appearance was to Dad's in his throes of death. Mom had the same skeletal look about her and the same shallow labored breathing. But with her, something did seem different. She had a look of fear to her eyes. Dad hadn't. His eyes had looked clouded.

Nora and I sat by Mom's bed. We cried and talked to her. Now she seemed wide awake, her breathing becoming more and more shallow and labored. It sounded much like a little dog's panting. She looked back and forth at the both of us with intense eyes. We told her we loved her. Nora told her through sobs that she could let go and be with Dad. A few minutes later, her head shot straight up toward the ceiling with an intense gaze. Her eyes had a brightness like I'd never seen before. It was as if she was seeing something that filled her with awe. She held this gaze for some time, and then suddenly, she averted her attention and stared first at Nora and then at me. Her eyes still had that bright, intense look to them. Her mouth started to move as if it was made of rubber, and with great effort, she seemed to be making an attempt to speak to me. She stared at me and her mouth kept moving in this gyrating manner, but no sound was ever uttered. And then she was gone. I didn't trust that she was gone right away, though. The whole experience had been so surreal that I didn't trust my senses. I half expected her eyes, that had suddenly turned dull and unfocused, to resume their life and intensity. But that didn't happen. Nora had called Doug right after she had called me, but by the time he and Diane arrived, it was too late. It had all happened that fast. I called Leo and asked if he wanted to come over. He cried and said he couldn't and that he was sorry he couldn't be there for me. I said that was OK. The four of us sat quietly around the bed and waited for the mortician. Mom had received her last rites a few weeks earlier.

Diane and I left the room so that the mortician could prepare Mom's body for transport. Nora and Doug remained. We sat in one of the studies down the hall. Diane called her family and walked the hallway while on her cell phone. When she returned, she told me that one of the residents had pulled his pants down and peed in one of the planters. His pants were still around his ankles when I looked down the hallway. We couldn't help but chuckle a little. She alerted one of the staff about the old guy's predicament. I had appreciated all the love and care Mom and Dad had received here, but part of me was glad about not having to be around all this for a while. It was all very sad.

The next day, Doug, Nora, and I went out for lunch together and then went shopping for Mom. It was Doug who wanted to make sure she had a brand new outfit. It was the most intimate thing we did together for her. We looked through some of the ladies' shops at the Old Mill District. I talked them into looking at J. Jill. (I bought her things there for the past several years, some of which she would actually wear. She hadn't always been pleased with some of my purchases for her). We found the nicest outfit—a flowered sweater with fall colors, an ivory silk blouse, dark olive slacks, and a bright paisley scarf. Doug was the one who spotted it, and it finished off the whole look. He also wanted her to wear her brown Ferragamo shoes even though no one would see them in the casket. (She had an assortment of these shoes in different colors that sat in her closet, unused over the past few years. She had resorted to wearing only slippers even when she went to her doctor's appointments). I felt good about knowing she would be well dressed at her own funeral and later, there next to Dad in his snazzy suit and tie. One of the girls at the facility had given her a rosary after Dad died, and it had been placed around her neck while she was on her death bed. We decided she should be buried with it. (The rosary that Doug had placed on Dad's chest before he died had disappeared that evening, as I've mentioned. While all of us had gone for dinner, it had gone missing. Doug fretted about it for days afterward, as it had been a keepsake given to him by Dad and passed down from his father. A few weeks later we asked about the rosary. One of the staff had an idea where it might be. She said that Mom liked to collect things in her purse—an item she had to have with her at all times and that she fretted about if it was out of sight. So we went to Mom's room to look through her purse and, among other things, there was the rosary. She must have put it in her purse the night Dad died while we were gone for dinner and she was alone with him. I wondered if it felt like a keepsake to her, recognizing on some level that Dad would be departing soon. I also wondered, during the time she had been alone with him, what might have transpired between them). We gathered a few other things to place in her casket—a photograph of Dad in his sailor suit with a kiss mark she had left on the photo years earlier, and her purse, which we felt she would fret about if it wasn't right next to her wherever she would be.

Before Mom died, John and I had planned a weekend trip to the beach. Sandy and Dave purchased a condo there for their retirement, and she had given me a key to use it for free. Mom's death made me reluctant to go ahead with our plans, but Doug suggested we go, as we had completed all the plans for the funeral. So John and I shortened the mini-vacation and headed out to the coast a few days before the funeral. I was having some eye problems and had been diagnosed with latent tuberculosis, probably related to the immunosuppressive treatment for my disease and maybe my having worked with vulnerable people during my years with the county. After the tuberculosis diagnosis, I was placed on medication to prevent it from becoming active. It has to be taken for nine months and has side effects and food restrictions during its use. One potential side effect is a stroke. This can occur because the medication can prevent the body from discarding a substance called tyramine that is found in certain food and drink. A substantial buildup of tyramine can cause the blood pressure to become severely elevated, which can lead to stroke. Needless to say, I was cautious about what I ate. A few days before we left, I had noticed a red circle impeding my vision in my right eye. Even when I closed my eye, it was still there, but it would come and go. I called my TB doctor, but I missed her return call in my hurry to get ready to leave. I had hoped it would be gone by the next day, but it wasn't, so before I left town, I called my optometrist and went a few blocks to his office. He said he thought it was a migraine symptom. I had been diagnosed with non-painful migraine in the past. A pulsing star would appear to impede my vision and remain even when I closed my eyes. It usually remained about twenty to thirty minutes and would then dissipate. This red circle seemed different to me, but I was anxious to get out of town for what I hoped to be a relaxing few days before the funeral onslaught. Before I left town, I called Nora to check in with her, and she didn't sound right. I asked her if everything was OK, and she said no. She told me that her best friend had just been diagnosed with ovarian cancer, and the level of the disease wasn't good. Nora had driven up to Portland a few times to be with her friend. I told her that I was heading for the beach before the funeral and that I'd see her in a few days.

So off we went. As we started into Salem and headed toward the beach, I noticed that the red circle had reappeared, and now there was a dark translucent curtain to accompany it. I decided to call my TB doctor, just in case. I left a message for her, and just after we got through Salem, she called back. I described my symptoms to her, and she told me to get to the closest ER right away. She said that would be Salem. We turned around, and John and I drove around Salem looking for the hospital, but the signs were confusing, so we parked the car and walked around town asking for directions. A young woman escorted us to a business establishment that she said would be able to help, and we were given instructions to the hospital. When we got there, we could see the hospital, but it was like a maze and difficult to determine where we were supposed to park. He let me off in front and left to find a parking place where the car wouldn't be towed. Meanwhile, I started the process of getting checked in. The waiting room was quiet after he joined me, but as time went by, more and more people piled in. While we waited, a tall attractive young man came barreling out of the emergency room doors, yelling for everyone to take cover and then ran out the front doors of the hospital. Everyone in the waiting room ducked under furniture or ran to the back of the room. I was half expecting some wild-eyed maniac to start shooting any minute, but we found out later that the maniac was, in fact, the man who had run through the waiting room. I found this out while we were escorted to the examination room. I asked the staff about the incident and was told that the man was a frequent flyer at the hospital. All in all, we were there for six hours. I had all sorts of tests done and was told it didn't appear to be a stroke but to follow up with my ophthalmologist and internist after my return to Bend. We were both too tired to consider the coast at this point, so we found a hotel, spent the night, and drove back to Bend the next morning. I called Nora after I got home, and she asked how my beach trip had been. I told her all about the fiasco and my visit to the ER. Then she told me that she too had been in the ER with Todd during the same time. He had collapsed on the field during a softball game. She got a call from one of the team members, and she had rushed to the hospital. It was discovered that he had some sort of heart condition that would need surgery, and the sooner the better.

The next few days, family gathered for the funeral—Cameron came from Springfield, Sandy and Dave from West Virginia, Byron from Connecticut, Todd and the girls from Medford, Cindy and Gary from Chicago. Diane's parents were also there. The evening before the funeral, Doug and Diane had family over to their house. Cindy told me about her daughter Liz's plans to travel to Slovenija with her husband and baby in the fall. Liz had married a Croatian, Dominic Sepich, so they would be visiting his relations in Croatia too. I was glad that this new generation was still keeping in touch with our relatives abroad.

The next day was Mom's funeral mass at the old St. Francis Church. The viewing and the Rosary beforehand were for family only. Others trickled in afterward for the mass. The older one gets, it seems the fewer people attend one's funeral, and this was the case with Mom. Dad had always been more outgoing, and Mom was the introvert. Her social circle had revolved mostly around Dad. Four of the picnic group ladies who were still alive were in attendance. One of Dad's doctor friends and his wife showed up at the church as well as two of his ex-partners. My friend Peggy sat in the back pew. I was touched that she had come. She never really knew my mother, so I felt it had been for my benefit. Nora's best friend came too. There were some others. When we went out to the cemetery, there was Mom's place next to Dad, a big hole in the ground. They shared the same headstone, and soon they would be lying next to each other. The reception at The River House (where Mom and Dad had enjoyed brunches together on Sundays in better days) was even more poorly attended than the service. It was mostly family and a few others. Then it was all over.

Shortly after Mom's death, I asked Doug if I could come up and take a look at the family photo albums he had been storing since Mom and Dad moved out of the Ninth Street house. He invited me up for dinner, and we looked through the albums together. I was looking for photos for my book, but it was just fun to see how life had been before our parents had gone to pot. It had been so long since we had seen them in a good state that we had almost forgotten what they had been like. But the most amazing thing about the evening was finding the album that didn't contain pictures at all. In it were love poems Dad had written Mom over a span of fifty years. We all knew of Dad's bent for poetry writing. He had written ditties in our beach spot journals almost since the hotel's inception in 1970. One time, Leo had photographed Dad's poems in the journals, which are still in the apartments that we've visited for so many years. It wasn't difficult to find Dad's poems because of his very distinctive cursive, except that the longtime owner of Unit 6 (my favorite unit) had a very surprisingly similar cursive and writing style. His sentiments were also very similar to Dad's, and I felt that I got to know the man through his entries in the journal in spite of the fact that I never met him. His wife had been a poet herself. She was taken with the tranquility of the place too, and some of her poems are about just that. The poems she wrote in her last chapter about her twilight years were the most powerful though. This was after she started losing her eyesight and felt her mortality.[40] I felt a connection with her too. After their deaths, a few of the adult children decided to keep the place rather than sell it. They placed a book of their mother's poetry on the coffee table in the living room for guests. When I next visited, I read her poetry book.

Anyway, I started reading the poems in the newly discovered album at Doug's house. I was blown away. I had Doug read a few, but he just couldn't do it. As the days went by and I got through

[39] Mary Hyatt Day, A Song of Myself: A Collection of Poems, October 2004 (Unpublished).

them all, they provided me with a new perspective on my parents' relationship.

I usually spend weekend nights at John's house. I have my own bedroom there because I've always been an insomniac and a light sleeper, while John's a restless sleeper—not a good combination. It was a few weeks after Mom's death. We made dinner together and watched a movie on television. I always spend a little time in bed with him before I go to my bedroom for the night. Then I headed to my side of the house. Both bedrooms are on the second floor. I had just gotten in bed and turned toward the bedroom door. The room is normally pitch-black after I turn off the lamp on the side table. But this time, there was a bright light coming from the closet on either side of the two sliding doors. The closet is shallow—only enough room for a row of clothing to hang on a rod. There are also a few shelves for storage above the clothing rod. I was quizzical about the light. I hadn't been aware of any light source in the closet but thought maybe I had just never noticed one before. Maybe it got turned on by mistake somehow. So I got up and turned on the overhead light in the room. I opened the sliding doors of the closet and inspected the ceiling and all around. I took everything out just to make sure, but there just wasn't any hidden light source there. Then I turned the overhead light back off and looked to the window to see if anything could be shining in from there, but there wasn't. I decided not to worry about it, but when I turned to look back at the closet doors expecting everything to be dark again, there it was again—the bright light coming from the sides of the sliding doors. I got up again and repeated what I had done the first time, but with the same result—nothing. I got back in bed and turned out the light again. This time I felt uneasy about looking in that direction again, but I did. Now the light on either side of the closet sliders was gone, but there was a luminescent little cloud right above the closed bedroom door. It hovered there—the only light at all in the room, which was now otherwise pitch-black. I ran out of the room. I knew at this point that my mother had been to visit me, but the thought hadn't occurred to me until just then. I felt petrified. I ran into John's room and told him what had happened. I knew he thought I was crazy. He said it must have been an illusion of some sort, but I knew better. I was so afraid that I couldn't go back into my bedroom. First, I tried to sleep with him, which sure didn't work out. Then I tried piling up blankets on the far end of his bedroom, but this didn't work either, so I went out on a love seat on the landing and threw blankets and pillows down. I was up most of the night.

The next day, I questioned my fear. Why would I be so afraid of my mother's presence? I didn't expect she would want to harm me. After contemplating the whole thing, I came to believe that she hadn't been able to communicate what she wanted to on her deathbed—I remembered the struggle she had made to speak to me. So she had come back to let me know she was still with me but in another form—one that only those who have left this world understand. I also decided that she picked John's home rather than my own so that I would have his comfort if her presence did in fact frighten me. But then another thought crossed my mind—she was still silent as she always had been inside the closet—the light emanating from around the door's corners were the only sign of her presence. But then who was I to talk.

All this contemplation did prevent me from returning to my bedroom, though. I slept elsewhere for some time, and after a few weeks, I returned, but I still leave the door open and the bathroom light on down the hallway. Without doing so, I feel a sense of claustrophobia. I guess the experience has just been too surreal to feel at ease with it and also left me with the same feeling I always had about Mom. It was all smoke and mirrors. I never really got to know her as I would have liked, and now she had sort of made an appearance but not entirely. Not long after, John started reading the book by Billy Crystal, Still Foolin' 'Em. John showed me the excerpt from the book where Billy describes a similar occurrence to mine, only his apparition appeared and spoke to him. He tells of his concern that if he mentions his experience, others will think he's nuts, but he knows better and doesn't care if others don't believe him.[41] He knows what he saw. And that's how it is. After John read this excerpt, he seemed more accepting of my insistence that something really did occur with my mother in the bedroom. It brought back memories of a professor he had in graduate school named Kenneth Ring. The psychologist was doing qualitative research on near-death experiences. John recalled how influenced he was by his professor's lectures on the topic, and so he bought and read the first book that came out about a year later—Life at Death. We went up to Portland for a weekend and found a few of the author's books at Powell's that were available and bought them. I ordered a few more on Amazon, and we both started reading them all. They were very helpful in validating the experiences I had during my parents' deaths and also mystical experiences I've had of my own.

Not long after the bedroom incident, there was another peculiar happening. When Nora had visited Sandy in the summer, Sandy told her she was getting rid of the family dining table that she had inherited after Mom and Dad moved out of the Ninth Street house. This is when they gave a lot of their belongings to us kids. Nora thought the dining set, which had been witness to many family meals and holidays, should remain in the family, so she called around to see if anyone wanted it. She didn't have room,

---

[41] Billy Crystal, Still Foolin''Em (Henry Hold and Company, LLC, 2013),245–246.

and neither did I. Doug inherited our grandparents' dining set, so Nora called Leo. He had sat around it as we had since he was fifteen, after he and I started dating. He decided he would make room for it. The trick was to get it to Bend from West Virginia, but it arrived a few weeks later, unscathed. Leo made it look brand new and remodeled his house to accommodate the set. He called to let me know that the chairs seemed to have gone catawampus every so often, but at first, he hadn't thought much of it and would rearrange them. On one particular night, he made sure to push each chair in around the table. The next morning, he walked down the hallway from his bedroom, and the first thing he noticed as he entered the dining area was that the two chairs Mom and Dad had claimed during their years with the set were pushed way out and facing each other, as if they sat in their places, departed, and then just left them pushed away from the table. Leo decided that he had had visitors during the night and said they were welcome anytime.

Sandy had a weird story of her own that she just recently described to me. It too was shortly after Mom's death. She started noticing that every time she walked across her kitchen tile, it felt as though there was grit or crumbs underfoot, so she would mop the floor thoroughly. If that didn't suffice, then she took her shoes off and wiped them off too. None of this seemed to take care of the problem, and no matter what she did, she felt the grit underfoot. This sensation continued every time she walked on the kitchen floor for a few weeks and then never happened again. Later on, she recalled Mom being perturbed anytime the kitchen floor wasn't spotless and cleaning the floor whenever she thought it was soiled. Sandy confided that she knew she wasn't imagining the sensation of the grit on her own floor and decided that Mom had paid her a visit too.

I had called Pietro after Dad's death to let him know. I also called him about Mom on November 11. It was good to hear his voice. He expressed his condolences. I knew he would be able to recognize my remorse because of his close though complicated relationship with his own mother. He went on to tell of the poor conditions in Italy. "There are no jobs," he had explained, and this was leading to his having to search elsewhere—maybe Germany or England again. I could hear his little boy babbling in the background and Pietro laughing and talking back affectionately to him. I asked about his marriage, and he said, "We fight a lot" and laughed after this comment too. He asked if I had the same boyfriend, and I said yes.

John had been having trouble with his hip for over a year, and it was getting difficult to sleep or walk due to pain, so a hip replacement was scheduled for December 20. Nora was able to arrange for Todd to have his heart surgery done in Bend on December 7, and they would all stay at the condo while he recuperated. Todd got through it all but had to remain in the hospital for about a week and then stayed with his brother for his rehabilitation before he could go home. It was about this time that John went in for his surgery. The whole experience was scary. Before he left the hospital, I gathered all the items that would be needed for his recuperation. I'm not exactly the nurse type, but I tried my best. He had to wear a contraption on his legs after he got home. There were wires all around and I had to fit both legs with a motorized compression wrap. He had to wear the controls around his neck. The purpose was to reduce the risk of blood clots. The weirdest thing was the noise it made as one leg's wrap would contract and then the other. It sounded like the thing was alive. I stayed at his house the first three weeks. He couldn't do much on his own but gradually got better. What's discouraging is that other joints seem to be going south too. Both of us have been in touch with our mortality. You start to have a different perspective for sure.

I took stock of all the deaths that had occurred around the time of my parents' demises. It was curious to me. I hadn't expected such a flurry of activity of this sort. There was Mike M.'s death in February 2012, a few months before Dad died. He was Sandy's ex-husband Mark's best friend in high school, the one who had gone on the double date with Mark, Sandy, and Sandy's nymphomaniac college friend. Over the years, I'd visit him when he worked at the service station down the street. The guys there were all characters, which made it fun to get my tank filled there. Later, he found work at the hospital and then as a clerk at Sears. He married a divorcee later in life who had a couple of kids. He seemed happy. He went in for a routine surgery and never came back. His service was out at the grave site on Highway 97, in bitter cold weather. Then, as I've mentioned, there was Arlie in April 2013, one year after Dad's death and a few months before Mom's.

In December, I got a call from Doug. He had received a call about Sandy's ex-husband Mark from his sister, Kim, who told Doug that Mark had died on Christmas Eve. According to Kim, he was on his way home from work in DC on July 18 (Mom's birthday) and had fallen onto the TriMet Train tracks and was run over. He survived the accident but spent months in the hospital recuperating and developed a series of infections. He had been newly married a few years earlier after years of the single life after his divorce from Sandy. He spent months away from work, at home, after he was discharged from the hospital with continuing complications, depressed and discouraged. His wife found him dead after she returned from work on the evening of December 24. Doug told me he worried about what Sandy's reaction to the news might be, but he called her anyway. So did Mark's sister and numerous old mutual friends of her and Mark's. She was really heartbroken about his death and called me for weeks afterward to reminisce and to express her own feelings of guilt for their failed marriage years earlier. I told her that I thought she had made the right decision in her leaving him in spite of the fact that I always liked Mark. I wouldn't have wanted to live with him, though, nor did I think Sandy should have had to live with his dark moods and drinking. There was something particularly sad about his passing for her and for me too. I think it's because of some of the tragic nature of his life and because his brilliance in his career didn't necessarily make up for his suffering and also because neither he nor Sandy ever really got over each other, and there had been such potential in the beginning. It also seemed that maybe he would have a chance at happiness again with his new wife, but if this occurred, it was short lived. A few months later, Kim posted an obituary in the Bend newspaper and sent a copy to Sandy. In it, was mention of their high school romance and marriage.

I hadn't seen my friend Jan C. (from my Seattle U days) for several years. She called out of the blue a few years back. She was one of the bridesmaids at my wedding. She and Eric were planning their retirement, and they were reconnecting with old friends from the past. We talked about getting together. About six months after her first call, she called again and told me that she had collapsed while on a cross-country ski outing with Eric. Her legs had just buckled underneath her. He had taken her to the hospital, where tests were done, and she was diagnosed with a malignant brain tumor—the same kind that Ted Kennedy had. Eric had a conference coming up in Bend, and so Jan and I planned a get-together while he was attending the conference. He dropped her off at my house for the day. She wasn't driving any longer. We spent the day looking through Seattle U yearbooks, called our friend Lynn who, Jan explained, also had cancer, was still working to keep her insurance, and also taking care of her ailing mother. We went to lunch, and then John and I met her and Eric for dinner that night. Jan couldn't see well, had difficulty walking, and she described having difficulty with her memory and speech. All this was apparent during the time we spent with her. I got a call from Eric in November 2013. He said that she was now bedbound and no longer very communicative. In December, he called to say the end was near, and in January, he called again to say that she had died and that a memorial would be held in March. I said I would try to make it. John and I traveled over. We got lost looking for the Catholic church in Aumsville, found a hotel this side of Salem, checked in, and got directions to the church. We hadn't eaten, and the hotel offered a discount coupon at Denny's, so we headed over. It was across the parking lot. The place was packed, and it took forever to get our meal.

By the time we got to the parish hall for the memorial service, we were already an hour late. We missed the readings, which wasn't all that much of a disappointment. The first thing we noticed upon entering the parish hall was the slide show. A celebration of life type of gathering—in style on the West Coast as opposed to the more traditional rites in the Midwest and East Coast—was underway. I rather prefer the traditional funeral, but the one thing I like about the more casual West Coast thing is the mandatory slide show. The family gathers pictures and slides of the loved one's life are presented on large screens. In this case, there were all manner of representation of Jan's life events and stages. They were joyful.

When Eric saw me, he came up with a smile and a hug. I apologized for our being tardy. There were a few people I hoped to see there. I scanned the crowd and recognized some of the faces. One was Joel, Jan's eldest. I introduced myself, and he remembered me. He introduced me to a friend of his sitting at a table next to him, saying, "This is my friend who barfed on your couch that time." I asked his friend if he remembered the event, and he said he did, and the main thing he remembered was how embarrassed he had been. This was when they visited us once when our boys were in pubescence. The next faces I recognized were Jan's brothers, standing next to each other. They resembled her. She had arranged a blind date for me with one of them while we were in college together. I wasn't sure which of the two had been my date, so I approached the one closest to me. The brother she hooked me up with had attended the University of Washington, and the other was older and had gone to Seattle U. I said that I thought maybe we had gone on a date years ago. He started laughing and described his memory of it—we had gone to a Planet of the Apes movie marathon, and then after we got back to his car, someone in the dark had peered into the window at me. I had shrieked from fright. He added that he didn't think he had been a very thoughtful date, but I barely remembered what he had been like. What I did remember very clearly was his providing a tour of his fraternity and my observing students sitting, lined up against a wall in an upstairs bedroom with strobe lights and psychedelic music playing. They all seemed wasted and out of it. It was disturbing to me at the time and reminded me of Haight-Ashbury with Dad a few years earlier. I told him that's what had really scared me that night. He commented that he could understand that given the difference between Seattle U and U of Washington, with the latter being the much more liberal school. (I remember at the time being glad I had chosen SU because I had looked at U of W with my folks and thought it too big and intimidating.) I asked who the girl next to his brother was. He said, "That's my daughter." She was the spitting image of Jan. She came over with her partner, and we talked. She commented that she was glad things hadn't worked out with her dad and me. I said that she had nothing to worry about—that her aunt had arranged the date and there had never been any signs of attraction during our one date, only mild discomfort.

John and I returned to the hotel and watched some TV before we went to bed. Our plans had been to get up and have the free breakfast at Denny's that the hotel provided and then head over for the funeral mass and buffet afterward. The next morning, we both woke up at 10:40 a.m., and the funeral mass started at 11:00 a.m. John never uses an alarm clock because he always wakes early on his own. But here it was. We scrambled around the room in semi-conscious states—so much for the free Denny's breakfast. We drove to the church and sneaked in the back row. We had managed to make it by 11:15 a.m. in spite of everything, but it was embarrassing being late two days in a row. Eric got up at the end of mass to give a moving commentary of Jan's life while maintaining his composure and without shedding a tear. After mass, the burial ground was on the church property. Jan had been cremated, so the urn was her coffin. Then we proceeded to the parish hall again for the buffet.

Eric told me that a friend of ours, Jerry, was expected to be present at this gathering, so I looked for his face in the crowd and recognized him almost immediately. He had been a friend of Jan and Eric's during college. They had arranged a date for Jerry and me because Jerry had a girlfriend out of state and I had a boyfriend out of state. They thought it would be fun to double date, so we did. On one particular night, we went over to Jerry and Eric's house. We drank wine and were up 'til four in the morning. By that time, Jan and Eric were an item, and their main interest that night was to make out. So Jerry and I found ourselves alone together, so what the heck. But our time together may have made him feel guilty or maybe just disinterested because after that evening, he became more formal and aloof with me, and I think it was the last time we went out together.

I asked John if he minded if I went over to talk to Jerry. When I approached him, Jerry smiled and gave me a hug. He said Eric had told him I might be here. I pointed out John sitting at a table across the room, and Jerry said that after he got something to eat, he would join us. He was pleasant, and I felt the three of us got along fine. He told of his career as a Lutheran minister and his uncle's gift of providing him the tuition he needed to continue on at Seattle University. He seemed to have been OK with it being a Catholic school in spite of his affiliation with the Lutheran Church. I asked about the girl he had been involved with in college—the long-distance romance—and he had, in fact, married her. She was a teacher. They had two boys, and she had died a few years back—just dropped dead of an aneurysm while teaching. He told of going into a depression after her death and also of still dealing with a difficult childhood—so he started writing poetry about all this and was published. He left his Lutheran ministry and started on a different course. I told Jerry that John had been in the seminary himself many years earlier. They discussed their experiences. Jerry told us that he was engaged again to a divorcee with grown children and whose husband had been unfaithful. Jerry said he was in awe of his fiancée who had been able to forgive her husband and even maintain a friendship with him after his betrayal of her. I wondered silently what he might have thought of me had he known of my past.

Over the next few months, there were several other funerals that I attended—close friends of my parents or their grown children. These gatherings presented themselves with additional reunions, and I came across people I hadn't seen in years. It was nice to see them again despite the circumstances. The past few years of experiencing my and others' health problems, deaths of my own friends and relations and my parents' friends and relations piled up within a relatively short period of time. And then we had a call about Rosemary. John's brother Paul called me on my cell phone while I was at John's over the weekend. He had been trying to reach John, but the line was busy. I called down to John from upstairs that his brother was on the phone for him about Rosemary, and he took the call. Paul told his brother that it looked like the end was near for Rosemary, and about a week later (April 9, 2014), the call came that she had died. When John called me with the news, I went over. He had a hard time with this loss. He dedicated a mass for her at the Old St. Francis Church that we attended together. When the priest announced Rosemary's name, John wept just as he had done upon hearing the news of his sister's death and when he read her obituary. The obituary family sent John described their sister as the family's angel on earth who provided her family with great joy.

Right after Rosemary's mass, John and I headed up to Portland to stay a few days and attend a concert with Jesse Cook and his band. We had seen him once about a year earlier. This time, we had seats right in front. The concert was stupendous. They played a mix of Cuban, African, Gypsy, Latin music—all my favorites. The band members were engaged with their audience, making the experience lively and energized. The music was haunting and hypnotic, the epitome of the life force itself—the guitars, drums, fiddle, flutes, and other instruments all harmonizing with a complex interaction. The haunting melody of the fiddle lent the music melancholy and depth. I felt alive. I wondered about the intensity of my emotional response to the music. I had always responded in a similar manner to like music-music that, I felt, put me in touch again with my heritage, antiquity, and emotional makeup.

The next day, we started out doing what we usually do in Portland— visiting Powell's Books, doing a little shopping, and finding a good restaurant. But this time, things were different than usual. John could barely get through a few hours of walking. His knee was so painful. We finally got back to the hotel, and he decided he couldn't make it to our favorite restaurant, usually about a fifteen-minute walk. We had to improvise. So we called for a cab. The cabbie spoke broken English and seemed not to understand where our destination was at first. And then we found ourselves in wall-to-wall traffic. While the meter kept adding up time, we remained stationary but finally inched our way about a block. The cabbie finally took an alternate route, which got us there in twice the time it would have taken to just walk. On the way back, the young female cabbie, with her dyed black hair and tattooed arms, empathized with John's infirmity. She told of a serious bicycle accident at age fourteen. She was in a coma, suffered multiple fractures, and still had manifestations of her accident. All in all, the experience had its merits. There was some humor attached to the initial slow cab ride with the language barrier to boot. And then there was the interesting young woman cabbie able to appreciate the suffering of John who, to her, must have seemed an old man.

After our return home, John told me about Rosemary's crush on Bobby Sherman, a teen idol of the 1960s and 1970s. I vaguely remembered who he was. I'm not sure what brought up the subject. Anyway, he said she put up a poster of her heartthrob on her bedroom wall and would exclaim to her brothers that she loved Bobby Sherman. As was usual, they teased her unmercifully. Paul would say "I hate Bobby Sherman," and then Rosemary would counter with "But I love him," and so it would go. John's telling me this story left us both whooping it up. It lay to rest (at least for a while) the somber state he had been in about his sister's death. During the upcoming summer visit to Connecticut and Coventry Lake, we would visit Rosemary's grave, one she shared with her parents.

John's favorite comedians are Lewis Black and Bill Maher, so we go see live performances whenever they are in our vicinity. (He also likes Stephen Colbert and Jon Stewart, but I don't think they travel around). The first time we saw Lewis Black, we were visiting family in Connecticut, and he was performing at Mohegan Sun casino. John invited his brothers and their wives to join us. Later on, we went to see the comedian in Portland, Oregon, at the Schnitzer. The first time we saw Bill Maher was also at the Schnitzer, but when we went to his show at the Britt in Jacksonville, Oregon, it was even better. We had great seats, the weather balmy in the outdoor venue. I thought of how connected we humans are. Min Yi had worked for him years earlier and even stopped by to see him during a visit to see her family in NYC with Cameron and their kids in tow. And here John and I were in the crowd across the country at his show. Motown is another favorite of ours, and we have seen The Temptations, the Four Tops, and Michael McDonald at the Britt too. We walked right by Michael standing next to his tour bus before the show started. And then last summer while in Connecticut, I went with Byron and family to Savers discount store. Angie and the girls ran around the gigantic discount store looking for deals on clothing, shoes, trinkets, and sundries. I remained in the front of the store with Byron and the rows of used books. I finally picked Don't Fall Off the Mountain by Shirley MacLaine to read in front of the lake. After I got home, I told Laura about the book—its tales of adventure and the author's interesting perspective on life. "Well," she replied, "she was at the Golden Globe party, don't you remember?" I told her no, I didn't, but she assured me that I had been the one who pointed the actress out to her. So I guess my preoccupation with the male celebrities there took precedence in my memory. But again, it all reminded me of how connected we all are. I had been in the same place with her without even remembering it.

Life seems different now. In some ways, this is the sweetest time in life. There's reflection, wisdom (I hope), and serenity. I think of all the people I've met along the way that have meant something to me and made life more meaningful. Some relationships true and enduring, some fleeting, and still others fleeting but still enduring. Losing touch and reconnecting or losing touch and never reconnecting. And a few I still despise. I reminisce about good times. I try to keep in touch with family and friends. I see the end in sight now for myself and others I care about. Something has changed for me in that the loved ones who have left this earth feel as though they're still with me. I find solace in other baby boomers that seem to stick together. Many of us are dealing with the same hardships—death of parents and other loved ones, illness, and infirmity. It's good to have understanding going back and forth. I told my mother on her deathbed that I was encouraged by Pope Francis and that I hoped he would take Catholicism in a new direction. I talked to my cousin Irma in Argentina right after he was appointed, and she was ecstatic. So John and I attend mass sometimes—once was a mass for my mother, one for a niece of his that died (Pascal's daughter), and another for his sister. I try to appreciate what I have left and do what seems important to me. I hope for the best. I still remember Dad contemplating his death in his later years. He would sometimes say he hoped that there would be nothing after he was gone. Maybe an afterlife seemed too complicated to him. But then years ago, he had waxed poetic about observations that led him to believe there is some sort of order and intelligence amidst the chaos in the universe—a supreme being. I also think his scientific/mathematical bent along with his spirituality led him to this conclusion. So I have wondered if he ever changed his opinion about an afterlife and if he found out for himself. I do know that my experiences with mystical events in the hours before and after my parents' deaths convinced me. And when my mother came to me with the light, it was the beginning of a spiritual awakening for me. I have confidence that when we meet again, I'll get to know her better.

Laura wrote to Leo on her Facebook page for Father's Day on June 15, 2014: "Thank you Dad for never grounding me, thank you for letting me be free. Thank you for riding It's a Small World 30 times over, and staying with me on cross country ski trips when I complained that my legs were broken. Thanks for comforting me, teaching me how to gut fish . . . thanks for wine and steak Fridays. Thanks for never encouraging me to love those silly guys that never loved me enough. Thanks for BBQ ribs and artichokes. Thanks for being strong and taking out slivers. I am happy you are in my life (not just because you give me loads of fish when you catch them, but thanks for that too). I love you, happy Father's Day." He responded, "Thank you . . . it wasn't hard with a special daughter like you."

Laura ran into her old grade school gym teacher the other day, Ms. B. In fact, the boys had her for gym class too. Ms. B is getting up in years, but that hasn't slowed her down much. She still runs wherever she goes, travels all over the world with any number friends—mostly male—who share her enthusiasm for rock climbing, bike riding, racing, running, you name it. Ms. B came in third in her age category in the Boston Marathon a number of years ago. She has been a fixture in Central Oregon, recognized by many because she literally runs everywhere she goes in her tennis skirt, halter top, sun visor, pom-pom socks, tennis shoes, and always with a big smile on her face. If she decides to pause for a chat, she continues to jog in place or runs circles around you as you converse. It's only in the most inclement of weather that she resorts to tights and a jacket. She told Laura that she had just run into someone who disapproved of her lifestyle in some form or manner and added that she has never cared much about what others might think of her. I am reminded of this when I recall Ms. B years ago at one of the Cascade Cycling events. There she was in her tennis dress, a bare midriff, etc. We chatted a few minutes, and then she jogged off as usual. Someone (a male who will remain unnamed) was next to me and made a snide remark that a woman "her age" ought not to dress and act that way. I suggested she ought to be any way she pleases, so he dropped the subject.

I also recalled Laura coming home from school one day and telling me she wanted to be Ms. B for Halloween. Her grandmother Frances found a blonde wig and jogging garb for her costume, and Laura headed to school. I wasn't sure how Miss B. would react but she was so pleased that she got someone to take a picture of the two of them together. It showed up in the school newsletter. Ms. B told Laura that it was the highest form of compliment and that this was when she recognized that they were both free spirits, two peas in a pod, and didn't give a damn about others' opinions of their lifestyle. Ms. B is still a hero to Laura and to me.

I recently visited my old home on Ninth Street in Bend. The couple who purchased our Ninth Street home graciously invited me to visit. I was introduced to their two beautiful adolescent children at the beginning of my tour. I had seen an article in the newspaper about the remodel after their purchase of the home and I had been impressed with the story and photos in the newspaper article. The garden in the backyard that Dad and Mom had built had matured and was beautiful. Bill (the person who sang at Cameron and MinYi's wedding) said that this had been the reason he wanted to buy the home. Tiffany described the changes they had made. There were bright green and teal walls, a more modern kitchen, and colorful artwork, vases and flowers all around. The couple had discovered hardwood floors under our old living room carpet and had stained it a dark walnut. Different spaces had been rearranged. They had done some changes to the patio and during the process had discovered the layers of our patio-the cinder, the slate and cement, and the brick. I thought about how years earlier, I had wondered if anyone would ever discover all of it, and what they might think of it. So I explained how the three layered patio had come about. Bill asked about the reason for the brick flower planter and the manhole next to it. I let them know that these were created to allow access to the septic system that used to be functional. I had forgotten that the slate walkway on the side of the house had not been covered by the brick, so some of Dad's (and our) creation still remained. Our names were still present in cement outside the guest house too. We all told our own stories about the place. I even mentioned the balloon that had landed in front of the master bedroom on that weekend morning many years ago. I also pointed out the chicken coup in the back yard. Bill suggested that it would have made a great playhouse for us and I told him that, in fact, Dad had rearranged it so that it remained a chicken coup but also acted as a playhouse for us.

The most interesting aspects of our meeting, though, were yet to come. Bill described the photograph of Dad in his sailor suit that was discovered when they tore up a wall for a remodel. We all wondered how it got there. They also discovered Dad's old tennis racket inside the wall. Tiffany had called my brother Doug about the discovery and sent the photo to Doug. Bill wondered if the racket had been stored in the attic and could have slipped into the wall from there. Doug explained that he and Sandy used to throw things at each other up there—maybe that's how the racket got there but our photos were never stored in the attic. Bill ran out to the garage and came back with the racket. He gave it to me. Anyway, the most interesting topic of all came up next. Bill smiled and shyly asked if I had any experiences with hauntings while in the home. He described peculiar events—his daughter noticed figurines that seemed to change positions on their own in her room. Bill and Tiffany felt a presence following them down the hallway on occasion. She said that Bill, in particular, was sensitive to such things. I said that I had experiences similar to this but not in this home. I didn't say anything at the time but later on I wondered if Dad had visited. Much of this had occurred before his death but one never knows. In his altered state, maybe he was able to visit his beloved home anyway.

I think back to my time in Elmhurst while living with my aunt Jean and family. I recall my sister's and cousins' fascination with ants. We spent hours watching them build their dirt mounds, marching one behind the other in a long line, looking for scraps of food, and carrying their finds (often much larger than themselves) underground. They'd build their home, rearrange it, and sometimes we would inadvertently destroy their home, but they'd just start all over again. I was only six, but even then I wondered about their seeming obliviousness to our human existence. If we walked by, did it seem to them there was an earthquake occurring? If we destroyed their home, did they perceive this as a natural disaster? I suspected they couldn't comprehend the complexity of human existence and wondered if we humans are like them—having no real clue about what really lies beyond our human experience—a whole-ness and a holy-ness which equals (w) holy-ness? And evolution is creation.

John and His Dad

John's Dad

John

John and Joe Tied Up

Pascal, Joe and John in Wagon

John and Joe

Joe, Pascal, John

John's Family in Dining Room

Angela and Rosie

John with Broken Nose

John in High School　　　John

John on Lake Pier

John with Younger Siblings

John in Kansas

The Lake Cottage

John at the Boat House

Me in Manhattan

New York Tenement Building

John on Right and Brothers

Laura and Chris Rathje

Jing

Clay

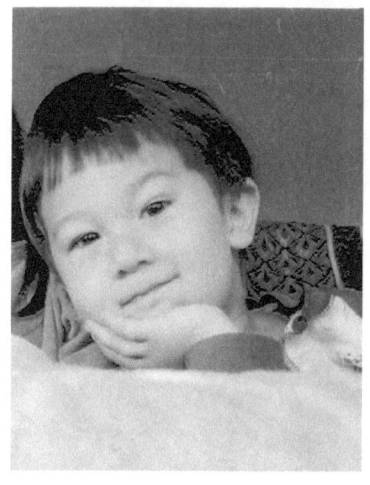
Burion

Laura and Jasper (2012)

Laura and the Boys

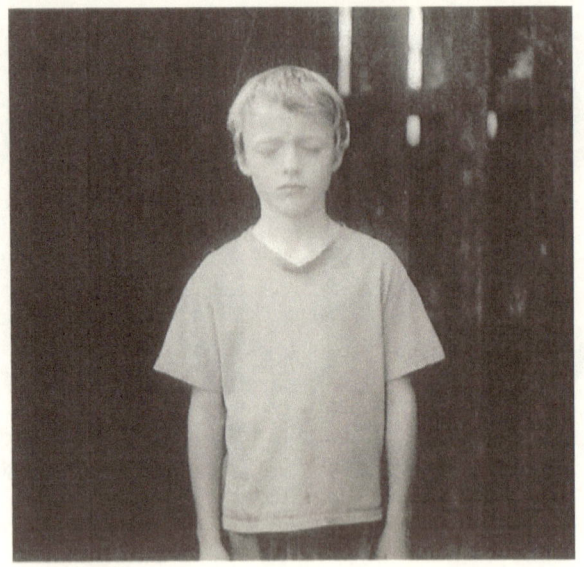

Nico

Ori

Jasper

Liz Graduates (2014)

CHAPTER 8

Growing up with my Slovenian family as a child instilled a curiosity about my heritage that has lasted my lifetime. When I first traveled to Slovenija and Italy with my father, aunt, and uncle, I knew that I was home. And when I traveled to Italy with my daughter later on, I sensed a connection to and affinity for the land, culture, and people that was deeply moving for me. Perhaps I was in touch with my lineage and its antiquity and just didn't know it. During the course of writing my memoir, I've explored my genetic makeup with the use of Ancestry.com and 23andMe. I've also read research on Slovenian roots and the history of Slovenija, Italy, and surrounding areas, which has made big strides with DNA and radiocarbon studies as well as archeological and linguistic findings. All this has challenged what have been considered accurate portrayals of history in this part of the world. I present articles that were the most enlightening on the subject. That my niece Andrea was able to locate a Luca Krkoc on the Internet (who told of the family having roots near Verona in the Veneti province of Italy) has made this information even more convincing. I offer excerpts from the following articles and information that Pauline Remec Moltzen provided about the Elmhurst Slovenians.

*Veneti and Slovene History/January 24, 2010:

"That the Veneti were part of Slovenian History came into sharp focus in 1989 when three Slovenian researchers, Dr. Jozko Savli, academician Matej Bor, and Father Ivan Tomazic published their findings in the book Venteti: nasi dauni predniki. The gist of their positions is as follows: 1) Slovenians lived in their lands long before the presumed settlement in the 6th century, 2) the name Veneti related to west Slavs, 3) Slovenians are their descendants and 4) Venetic and Slovenian languages were related". The English version of the book is Veneti: First Builders of European Community".[42]

*Venetian Language-History of Venetian People:

"Venetian identity is deeply rooted in very ancient times, prior to roman conquers: the civilization of ancient Venetians ... lasted for over 1, 000 years ... [and its] people is one of the few of the Italian peninsula to boast a continuum from the dawn of the history, if not prehistory. We have news of the first Venetians settled in the north-east of the peninsula, but in a much wider area

---

[42] Anton Skerbinc, "Veneti and Slovene History", http://anton-skerbinc. blogspot.com/2010/01/veneti-and-slovenian-history.html.

than today, since 4th century B.C. considering all the archeological findings, from situle-bronze funerary vases-to venetian findings even in Slovenija, Istria and in the present Austria-Corinthia, up to Adria ...

The Serenissima Venetian Republic was a model of parliamentary and federal State unique in the world, from which, among others, the Founding Fathers of the United States of America also drew their inspiration."[43]

*Etruscan Civilization:

"Etruscan civilization is the modern name given to a civilization of ancient Italy in the area corresponding roughly to Tuscany, western Umbria and northern Latium... [and the] ancient Romans called its creators the Tusci or Etrusci... As distinguished by its unique language, this civilization endured from the time of the earliest Etruscan inscriptions (ca. 700 B.C) until its assimilation into the Roman Republic in the late 4th century B.C. At its maximum extent, during the foundational period of Rome and the Roman Kingdom, it flourished in three confederacies: of Etruria, of the Po Valley with the eastern Alps, and of Latium and Campania."[44]

---

[43] "Venetian Language—History of Venetian people," http://w w w. linguaveneta.it/en_storia.asp.

[44] "Etruscan Civilization," *Wikipedia, The Free Encyclopedia*, http://en.w ikipedia. org/wiki/Etruscan_civilization.

*Glasilo Magazine Excerpt: Etruscans, Veneti and Slovenians by Joze Skulj/October 2004:

"There is a genetic continuity between the ancient Etruscans and Veneti and the present day Slovenians. Genetic information makes it evident that the Slovenians are indigenous to their land as indicated by the mtDNA relationship with the 2,500 year old skeletal remains of the Etruscans, particularly those from Adria in Veneto. Genetic information supports the historic quotation from the biography of St. Columban written in 615 A.D and cited by Toma'i-"Termini Veneiorum qui it Sclavi di cuntur"- the land of the Veneti who are also called Slavs (Savli 1996)."[45]

*Pan-Slav Theory a Fiction Story (II)-Etruscans, Veneti and Slovenians, genetic characteristics (posted on January 22, 2011) (continued from 8/9/2010):

"Copper metallurgy appears to have been underway in the Balkans at an early date-earlier than in Greece... but it didn't challenge the basic assumptions underlying what they had written: the position of the ancient civilizations of Egypt and Mesopotamia as the innovators, illuminating the rest of the Old World with... their culture wasn't challenged.... (Renfrew 1973).

---

[45]   Jose Skulj, "Glasilo Magazine Excerpt: Etruscans, Veneti and Slovenians," October 2004, http://www.theslovenian.com/articles/skulj.htm.

..."4 out of 5 or 80 % of the Venetic' sequences are found in Slovenia"... [and]... in addition to the haplotypes found in the ancient Veneti from Adria, Slovenians also share haplotypes with the skeletal remains of Etruscans from Etruria proper, names from Volterra (Vo) and Maglianoa/ Marsiliana (M/M)... [with no] abrupt genetic difference between skeletal remains from Etruria proper and the present day Slavic populations in Balkans... [which]... shows the relatively strong genetic mtDNA relationship between ancient Veneti and modern day Slovenians".[46]

*Indo-Aryan and Slavic Affinities:

"The most important part of the linguistic families of India, Pakistan and Ceylon (Sri-Lanka) is the Indo-Aryan, of which the ancient and classical form is Sanskrit... Sanskrit, especially Vedic Sanskrit, which is the oldest, exhibits more similarities to Slovenian than Hindi or Punjabi... In addition to linguistics, there are also genetic similarities between Slavs of Europe and the people of the Indian sub-continent."[47]

---

[46] J. Skulj "Pan-Slav Theory a Fiction Story-Etruscans, Veneti and Slovenians, genetic characteristics," January 22, 2011, http://spacezilotos.wordpress.com /2011/01/22/pan-slav-theory-a-fiction-story-ii-etruscans-...

[47] Joseph Skulj, Jagdish C. Sharda, "Indo-Aryan and Slavic Affinities" Hindu Institute of Learning, 11 Westacres

My aunt Jean sent my dad articles by Pauline Moltzen, a Slovenian woman who lived in the Elmhurst suburb of Chicago and who also had the same maiden name of Brecelj as my grandmother. Her mother (Franziska) and my grandmother were cousins. Franziska sponsored Francesca when she came to America. I offer some of the excerpts from an article that was submitted by Pauline and published in Slovenija Quarterly Magazine, from Ljublana, Slovenija. It is circulated in countries where Slovenians immigrated.

"A gift subscription to Slovenija was given to me by a Slovenian cousin who lives in Illinois. It has been a joy and a revelation to read about our ancestry, to learn about Slovenija's history, to see pictures of the country's majestic beauty".

"I've read with particular interest Janez Keber's Origin of Slovene Surnames but with only a few exceptions, I have found none of the names of our people who settled near Chicago in Elmhurst, Illinois, at the end of the 18th century and in the early years of this century—Slovenians who came from villages near Trieste (Italy). Probably because various armies occupied this strategic area over the centuries, our surnames are of Italian, German, French and Slavic origin. These are the surnames of the Elmhurst Slovenians: Besednjak, Bratina, Brecelji, Cigoi, Cermelj, Dezutel, Fagenel,

---

Drive, Toronto Ontario, Canada, Mc M-2B7.

Feuce, Fisher, Hrovatin, Habazin, Krkoc, Komel, Leston, Lisjak, Maloit (or Milost), Podgornik, Rebek, Remec, Fojic, Succeeda, Sustersich, Volk, and Vertovec ... my mother's maiden name was Brecelji, but she was often referred to as Brsljanka because her home in Gojace had thick ivy vines (brsljan) on the walls. My father's people evidently made baskets for they were known as the 'Kosh' family (kosara = basket)..."

"Our first family was the Milost family. Their name changed in the United States to Maloit because a teacher in the public school wrote it down that way when their daughter went to school.... Franz Milost came to the United States from Trieste where he had been a coachman for a wealthy family. In Trieste he met and married his wife, also Slovenian, who was employed by the same family as a cook.... Leaving his family behind, Franz came to the United States, probably in the early 1890's ... when financially able, he sent for his family. The day of their departure found Alvin [one of his three children], the youngest ... too ill to travel. Reluctantly, he was left behind to be cared for by family until he could come later. The reunited family [settled in] Elmhurst ... and after hard work and frugal living, they built a substantial brick two-flat house. This was the welcoming home [of Franz and Karolina Milost] to which our Slovenians came".

"I am eighty-two years old and it seems that those ever so long ago days are more vivid to me than the recent past. I wish I had paid more attention and asked more questions of my people. Certainly, despite the poverty left behind, it must have been wrenching to leave home and family for an unknown land. I did not realize it then, but now I believe I know what my dear mother meant when she would say, 'I miss the sound of the church bells reverberating through the hills.' And more poignantly, 'the stars seem to be so far away here!'"[48]

[Regarding Karolina Podgornik Milost] "Karolina not only fed and housed the new arrivals, but found them jobs, hosted wedding parties, and as a midwife, delivered their babies. She was a remarkable woman with many talents, a great cook who always had a big flower garden, flowers as well as vegetables, chickens, but her great love was people, especially children. When she died, a great loss was felt by all who knew [her]".

"Saint Mary's cemetery on Alexander Boulevard in Elmhurst dates back well over 100 years, way before we came to this country, but I tend to think of Saint Mary's as OUR cemetery for so many of the people I have written about are buried there. If you ever visit this small and interesting burial ground, there is an impres-

---

[48] Pauline Remec Moltzen, "The Slovenians of Elmhurst, Illinois." *Slovenija Quarterly Magazine XIII*, no. 1 (1999).

sive tall monument to the left of the entrance at a gravesite which reads: NO TEARS, NO CARES, NO ANXIOUS FEAR CAN REACH OUR LOVED ONE SLEEPING HERE. May they all REST IN PEACE!"[49]

I talked to the now 98 year old Pauline recently, asking her about my family in Elmhurst and the Slovenian community there. She told me stories about it all—her being in attendance at my grandparents' wedding—a girl of nine years and also with her younger brother, Ade. She told of Dad's birth in her own home with Mrs. Milost as midwife. She told of the atmosphere of her hometown of Elmhurst, where she grew up a daughter of immigrant parents and the death of her father during the 1918 flu epidemic. Her brother was born the day he died. She described the populace of her hometown as follows: "When our people arrived, Elmhurst was inhabited by WASPS and then more recently by the arrival of Germans in the early to mid-1880's and from their perspective—"we may as well have been from Mars"

Pauline also sent me her Slovenian folder. In it I found out more about my family. My grandmother Francesca was a member of a Slovenian women's group formed in Elmhurst in 1940. The group's purpose has been to preserve the heritage of the Slovenian people.

---

[49]   Pauline Remec Moltzen, "The Elmhurst, Illinois Slovenians," Elmhurst Historical Museum Archives, August 1999.

Aunt Jean joined the group in 2003 and acted as vice president. She inherited the SWUA badge from her mother, Francesca. This is about the time Jean wanted to study the Slovenian language, in spite of the fact that in her youth she would have nothing to do with it. In addition to taking lessons from a Catholic Slovenian priest in Chicago, she and Yanko wrote back and forth so that each of them could learn the other's language. She translated one of his letters to her dated March 21, 2005. "January 17, I had an operation. Now I am walking with 4 legs (he used a 4 pronged cane). It is good, doesn't hurt. Happy Easter Holidays. HABUNSA (I am laughing). It is written GOBANCA. Good wishes to you and your family. Yanko."

I contacted Pauline to get permission to use some of her published article excerpts in my book. She sent me written permission along with the following letter. I could not have expressed the feelings she described any better.

Letter from Pauline Moltzen Remec-

July 18, 2015

Dear Cheryl,

I have nostalgia when I remember the early Slovenian years, and I think you have the same writing about your family.

SENTIMENT; A MEMOIR

Families are so scattered these days. Your dad went west and I went east, and many others did so too. Financially it was the thing for us to do, and no doubt it was so for your father.

But sometimes I wonder. We were a close knit group of people and that provided a certain stability of belonging. Your dad was so close to Joe Remec, probably the best friend he ever had. I was close to your Aunt Jean Gale and to my cousin Dorothy Hrovatin and Virginia Hrovatin too. I have made friends while living in Pennsylvania, in New Jersey and here too, but it is not the same.

You and my granddaughter, Molly, are cousins. There are other grandkids from my adopted daughter, Kathy. Paula Jean is married to a scientist and they have two children and live near Boston. Her brother Robbie is married to a beautiful Guatemalan girl who came to the U.S. while quite young. They have two small boys, live near me, but are moving to Virginia soon.

Some time ago your dad sent me a picture of him and his progeny. You can surely tell some stories too.

To get back to Molly. She is a graduate of Boston College 2 years ago. She and John live in Austin, Texas. Who gets married first these days? He is a Notre Dame graduate. I will be 99 in November. My husband died in 2002. I live alone here on the hill- a place we bought years ago as a hunting property. It is quite beautiful here, but winters are long. Thanks for keeping in touch. Any questions I will be glad to answer if I can.

Love and Remembrance, Pauline.

Joe and Frank Brecelj
(In B. Aires)

Marija
(on right, Francesca's Sister)
with a Friend

Jozko Krkoc (Francesco's
Brother in South America)

Olga and Cirila in B. Aires
(Francesco's sisters)

Francesca's Siblings in Buenos Aires

Nelida and Albin (Francesca's brother)

Olga and Josef's Wedding

Olga, Josef and DTR Irma (seated) DTR Neli and son-in-law (standing)

Yanko in Slovenija

Relatives in Argentina

Yanko saying Mass — Vida and Rafl – Yanko's Parents

www.ingramcontent.com/pod-product-compliance
Lightning Source LLC
Chambersburg PA
CBHW021421070526
44577CB00001B/1